In the COMPANY of ANGELS

In the COMPANY of ANGELS

DAVID FARLAND

Bonneville Books
Springville, Utah

This is a work of fiction. The characters, names, incidents, places, and dialogue are products of the author's imagination, and are not to be construed as real.

This is not an official publication of The Church of Jesus Christ of Latter-day Saints. The opinions and views expressed herein belong solely to the author and do not necessarily represent the opinions or views of Cedar Fort, Inc. Permission for the use of sources, graphics, and photos is also solely the responsibility of the author.

ISBN 13:978-1-59955-888-2
Published by Bonneville Books, an imprint of Cedar Fort, Inc., 2373 W. 700 S., Springville, UT 84663
Distributed by Cedar Fort, Inc., www.cedarfort.com

LIBRARY OF CONGRESS CATALOGING-IN-PUBLICATION DATA

Farland, David, author.
In the company of angels / Dave Farland.
pages cm
Summary: Eliza Gadd crosses the Great Plains by handcart with her Mormon husband on the journey from their native England to a new home in the Rocky Mountains. Baline Mortensen, a nine-year old Dane, is a member of the handcart company as well. Together they suffer unimaginable deprivations. Based on the true story of the Mormon pioneers in the Willie Handcart Company of 1856, who leave for the Rocky Mountains too late in the season and are stranded on the plains in the early onset of the coldest winter in US history.
ISBN 978-1-59955-888-2
1. James G. Willie Emigrating Company--Fiction. 2. Mormon handcart companies--Fiction. I. Title.
PS3556.A71558I5 2011
813'.54--dc22

2011006355

Cover design by Angela D. Olsen
Cover photo by David Farland
Cover photo effects by Howard Lyon
Cover design © 2011 by Lyle Mortimer
Typeset by Heidi Doxey

Printed in the United States of America

10 9 8 7 6 5 4 3 2 1

Printed on acid-free paper

Praise for David Farland and *In the Company of Angels*

David Farland is derivative of no one, yet he writes within a tradition that is as old as storytelling. The tale is set in heroic times, in a land glimpsed only from a distance, but serves only to clarify and magnify tales that are also true for us in our relentlessly unheroic times.

Orson Scott Card
New York Times bestselling author of *Ender's Game*

Aside from being a talented writer, David Farland is an excellent writing teacher. Hearing him teach live and reading his written advice has helped me focus many of my own thoughts about the writing process. Those who would like to learn more about the craft of writing would be wise to pay attention.

Brandon Mull
New York Times bestselling author of *Fablehaven*

David Farland once again proves himself to be a wizard at storytelling.

Publishers Weekly

It is like being a member of the 1856 Willie Handcart Company.

Michael De Groote
Deseret News

In the Company of Angels is a beautifully written, powerful account of a perfect storm on dry land.

Kenny Kemp
Author of *Dad Was a Carpenter*

Additional Works by David Farland

Novels

On My Way to Paradise

Wheatfields Beyond

A Very Strange Trip

Novelettes

The Sky is an Open Highway

My Favorite Christmas

We Blazed

In the Teeth of Glory

The Stone Mother's Curse

Series

Serpent Catch

The Golden Queen

The Runelords

Mummy Chronicles

Star Wars: The Courtship of Princess Leia

Star Wars: Jedi Apprentice: The Rising Force

Benjamin Ravenspell: Of Mice and Magic

Contents

ACKNOWLEDGMENTS

When writing a novel, an author often receives help from dozens of people. In this case, particular thanks are necessary to Jeanie Walker, who first introduced me to the story of the Willie Handcart Company, and to Larry Walker who helped clarify so many questions and provided research materials, then went the extra mile and read the first draft of my manuscript. I'd also like to thank Laura Anderson, who led me to some excellent sources and also helped with my rough draft. I'd like to thank Scott Bronson, Linda Adams, Dave Doering, and Noelle Perner for their help in editing and proofreading the manuscript. My niece Courtney Heirtzler posed for the cover, and I'm especially grateful both to her and to her parents for letting me take her out into the snow to get thoroughly frozen during a photo shoot. Thanks should also be extended to Howard Lyon for his help on the cover, to Nathan Best for his excellent work on the website, and to Tim Schulte for his sound advice on publishing. Last but not least, I'd like to thank my wife, Mary, for her understanding when I took those long and expensive trips away from home to do my own peculiar kind of research—studying flowers and bugs, and getting a better feel for the land that the pioneers had to cross.

Prologue

High on the plains in central Wyoming, up near the Continental Divide, is a desolate place where it is said that the spirits of the dead can often be encountered.

It is a place far from human habitation. Fat sage hens wander about, plump and dark and as approachable as tame chickens. Away from the rivers, antelope race over the barren prairie, while mule deer make their homes among the willow reeds that cover the banks of the Sweetwater River and its feeder streams.

Even with water, few trees can survive the icy storms that blow down from the Wind River Mountains, whistling through sagebrush and rolling over the dry prairie grasses and sand-colored stones, but in the shelter of the valleys, one can find a few quaking aspen trees with bark as white as snow and leaves that shiver like a freezing child in the slightest breeze. Dark pines fill some mountain folds, creating a perpetual twilight beneath their canopies.

It is upon the banks of one silver brook called Rock Creek that many have sensed the spirits of the dead, in a place called "The Temple of Wyoming."

It is a temple formed without human hands. Nature enforces a code of reverence there. A single rock wall along the north of the creek provides shelter from the worst of the wind, and red-barked willow reeds grow tall along the brook, shushing all sound. Heaven forms the temple's ceiling, and beneath its floor lies a grave.

Thirteen people are buried there, laid out toe to toe. Beside them rest two more men who died while digging the large grave. In 1856, they tried to cross a continent, hauling all that they owned in handcarts, and were caught in an early storm. Most were men who died struggling to save their families from the brutal blizzard, but others were children, weakened by starvation. They are but a few of those who died along the trail.

Their story is not a common tragedy. Theirs is a story of courage, hope, and heroism that may be unparalleled in the American West.

Few have tried to tell their tale. It is not an easy one to tell. Though survivors, and even many of those who died, left biographical accounts, it is an odd tale—a story of revelations, of angelic visitations, of people struggling to find religious freedom in a harsh world.

A cold-hearted historian would tell the story differently than I. Some have labored to dissect the errors made and assign blame for the tragedy, or to apologize. Others have focused on what was in its time the most expensive and massive rescue operation in known history.

I've read hundreds of biographical sketches by those who survived. Few of those who lost limbs to the cold ever complained, and nearly all expressed endless gratitude for their rescuers—both human and divine.

In deciding how to approach this story, it seemed that it was not mine alone to tell. It belongs to those who lie buried along the trail. I cannot present it as an episode devoid of religious overtones, as a historian might. I cannot exclude the testimonies that were borne on that grueling trek.

Nor can I gloss over the hard and sometimes uncomfortable truth of what really happened—how the callousness of average Americans combined with the oversights and errors of a few leaders to create such a high death toll.

I will try to tell the truth as best I can. I cannot tell it perfectly, for despite the biographies, despite the journals kept, not every word spoken along the trail was recorded. In some places, the record is as quiet as the barren hills along with Wind River, but I will fill in the silence as best I can. . . .

Send me the worthy poor, the humblest of our saints who long to sail to Zion, though they have not a sixpence in the world.

Brigham Young, in a letter to
Franklin D. Richards, 1855

1

THE END OF THE WORLD

"Doff your cap, Mormon, and show us some horns!" a man cried.

Eliza Gadd's stomach twisted into a knot. The stranger was glaring at Eliza's husband, Samuel, who tried his best to ignore the man.

The stranger stood on the pathway to his house on the outskirts of Council Bluffs, Iowa, wearing nothing but some threadbare overalls and a battered black hat, his legs shaking from fear, his face reddened and twisted with rage. He gripped an ax, as if ready to take a swing at the first Mormon that drew too close. He rushed to the front gate of his white picket fence, one hand hovering near the latch, and demanded again, "Doff your cap, Mormon!"

A few feet ahead of Eliza, her husband Samuel pulled a handcart along the road, his blue denim shirt soaked with a V of sweat down his back, his floppy broad-rimmed felt hat hiding his sandy hair. The handcart squeaked and rattled as if it would split apart at any moment. It was a little larger than a wheelbarrow, and it held all of the family's possessions—clothes for Eliza, her husband, and seven of their eight children, along with a frying pan, a pot to boil water, and a few spoons and cooking implements.

Samuel nodded, but kept walking. The ax-man leaned over the gate and screamed, "Look at me when I talk to you!"

He was an unsavory fellow. His sunburned arms were knotted with muscle, and sweat seemed to have permanently left a greasy stain in the armpits of his overalls. "Show your horns! Show 'em to me, you Mormon devil!"

The farmer trembled with anticipation and terror, as if both eager to see a Mormon's horns and terrified by the prospect.

Horns? Eliza wondered. *He can't seriously believe that Mormons have horns.* In a saner world, she would have hoped that he was jesting, but she spied his two daughters in an upper bedroom, peering out the window with eyes made as round as hens' eggs by fright. These buffoons really did believe that Mormons had horns.

Similar scenes had greeted them in town after town. The locals would gather at their doors to gawk and to jeer at the poor deluded Mormons who were hoofing it off into the wilderness to starve.

Eliza and Samuel were traveling with five hundred Mormons in the Willie Handcart Company, trying to reach Utah—the promised land of the Mormons, the American Zion.

Before they could reach Zion, they had to pass through Council Bluffs, a few hundred rough log-and-mud houses sheltered in a small valley between two rows of hills; the town boasted nearly a dozen taverns and little else. Rail fences partitioned off the gardens behind the houses, where corn grew tall in mid-August. Chickens, black and red, raced about the street, while a few hogs wallowed at the roadside.

In all of human history, no group had ever traveled so far to escape persecution. The Jews had fled Egypt and traveled only a few dozen miles, while the gypsies had spread several hundred miles across Europe. But most of the folks in this company had left their homes in England, Scotland, Denmark, or France and sailed thousands of miles across the ocean—only to march across a continent. One member of the party, Sister Tate, was a Hindu, all the way from India.

The immigrants in the handcart company dressed shabbily. Most of the children and even many adults could not afford shoes, and so they walked barefoot. Half the women in the band were widows, and so women outnumbered men three to one, and of the folks in the company, a dozen were cripples, senile, or mad, and thus had to be carried in the carts.

Eliza had been born to an upper-class family, but she had landed among the poorest of the Mormon poor.

The signs of poverty among the group went well beyond the immigrants' threadbare attire. Most were stunted from malnutrition, and many suffered from lice, strange rashes, and scabs that would not heal.

So the poor were walking to Utah, unable to afford the wagons that a wealthier man would consider necessary.

In every town that they had passed, the company had been forced to run a gauntlet as the locals came to ogle, mouths agape. The Willie Company had given them a free freak show; secretly Eliza knew that she was the biggest freak of them all.

She held her chin up, tried to show no fear. Her cheeks burned with shame. She had been walking down a hot road all day, and the clouds of dust raised by others had powdered her face. She only hoped that it would hide her embarrassment.

Eliza straightened her little white cap, a stylish thing that her mother had left her.

She strode past the ax-man, smiled genteelly, nodded good-day, and tried to ignore him, even as every nerve in her body warned her not to turn her back. The fellow stood trembling, a crazed look in his eyes, and shouted at Samuel. "Don't you—don't you walk past me, Mormon. Don't turn your back on me. I'm talking to you!"

Eliza was just congratulating herself on making it past the ax-man when her seventeen-year-old daughter, Jane, strode up to the fellow, bouncing baby Daniel on her hip.

Jane smiled, affected a silly American accent, and said, "Sorry to disappoint you, feller, but we filed off our horns just yesterday. Makes it easy to hide among you gentiles!"

Eliza wanted to warn Jane away from the madman, but she was a pretty girl, as lissome as a swan, with hair that shone like spun flax, and Jane seemed to think that her sway over men held no bounds.

The ax-man's eyes bulged and his Adam's apple bobbed as he vainly tried to figure out something intelligent to say. It was common to file off cows' horns, so that they wouldn't gore their owners.

Obviously the poor man was trying to figure out if the ploy might work on a Mormon.

Jane laughed and thrust out her tongue at him, waggling it in snakelike fashion.

The American stumbled backward, retreating, and tripped over one of his uneven paving stones.

The clown! Eliza thought. *His entire senses have gone derelict!*

She'd faced unreasoning persecutors back in England, yet she'd never seen anyone so frightfully dense as this.

Still, she'd been surprised by the impoverished intellect of Americans all along her trek. After arriving by ship in New York, the saints had been harassed at every stop—assailed by men with foul mouths, threatened, denied shelter at hostels, brutally treated by railroad executives who forced the immigrants to sleep in cattle cars when they'd paid for better.

Illinois had been worst. The immigrants had taken a train up to Lake Superior, and then gone by steamboat to Chicago, and from there rode to Rock Island, where they crept into the town by night and hid in a train house to wait out a thunderstorm. A mob gathered, two hundred men with guns and torches, demanding that the Mormons "send out their women" amid threats of rape and murder. They'd hurled insults and rocks at the train shed for five hours, while the immigrant men huddled behind the doors armed with nothing more than a couple of pistols and sabers.

The immigrants hoped that the local peace officers might come to save them. But Captain Willie informed them that there was no law that would protect a Mormon in Illinois.

Ten years earlier, in 1846, Illinois had placed a bounty on Mormon scalps, offering thousands for the heads of the church's leaders. Even the hair of Eliza's young babes was worth a dollar a scalp.

Illinois was just one of more than a dozen states that had passed such laws against various religions in an effort to drive out Mormons, Jews, and other undesirables.

Over the years, only luck had saved any Mormons from losing scalps in Illinois. The first pair of bounty hunters that had ever tried to bag a Mormon attacked a passing wagon, killing a man, his ten children, and three "wives." Fourteen people had been butchered. Yet when the authorities researched the case, they discovered that the alleged Mormon was just an innocent Methodist minister, traveling with his large family and two aunts. The scandal over the murders had spurred state officials to withdraw the bounty, though the laws remained on the books.

At eleven that night a sheriff had finally come with enough deputies to disperse the fatigued mob, though a summer storm deserved most of the credit for scattering the killers.

Eliza had learned to be wary of the mobs that formed in nearly every city they visited. Sometimes even the lawmen joined in. A week earlier, a sheriff from Powesheik County, Iowa, had come with a small army and forced the handcart company to unload all of its supply wagons on the pretense of searching for women tied up under the floorboards. The charge was insane.

Yet rumors spread by the eastern press persisted in telling of Mormons abducting women and hiding them in compartments in wagons—or carrying them through secret tunnels under the Rocky Mountains—all in an effort to get them to Utah, where the women were used to sate the monstrous appetites of Brigham Young, the Mormon leader.

Eliza thought that you'd have to be as dumb as a fencepost to believe such tales.

But there it was.

The whole United States was in turmoil, everywhere Eliza looked. It wasn't just the attacks on Mormons. There was a war breaking out in Kansas between the slavers and the abolitionists. In May, Old John Brown had gotten up a gang of men and gone through the countryside in Kansas stabbing to death every slaver he could roust out of bed while the slavers continued murdering abolitionists in a bloodbath. The federal government had called in troops from all over the frontier and begun blowing houses down with cannons. Now they'd arrested the governor and were threatening to hang him for treason—all for failing to stop the violence.

It seemed to Eliza that the federal government was to blame.

It was an election year, and the newly formed Republican Party was calling for an end to the "twin relics of barbarism"—slavery and polygamy. Mormons were opposed to slavery, but while polygamy was widely practiced on the American frontier—mostly by fur trappers and settlers who had taken multiple Indian squaws as wives—the Mormons were the only American religion that openly condoned polygamy. Joseph Smith, the church's first prophet, had proclaimed that polygamy was sanctified by God if it was practiced, as by Abraham, with the goal of raising children in righteousness. So a select few members of the church were asked to enter into plural marriages.

President Buchanan, a Democrat, was responding to the Republican threat by promising to "get tough" on the Mormons. By making a sufficient example of them, he planned to cow the southern states into giving up the practice of slavery, and thus avoid a civil war. Whether that meant that Buchanan would send an army across the plains with orders to exterminate the Mormons, as had been done in Missouri a dozen years earlier, or if he had something else up his sleeve, no one could yet guess.

It wasn't a good time to be a Mormon.

So Eliza had learned to fear these "Yankee yahoos" as Brother Savage liked to call them.

Eliza sighed wearily as she lifted her sleeping babe, Isaac, higher on her shoulder. She waved away a trio of mosquitoes bent on carrying the child off to eat.

Her calves and back ached from walking the past three hundred miles, and this had been the easy part of the journey. There had been good roads and an occasional town, where one might buy what one needed. Ahead of them was nothing but wilderness. Eliza licked her sunburned lips, sucked in her hungry belly, and lifted her chin.

Ahead were more houses, and the gawkers were streaming out to greet them. She wanted to make sure that her children stayed near, that they presented themselves well.

Jane looked fine. Sarah, age five, was riding in the back of the handcart and had fallen fast asleep, her head lying on a bundle of clothes. Mary Ann, age seven, was old enough to walk much of the way, but her father was letting her ride, too.

Thirteen-year-old Bill plodded behind the cart, ready to push it if need be. Her oldest son, Albert, was working the cattle drive, so Bill had taken over many of Albert's former duties.

She half-turned to see little Sam Junior, age ten, who walked well behind the cart, talking softly to one of the Danish emigrant girls that he played with, a bright-faced little blonde girl with a blue dress and golden hair. Her name was Baline.

"That there is a dragonfly," Sam Junior told Baline. "Can you say dragonfly?" He gestured to a streak of red that buzzed nearby. The dragonfly hovered near Baline's white apron, seeking a place to land.

"Ya, I say it, ya," Baline answered merrily. "Is like two vords, dragon and fly, dragonfly. Ya?"

"Precisely," Sam said, sounding for all the world like some school proctor.

"Sam, catch up—and watch your posture," Eliza called. "We're coming through town. Remember your station."

Sam glanced at her and suddenly began marching with his back ramrod straight as he hurried to catch up. She didn't have to say more.

Eliza frowned at Baline. She was a bright child, a magnet for other children, and that was what worried Eliza. Though she was only ten, Sam Junior might find himself attracted to such a girl, and Eliza didn't believe in interracial marriage. Most Mormons saw all people as brothers and sisters and treated the Danes and even the French as equals. However, it was bad enough when an Englishman married a lowly Irish woman or a Scot, but Eliza wouldn't have her son chasing after a brutish, ill-mannered Dane.

At the front of the column of weary travelers, Captain Willie, a bearish man of forty, called out, "Let's give them a song!" Obviously he hoped to drown out the voices of his detractors.

The Mormons, as obedient as sheep, began to sing the anthem of Mormon pilgrims:

"Come, come, ye saints, no toil nor labor fear,
But with joy, wend your way.
Though hard to you, this journey may appear,
Grace shall be, as your day.

'Tis better far for us to strive,
Our useless cares from us to drive,
Do this, and joy, your hearts will swell—
All is well. All is well."

Eliza refused to sing. She wouldn't even mouth the words. Still the music began to ascend around her as the immigrants plodded into town, handcarts creaking and rattling. Their practiced voices rose in harmony, echoing from the small hills along the road, frightening chickens, drowning out the voices of the locals, many of whom ran from their houses and stood at their gates to jeer.

"Say 'hi' to the injuns for me," one man cried from a rocking chair on his porch as Eliza passed his white house. He took off his hat and revealed a massive scar on the crown of his head, circled by scraggly hair.

"Mother," ten-year-old Samuel cried at her back, "that man has been scalped!"

The fellow laughed derisively. His antics had had their desired effect.

"Don't let him alarm you," Eliza warned. "It will only encourage him."

Two doors down, a portly matron in a faded cotton dress accosted Eliza. "Don't go," she shouted, reaching out as if to stop her, or perhaps grab baby Isaac from her arms. "Please don't go. It's too late in the year to cross the mountains!"

Eliza smiled and nodded at the woman kindly; she whispered, "Thank you," but kept walking.

The matron shouted desperately, "At least leave the babe with me! If you love it, you'll leave it behind."

If we were back in England, Eliza told herself, *I should want to be her friend.*

Eliza wasn't the kind of woman that could leave her child behind. She walked on. For three houses, people just stared sullenly as the Mormons passed.

Now came the mockery. "Gee-haw," some teenage boys shouted

as they perched on a fence, taunting the men and women who pulled the carts. "Get up, mule!"

Eliza kept her eyes forward, ignoring the taunts, even when a green apple flew through the air and rebounded off of Samuel's back.

The rules of the handcart train were strict. The saints were to ignore any abuse, to say nothing in retaliation, and to follow the Savior's example and turn the other cheek. To revile one's tormentors in any way or to seek to rebuke them tended to only invite further attacks.

So the immigrants trundled down the street, voices rising in song just enough to drown out the worst of the insults, until they entered the merchant district.

Eliza's feet hurt. She'd only carried her babe five miles this morning, but her feet were swollen and calloused from weeks of abuse.

She passed a barbershop and an apothecary, a dry goods store, and a pair of blacksmiths with the bitter scent of coal smoke coming from their open doors. But there were also the taverns where scantily clad prostitutes leaned from the upper windows, their breasts nearly falling out of their flimsy attire, as they shouted down to Jane, "Hey, you—you're a likely one. Show us a bit of leg."

Suddenly the handcart at the front of the column came to a grinding halt, blocking the road so that all one hundred carts behind had to stop, too.

Captain Willie stood at the head of the column talking with a strange, heavyset man in a cheap brown suit.

"Who do you think that is?" Eliza ventured to ask her husband.

"Church agent, I imagine," Samuel answered, removing his cap and wiping the sweat from his face with the worn sleeve of his shirt. "There's a church outfitting station across the river where we're supposed to acquire more supplies."

The church agent, a young broad-shouldered man with a thick beard the color of chestnuts, gestured toward the banks of the river. His voice suddenly grew loud and carried as he told Captain Willie, "Give 'em a couple of hours to rest and to shop, then we'll ferry across."

Captain Willie nodded in acknowledgment. Docked just

downhill at the side of the river was a huge ferry, a brand new steamboat, gleaming in the midday sun.

Eliza relished the idea of shopping. She didn't have much money, only twenty-eight cents left to her name, mostly big American pennies. Rations had been scant on their journey, so she hoped to buy a little candy for the children, and perhaps some buttons or extra needles.

The volume of the Mormons' voices rose as they came to the climax of their song:

"And should we die before the journey's through,
Happy day, all is well!
We then are free, from toil and sorrow too,
With the just, we shall dwell.
But if our lives are spared again
To see the saints their rest obtain,
Oh, how we'll make this chorus swell!
All is well. All is well!"

Eliza was embarrassed to be here, to be among the ill-bred Mormons, to be so filthy. The trail through Iowa had been filled with tumultuous hills. The tops of the hills found the ground dry, with dust as fine as talcum, while down in the valleys, recent thundershowers had left mud holes and ruts, so that one man could not pull a cart alone. Thus, everyone's feet were caked with mud. Her son Bill was as sooty as a chimney sweep, and nothing could be done about it.

"Tuck in your shirt," Eliza whispered to him,"and comb your hands through your hair."

Jane stood with the other twin, Daniel, who was just shy of his second birthday, bouncing the babe on her hip.

In the profound silence that followed, a rough-looking fellow in front of the tavern called, "Gee-haw, mule," at Samuel and grinned like an idiot, as if he were the first to come up with the insult. He'd been leaning against the hitching rail, but now he reached behind his back and pulled out a bullwhip.

A couple of the man's friends stepped forward, too.

Crack! The whip snapped just inches from Samuel's ear. Samuel cringed but made no move to run, nor to defend himself. He stood with legs trembling, quivering, head bent, cowering. Sickness and hard labor had taken thirty pounds from him in the past month, and his poor clothes hung on him like rags.

Samuel would not fight, Eliza knew. He'd been the branch president in their tiny congregation back home, a sort of lay minister. He wouldn't break the rules of the handcart company.

Suddenly a memory exploded into Eliza's consciousness: "Don't marry that man," her father had commanded in a severe tone. "Don't even think about it. 'Ye, gad!' Can you imagine the taunts your children will suffer? 'Look, there goes a Gadd—or is it a gadfly?' "

"Gadd is a good name. It's Welsh. It means 'gate.' "

"Wales," her father snorted. "You mean you couldn't find a man of low enough breeding in England?"

"He's a good man, Father," Eliza had said, "not a low sort or a mean man at all. Though he might not be the first in consequence in Wimpole, many hold an elevated opinion of him."

Eliza's mother had chimed in more sympathetically, "It's not that he's a low man, Eliza. There is no discernable flaw to his character, no overpowering defect in his intellect, but he's a common man, common in every way. He's got a common man's intelligence, a common man's education and lack of ambition. He'll never be a superior provider for you, and heaven help you if you should bear offspring."

Twenty years ago her parents had spoken that warning, twenty years ago and four months, almost to the day.

It's funny how a few words can come back to haunt you, Eliza thought. Her father had been dead for three years, her mother for five. Yet their warnings rang in her ears, almost as if their ghosts were at her back, whispering.

Her parents had been right. Samuel was not the first-rate provider her parents had aspired to. He'd made a marginal living as a middle-man, renting fields from lords and then advancing the land out again to tenant farmers. Though he was not poor, he'd never brought home enough to keep the family comfortable, and once

Samuel had united himself with the Mormon church, many a lord had refused to do business, hoping to starve him into submission; thus Samuel's income had shriveled away until Eliza had been forced to take a position as a nurse just to keep food on the table. Now the whole family was destitute, beyond the verge of ruin, and Samuel had brought them six thousand miles to escape their persecutors.

Still, Eliza thought, *I'm fully prepared to follow him off the edge of the world.*

So Eliza's parents had been right about Samuel. He had no great intellect for extracting an advantage in a business deal. She had argued, "Samuel is not a common man. There's uncommon goodness in him." Eliza had been right, too. Samuel was unflaggingly faithful to his lofty standards, firm in his decorum. He would not engage in an altercation now, not even to save his own life.

"Oh, he don't like that whip," one bully chortled. "He don't like the whip one bit. He's an angry old mule, ain't he?" The bully turned from his companions and taunted Samuel. "You got something to say to me, mule?"

One companion pointed at Jane and sniggered, "Forget him—now she's more like it! Hell, I'd be glad to put my spurs to her. What do you say, boys?"

Eliza's jaw clenched at the insult. She looked at her husband. Samuel was a brave man in his way. Though his shoulders were tense and angry, he just stood like a dumb ox and would not answer the men.

Nor would any of the other Mormons come to their rescue, Eliza knew.

One man jested, "She looks plenty skittish to me. Might just buck you off."

Eliza handed baby Isaac off to her thirteen-year-old son, Bill, and strode toward the brute that had last insulted Jane, but the bully with the whip stepped into Eliza's path, intercepting her. He was thin, perhaps thirty, with dark-brown hair, a hatchet face, and a bushy mustache that dripped down well below his chin. His hat was slung low over his eyes.

"Sir, you and your friends owe my daughter an apology," Eliza demanded, though she instantly regretted bestowing upon him the honorary "sir." He was obviously a lout.

The bully smirked, dark eyes flashing. He was chewing slowly, and now he spat a wad of dark tobacco. He made it look as if he was aiming at the ground, even as he soiled Eliza's skirt.

She glared at him and then explained as calmly as possible, "Mister, these immigrants are Mormons. They adhere to strict rules that prohibit violence, and so, as I'm sure that you suspect, you have nothing to fear from them."

The bully smiled. "Hell, I know that. I was Mormon once't, for about a week—until old Brigham started preaching polygamy."

"Then you should understand this:" Eliza said, "though my husband and children are Mormons, I am not. I don't partake of their perplexing notions any more than you. As a 'gentile,' I'm free to give you the rebuttal that you deserve." With that, Eliza slapped the bully's face so hard that spittle flew from his mouth. She hoped that she'd knocked out a couple of teeth.

There, she'd finally admitted it in public. Here she was among five hundred Mormons heading to Zion and she didn't give a hoot about their uninformed beliefs.

More the fool me, she thought.

The bully fell back. Rage flashed across his face, and she thought that he'd repay her blow. He grinned broadly. "Well, ma'am, if'n you ain't a Mormon, then maybe there's hope for you yet." He took off his hat, revealing a full head of hair slick with grease. He put the hat over his heart and said, "I apologize to you and your kin. I'm mighty sorry."

Eliza nodded.

"Zeb Walker, you leave that woman alone!" a fellow shouted. It was the church agent that had been giving orders to Captain Willie. He came rushing down the street in his cheap suit.

Zeb whirled to meet him. "Or what, McGaw—" Zeb demanded, "you gonna sissy-slap me, too?"

"Shut your mouth, you damned apostate," McGaw growled.

Zeb Walker turned toward Eliza, and she saw a fiery light in his dark eyes. He was enjoying this.

"I don't take orders from you," Zeb yelled, "ya evil old slave driver. You're fixing to lead these folks straight down the throat of hell, and you act like you're better than me?"

Suddenly, Eliza realized that this is exactly what Zeb had wanted—an audience. He'd staged his insult, cracked his whip, in order to command the immigrants' attention. It was an old street-preacher's trick. You do anything to get a crowd to stop and give ear.

My, she thought, *we* are *giving them a freak show today.*

Now Zeb stepped up onto the sidewalk to gain a little elevation; he waved his hands broadly and shouted to the folks in the handcart company, "Has McGaw warned you good folks about the Grasshopper War?" Zeb shouted. "They got Mormon crickets back in Utah as big as your thumb and as black as sin. Millions of 'em come swarming over the hills eight weeks ago, turning the land black, eating everything in sight—gardens, trees, your Sunday go-to-meetin' clothes. Folks are starving in Utah! Their children are starving. Has he told you that?"

"You shut your mouth!" McGaw cried. His knuckles had turned white he was clenching his fists so hard. "They know what they're getting into!"

"Oh, do they?" Zeb shouted. "Summer's nearly gone. Up on the Great Divide, winter starts in September, two weeks from now. And you've got a whole passel of cripples and old folks in your crew. Not one in three of yer kids even got shoes." He turned to the crowd, staring straight at Bill and Sam Junior. "Do you kids know what you're gettin' into? You'll never make it over the Rocky Mountains without freezing! Don't go. Don't listen to your leaders, I'm begging you!" Zeb choked up. His concern for the children was real. "There's work here in town for any man who leaves this company. I promise. I've got a mill, and I'm paying two dollars a day for an honest day's work. I need haulers and drovers. Stay here in town. For heaven's sake, I'm begging."

"I'm warning you for the last time!" McGaw raged. He moved in closer, as if to strike.

Interesting, Eliza thought. None of the Mormons would stand up to defend the honor of her daughter, but McGaw looked as if he'd tear this apostate's head off in order to shut him up. It made her wonder what McGaw and the other church leaders might be hiding.

"Has he warned you folks about the wildfires?" Zeb called to the crowd. "The Sioux set the prairies on fire each fall to stampede the buffalo onto their killing grounds. You're set to walk straight into the wildfires."

McGaw growled like an animal and stepped up to Zeb, glaring face-to-face. "They'll make it across the prairies, by God. They'll make it. The handcart system was instituted by a prophet. They'll travel faster than ox-drawn wagons. They won't be hunting stray animals every morning and won't be tied to trails where the grass is deep and the going rough. You'll see!"

The apostate flashed a superior grin at McGaw and goaded him. "Brigham Young ain't no prophet. He's a lying womanizer. The doctrine of spiritual wifery comes from the devil, and Brigham will lead you all straight to hell."

Eliza wasn't prepared for the sudden attack.

An old white-bearded geezer stood on the tavern porch, leaning on a cane. McGaw snatched the fellow's cane in one fluid move and swung, hitting Zeb on the shoulder and driving him back, then stabbed low, catching Zeb's ankle in the crook of the cane, and pulled Zeb's foot out from under him.

Zeb fell with a crash, but one of Zeb's cohorts leapt on McGaw from behind, knocking his hat off and grabbing him by the hair, and held McGaw's head fast while he shouted to the others, "Hit him! Hit him!"

McGaw grappled with his attacker, squirming and shouting, "I'm tired of your foul mouths, you apostates!" For a moment it was hard to see who was holding whom.

Samuel grabbed Eliza and pulled her away from the fight. She heard pistols cocking and turned to see that a couple of handcart pioneers had drawn weapons, while others reached for axes, knives, or anything else handy. Several townsfolk did the same, and there was an uneasy moment as both sides took stock of the situation and came to a truce, agreeing to let the men brawl.

One apostate had his arm around McGaw's neck from behind

and was trying to choke him while he waited for others to hit him. Yet McGaw was big, and he managed to duck and weave just enough to save himself. Blows glanced harmlessly off of his cheek or missed altogether.

"Samuel," Eliza urged, "it's not a fair fight, three on one."

Sam grunted, "It's fair enough."

At that moment, McGaw ducked, pulling from his attacker's grasp. The man grabbed McGaw's long hair, and part of his scalp came away. As McGaw broke free, his fists began to fly, and blows landed with loud smacks.

Within moments, McGaw landed a punch to Zeb's gut that folded him instantly and left him gasping for air. Another strike sent one of Zeb's allies flying backward over the hitching post. The third apostate was already grasping his shoulder from some hurt, and McGaw grabbed him by one arm and swung him in a circle twice, then sent him flying headfirst into a water trough.

McGaw stood for a moment, glaring at his fallen enemies and huffing like a wounded bull, then reached down and picked up his hat. While he was at it, he grabbed the clump of his own bloody hair and stared at it mutely, as if trying to determine how to reattach it.

"How could you call that exchange fair—" Eliza demanded of her husband. "There were three against one!"

"Three against two—" Samuel corrected. "McGaw had God on his side."

2

The Weak

With the coming of trouble, Baline Mortensen raced down the line of handcarts to join with the Danes. The handcart company was divided into "hundreds," each with its own leader, who was responsible to make sure that his people were safe.

Her thoughts were a torrent. She'd seen the cold look that Eliza Gadd had given her earlier, and then the woman made everything worse by slapping one of the townsfolk. The company had traveled six thousand miles without such trouble, and just when it looked as if they'd make it across America safely, this had to happen.

She found Father Jens sooner than she'd imagined. He'd wandered up to a store and stood peering through a window at a red coat. Around him, there were only English and Scots.

So Baline took the opportunity to speak to Jens privately about something that was bothering her. She would never have asked the question if other Danes were near, but the English that surrounded them could not understand her, so she spoke freely. Baline felt that it was like being invisible, but only her words were invisible.

"Father Jens," Baline asked, "why are the English so weak?"

Jens Nielsen was not her real father. He had been a missionary back in Denmark and had lived with her family for awhile. Baline's real parents had not been able to sell their farm this season and had therefore not had the money that they needed to emigrate. So Jens had offered money to the family to send Baline ahead, as they had done with her older sister Margrethe, a year before.

Baline's parents jumped at the chance. In Denmark, the Lutheran church was an official arm of the government. The parish priest was in charge of the schools, and the local priest on their island of Falster, Peder Kock, hated Mormons. He regularly published slanderous articles in the paper and stirred up mobs, encouraging them to attack and even kill the Mormon missionaries, and to destroy the homes of Mormons.

Jens Nielsen had been attacked more than once and had even tried to swear out a warrant against his foes. Yet the judge had told him, "There is no law that protects Mormons in Denmark."

At school, Baline had found that she, too, incurred Peder Kock's wrath. The boys often pulled her hair or pushed her to the ground, and when they did, the priest would look away. She felt sure that the boys did it only to win his approval. Once, after school, some boys had pushed her into a filthy mud puddle, yellow with cow pee, and rubbed her face in it.

Baline didn't think that this was too bad. Christ had suffered worse things for the gospel's sake. Yet it terrified Baline's mother. Baline had heard her parents whispering at night when they thought she was asleep.

"We must send her away," her mother had said. "Baline will soon be ten years old, and she will begin budding into womanhood. The boys will try . . . they will rape her, as they tried to do with Margrethe."

Baline's mother had begun sobbing while her father comforted her.

Baline hadn't known the meaning of the word "rape" at the time, and still wasn't quite certain what it entailed. She had asked one of the women at church, and the woman had responded by telling her about how dogs mate and then have puppies. She said, "That is what the men try to do to you."

Baline had turned red with embarrassment and grown dizzy at the thought. She had run out the back door of the meeting house and nearly vomited. She had never imagined anything so vile. She was terrified that some evil man would try to make her have puppies.

"Weak?" Jens asked, pulled from his reverie. "What makes you think the English are weak?"

"You know what I mean," Baline said. She didn't like talking this way about the English. Some of them, like Mary Hurren and Agnes Caldwell, were quickly becoming her best friends. "Sister Gadd just slapped a man. She thinks the English are better than me, but they're not. They are uglier than Danes, and smaller. They have the crooked teeth. And they are more evil: on the ship, some English boys and girls were caught kissing. No Dane would ever do that! And then last week, Captain Willie had to reprove them. He said that some of the English men were sneaking into farmers' barns at night and milking their cows, stealing milk, and one of them had even killed a piglet!"

"A man will do terrible things when he gets hungry enough," Jens said, apologizing for the English saints. "We should not speak evilly about others, especially our own."

Baline reached up with one toe and scratched the back of her leg. The mosquitoes were terrible here near the river. Her legs felt as if they were made of lead. She'd just walked five miles today, over three hundred miles in the past month. So her legs were lead inside and covered with burning welts on the outside. She was weary and looked forward to the rest that was promised for the next day as they prepared for the hard part of the journey, but she didn't relish staying here with all of the mosquitoes.

"We must also be truthful," Baline said. "And the truth is that the hard part of our journey has not yet begun. Yes, the flour we get isn't enough to keep us from staying hungry, and many of the children cry at night, but the pangs are not too bad.

"And even if they were worse, my hunger does not excuse me from stealing another person's food," Baline said with the kind of pure wrath that is felt only by the very young. "You are the one who taught me that!"

Jens sighed and seemed to think. Then he admitted, "You are right. Their hunger does not excuse their sins. Yet there is more to it. Perhaps their hunger is greater than yours, or perhaps they have less tolerance for it. Did you ever think of that? A thousand years ago, our ancestors were the kings of the sea, the Vikings. You know of them?"

There were old Viking ruins near her school back in Denmark.

Rounded stones were carved with ancient runes for Freya and Thor, the gods that her ancestors believed protected the village. "Yes," Baline said. "I know of them."

"Then you know that they sailed across the ocean each summer, plundering villages and carrying away the women to make them captive, in order to prove their courage to the gods. They went to England, and to the shores of France, and always they took away the most beautiful women and brought them home to wife."

Baline nodded, for she had heard this. "So?"

"A woman and a man, they are like horses. If you mate two fine horses, they will give you handsome foals. People are the same. If a handsome man marries a pretty girl, their children will be nice to look at—like you!"

He reached down and pinched Baline's nose. Baline knew that she wasn't really pretty, not like some girls. She had the big bones of a farmwoman or a warrior, but she also had a winning smile, and she was happy all of the time, so other children flocked around her.

"So, that is why Danes are handsome?" Baline asked.

"The ugly girls, and the weak ones that no Viking wanted, they stayed in England, and got married. They gave birth to children with crooked teeth, like trolls, and ugly faces. But the pretty women in Denmark, they gave birth to handsome children. And that is why, today, the Danes are the most beautiful and the strongest people in the world.

"And that is why the English are weak today and are so easily overcome."

Jens fell silent for a moment, then whispered, "Don't tell this to your English friends, okay? We don't want to hurt their feelings."

Baline stood for a moment, feeling sad and in shock. Agnes Caldwell had the crooked teeth, a little. Her face was pretty, almost elfin, but she was imperfect. Even Mary Hurren had kinky, brittle hair.

"Then it is our fault that they are weak?" Baline asked. "We stole the strength from them, and the beauty?"

"It is not your fault," Jens said. "You stole nothing from them. It was your ancestors a thousand years ago who did it. And now, you have a chance to return it. Because they are weak, they will need the strength of a good person like you. You can be their example."

Baline nodded solemnly. Because they are weak, she realized, they have little self-control. That is why Agnes Caldwell falls behind the handcarts so often. That is why Mary Hurren weeps so bitterly when she gets hungry.

"So, they will need me to be strong," she said. "Not just strong enough to pull their handcarts, but strong enough to be faithful even when their hearts are breaking."

Jens said thoughtfully, "If you would really be strong, there is something you should know. You can do more good with God's help than you can ever do on your own. Did you know that you can be like an angel?"

"When I die?" Baline asked.

"No, you can be one now," Jens said. "The word *angel*, it means 'one who speaks for God.' If God inspires you to say something to another person, to give them words of warning or of comfort, it is the same as being an angel. In the Doctrine and Covenants, God says, 'Whether I speak by my own mouth, or by the voice of my servants, it is the same.' And so, when you speak under inspiration, it is the same as if you were an angel."

"I see," Baline said, but only because she was afraid to disagree with someone as wise and kind as Jens.

"Let me tell you a story," Jens said. "When I first joined the church, I was sad one day because I felt like I was of no use to anyone. I wanted to preach the gospel, but I was not very good at reading, and so I did not know the scriptures. So, one morning, I prayed to God to help me do some good in the world.

"That morning I got up very early to take some ducks to the Saturday market. The fog in the streets was so dense that it made the cobblestones as slick as if it had just rained. I was walking through the streets, almost blinded by fog, when I thought I heard a distant sound of crying.

"Almost, I paid no attention to the sound, but suddenly I remembered my prayer, and I thought, perhaps this is my chance to do some good.

"So I began walking through the fog, searching for the girl that was crying, and as I did, I began to get frightened. Whoever it is, I thought, she will be a stranger. How will I introduce myself? She will think I am being forward, and make fun of me.

"Besides, I thought, it is probably nothing. It is probably some girl crying because her cat got trampled by a horse or because her nose has a hump on it.

"At last, after walking nearly eight blocks, I found the girl. She was huddled in an alley, shivering with cold while her head rested on her knees.

" 'What will I say?' I wondered. Then she looked up at me, and I did not have to say anything at all. The girl that I had thought would be a stranger was someone I had known as a child, back when I lived in Lolland. She was living a hundred miles away from me, and I had not seen her in seven years. She was my best friend's little sister, Mareska. When last I had seen her, she was a child no older than you, but now she was a young woman.

" 'Mareska,' I said, 'what are you doing here? Why are you crying?'

" 'I came looking for you,' she said, 'but I could not find you.' It turned out that she had joined the church in Lolland, but the persecution was so bad, her brother begged her to come to Copenhagen and find me, hoping that I could take her in and she could live quietly where no one would know that she was a Mormon. She did not know that I had become one, too! The poor thing, she had run out of food and money and had not eaten for three days."

To Baline, it sounded as if Jens was speaking of things that had happened long ago. It was like listening to stories from the Bible.

"Did she live through it?" Baline asked.

Jens laughed. "Of course she is still alive. She is Mareska Knutson. She is standing right over there!"

He jutted his chin toward a young woman who stood down the street, holding her two-year-old son up on her shoulder so that he could see.

"Oh," Baline said, feeling in awe.

Jens spoke softly, more solemnly, "Now, every night, you see me walking in the evening through the fields. My wife will tell you that I am thinking, but really, I am listening, listening very hard to see if I can hear the voice of God. Most of the time, he speaks so softly that even when we struggle to hear him, we find it hard to understand what he wants. But if you listen sincerely, Baline, sometimes he will call you to be his servant. He won't command you all of the time, for he does not want to be our puppet-master. So he asks that we study the word of God as found in the scriptures and do good to others of our own free will. Yet when the need is great, he will ask you to help. And why should he not ask you instead of some angel? Isn't it easier to ask you to help someone next door, than to send an angel all of the way from heaven?"

Baline fell silent and stood listening for a still, small voice inside her, to see if God wanted anything now, but she didn't feel anything.

From down the line, Captain Willie shouted, "Move out! Move 'em on out!"

He was pointing north, away from the ferry docked on the river, as shiny as a new coin.

"What is this? What is going on?" Jens asked.

Jens, like many Danes, couldn't understand more than ten words of English, but Baline was studying her new language diligently. Brother Peder Mortensen was wealthy, and he had a book of English words. He let Baline read it all that she wanted so that she was learning fifty new words a day. Beyond that, she tried to play with the English children almost exclusively. So that even though she did not speak English like a native, she could usually understand what she heard. Many of the Danish saints were in awe of her mastery of the language, and they whispered that she had "the gift of tongues."

Baline listened for a moment as some of the settlers relayed orders down the line.

"We must leave the town," Baline said, "because of the trouble that Eliza Gadd started. It is too dangerous to stay."

"But what about our shopping?" Jens asked. This was the last city they would find for more than a thousand miles. Like everyone else, he had wanted to buy some supplies.

Baline just shook her head and went back to her handcart. She had hoped to be able to ride the boat upriver, but Captain Willie did not want to leave his people in town, not with the present threat.

So the whole company marched along the Missouri River for ten more miles, taking no rests, not even stopping for a bite to eat. The sun was sweltering, and it grew humid beneath the cottonwood trees along the river. Mosquitoes flocked around them.

As they walked, Baline wandered among the handcarts, listening to people.

Even some of the Danes had begun to complain. One of the men, Brother Hansen, had stopped in town long enough to talk to a Dane who worked as a teamster. The Dane had left a Mormon wagon train two years earlier, and he'd told Brother Hansen about the high wages paid here in town, and now Hansen spread the news as if he were the town crier.

So it was late in the muggy afternoon when the company stopped to rest. Across the river, not half a mile away, were green fields thick with cattle. A settlement had been built there by the church, and a town was springing up around it—one with a gristmill and a new bank and a few houses in various phases of construction.

The ferry came up around the bend after they stopped. It had a genuine steam engine that belched as its piercing whistle sounded. It drew up to shore, and a man shoved a gangplank onto the shore and began loading.

Not everyone could fit on the boat at once. The Scotts and some of the English were ferried across first. Then it was the Danes' turn.

But as the ferry was loading, Brother Hansen stood beside his handcart, his wife in his shadow, and watched everyone leave.

Some of the men went to talk to him, and an argument ensued. "I am staying," he said adamantly. "I have an offer of a good job!"

The leader of the hundred for the Danes was Johan Ahmanson, a tall young Swede with sandy hair. He stood with Hansen, who was a younger man with only a mouse of a wife, and tried to reason with him. "We did not come for money," Ahmanson said. "We came because it is God's will."

"We are going no farther!" Hansen bellowed, and he glared up at Ahmanson. "This is my decision to make."

Many people had left the company along the way—some in New York, others in Chicago. It was a bad thing to separate from the saints. Those who did so often apostatized from the church. Only a couple of Danes had left the company up until now.

Secretly, Baline felt glad to see him go. Hansen was a pudgy man who found it hard to pull a handcart. At the end of the day, he would eat his own rations and then demand that his wife give him her food, too.

No one liked him.

Ahmanson shook his head sadly, as if sorry to see him leave. "Yes, it is your decision to make. I won't try to stop you, but we will have to settle accounts . . ."

At this, Hansen's face turned red, and he got blustery. "Settle accounts?"

Ahmanson nodded. "Of course. You borrowed money, and now you must make arrangements to pay it back."

Hansen had not been a wealthy man. He had not been able to pay for his passage across the ocean or for his train fare to Chicago. Most of the money that he'd used was borrowed. Now, if he wanted to leave the company, he would have to pay up.

Brother Madsen, the clerk for the Danes, got his ledger and read off Hansen's debts. He had spent all that he had to get here, and he still owed seventy dollars for boat fare to Peder Mortensen, a wealthy old crippled cobbler. He owed another $3.82 to Father Jens for some tin pans that he had bought in New York.

Hansen had no money at all, so he wrote a note swearing to send money to Peder Mortensen. It was money that Baline felt sure the Mortensens would never see.

Father Jens tried to discourage Hansen from leaving the company. "I don't want you to send money to me," Father Jens said reasonably. "It costs seven dollars to send a letter across the prairie. It would be cheaper just to give me the pans!"

Of course, giving Father Jens the pans would create a hardship on Hansen. He would have no way to cook his food until he bought new ones.

"I can't give you the money, and I won't give you the pans back!" Hansen said.

Father Jens was a big man. At six feet six inches tall, he towered over almost everyone. He wasn't just tall, he was strong, too. Hansen didn't dare lift a hand against him.

"You can't just keep the pans," one elder in the group said. "To do so would be like asking a man if it is all right to rob him."

Several others nodded sagely, and some of them crowded close to Hansen. There had been much anger in camp at how he mistreated his wife, and it was obvious that some of the men would have welcomed a reason to fight.

Hansen was growing angrier by the minute, his face turning red and his eyes widening. He said, "This is robbery! This is robbery!"

Captain Ahmanson reached into the back of the handcart and took out the pans. "No, stealing a man's pans is robbery. We are only doing what is right!"

Hansen glared at Ahmanson, then at Father Jens, but all that he could do was run to his handcart and march away, his legs stiff from wrath.

"He will make trouble for us," Father Jens said with certainty.

Captain Ahmanson carried the tin pans to Jens's cart and put them in. He asked, "What trouble could he make?"

Jens shook his head. "I don't know. And that's what worries me . . ."

Because of this altercation, Baline had to wait for the boat to come back on its third docking. Even then, it was crowded with settlers and handcarts. Jens Nielsen, his wife, Else, and his little five-year-old son, Niels, all got boarded off toward the bow of the boat.

A few feet away, young Samuel Gadd stood on the ferry, hanging over the rail, staring west with a dreamy gaze, a sweet grin plastered on his face as if he'd just gotten his first kiss.

Like Baline, he was ten years old. He had brown hair that fell into his hazel eyes, and his skin was freckled.

"Vat are you smiling at?" Baline asked.

Samuel licked his lips. "I had a dream last night," he said. "I dreamt that we reached Zion. It was so beautiful!"

Baline was immediately riveted, for she had often heard fascinating stories about prophetic dreams, but to her surprise, Samuel's mother glanced down at him, her eyes pinched with concern.

"I dreamt," Samuel said, "that I was walking through a desert of sand so red it was like rust. It was so deep that my feet sank with each step, as if I was trudging through snow.

"The sun was going down, and over a hill I saw glorious lights, pale blue, and so I ran to the top of the hill and looked down on a city, a fantastic city, unlike anything I've ever dreamt or could imagine. It had spires like the House of Commons, but they rose up impossibly tall, and there were broad domes in the city, too, held up by slender columns. All of the buildings looked as if they were made not with stone or brass, but looked as if the walls were sculpted of light. They shone like clear glass. And all of these spires and domes rose up high into the air, glimmering, like monuments.

"At the heart of the city was a great light, burning and smoking, as if the sun had fallen to earth and set fire to everything around it, and I knew that God was there, giving it light.

"So I ran out of the desert, onto a street of gold so clean that it was like . . . like a clear pool on a spring morning, hidden deep within the forest."

Now there were several people around Samuel, hanging onto every word. The Mormons believed in dreams, believed that God could talk to a man in dreams, and Baline felt sure that this one was of God.

"I saw marvelous things there, things that I cannot even begin to describe," Samuel said. "Now I know that the artistry of people is nothing when compared to the artistry of God: I saw a sculpture of a beautiful woman carved from water, as clear as leaded crystal, only the water hung in the air above me as if just waiting for permission to drop.

"I saw a bench in the park that was more comfortable than any bed I ever dreamed of, and the Holy Spirit told me that God had made it just for me, as a place to rest, and that he knew every inch of me, and there could not be a more perfect place for me to sit.

"I saw the Prophet Joseph riding a fine, tall roan horse down the streets, and—"

"Birds?" Baline asked. "Did you see any birds in Zion? Or flowers?" Baline had always hoped that there would be birds in heaven.

"I saw a place, a huge archway in the city, and hanging vines swept down the wall for hundreds of feet, with their white flowers glittering in the shadows like stars, while hummingbirds darted from blossom to blossom, sparkling like emeralds when the sun took them!"

There were nods of approval from the listeners, and one woman declared, "It is from God."

But Samuel's mother, Eliza Gadd, looked sad and hurt. "Don't get your hopes up, Samuel," she said. "I don't want to see you break your heart. There won't be any castles sculpted from light when you get to Salt Lake City, just a few houses made of mud, all plastered over logs. And you won't see God burning in any bushes, just fat old Brigham Young squatting there like a toad."

Baline gasped to hear her speak of the prophet in such a manner, but then remembered that Eliza was just a gentile.

"But," Samuel explained to his mother, "it wasn't a dream about Zion as it is now. This is just the beginning. I saw Zion as it will be, someday, when God makes it his home."

Sister Gadd just shook her head. "Don't get your hopes up," she said again.

Baline wished desperately that she could have seen Samuel's dream of Zion, but she had to console herself with the thought that she could help build it.

As the ferry carried Baline across the Missouri, she glanced up at Jens. He was a good man, but didn't understand a word of English.

He was gazing back toward the retreating shore of Iowa. A dozen families stood staring sadly at the boat for a long moment, some waving, some hiding their faces in shame; almost as one they turned away and began trudging sheepishly back toward town.

These were the English deserters.

Baline had finished the easy part of the journey, the walk through Iowa, and even that was too hard for many people. Three hundred miles had worn out more than just shoes. Some of the deserters said that they planned to come west next year, when they had earned enough money for teams and wagons, but everyone knew the truth: such people would probably never earn enough money. They were joining the old world, full of its strife and corruption. They were apostates.

But Baline was determined to walk to Zion, barefoot as she was, to make a new world among the people that were one in heart, where she would be free to live the gospel without interference from the mobs and the government.

Now Baline looked up to Jens. He was staring off at the apostates, lost in thought. Obviously he felt bad, and perhaps he wondered if he should have just let Niels take his pans.

The waters of the Missouri were dark and brown and seemed to roil like boiling coffee as they rolled swiftly along. No fish jumped in the river, though many mosquitoes danced upon its surface.

Baline went to the handcart and shoved the tin cookware that they had taken from the Hansens under a tarp. It wasn't much—a couple of thin sauce pans and some plates. The cooking fires had blackened their bottoms.

"What will you do with this?" Baline asked Father Jens. "Try to sell it?"

"Maybe we can use them to fix the handcarts," Jens suggested. "I will nail those pans over the hubs, to keep out the dirt, and I will nail the plates around the rims of the wheels, to strengthen them."

Baline had seen others using makeshift bits of tin to fix their carts. Now it would be their turn, and she understood why Jens had kept the cookware.

Suddenly the ferry lurched as it hit the Nebraska shore, and all across the ferry, men shouted and threw their hats into the air, and some men hugged their wives and kissed them right in public.

"What happened?" Jens asked. "Why are they celebrating?"

Baline cocked her head and listened. "Say good-bye to the United States," one of the men was shouting. "Woo-hoo! And hurrah for Zion!"

An old woman began to sob as her white-haired husband held her close. "No more mobs," she whispered, tears streaming down her cheeks, "no more worrying about every sound in the night."

Baline reported, "They are celebrating because we have left the United States. There are no more cities for a thousand miles. Never again will we have to face the persecution."

Baline suddenly felt as if a weight had been lifted from her, a weight that she'd carried so long she'd forgotten that she sometimes stumbled from the load.

Joseph Smith had taught that the United States was founded by inspired men, the first country ever created where men could worship as they pleased. A month ago, she had been so happy to arrive, but that was before she'd faced the mobs in Indiana, Illinois, and Iowa. Now she was overwhelmed with relief at having escaped.

"We are now truly free," she said, and tears began to stream from her eyes.

"Yes," Jens whispered, and he leaned over the rail of the ferry and wiped his eyes with the back of his sleeves. "We are free. Thank God."

3

Lightning Out of a Clear Sky

After the tents were set up on the Nebraska shore of the Missouri, after dinner was done and the dishes were cleaned, Eliza and four other women went to the banks of a nearby creek to wash. The sun was rapidly sinking toward the western horizon, and there was just enough time to wash their sweaty dresses and hang them out to dry before nightfall. Dense foliage provided a screen for the women to undress behind, and added to this was some just-washed bedding which hung in billowing walls. As the women stripped, "Sister" Linford—for among the Mormons, every woman was called sister and every man was brother—made sure that no one drew close, lest one of the men or children barge through the brush and catch the women disrobed.

One woman in the group was a longtime family friend, a young widow named Martha Campkin. When Samuel Gadd had been the president of the small branch in Wimpole, the Campkins had been members of the congregation. Martha still thought of Samuel Gadd as being her spiritual leader, but their relationship was drawing tighter than that.

Martha's husband had died only a few months past, and now her sons looked upon Samuel Gadd as a surrogate father. The boys followed the Gadd family handcart all day, every day, and Samuel was so good-hearted he could not discourage the relationship, even as Eliza saw signs that Martha was growing ever more dependent on

Samuel, forever asking his opinion on this or that topic, and encouraging her children to hang onto his every word and follow in his footsteps.

Now Eliza was concerned that Martha might be hoping that Samuel Gadd would take her as a second wife.

As if that were not bad enough, the young Hill sisters were always hovering nearby. Everywhere that Eliza turned, there seemed to be women vying for her husband's affection. Eliza didn't like the situation. "Too many hens in the house and not enough roosters," her mother would have chided.

Neither Eliza nor Samuel could escape the women, not even in their own tent. The Willie Handcart Company had one tent for each twenty people. The tents were like large, white, canvas teepees.

Eliza's family, with her husband and seven of her children, took up nine slots. In addition, the Linford family with their three boys, ages seventeen, fourteen, and eleven, filled up five more slots. Four more slots were all taken by single women. True, one of the women, Grandmother Funnel, was in her early sixties, but Grandmother Funnel's daughter Lizzie was only three-and-twenty. Marian Miller and Ann Howard were both about ten years younger than Eliza. Having the benefits of youth, all of the younger women in Eliza's tent were prettier than she.

It felt as if it were a plot on Captain Willie's part, though in all honesty, all of the tents had more women than men, and some of the tents had only single women in them.

Still, Eliza worried that the church leaders were grooming her husband, preparing him to accept the doctrine of plural marriage at the journey's end.

Eliza's mind was muddled with alarm, and not just about the women, either. Everyone in the camp was wondering what to do. The townsfolk in Council Bluffs had been right. It was too late in the summer for them to continue on to Utah—that seemed certain. But neither could they turn back, not in the face of the prejudice and hatred that had been cast into their faces at every turn.

As Eliza had gone through camp, speaking to various sub-captains and to the church outfitters, hoping only to make her own informed choice, she found that sound information was hard to come by.

An informed choice, Eliza thought. *That's what I need to make today.*

As Martha Campkin slid out of her dress, all sweaty and dusty from the road, she said softly, almost as if in a daze, "Eliza, I couldn't help but notice that Samuel has his cough back." Samuel had developed a cold after standing guard duty in a summer storm two weeks earlier, and now it nagged him. "I heard Captain Savage tell him that it's his turn for guard duty this evening. I don't think that he should be pulling a handcart all day, then pitching the tents, then standing guard all night—not in his condition." Her tone was more than kind. It was intimate, dreamy.

Eliza glanced over, saw Martha naked, hugging her dress.

Without thinking, Eliza snapped, "You worry about your own husband."

The words fell like a slap, and Martha stood for a second, the blood leeching from her face.

Silently Eliza cursed herself and wondered why she had said such cruel words. The answer was simple. For just an instant, Eliza had forgotten that Martha was a widow.

Martha's husband had taken sick with smallpox back in England just a few months ago. He'd seemed better when the family had sailed from England, but he took a turn for the worse aboard ship. By the time they'd landed in New York, Martha's husband's face had gone gray, and he suffered from constant fatigue.

He should have been given time to rest. But he couldn't afford it. Some missionaries back in England had borrowed six hundred dollars from Martha's husband, promising to have the money waiting in New York. But when the family arrived, the money did not materialize. The missionaries had stolen their life savings. So her husband had taken the family to Missouri by train and tried to open a shoe shop in Saint Louis. Within eight weeks he had worked himself into the grave.

Martha was understandably bitter. She'd been defrauded by a pair of missionaries, and the loss had led to her husband's demise.

But instead of an angry retort now, Martha only stammered in confusion. "I—I'm sorry, Eliza," she said. "I didn't mean a thing by it. I wouldn't wish ill fortune on you or your family."

Eliza knew that Martha had not meant to insult. She wasn't accusing Eliza of being neglectful of her husband's needs. Rather, Martha's concern was genuine, loving—and that was what had raised Eliza's ire so precipitously.

Loving, Eliza thought. *She sounds like she's in love with my husband.*

Emily, ever the peacemaker, struggled to steer the conversation toward safer ground. "Perhaps I should trade places with Samuel on guard duty tonight."

"You?" Julia chided. "Could you shoot a man?"

"Of course," Emily said. "A woman can do anything that a man can do. And she has a right to defend herself, even if it comes down to blood. Arapahoes, mobsters—bring them on! I'll let Eliza here slap them silly, then I'll shoot them while they're trying to spit out their teeth."

The younger girls giggled, and Eliza's face went red. The families in camp had all retired to their tents to hide from the swarms of mosquitoes rising from the Missouri. Eliza imagined that in every tent, people would be talking about what she'd done today.

Martha studied Eliza from the corner of her eye, saw her embarrassment, and chided the Hill girls, "Don't laugh. What Eliza did today was very courageous, and we all owe her a debt of gratitude."

"Here, here!" Emily said, and Eliza turned away.

She didn't want their praise. Yes, what she had done was courageous, but they were more than courageous, for they were willing to take their abuse without venting their anger. They had both Eliza's courage and a level of self-control that she lacked. She didn't want their praise. She didn't want their advice. Right now, she realized, she just wanted to be away from everyone, somewhere off alone.

There were too many hens in Eliza's camp. "Never let another woman under your roof," Eliza's mother had told her years ago, when the first rumors began to spread that Mormons were practicing polygamy, "even if it's only for a few days. Men have a rutting instinct, just like bulls or rams. Let a young woman under your roof, and you'll suddenly find that your husband's affections are divided."

Eliza heard the words ringing in her mind, even after five years. That damned haunting voice. She glanced around the wooded glen, as if to find the source of it, almost as if expecting her mother's shade to be hovering in the shadows beneath the trees.

Julia pulled off her muddy dress and just stood for a moment, stretching. At nineteen, Julia was a beautiful young woman, with luxurious dark hair and the eyes of a doe. Her body was lithe and slender, much as Eliza's had been twenty years ago when Samuel first took her to bed. Julia was a dainty girl, very pretty, and men were naturally protective of her.

Yet Emily Hill was just as tempting a morsel, if not more so. Emily was a poetess, and Eliza could see how her sly wordplay and powerful mind amused and attracted Samuel. When he spoke to Emily, his voice often became soft and husky.

Eliza worried. She didn't believe that her husband would ever reject her. He'd never push her out of his bed, but she worried that he just might invite another woman into it. It wasn't that Samuel was lusty. Nor was he unfeeling toward her. He was as kind as a man could be.

That was the problem. Kind, hard-working, well-spoken, diligent in his studies of the scriptures, a large family—he was just the kind of man that the leaders of the church would want to head a congregation. Once they reached Utah, he'd probably be called to be a bishop, the equivalent of a priest in most other churches.

As a bishop, he'd be expected to show his support for the doctrine of polygamy by taking a second wife. Not that he'd ever love another woman as he did Eliza.

When Joseph Smith had introduced polygamy, it was said that he did so after prayer. He had asked God how it was that ancient prophets like Abraham and Solomon had been allowed to take multiple wives when the teaching of Jesus in the New Testament clearly indicates that a man should have but one wife.

The answer, according to rumors spread by those who knew

Joseph, astonished even him. He was told that the Lord allowed such marriages so that the families might raise children in righteousness.

Thus, the Mormons now practiced polygamy on a limited basis. Good men were typically asked to engage in the practice. It wasn't about lust. It was more often a church calling, and the marriage was only sanctioned if the man's first wife agreed.

Thus, plural wives were often charity cases—widows like Martha Campkin who would find it a struggle to raise her children without a husband out on some homestead in the Utah desert.

Because the first wife had to sanction a second marriage, a plural wife was seldom more attractive than the original wife—either in appearance or in personality.

In theory Eliza would have the power to veto any match that her husband might be asked to enter. But sometimes Eliza worried. She wasn't a Mormon. What would Samuel do if the church leaders asked him to marry? Would he be obedient to the will of God as revealed by his church leaders, or remain faithful to his wife?

"I'm going for a walk," Eliza said.

"Sixteen miles wasn't enough today?" Emily teased.

"Apparently not," Julia chortled.

"Aren't you going to stay and do your wash?" Sister Campkin asked, a fretful tone in her voice.

"Tomorrow," Eliza answered as she hurried from the screen of brush. She couldn't stomach the thought getting naked right now, not with this herd of cows.

Behind the screen of brush and sheets, Eliza heard Martha Campkin whisper, "You shouldn't have teased Sister Gadd. Eliza's a proud woman and can't stand to be teased."

With her back to the tent, Eliza said coolly, "I'm not your sister."

There was embarrassed silence behind the screen as the women realized that they had been overheard and then Emily said, "We love you like one anyway."

Eliza walked back to her tent.

Outside the tent, the children were dashing about, playing tag. After walking all day, it only took a little dinner to help the younger ones recover.

Eliza didn't fret about the children much. The Mormons watched out for each other, as if they were all one big family. If she left little Sarah out to play, other mothers would be watching her as if she were their own. If Eliza left a pan unwashed and went into the tent for a moment, she'd find that someone had cleaned it in her absence.

Usually, if Eliza found a witness, she would learn that Ann Howard was behind the good deed. The woman was notorious for going about and committing random acts of kindness.

Baby Isaac was sitting in the dirt outside the tent, trying to push his thumb on top of a beetle. A quick peek showed that Daniel was inside the tent, asleep. Jane was watching the twins, but Eliza didn't like the idea of leaving the young woman with such a huge responsibility. Eliza picked up baby Isaac, slung him up on her hip, and told Jane, "Watch after the little ones while I'm gone."

The river was full of mosquitoes, so she walked west, away from it.

The saints had camped that night at an old Mormon outpost near the small town of Florence, Nebraska. Florence consisted mainly of the ruins of a settlement built ten years back, when the Mormons had first fled the states to Salt Lake. Nothing much remained of the Mormon settlement. Indians had burned the ruins years ago. But there was an old flour mill beside the creek up north. The abandoned building had just been restored, and now there were five new houses built, like pygmies huddling in the shadow of a giant, and dozens of others were now under construction. A brand new bank had just been built in Florence, too. Florence was booming, thanks to a handful of scheming investors who were promulgating the notion that in ten years Florence would be the next Chicago.

Fools.

The hills rising above the river were denuded of all but grass, for wildfires often spread across the prairie. But unlike the eastern shore of the Missouri River, which had been logged off, there were plenty of trees still here on the western bank, especially near the small creeks that fed into the river to the north and south of town.

Here, the Mormons had bought several hundred acres of land to act as a staging area for immigrants. Five hundred head of cattle were grazing in the tall grass, and a sizeable warehouse had been built of cottonwood logs to hold the flour, bacon, beans, salt and other provisions that the immigrants would haul west.

Eliza carried Isaac through tall grass. The slanting sun shone on it from behind, and full heads of grain glowed in the light in odd colors, a golden so luminous it was almost silver, a rust so dark it was almost cinnamon.

The grasses had no names that Eliza knew. They were not wheat or oats or barley or rye. She had asked Captain Willie once what the names for the grasses were and he had replied, "Buffalo grass," though there were dozens of varieties. Any grass that had no name out here on the prairie, he simply referred to as buffalo grass.

Probably, she thought, *the grasses don't even have a name yet. I'm that far from civilization.*

With every step, her feet threshed the grain, scattering hard seeds to the ground. Grasshoppers rose up and flew ahead of her, as if to herald her arrival.

Eliza climbed a long hill, and at its peak she could see an endless line of downs rolling off into the distance. She had never seen hills like them. They reminded her of waves on the sea, like high waves just before a storm. It was as if the earth had been molten one moment, then frozen solid the next.

I wish I were Emily, Eliza thought. *I wish I could capture the sight of these hills in a poem, like she does, and capture the beauty of the rolling grasslands, so ripe and wholesome.*

I wish I had her soft breasts and firm belly, her slender hips . . .

At her feet, in the tall grass, Eliza noticed a tombstone, and saw others poking up through the straw around it. The name on the tombstone said, "Elizabeth Willie."

She gave a small cry, making two realizations at once: ten years ago the Mormons had come through this town, leaving hundreds of dead in their wake, and at the same time she realized that this woman's grave might well belong to someone in Captain Willie's family.

Eliza studied the grave, wondering. Mother, sister, wife? What had the woman been to Captain Willie?

She strolled for a moment through the old graveyard and came across another grave, one belonging to a man named William Woodward.

There was a William Woodward in the Willie Handcart Company, too. Captain Willie was in charge of the company as a whole, but each one hundred people had a sub-captain over them. William Woodward was a missionary returning from England, one of the young sub-captains.

Could this be his father's grave? Eliza wondered.

Downhill behind her, more than half a mile away, she heard a child wail loudly, as if hurt. Not one of her own. Even at this distance, she knew her children's cries.

But the sound was sobering. There were dozens of people in the camp who had taken sick with various fevers and chills over the past couple of weeks. Some of them had to be pulled in the handcarts. Over half a dozen people had died on the trek already.

There was talk of staying here for a couple of days to fix the handcarts, which were rapidly falling into disrepair.

If we stay for a day or two, Eliza realized, *we'll probably donate some of our sick to the graveyard.*

She sat in the shadow of a headstone and let little Isaac trundle about. The grass was over his head, and he soon found himself exploring the ground, picking bright golden dandelion flowers and discovering ants, experimentally shoving them in his mouth. Sometimes he'd point at a flower or a rock and ask, "What's this, Mommy?"

After a bit, he came and pulled at her blouse. Eliza unfastened her buttons and gave him a breast. With all of the walking in the past month, she was rapidly losing her milk. So she let him nurse, silently willing her milk to flow, and whispered, "Drink while you still can."

Eliza leaned back against a headstone and tried to stop her troubled mind from racing. *The problem,* she thought, *is that we keep getting surprised. You cannot forearm yourself against that which you cannot foresee.*

In England, we were all packed and ready to go when we discovered that the church officials hadn't been able to book passage on a ship. Once they found a ship, we were allowed fifty pounds of belongings per person.

But when we got to Iowa City, Iowa, we discovered that we could only bring seventeen pounds per person on our handcarts.

Thus each family had to dispose of two-thirds of their possessions. Some had tried to sell family heirlooms and found that the locals, who seemed to universally hate Mormons, would only pay a trifle. The money earned would not even pay for shipping the goods.

Eliza had joined some of the other women in packing a few of her treasures into trunks—filling chests with the family silver, with silk tablecloths and fine china. Then they had hurled the trunks out into the Mississippi River. She felt it better to lose everything than to enrich those who hated her family.

Now, Eliza wondered what she had gotten herself into. She'd asked some of the sub-captains in the group, and most of the answers seemed patronizing and uninformative. "Don't worry your pretty little head about it," one man had said.

The sun settled in a pink ball that cast long rays through some purpling clouds on the horizon, painting the sky. Baby Isaac fell asleep in her arms, and Eliza didn't dare move him. It wasn't until the darkness came full and an orange moon as bright as a pumpkin began to spring up in the east that Eliza decided to return to camp.

Eliza buttoned her blouse with one hand, gathered Isaac into her arms, and rose to leave.

A man gave a startled cry of "Wha?" and leapt backward, nearly tripping over his own feet. It was Captain Willie.

"Gol," he laughed when he saw that it was Eliza, "I thought you was a ghost."

"Not yet," Eliza said.

He stood for a moment in the moonlight, holding his heart and trying to get his breath. "Gol, my heart is pounding!"

"I didn't mean to startle you," Eliza said.

"What are you doing out here at this time of night? Don't you know that there are redskins about? The Omahas are friendly, but the same can't be said for the Sioux. They sometimes send raiding parties this far east."

"Then," Eliza said, "perhaps you will be kind enough to escort me back to camp?"

Captain Willie grunted, stood reverently staring down at a tombstone for a long moment, then laid a handful of wildflowers on Elizabeth Willie's grave.

"What was she to you?"

"A cousin," Captain Willie said. "Just my cousin. Sweet girl."

He patted the tombstone, whispered something under his breath, speaking only for the ears of the dead. Then after a long moment he invited Eliza to walk.

"How did she die?" Eliza asked.

"Dysentery," Captain Willie said.

"So many graves."

"We had three thousand people here," Captain Willie said. "We left three hundred of them in the ground. Most died from dysentery. In our weakened state, if you got it, the chances were that you'd be dead within a day. Black-leg took most of the rest."

"Are you angry?"

"That they're dead?"

"That Brigham Young dragged you through this?"

"I made it to Zion," Captain Willie said. "We lost one in ten that winter, and a few more crossing the plains. It doesn't seem too high a price to pay."

"Captain Willie," Eliza said in her most professional manner, "I've been talking to some of the sub-captains, trying to make an informed decision about whether to continue our journey now, or wait out the winter."

"Oh," Captain Willie said thoughtfully; then he teased, "Well, I'll be happy to inform you of my decision, once I come to it."

"I'm not in a joking mood," Eliza said. "I would very much like the answers to some questions."

"All right, Eliza," he said, "if it will help."

"We are traveling a thousand miles, and we are bringing seventy days' worth of provisions?"

"That's correct."

"So you plan on making fifteen miles per day." That wasn't a question. Fifteen miles wasn't too hard to do, Eliza knew, when you walked on good roads. But on days when it rained and you found the handcarts stuck in mud up to their hubs . . . "Will we be traveling on Sundays?"

"I think that the Lord will forgive us," Captain Willie said, "considering what we're up against."

So that meant that they'd have to travel fifteen miles per day. Even on good roads, some of the children couldn't be asked to walk fifteen miles in a day. That meant that the adults would have to pull them in the handcarts in order to give them a little rest.

That was tough. It became much harder when you took into account the other factors that might slow the company down. If there were deaths, people had to be buried. If people fell sick, the handcarts couldn't move. One old man, his mind dazed from heat and fatigue, had wandered off a couple of weeks ago, and it took a rescue party most of the night to find him. Then, of course, the weather could stop you in your tracks

So to be safe, the carts really needed to make something closer to twenty miles per day.

"There are a couple of forts where we can re-supply along the way, correct?"

"Yes," Captain Willie said slowly. He sounded evasive.

"But we can't stop at Fort Kearny," Eliza corrected. "That's what McGaw told me."

"You talked to McGaw?" Captain Willie sounded worried, as if McGaw might be some sort of a traitor with a loose tongue.

"He was very helpful," Eliza said, knowing that Captain Willie would be forced to tell her the truth now, for he wouldn't know how little McGaw had really said. "Why is it that the commander at Fort Kearny won't allow Mormons to camp nearby? Isn't he supposed to protect us?"

Captain Willie shook his head and sighed. "I don't know. All I know is that he'd rather see us all dead than let us camp in the shadow of his fort."

"In fact," Eliza said, "I understand that there won't be any protection from the army along our route. The army has all been drawn off to Kansas?"

"To handle the uprising there," Captain Willie said. The

company had been hearing terrible rumors all through Iowa. A bunch of abolitionists had moved into the Kansas Territory in order to sway it toward becoming a free state. Ruffians out of Missouri had responded by riding across the border and hanging the abolitionists. The whole country was on the brink of war, and the federal troops were engaging in skirmishes with the various factions on almost a daily basis.

"And after we pass the fort," Eliza said, "I understand that the water is of poor quality for a hundred miles, and there are no trees. How will we keep warm at night? How will we cook?"

"You'll keep warm at night by staying in your bedroll. And you'll cook with dried buffalo dung." Captain Willie must have heard Eliza's indrawn breath. "It's not so bad, cooking with buffalo chips. It adds an interesting savor to whatever you're cooking."

"And after we reach Ash Hollow, the grass gets bad and the game is scarce?" Eliza said. She had heard rumors.

"That's why we're taking beef cattle with us," Captain Willie said.

"When we cross the Continental Divide, what exactly is the elevation?" Eliza demanded.

"I wouldn't know," Captain Willie said. "Why would you care?"

"I met a man who sometimes climbs mountains in the Alps. He once told me that glaciers could be found at the ten thousand-foot level.

"I also understand that you have a book in your possession," Eliza said, "called *Peercy's Guide*? The church leaders should have provided it to you in New York. It might have the information I'm looking for."

"Just how much information do you need to make an 'informed decision'?" Captain Willie asked.

"All that I can get," Eliza said. "It's really not so hard. It's simple math. I list the pros and cons to each choice, assign a probability modifier to each potential outcome, and add up the points."

Captain Willie sighed in disgust. "Woman . . . you could have the whole US Cavalry marching at your back, watching for Indians. You could have a castle to sleep in at night, rolling on wheels. You could have enough food to feed all of England being carted for you by Indians, and you could still step in a prairie dog hole and break your neck. You can still be stung by a bee and keel over. You can still catch a cold one afternoon and cough your lungs out by breakfast. I've seen all of them happen. It isn't simple math. There's too many things to go wrong."

Eliza bridled at his patronizing tone. "May I peruse your book?"

"Send one of your boys to my tent in the morning," Captain Willie said.

He suddenly lengthened his stride and veered downhill, toward the shadows of a small creek where stately cottonwoods reared their heads. On the plain below, campfires were blazing merrily, and people had begun to gather around them for the nightly prayer meeting.

Eliza knew that she had been asking too many questions, and they were bound to upset Captain Willie. The company was being asked to travel across the plains, but as she calculated it, they didn't have sufficient provisions in food or clothing, and there was absolutely nothing to spare. There was no margin for error.

"Here's something worth knowing," Captain Willie whispered as he strode downhill. "We're in Indian country. Don't walk along the skyline from here on out, day or night."

"Surely, you're trying to frighten me." *Or change the subject*, Eliza thought.

Captain Willie said, "No, I don't take pleasure in frightening people needlessly."

They walked silently toward the tree line. As they neared it, fireflies flew up out of the grass, green comets that rose like cinders and then winked out. Little Isaac clung to Eliza's neck, but reached out toward the lights.

They're like fairies, Eliza thought, *recalling tales of fairies and pixies back in England, with their tiny lanterns. We should have had these where I grew up.*

Ahead, down among the trees, children were laughing and hooting, running about as they played cat-after-mouse. She spotted Sam Junior chasing Baline Mortensen and Agnes Caldwell around a tree.

Suddenly, lightning flashed on the horizon. Then dozens of tiny fireflies lit up at once, each tiny light answering the call of the greater light.

"A storm's coming," Eliza said.

Captain Willie peered up at the horizon. "Nope. I don't think so. It's dry lighting. Watch."

The lightning flickered again, and Eliza saw it on the horizon, green and sickly, like a bruise in the heavens.

Captain Willie said. "See, there's no clouds in the sky."

"Lightning out of a clear sky?" Eliza asked, incredulous. But she knew that he was right. She'd seen lightning but no clouds—only a hazy nimbus.

"There's dust in the air, high up."

"I've never heard of such a thing."

"Happens a lot out West," Captain Willie assured her. "The buffalo are raising clouds of dust, vast clouds. Them buffalo get nervous so close to winter, and they begin traveling south in herds so huge that you can look from one horizon to the other and see only buffalo. They stamp their feet and roll in the dry wallows to get the flies off their backs. The dust rises up in the air, causing dry lightning."

"We'll see buffalo soon?" Eliza's heart raced at the thought. The creatures were legendary in England. A male buffalo could stand six and a half feet tall at the hump and might top over two thousand pounds. The conventional muzzle-loaders used for hunting and warfare throughout Europe weren't powerful enough to bring the beasts down.

"Soon enough," Captain Willie said. "Once we hit Lone Tree, you'll see more buffalo than you ever wanted."

"You sound frightened of them."

"Driving a wagon team through a herd of buffalo that's forty miles across can be kind of nerve-jangling," Captain Willie admitted. "Lord knows what will happen when we try to creep through with our rickety handcarts." He fell silent for a moment, as if cursing himself for expressing his fears, then nodded toward a large cottonwood. "Last I saw your husband Samuel, he was leaning against that tree. I figure you might want to say good night."

Eliza halted and said softly, "My husband has been ill, as you know. His cough is back. I wonder if we could take him off guard duty tonight?"

"Has he asked to be relieved?"

"He won't ask," Eliza said. "You know that."

Captain Willie considered, and Eliza imagined that she could read his thoughts. There could be redskins about. But even more likely was a threat from the apostates across the river. If a couple of them were to bring a skiff out on the water, they could take pot shots from their boat into the tents.

Of course the fact that Captain Willie had to worry about such things at all was mostly Eliza's fault.

"I think we need him," Captain Willie said, "at least tonight. But if the weather turns wet, I'll have him relieved."

"Thank you," Eliza said.

She hurried up in the darkness to the large cottonwood, but didn't see Samuel. Around her, cicadas were making ratcheting sounds, and off in the brush she saw a raccoon prowling the edge of the creek, the gray tips of its hair looking ghostly and silver in the moonlight.

Samuel cleared his throat, and Eliza looked up. He was twenty feet high, sitting in a crook of the tree.

He cleared phlegm from his throat, then climbed down beside her. "Imagine that," he said, "a vision of loveliness here in the wilderness."

Baby Isaac looked up in the darkness, "Da da?"

Samuel took the baby, and Eliza studied him for a moment in the moonlight. Something seemed to be missing.

"Didn't they give you a gun tonight?"

"I have this!" Samuel said, reaching into his pocket. He pulled out a snub-nosed derringer, the kind a gambler might hide in his vest.

"Not that," Eliza said. "I mean a real gun."

"It shoots," Samuel assured her. "It makes a little popping noise, like a log splitting in the fire. I imagine that should Indians attack, I could throw it at them."

Eliza smiled.

Samuel stifled a cough.

"I think you should be in bed," she said.

"Always trying to get me in bed," Samuel teased. He leaned forward to kiss her, and she backed away. It was improper to kiss in public. Even for married couples it was scandalous. But she glanced around. It was dark, and no one could see, and she had not been able to show him proper affection for months. She kissed him briefly, then pulled away.

Samuel cleared his throat.

She frowned. "You should be in bed."

"Seriously, I'm fine. It's a good night to stay up. The weather is warm; the moon is full. Maybe someone else can stand guard in the rain for once."

Eliza worried. She thought of Martha Campkin. The poor woman's husband had died like this, from a nagging illness that wouldn't go away. As far as Eliza was concerned, it was the missionaries that killed Brother Campkin.

But if my husband dies, Eliza thought, *I'll have to blame it on the mobs*. There hadn't been any redskins to disturb the camp in Iowa. Her husband had been forced to stand guard duty in order to keep out the mobs that had threatened at every turn to harm the saints.

She smiled sadly at him, and Samuel leaned into her and stole another kiss.

He stood for a moment, trembling, while the baby clung to his neck. Samuel seemed on the verge of saying something important, but then he held his tongue.

Eliza leaned her head into his chest and hugged, listened to the beating of his heart, pounding strong.

He has a good heart, her nurse's training told her. *But then*, she added, *I always knew that.*

She shifted her head a tad, listened to his breathing. The left lung was clear. She hugged him, continued holding him, not letting Samuel know what she was doing. She shifted her head a tad, listened. The right lung sounded mildly congested. She could hear wheezing.

Maybe if I go through camp, she decided, *I could find someone with eucalyptus serum or horehound. Even a little mint tea might help. As a last resort, I might buy some in town.*

"Are you mad at me," Eliza asked "for slapping that man?"

"No," Samuel said. "I'm proud. You're a strong woman, and I need that. The weak ones die out where we're going."

Eliza winced.

"I've even been thinking," he continued, and seemed to hold his breath. "I wanted to ask, 'will you marry me?' "

Eliza laughed nervously. For the past month, a hundred times a day, she had worried about her marriage, about the effect that all of the hens in camp might have on her husband. Now he was asking her to marry him again, and all of her worries seemed to slide off of her shoulders like a soiled garment. "What do you mean? In a new ceremony?"

"When we get to Utah," Samuel said, "they're building temples—and an endowment house right in the center of Salt Lake City—places where we could be married for eternity—not just 'until death do you part.' "

Eliza smiled sadly. She could tell how much this meant to him. Mormons believed that they could be married forever. But Eliza had never known that Samuel wanted this from her. After twenty years, he was confirming his love.

"And you'll marry just me?" Eliza demanded. "There won't be anyone else?"

"Who else would I want to marry?" Samuel asked as if the thought had never occurred to him.

Emily Hill, Eliza thought, but she dared not say it.

Instead she only whispered, "I'm sorry. I can't."

"Why?" He sounded hurt.

"Because . . . because I don't believe in your church. It wouldn't be right." Only members of the Mormon church would be allowed into the Endowment House, Eliza knew, and even they had to pass through interviews in order to be found worthy. "I couldn't lie about it."

The air went out of Samuel's lungs in a soft sigh, and it seemed for a moment that his heart would break.

"I know," he said reassuringly. "I know. But if you can't manage it, even if you can't find the faith, I want . . . you to know how much I love you." He fell silent.

She put her arms around him and tried to comfort him.

"You should get to bed," Samuel said. "Captain Savage says that we won't be traveling tomorrow, or even the day after. We're going to have to take on more food, fix the handcarts. Don't worry about me. I'll have plenty of time to rest."

Eliza took the baby. Isaac fought her, wanting to stay with his father, but Eliza was still nursing them with what little breast milk she could. In a few minutes, Isaac would want her again.

She walked back toward her tent, and green lightning flashed on the horizon, while lightning bugs burst into flame all around.

Samuel coughed, a hacking sound, muted by the ratcheting of cicadas.

She stopped to peer at Samuel, but there against the woods he was just a ghostly shadow, a specter at the edge of the trees.

4

THE DEBATE

Fixing the handcarts didn't take a day or even two. It took three full days, which the saints could ill afford.

It was nobody's fault, really, but at every turn, the saints had been delayed.

The first delay took place in England. The Crimean War had broken out last fall, and it held an unheard-of-horror—the use of underwater mines to guard harbors and terrorize the shipping lanes. With France and England buying up all of the ships to fight the Russians, it had been impossible for the saints to book passage to America. For two months the saints had been forced to wait while church leaders sought to buy passage. Almost, the whole trip west was cancelled then. But most of the families that were emigrating had already sold their homes, their businesses and other assets, and quit their jobs. They couldn't afford to wait another year.

The saints should have set sail by February first. Instead they left England in May, more than three months late.

Because they had departed on a minute's notice, the church's outfitting company in Iowa never received word that they would be coming. So when the saints arrived at Iowa City, Iowa, they found that not only had their handcarts not been finished, they hadn't even been started.

Immediately the camp was thrown into turmoil. The young men were sent to Kansas on a cattle drive to get the beef and milk cows that the company would need to feed them on the trip. The women were put to work sewing tents as fast as they could, stitching until their fingers bled. The older men began cutting trees in order to build handcarts as best they could. But there was little in the way of wood and metal at that time of the year. The frontier was booming, and good cured lumber was impossible to come by.

As a result, the saints were forced to make do. They bought a little stout ash, partly cured, to make wheels for the handcarts, then rimmed the wheels with iron. But the boxes of the carts, along with the axles, had to be hewn from green hickory and oak.

As a result, the green wood was shrinking as it dried, so that the carts fit together poorly, and the weak axles were grinding down to toothpicks under the heavy loads. Wheels were popping off right and left.

The saints couldn't just fix the problem along the way. West of Florence, Nebraska, hardwood was almost impossible to find. With the wildfires on the plains each year, the land had been burned barren. On some stretches of the trail, a man could walk for a hundred miles and the only shade he was likely to find would be under his own hat. Even if he did see a tree, it would likely be a cottonwood, which rotted from the inside and thus could not be used for making axles.

So it was on the night of August 16 that Captain Willie called a meeting. There had been much grumbling among the saints about the lateness of the season, and many in camp had begun to suggest that the group should head north and winter at Wood River, or head back east to take shelter among the towns of Iowa where the people might find work.

Well, Captain Willie had a few words for such folks.

The full moon rose red on the horizon that August night, stealing up over the eastern hills, painting the hills with a reddish glow, like some lost world out of a dreamscape. The Missouri River flowed as brown as chocolate beneath it, its dark waters swirling and making slapping noises in the flow, while mosquitoes buzzed in annoying clouds around the settler's faces, and bats hunting on the wing danced in and out of the smoke from the bonfire.

For three days now the settlers had been stalled on the banks of the river, gathering their courage for the grueling trek ahead.

Captain Willie got up to speak. He climbed atop a handcart,

and a flickering flame leapt up, lighting his round face from below, while the rising moon rested on his shoulders.

Captain Willie was not tall. He normally spoke softly and gently, and relied upon his stout physique to give force to his words. But as he stood looking out over a crowd of five hundred brothers and sisters, he judged that he needed to speak loudly. He had often stood on street corners in England, climbing atop a box or stool, and preached the gospel to all those who passed him by. So he was used to addressing crowds. Normally, on the streets of London, he could count on the brick buildings to let his words echo back, let him save his voice. But not here, not tonight. The lapping water in the background was too loud, and the buzzing of the cicadas in a nearby grove was like the sound of a policeman's whistle. More than that, there was nothing here to reflect his voice. To the east was the river, and to the west the plains gently swelled up in rolling hills. The elements would conspire, he knew, to steal his voice.

"Brothers and sisters," he shouted, "we have heard a great deal of muttering and discontent in our camp as we prepare to undertake our journey. It is now the sixteenth of August, and there are those who worry about the lateness of the season.

"It's true, the end of summer is drawing nigh, and we will be well into fall before we reach our brethren and our beloved prophet in the Great Salt Lake territory! We may be at risk of getting some cold toes here and there.

"But we are about the Lord's errand. It was he who commanded through his prophet Brigham Young that we gather to Zion and create a community where all men live as equals, and all are one in heart. It was he who commanded that we become a people ready to receive the fullness of the everlasting gospel, so that we might prepare the world for the great and dreadful day, the Second Coming of our Lord and Savior, Jesus Christ.

"It is the Lord's desire that we gather to Zion. As it says in the Doctrine and Covenants, 'What I the Lord have spoken, I have spoken, and I excuse not myself. And though the heavens and the Earth shall pass away, my word shall not pass away. Whether it be by mine own voice, or by the voice of my servants, it is the same!

"And so, brothers and sisters, we heed the call.

"As long as we obey the Lord's will, he is bound to give us aid. He is bound to strengthen us and make our paths straight.

"When Brother Brigham wrote to us last winter, urging us to try this trek, he said that the elements would be tempered for our sake. The storms may threaten and floods may rise, but we will get through victorious!

"I urge you to go forward, brethren. Follow the call of the prophet. We are on the Lord's errand, and though the devil bar our way, we have nothing to fear. Go forward, even at the risk of death!"

Captain Willie halted to catch his breath. The moonlit faces in the audience were thoughtful, worried.

I shouldn't have used the word death, he thought.

He knew what he wanted to say. He wanted to exhort them as with the tongue of an angel.

But I can't bear this message alone, he thought. *The Spirit of the Lord needs to carry it to the hearts of these people. It is by the mouth of two or three witnesses that God's word must be established.*

Levi Savage cleared his throat and stood up in front of Captain Willie's makeshift stage.

Captain Willie paused. Levi was one of the captains of a hundred, and a seasoned frontiersman; as such, he commanded great respect. But Levi had softly voiced his worries about coming on this trek.

Like Captain Willie, he knew the trail. He'd ridden with the Mormon Battalion in the war against Mexico, and Levi had a reputation. He was solid grit and leather, as tough a man as you could find on the plains. He didn't have the meanness of Wild Bill Hickman, or the killer's instinct of Porter Rockwell, but he was every bit as tough. He was a kind man, a faithful member of the church. For the past four years, he'd served as a missionary in India and Siam.

It's possible that he has changed his mind, Captain Willie thought, *and that he will side with me now*. Regardless, Captain Willie dared not try to silence someone who had won the hearts of so many.

"Brother Savage," Captain Willie said hopefully. "Do you have something to say?"

Levi pulled off his hat. "Yes, Brother Willie, I do."

"Then, please, say a few words."

"If I speak," Levi said, "I'll speak my mind, no holds barred, and let my words cut where they will."

So, Captain Willie thought, *he is still against me. Well, let these people hear the doubter's and the devil's plan. The devil might cloud these folks' minds for a moment, but the Lord's word will blast through it like a summer's morn, and that will be all the better.*

"Have your say," Captain Willie said, stepping down from the wagon bed. Levi Savage sprung up lightly and stood for a moment, peering over the crowd. He was in his mid-thirties, with curly brown hair cut short. He didn't have Captain Willie's powerful bearing or strong voice. He tensed and considered his words before he spoke. "Brothers and sisters, this is a hard thing that you're about to do, trudging across the prairie, pulling your young and your sick in your handcarts. This trail ahead is not just harder than you know—it's harder than you can imagine right now.

"The church has asked me to do some difficult things in my life, but never have I faced a challenge so cruel as this.

"I want to say to you with all of my heart:" Levi said with his voice rising to a shout, and then whispered with all sincerity, "Don't go. Don't you dare go!"

A stunned silence fell over the crowd. Everyone in the camp knew that Captain Willie was all for hurrying ahead, making time as fast as possible, and in the Mormon church, where leaders were inspired by God, to oppose a leader was considered the equivalent of opposing God.

Now, Levi Savage stood, a sub-captain, opposing God, with his legs trembling in fear, and his voice grew thick with emotion. Tears began to stream down his face, and more than anything those tears stunned the audience, for Levi had a reputation for courage that yawned as wide as the whole West.

"Look at you folks," Levi said. "Take a hard look at yourselves. You aren't a proper company. Half of you folks have never slept in the open until last month. We got no men to pull the carts, hardly enough to stand guard at nights or pitch a tent. You're mostly women and children. We got old folks and cripples that couldn't hobble a mile in a week. It isn't their fault that they can't walk. We got a sister that's out of her mind, and we'll have to tie her down to keep her from running off before we're through. We've got so many children crawling around, trying to negotiate through them is like trying to walk through a field of cow pies." The audience laughed. "So, we'll have to pull those that can't make it on their own—the old, the children, the cripples. I'll tell you, I never seen a sadder company." Someone coughed. "Oh," Levi added, "and I near forgot: half of you are sick. One Danish sister died tonight, not more than an hour ago—Maren Hansen. Did you know that? She's the sixth or seventh to die in the last month. You folks are dropping like flies at the first sign of frost.

"Your clothes are all worn, what little you have. That isn't your fault. But I've crossed the Rockies at this time of year, and I'm telling you, we haven't got what it takes to make it alive, either in the way of clothes or food.

"You're liable to have to wade through snow up to your bellies on this trip, and shovel it at night, then lay yourselves down in a thin blanket on the frozen ground."

Brother Atwood, one of the other sub-captains, shouted, "There won't be any snow! We have the prophets' word on that. I'll tell you what, Levi: I will personally eat all of the snow that falls between here and Salt Lake City!"

Levi gave Atwood a look that would make a grizzly bear back off, and Atwood fell silent.

"I've been in them mountains this time of year," Levi said. "There will be snow.

"And traveling with handcarts ain't like traveling in a wagon, where you can go wrap yourselves up as warm as you please.

"No, we're without wagons. You folks are destitute of clothing, and even if you had what you need, you don't have the strength to carry it. We must go as we are. The handcart system I do not condemn. I think it preferable to unbroken oxen and inexperienced teamsters. The lateness of the season is my only objection to leaving for the mountains at this time."

The tears fell freely now, and as he cried like a child, Levi trembled and shook his fist to heaven. "I'm telling you now, don't go. If you do, you'll regret it! If you try to take a mixed company of women and children across the plains at this late season of the year, the bones of your children and old ones will strew the trail along the way, as white as pearls, and only the wolves will rejoice that you made your decision. Don't go. Please, for God's sake, don't go."

Levi finished, and the crowd fell utterly silent. Some of the men's faces had gone pale with fear, while women sobbed, sick with terror.

This was a disaster.

Captain Willie leapt back onto the wagon and shouted at Levi's back, "You, sir, are a disturber of the peace! You are a menace to any proper society!"

Captain Willie fully expected Levi to launch an attack, and though Willie knew that he couldn't best the man in a fight, he'd have Atwood and others to subdue him.

Levi turned and said calmly, "I understand your concerns, and if you don't think I'm fit to lead my hundred, then go ahead and take my job. I wouldn't blame you, and there would be no hard feelings on my part. But I'll not lie to these people and counsel them to go when my heart warns me so strongly against it."

Captain Willie could feel blood rushing to his face. He was angry enough to strike Levi Savage. "The God I serve is mighty to save, sir. The God I serve can save a man in the uttermost extremity."

Levi shot back, "I won't argue with that, but I know enough to tell you that when it's rainin' God expects you to use some common sense and come in out of the storm. You, on the other hand, think it will all go away just because you're a man of faith."

"You shut your mouth, you spineless—," Captain Willie shouted. "I don't need any of Job's comforters preaching to me about faith. How dare you! How dare you! You've seen miracles as well as I have.

"You want honesty?" Captain Willie shouted, "I can tell the truth better than you. The truth is that we have no choice but to go forward.

"Some of you have spoken these past few days about wintering up at Wood River, or some other spot with adequate trees and shelter."

"We don't have to go that far," Levi Savage shouted. "We can stop here, at Winter Quarters."

Captain Willie roared, "Have you really considered such a plan? It's foolishness! You and I have both wintered here, hard on the edge of the prairie. Brigham had us stop at Winter's Quarters in June, in time to plant gardens and take in a harvest. We stopped in time to hew trees and build homes. They were poor and ugly, but they were mostly warm and dry. And you can see the results of our efforts lying buried up there on the hill. One in ten died, after all that we could do. One in ten dead. That's not counting the folks that died on the trail, or died once we reached Salt Lake. How much worse would these people fare if we stopped here now? We don't have adequate shelter. We don't have crops. We don't have provisions or the wherewithal to buy them! Choosing to stay here is the same as choosing to die."

Levi Savage looked as if he would fire back a retort, but he knew that he was beat, and he held his tongue.

"Others of you talk about heading back," Captain Willie continued. "Many of the Children of Israel also turned their tails and trudged back to Egypt. But you've seen how the folks around here scorn us. You know how they mocked us and spit on us as we came through. They threatened to rape our women, beat our men, and burn our tents. Babylon has no love for us. Are any of you eager to face more of their abuse?"

From the crowd, some folks shouted, "No!"

"Me neither," Captain Willie cried. "I'd rather winter in a grizzly bear's den.

"Even if you were to cower back into their presence," Captain Willie shouted, "there isn't a town within four hundred miles that has enough provisions to see a company this large through the winter. Think on that!

"Even if they do take you in, you know what they'll want. They'll demand that you deny your testimonies and become like them! Do you want to end up apostates, like those whoremongers in the taverns across the river? We've already seen the weakest of us file off and show their true colors. Do any of you want your children to become like them?"

Someone shouted, "You tell them, Captain Willie!"

Another cried, "Better dead than an apostate!"

"We've escaped Babylon," Captain Willie said. "We've escaped, and though our flesh is weak, our spirits are strong. We can't turn back. We must not go back. We can only go forward. At least I can only go forward!

"Now, Levi is right about one thing. If we move forward, some of you may die. But you'll die with your hearts full of hope and love for the Lord. You'll die with your faces planted toward Zion! Such a death is sweeter than any ambrosia that the apostates in Iowa might offer!"

"Amen!" someone shouted, and a dozen others chimed in.

Captain Willie raised his hands for silence. "There are some that worry about storms ahead, but the same God who parted the Red Sea for Israel and who calmed the Sea of Galilee guides us now. I must bear witness to his greatness and majesty.

"Ten years ago, when I drove down out of the Rockies into the Salt Lake Valley with Brigham Young, the mountain man Jim Bridger told us that corn could not be grown in that region. 'It's too cold there,' he said. 'The growing season is too short. Why, I'd pay a thousand dollars in gold for a bushel of corn if you can grow it in the Salt Lake Valley.'

"We reached the Great Salt Lake at the end of July, and though winter was not far off, we commenced to tilling the ground.

"I bear witness to you that God prospered our crops and blessed them. He lengthened the summer for our sakes, and come the end of October, with my own hands I harvested whole bushels of corn that I'd planted on the first of August!

"It shouldn't have happened. It shouldn't have happened. Every year since, the corn has died on the first week of September. But the Lord rewarded our faith, after we did all that we could do!"

Captain Willie looked down in the faces of his people. He saw rapture there. He saw hope and the overpowering influence of the spirit of God.

He had them now. At first when he'd spoken, he'd sounded as weak as a lark, crying in a bush amid a pounding storm. Now, his voice was like the surf of the North Atlantic, booming against a shore of stone, resonating so strongly that it carried through the bones of your feet and shivered up your spine.

It was bearing his testimony that had done it. The spirit of the Lord was carrying the truth of his words from his spirit to theirs.

"The Lord is with us," Captain Willie promised. "He who takes note of when a sparrow drops to the ground is with us, even if it feels to you as if he is far away. He knows our needs before we voice them. He knows our dire circumstances. And I feel his spirit whispering peace.

"I promise you in the name of the Lord," Captain Willie shouted at the top of his lungs, "that God will temper the weather this trip. Storms will pass us by on the right and on the left. He will lighten our loads, strengthen our weary arms, and heal our hurts. He can be with us as he was with Moses of old, traveling as a pillar of fire by night, and as a cloud of smoke by day, if we'll just hold on and keep our faith in him!"

Many in the crowd leapt to their feet. There were outcries of "Hosanna, Hosanna, Hosanna," and the women took out their kerchiefs and waved them in the air while men waved their hats.

They see it now, Captain Willie realized. *There is no going back.*

"Who will come with me?" Captain Willie shouted.

Hundreds of saints threw their hands in the air, voting to depart, and some broke into song.

Yet there were a few in the crowd that remained silent, contemplative.

Levi Savage leapt up onto the wagon, raised his hands, and shouted, "Quiet! Quiet!"

Captain Willie worried that he would try to produce some new argument that would weaken the faith of these people, and for an instant he wondered if he should drag Levi down from the stage, wrestle him to the ground.

But Levi cried out, "Brothers and sisters, if you vote to go forward, I can't stop you. I think you're wrong, but I can't stop you. You men and women, you might choose to go forward and die for yourselves, but I got to wonder. Do you have the right to make that choice for the babes in your arms?

"Captain Willie here doesn't want to turn back toward Babylon, and I haven't got the stomach for it either. But I'd do it gladly if it would save the life of my child."

Captain Willie had seldom wanted to strike a fellow Mormon, but at that moment, it was all he could do to stop himself. As if on its own volition, his hand curled into a fist, and he found himself aching to see if he could knock some sense into Savage's boney head.

One of the other sub-captains, William Woodward, raised his hands for quiet.

"I have some words for this people, if I might," he said mildly.

Captain Willie was tongue-tied, trembling in anger. Levi Savage glanced at him, his eyes red from tears. Both of the men leapt down from the wagon, yielded the stand.

"I've been listening to both of the arguments," William said, his voice as soft and soothing as summer's morn. "Both men are well spoken, and both are honest in their feelings. I have no doubt that both of them have the welfare of our souls as their single, most sincere desire.

"I cannot help but believe that both men are right. God is with us, and hard trials lay ahead. But both men may be equally wrong.

"The problem is, they each have one answer. But one answer may not be right for everyone.

"We have five hundred people in this camp. Some of you are sick. Some of you are crippled. Some of you are elderly. Some of you are failing. But many of you are strong. I think of Brother Hurren over there. We're short a couple of wagons, and that means that we won't be able to have the oxen pulling all of our provisions. Some of you have grumbled at the notion of carrying an extra hundred pounds of flour on your handcarts. But Brother Hurren has offered to put five hundred pounds on his handcart. He's got a wife with a new babe, and he'll be loading on his children besides. I thank God for great men like him. I do believe that if Satan himself with a band of wild Sioux tried to bar our way across the Rocky Mountains, Brother Hurren would run right over them."

At that there was some laughter and grumbles of agreement.

"The Book of Mormon teaches that each of us has a right to

choose his own destiny. You have the right to know what the Lord wants you to do.

"It is entirely possible that the Lord, knowing the dangers along the way, may warn you in your heart and in your mind to wait here for another season, or to go back to New York or somewhere else. Or maybe he'll tell you to go forward.

"The Apostle James said, 'If any of you lack wisdom, let him ask of God, who giveth to all men liberally and upbraideth not, and it shall be given him.' The Book of Mormon says that 'By the power of the Holy Ghost, you may know the truth of all things.'

"So, brothers and sisters, I urge each of you now to pray. I urge you to find out from the Lord what he would have you do. Search your feelings, and then make a decision."

A young English woman stood up in the crowd. She held a small boy in her arms, bouncing him up and down. "I don't have to pray," she said. "I already know. The spirit told me to come to America, and I came. My husband used to threaten to kill me if I went to church, and he'd hide my shoes. But the Apostle Wilford Woodruff gave me a blessing and told me that me and my children would make it safely to Zion. I left my drunken husband and sneaked down to catch a train to Liverpool. He followed me, and I saw him through the window of the train, carrying a pistol in his hand. He'd beaten me often, and I knew that he would kill me and the children, and so I prayed to the Lord for help. I had nowhere to hide. But suddenly I saw a woman next to me, wearing a bright blue bonnet, and I begged her to let me wear it. Then I grabbed my children and hugged them close.

"My husband walked down the aisle, gun in hand. He stopped for a moment and peered right at me, looked me in the eyes, and I begged the Lord to hide me. My husband walked on, never recognizing me or his own children. The Lord was with me.

"I believe that Captain Willie is right. The same God that protected me then will protect us now."

She fell quiet, then sat back down on the grass with the rest of the crowd.

"Sister Panting has her answer," William Woodward said. "Now

I urge each of you to get your own." His words were a release, a call to end the meeting peacefully.

"Wait a minute," Captain Willie said. "I want a show of hands tonight, if I may. I'm leaving in the morning, and those who would like to follow, may follow. But I need to know if the number will be large or small." He shouted, "Who is coming to Zion?"

With a shout, hundreds of people threw up their hands. Here and there, some people looked away, and Captain Willie knew that he had lost them. Due to Levi Savage's words, dozens of them would apostatize tonight.

All the better, he thought. He didn't need those who were cowardly, or weak in faith, or just plain lazy to slow the company down. Let them slink back to Babylon.

Levi Savage spoke up, demanding a final word. "Brothers and sisters, it seems that the vote has gone against me. I bear you no grudge. If the spirit of the Lord tells you to move forward, then go forward, and I will come with you. But I promise you this: there isn't a man in this camp who will work harder to bring you safely into Zion than I will!"

Captain Willie held his tongue, his jaw clenched.

Not a man will work harder, eh? he thought. *Well, that's a promise that I'm going to hold you to.*

5

Talking to God

The day after the mammoth argument, Baline Mortensen woke to the sound of two girls outside her tent, merrily chanting a rhyme.

"Baline-tay, Baline-tay, won't you come out to play? Answer yea or nay, for I am tired and going way! Baline-tay, Baline-tay."

Baline scurried out of bed to find Mary Hurren and Agnes Caldwell smiling and giggling at Baline's tent flap. Mary Hurren covered her mouth with her hand and laughed, for the rhyme was a Scottish one, and Mary had to twist her mouth funny to match Agnes's atrocious accent.

"What are you doing?" Baline asked.

"We're going to play all day," Mary said. She lunged forward. "Tag. You're it!"

Baline stood for a moment scratching. The mosquitoes had bitten her so much that she felt like she had little red-hot pebbles under her skin, and even places that weren't swollen were itching terribly.

Then she raced off through the camp, weaving through the tents.

So the morning began, as summer days should, beneath skies of blue in fields of gold. The children raced down to Turkey Creek and hunted for bullfrogs and salamanders in the shadowed waters, and some of the boys cornered a large white catfish in the shallows and then took it back to camp to eat.

At noon, three Omaha Indians came to camp, men who wore nothing but breech cloths and necklaces carved from claws and bones, and they demonstrated their archery skills to the settlers, shooting their stone-tipped arrows far across the fields. Their accuracy was so good that at a hundred yards, Captain Savage said that the bows were as deadly as muskets.

It was then that Baline began to notice something odd. The big steam-powered ferry had stopped a quarter of a mile south of camp, and a crowd of English saints stood on the shore waiting for it. Many of them carried bags. Some had taken their handcarts.

"Are they going to the town to shop?" Baline asked Mary.

Mary's face took on a sober expression. "They're leaving us," she said. "They're going back to live with the gentiles in Iowa."

Baline didn't quite understand. Brother Ahmunsen, the captain of a hundred who was in charge of the Danish saints, had not been able to translate most of what had been said at the meeting the night before, and there was so much shouting and so many "amens," and so many people talking at once that Baline herself could hardly understand.

"These are the weak ones?" Baline asked. She wondered if there was something that she could go say to them to change their minds, or if they would come if she offered to help them pull their carts.

"Some say that they prayed," Mary said, "and God does not want them to go. Some of them are too sick to make it. But Dad says that some of them are just laggards."

If I were an angel, Baline thought, *I would help them*. So she left her little group and raced down to the river, careful as she ran to watch the grass, for the bees were thick among the clover.

At the shore, the ferry had just landed, and people were marching up the gangplank. They all moved slowly, like old people, and most of them hung their heads. Some of the women were crying.

Baline called out to one woman, Sister McKay, "Don't go! You don't have to go. If you come vit us, I can help in the pulling of the cart!"

Sister McKay's head turned slightly, but she did not look in Baline's direction. Instead, she lifted her chin a little higher and hurried up the gangplank, then disappeared.

Baline called out to some others that she knew, but no one

answered. It was as if she were invisible, and inaudible, like a ghost trying to capture the attention of the living.

Last of all, she noticed a young boy in the crowd that did not belong. Joseph Oakey, age twelve, went sneaking along in the shadow of some tall Englishman. Joseph was easy to recognize. He was tall for a boy of twelve, and his hair was cut in the bowl style, making him look like a monk.

Baline knew him well, for they had often played together over the past two months.

"Joseph," Baline cried. "Vat are you doing? Vere are you going at?"

He did not answer. Baline scooped some mud from the riverbank and hurled it, hitting him square in the back. "Answer me!" she demanded.

Joseph turned on her, his face twisted in rage. "Shut up!" he cried. "I'm going away."

"But you mother and father," Baline cried, "do they know vat you are doing? You are running avay!"

"They don't care," Joseph said. "What does it matter what happens to me?"

"But vere vill you live?" Baline asked. "Vat vill you do?"

Joseph just stumped up the gangplank onto the ship, and Baline stood for the longest time, heart hammering, wondering what to do.

From the rail of the ship, Joseph came up with his final answer. He shouted, "Who cares?"

I do, she thought. *But he won't listen to me.*

The boat's steam whistle blew, a shrill blast that seemed to shake the trees, followed by two shorter blasts, and the ferry's engine made chugging noises as it began retreating from shore.

I must tell his parents, Baline thought.

She turned and ran back into camp. There were a hundred and twenty tents in camp, all of them exactly the same, all set in a huge circle. She didn't know which one the Oakey family was staying in, and it took her the better part of an hour before she finally found

Joseph's little four-year-old sister, Sarah Ann, who led Baline to the proper tent.

Joseph's mother became hysterical at the news, and she rushed out of the tents screaming until she found her husband chopping wood out in the trees. He dropped his ax and took his oldest son and raced to the river, staring longingly across the Missouri, whose brown waters roiled and churned dangerously.

"The ferry isn't coming back until tomorrow, Father," the oldest son said.

"I can't wait for it," the father said. "Grab the other end of that log. We'll swim across. Joseph won't get far."

So the two men, fully clothed, carried the log out into the river and began to swim. The log floated far out into the river and down around a wide bend, out of distance, as Baline watched.

Joseph's mother paced along the bank, tears streaming down her eyes, muttering, "They'll find him. They'll bring him back. They have to!"

Baline hoped that she was right.

But Baline offered up a silent prayer, and an odd thought came to mind. In playing with Joseph, he was always the best at hide-n-seek, and Joseph had all of land east of the Missouri River to hide in. After her prayer, Baline felt with utter certainty that Joseph Oakey would never be caught.

Camp was sad that night. Joseph had run away, along with a hundred English saints. To make matters worse, Maren Hansen was buried at noon. Baline had not known the old woman well, but Baline knew her son, Peter, a shy boy with a very sensitive nature. At thirteen, Peter was an orphan now and would have to travel to Zion all alone.

Like me, Baline thought. She had adults to watch over her, but they weren't her parents. Though Jens and Else Nielsen took care of her, they didn't love Baline as they did their own child.

In the evening, the solemn mood was broken when the Danish saints decided to hold some baptisms.

A handful of the Danes donned white clothing and went down to the muddy water where Turkey Creek emptied into the Missouri. There, Brother Madsen performed the baptisms, saying the baptismal prayer and then letting each person lean back until they were immersed in the water.

These weren't the kind of baptisms that were done when someone accepted the gospel and wished to become a disciple of Christ. These were baptisms done for the sick, for those who were often only sick with worry or grief. One small family was baptized, a husband and wife whose first child had died an hour after birth, just last week. Three others were getting baptized because they suffered from various maladies.

But most of all, Baline realized, they were getting baptized because they were unsure what to do, whether to go west to Zion or stay behind.

As one of the sisters was submerged, Baline pulled Jens Nielsen aside and asked, "Doesn't getting baptized wash away your sins? How does it help sick people?"

Jens told Baline, "It doesn't make them better, but it does help ease their minds. If they die from their illness, or if they die crossing the plains, at least they will die with a peaceful conscience, ready to meet God."

"That is silly," Baline whispered back to him as the sick woman disappeared for a moment under the brown flow. She came up gasping for breath, blinking the water from her eyes. "One doesn't need to die with a clean conscience; you have to live with a clean conscience."

Jens smiled at her. "I agree. These people are trying to prepare to meet God. But you never know when it could happen. You could get struck by lightning or fall off of a horse and break your neck. If you live with a clean conscience, you're always ready to meet God."

"Yes," Baline said.

Jens had suddenly become more serious. "Are you saying your prayers?"

"Yes," Baline answered.

"And has God helped you find people to serve?"

"I took some water to Maren Hansen before she died," Baline

answered. "Yesterday, Marie Mortensen got stung by a bee, and I took the stinger out quickly, so that her foot did not swell up much."

"Good," Jens said. "Have you felt impressed to speak for God?"

Baline shook her head. "I tried to talk Joseph Oakey into staying, but he didn't listen."

"People almost never listen to God," Jens said, "and so if you speak for him, they will not listen to you."

"What do you mean?"

"I am convinced," Jens said, "that God tries to talk to us all of the time. But he speaks so softly, that we can only hear if we listen very hard. Even when he does speak, we don't often like what he has to say."

"Why not?"

"Because, he asks us to do hard things, unselfish things, and it does not seem wise for us to do them." Jens reached down and squeezed Baline's shoulders. The sick woman had come out of the water, and now a man was walking down.

"Father Jens," Baline asked, "one of the English boys, Samuel Gadd, had a dream in which he saw Zion. He said that the buildings were made of light, and very pretty. Do you think that God could show me such a dream?"

"When Lehi had a vision," Jens said, "Nephi asked to see it too, so that he would know if it was true. I think that you can do the same, if you feel that it is important enough."

Baline nodded thoughtfully.

Jens said, "Have you prayed to know if you should cross the wilderness?"

"I thought that you'd do it for me," Baline said.

A flash of concern crossed Jens's face. He tried to hide it, but Baline saw it. "You are old enough, and wise enough," Jens said. "I think that you should ask God, and see what he wants for you."

A sudden worry took her. Baline wondered, *If I pray, what if God asks me to stay behind? Who would I live with? What would I eat?*

"Are you going west?" Baline asked.

"Yes," Jens said. But again Baline saw that worry on his face.

"Did God tell you to?" she demanded.

Jens hesitated. He licked his lips as he tried to figure out how to answer. "I think . . . I think we should go. But my heart is heavy, and I am worried. This trip, it will not be as easy as Captain Willie says that it will be. I think . . . someone in my family may die."

"You?" she asked. Jens was a large man, like her father. He was as sturdy as a hill, and she could not imagine him dying. But Else was a tiny woman, frail looking. "No, Else," she guessed.

"I don't know," Jens admitted. "I only know that my heart is heavy when I pray, and I can find no peace. I hope it is me. I pray that it is me. If I died knowing that the rest of you would make it to Zion, I would die peacefully."

Baline fell silent. She knew now that she had to pray. She supposed that if she had to, she could find the courage to grab a log and swim back across the Missouri, to live among the gentiles. Even if they tried to rape her and make her have puppies, she could find the strength to go on.

That night, after the games of tag were over, after all of the fireflies along the banks of the river had been caught, after the prayer meeting where various elders in the church urged the saints to go west once again, Baline Mortensen sneaked out of her tent to pray.

She went down to the banks of Turkey Creek, where the cottonwoods grew thick. The beef cows had been foraging here, and so she had to be careful to avoid the cow pies hiding in the grass, but the full moon was bright enough so that she could see the shiny places where the cows had been.

She wanted to be alone, and so she went past the washing grounds, where women had left clothes to dry on branches, where night shirts and aprons hung in the moonlight, swaying like ghosts in a silent breeze.

At last, Baline found the creek, its banks heavy with moss. A lone bullfrog was croaking. Cicadas in the trees above made ratcheting noises like the grinding of a watch's gears, while on the edge of the meadow, crickets played a lonely refrain.

Despite the soft night sounds, it seemed quiet. The heavens full of stars made Baline feel quite small and humble. The moss was cool under her bare feet, and small twigs crackled beneath her weight. Baline found an open spot among the trees, where moonlight limned the leaves with gold; there she knelt.

Like Joseph Smith, going to pray in the Sacred Grove, Baline thought. Only he had been older.

Still, God had come to speak with him, and that gave Baline hope. *God could speak to me*, she realized. *With a word he created the heavens and earth. Why could he not spare a word for me?*

"Lord," she whispered, so that her voice would not be heard among the burble of the stream. Then words failed her, so Baline poured out her heart in groans of desire. Her thoughts were complex.

I want to go to Zion, she thought. *I want to go there more than life itself. I want to turn away from this world of darkness and sin, to walk calmly away and never turn back. I want to live in the City of Light, where there is no need for sun or moon, for God lights the streets. I want to hear his voice and let his wisdom direct my every thought.*

When she finished, she sat for long minutes, her heart pounding, and she opened herself, listening, straining with every fiber of her being to hear God's answer.

At last, she felt a burning sensation in her bosom, and the spirit that filled her was so sweet and pure, it was as if it lifted her into the air and sent her floating. Though her eyes were closed, she sensed light all around her and knew that if she opened her eyes, she might well see cloven tongues of fire overhead. But the light didn't just surround her, it seemed to pierce her, to cut through her flesh and dissipate all of the darkness in her.

"Be at peace," a soft voice said in answer. "Thou seekest Zion. Go, and thou shalt lead the way for others."

Weeping tears of relief, Baline got up and made her way back to the camp, feeling her way through the brush more than seeing.

That night, in her dreams, she saw the beacon lights calling her to Zion.

6

An Informed Decision

Eliza pored over *Peercy's Guide* and fretted. The spine of the book had not been cracked. As far as she could tell, Captain Willie had not opened it. Perhaps he felt he knew the trail to Utah well enough. After all, he'd crossed it twice before, and each of the sub-captains also knew the way. But the information that she found inside seemed invaluable. It showed pictures of places she had been—etchings of Council Bluffs and even the ruins of Winter Quarters, just up the hill. It also showed the dead lands ahead, and told a story of cold and future struggle that Captain Willie would only shrug away.

I cannot trust that man, Eliza realized. He might have good intentions, but the truth was, his good intentions could get them all killed.

Nor did she really trust anyone else in camp. Levi Savage was the only authority that she trusted to any degree, but Captain Willie had apparently assigned guards to keep him quiet. At any rate, Savage was quartered in his tent, and when she had approached, William Woodward and John Chislett had stepped forward and informed her that Levi was busy writing letters and was not to be disturbed.

Even Ann Cooper, a widow that Captain Savage had taken a fancy to over the past few weeks, could not get near him. Ann was a sweet woman who had lived only a mile from Eliza, back in England. She was in her mid-thirties and had three children. Her youngest daughter had died on the Fourth of July, and Captain Savage had tried to comfort her. But now she paced outside his tent, fidgeting like some schoolgirl in love. Though some of the hens in camp gossiped about them, Eliza wished both of them well.

Failing a visit with Captain Savage, Eliza realized that there was information to be had outside of camp. There were other groups going west. A few days before the Willie Company had left Iowa City, another handcart company had come in behind them, the Martin Company.

Here in town, she had seen another man bustling about, a rugged, hawkish individual that all of the Mormons seemed to defer to. By asking around she learned that his name was Almon Babbitt and that he served as the Secretary of State for Utah. Some folks referred to him as "Colonel Babbitt," for he had been a militia leader among the Mormons and had worked as a lawyer for many years.

Now he was a teamster, hauling freight between Utah and Illinois or Kansas. But he wasn't just a teamster, she learned. He was Brigham Young's personal teamster, in charge of bringing across his most-prized possessions—steam engines, harvesting machines, pipe organs, money, and guns.

Colonel Babbitt had ferried across the Missouri in the morning, taken on some supplies, and hardly slowed. He held a brief meeting with Captain Willie and then went into Florence for some business at the bank.

That's where Eliza ambushed him.

The colonel was just stalking out of the bank, nearly at a run. He was a tall man, lean as a bullwhip. The hair hidden beneath his felt hat needed a cut, and his face was burned and leathery from the summer sun. A pair of Colt six-shooters hung low on the hip, as if he were a gunslinger.

"Colonel Babbitt," Eliza said, "may I have a word with you?"

He stopped dead, peered down at her. "You have me at a disadvantage, madam."

She'd expected some guttural grunt from this rough man. Instead, he spoke like a gentleman.

"Eliza," she said, "Eliza Gadd. I'm with the Willie Company."

"Pleased to meet you," he said with a slight bow. Until that moment, he had been all bustle and business as she watched him. Now he stopped. He didn't look longingly away, as if displeased to have been disturbed, or as if he wished to run off for a more important engagement. He was perfectly willing to give of his time, regardless of how much he valued it. He took off his hat, holding it in his hands respectfully, as a cultured man would in the presence of a woman.

"I understand that you're well acquainted with the Mormon trail, sir?" Eliza asked hopefully.

"Perhaps no one is more so," Babbitt said. His tone was honest, not boastful. "I'm making the trip for the fortieth time."

"I see," Eliza said. "Then perhaps you can tell me something. I have been reading *Peercy's Guide*, and I understand that there is a good possibility of snow as we cross the Great Divide, even in the summer."

Babbitt whetted his chapped lips with his tongue, considered his words. "True enough, summer storms are quite common, and I've seen snow up to six inches deep even in July, but it will melt away in a couple of days."

"And what about September?" Eliza asked. "Late September. By my calculations, we should be crossing then."

"Not bad. You'll get a night or two of freezing cold, maybe even bitter cold. But generally the weather holds until late October and on into the first weeks of November."

That was comforting, and Almon Babbitt seemed perfectly honest.

"Thank you," Eliza said. She had a million questions that she wanted answered, but she had already asked the most piercing one and didn't dare burden him further. She turned to go.

Colonel Babbitt hastened, "Whoa, there. Don't run off so fast. If I were you, I wouldn't worry about the snow so much. I'd keep an eye out for Indians."

Eliza looked at him querulously. "But *Peercy's Guide* says that our affairs with them are governed by treaties?"

"They were, three years ago when he wrote the book," Colonel Babbitt admitted. "But a lot has changed. You'll be traveling through

Sioux country, and things are kind of touchy. Hasn't Captain Willie told you?"

"He warned us last night that we should be on the lookout," Eliza said, "and he told the children that they shouldn't stray from camp."

Lines of concern broke out on Babbitt's brow.

He turned his head as if he would go speak to Captain Willie immediately, then thought better of it and spoke to Eliza herself. Eliza hadn't told him that she wasn't a Mormon. She wondered if he would have been so blunt if he knew. As it was, he spoke now like a military commander relating the movements of enemy troops.

"We had a Mormon wagon train that came through here two summers ago," Colonel Babbitt said. "One of the Danish saints had a cow that went missing, and when he went searching for it, he found that the Sioux had taken it to their camp. Seeing that he was vastly outnumbered, and being terrified of the Indians, he didn't dare enter their camp. But he was angry at the loss, and two days later he mentioned it to an army patrol.

"The patrol was led by a snot-nosed lieutenant named Grattan, fresh out of West Point. He was stationed at Fort Kearney and was out to impress his superiors. He heard about the cow and went looking for it, but if you ask me, he was looking for trouble.

"His men went to the Sioux camp, pulling along three howitzers. He had his men set up a picket line, guns leveled at the village, and demanded that the Sioux return the cow.

"Now it so happened that Standing Bear was in the camp."

Eliza asked, "Who?"

"Standing Bear, High Chief of all the Sioux nations," Colonel Babbitt said. "There are seven nations among the Sioux, and each has its chief, but Standing Bear was chief over them all."

"You know him?" Eliza asked.

"Met him a couple of times," Colonel Babbitt said, thinking back. "Some people seem to wear nobility the way that others wear a suit. They have a keen intellect, a genuine love for others, and a code of conduct that not only defines them, but demands respect. Standing Bear was such a man. He was a great man.

"Well," Babbitt continued, "Standing Bear came out of his teepee to talk to Lieutenant Grattan, and Grattan said that if he didn't get that cow back, he would begin blowing holes through the teepees with his howitzers."

"Sounds like a disproportionate response over one cow," Eliza suggested. She could tell by Babbitt's tone that this was going to end badly.

"Absolutely," Babbitt said. "Can you imagine someone threatening to kill the president and threatening to level Washington, just because one of his people stole a cow? Well, that is what Grattan did. So Standing Bear says, 'We didn't steal the cow. It just wandered into our camp. We thought it was a stray, so one of our braves butchered it.' "

Eliza stopped him. "But we've been told that Indians steal all of the time."

"That's true," Colonel Babbitt said. "Among the Sioux, stealing livestock—especially horses—is a way of life. A warrior who steals from an enemy proves his cunning and bravery. It is called 'counting coup.' And the Sioux are more likely to rob a man blind than most others. In fact, they brag about it and even measure time by it. For instance, they call 1840 'the year the Ogallala Sioux Stole 100 Horses.' And two years back they robbed a mail train of ten thousand dollars in gold. Thus, 1854 was 'the year of much money.' "

Down the street, a horse neighed as if it might bolt. Eliza glanced to make sure that it didn't come running down the street. It was a roan with an evil disposition, being ridden by some young man. Eliza had known many a horse that kicked at passersby or that would bite its rider. This one was trying to do both at once. The horse raced out into the street, bucking a couple of times, kicking at a buckboard.

Colonel Babbitt waited for the horse to settle down, lest it come after them. He settled a hand on his pistol uneasily, as if he'd shoot the animal if it drew near, then continued. "As I was saying, Grattan figures that Standing Bear is playing him for a fool, and he starts getting angry and threatening to shoot the place up. So Standing Bear offers to pay for the cow, proposing that he give his best horse, along with three other horses for it.

"Now, among the Sioux, that was a kingly offer. Some of the Sioux love their horses more than they love their own wives.

"But Grattan wants to arrest the Indian who stole the cow, a fellow by the name of High Forehead. Well, High Forehead had already left camp a week earlier, and Standing Bear tells Grattan so.

"But Grattan is using an interpreter," Babbitt said, "a French fellow that doesn't like the Sioux. Some folks say that the Frenchman had been drinking; some said he was downright mean. Anyway, he tells Grattan that the Sioux are refusing to turn over the culprit, and Grattan becomes furious and orders his men to shoot."

"When Standing Bear sees that Grattan is getting ready to open fire on the village, murdering innocent women and children, he raises his hands in the air to surrender and steps in front of the cannon, yelling for Grattan to stop. Maybe he thought that no one would dare open fire on him. Or maybe he threw himself in front of the cannon in hopes that it would save some of his villagers.

"In any case, Grattan's men let loose with gunfire, and the first volley nearly cuts Standing Bear in half. All thirty-five of Grattan's men begin shooting, and Grattan himself opened fire with a howitzer.

"Now, when the villagers saw that the howitzers were going off, most of the warriors ran for their teepees. Grattan might have figured that they were running away. But as soon as his men cut down a few warriors, he finds out that the Sioux were running for their weapons, and while Grattan and his men re-loaded, the Sioux came out with their war shields and tomahawks and split their empty heads open. Only one white man escaped to tell the tale."

"That was lucky," Eliza said.

"It wasn't luck," Babbitt said. "You don't escape a Sioux war band. I suspect that they let him go so that he could warn others that you don't mess with the Sioux. The way I see it, Grattan deserved what he got, and the matter should have been left to stand."

Eliza frowned. "Should have?"

Babbitt spoke softly, as if he did not even wish to discuss what happened next, but he was morally bound to tell her.

"So last summer, Washington responds by sending a full-blown general with some crack troops to avenge the so-called 'Grattan Massacre.' "

Eliza shook her head. Folly upon folly. "And?" Everywhere that she looked, this land was governed by fools.

"The general is named Harney. Steer clear of him and his men. He's a mean one, and he doesn't think twice about murder. So last summer, he goes looking for trouble. He goes up to Ash Hollow and finds a Sioux Camp down on the mouth of the Blue Water River. He sneaks up to the camp with his men, has them hide in the Sioux's corn fields, and waits for dawn.

"When the Indians awake, he calls out their chief and some warriors under a white flag, and once he has them in his camp, unarmed, he gets ready to destroy the village.

"One of the Sioux chieftains, realizing what Harney is up to, grabbed a knife from a soldier. In less than a minute, he cut down ten men. Them Sioux are trained to fight with a knife from birth. Even with half a dozen bullets in him, this chief fights like a panther, but it doesn't do any good. Harney's troops murdered the prisoners and then fired on the camp.

"Harney's men were armed with these new 1855 Springfield long-range rifles. The Indians have never seen weapons like this. Our muzzle-loaders are like pea shooters in comparison. These new guns, you can fire ten shots at a hundred yards, and there won't be an inch of spread between the bullets."

Eliza had never handled a rifle before, but she knew that with the Crimean War, new and terrifying weapons were being unleashed upon the world. She also knew that a muzzle-loader fired a round ball made of lead, and though that gun might have quite a kick, it wasn't very accurate. At a hundred yards, the ball could be carried by the wind, and a spread of eighteen inches between shots was pretty common. A poorly made gun might have a spread of thirty-six inches. Hence the expression that such a gun "couldn't hit the broad side of a barn."

Babbitt continued, "Of course Harney is eager to try these new guns out in battle," Babbitt continued, "so while the Sioux are retreating, he has his men cut them down. I've talked to a dozen soldiers under Harney's command. I've never seen such tortured souls. They're all damned creatures, hollow men. They're not eager to tell their tale. But if you can get them to spill their guts, their stories are all the same.

"The women and the children in the village hid in the teepees, and some fled into some caves. So after Harney had slaughtered the warriors, he sent his men through the village and executed the women. He had young squaws, girls thirteen and fourteen years old, begging for their lives, clutching their babes, and Harney ordered his men to shoot the babies out of their mothers' arms first, then kill the women."

Eliza was still nursing her twins, and the image that this news brought to mind knocked the air out of her lungs. She stood for a moment transfixed from shock and felt her breath come ragged.

"I'm sorry," Colonel Babbitt said. "I didn't mean to alarm you. But you need to know the truth. Harney is a stone-cold murderer. The Sioux call him 'Woman Killer.' Now there are a number of young bucks who are gathering to seek revenge. There's been talk of it all summer. I heard from some Arapahos that they're joining a war band of mixed malcontents—Sioux, Arapahoe, and Cheyenne.

"You see, the government's crimes weren't committed just against the Sioux. The government has a treaty that calls for payment for the passage of settlers. The government pays in the way of blankets, food, axes, and whatnot. But they've got this Indian agent over near Laramie, a fellow named Tippets, who is supposed to disperse the goods. The problem is that he's been holding back most of the trade goods and demanding 'presents' from the Indians before he completes the payment. This spring, he bought himself a 'squaw' that way—a pretty little girl of thirteen or so. So now all of the tribes are in an uproar.

"They're led by a young fellow named Crazy Horse, the son of a medicine man, who is said to have powerful medicine himself. These young bucks can't get their chiefs to lay their treaties aside, even though the US Government has broken the treaties all to hell, so they hope to stir up trouble, rally their rabble, so to speak. Some of these warriors have sworn to wipe out every wagon train that passes through this fall, and though they haven't struck yet, honor demands that they do so soon. You all picked a bad time to make the journey. I've talked to a lot of the old-timers, and they say that they've never seen such hostility before."

"Thank you," Eliza said. "I appreciate your honesty. I prefer the taste of one bitter truth to a thousand sweet fables."

Babbitt studied her face appreciatively, then bowed slightly, as if to excuse himself. "You're welcome."

He turned to go, but Eliza stopped him. "Colonel Babbitt, you have a wagon train, and I understand that a few other wagons will be joining our company, for protection. Will you be coming with us?"

"I'm afraid not," Babbitt said. "My schedule demands that I send my wagons on with all due haste."

"A pity," Eliza said. "I enjoy your company."

"Well, perhaps we will meet again," Babbitt said, and he was off, striding swiftly south toward the Mormon camp, as if eager to meet his destiny.

When Eliza returned to camp that afternoon, she found an Indian teepee set up just outside. Several men from the Omaha tribe were there. It was her first close sight of a wild Indian. Most of her knowledge about the red men had come from reading the novels of James Fennimore Cooper or horrific accounts of their savagery spread in English newspapers. Sometimes Indians were trotted out in circuses and sideshows, dressed in full regalia, so that the gentry might gawk.

As twilight approached, Eliza went to their campfire to speak with them. The men were shorter than she had expected and wore no war paint. She'd heard that Indians smelled of rancid bear fat, but these men were clean. They wore breech clothes of buckskin, shirts of poor-quality cotton, and necklaces made from bone. Their knives had blades of volcanic glass, and altogether Eliza found them frightening.

But she asked her question to one of the men who spoke halting

English. She explained that their handcart company was going to be traveling through Sioux territory, and she was worried about the dangers. She told the men that her company had five hundred people in it, but among them were only six firearms—two long-bore muzzle-loaders, a shotgun, a pair of single-shot pistols, and a revolver. In addition, the saints had two swords.

Of course, among the English and the Danes, firearms were rare. The nobility didn't like the idea of having an armed populace, and so guns were normally the property of a few lords who used them primarily for hunting and for guarding their estates. On this past Fourth of July, the Americans had celebrated by taking everyone in the camp out and having them fire the guns, so that they might learn how to retain their freedom. But even among American citizens, only about one in ten owned a gun. Sam Colt had invented his six-shooter revolver twenty years earlier, but it was only beginning to catch on. He was currently making his killing in an arms war, selling revolvers to the Turks and the Russians, the English and the French. By selling weapons to everyone involved in the Crimean War, Sam Colt had become a millionaire.

"Will our guns be enough to scare the Sioux away?" she asked.

The Omahas looked at one another, and they fought back the urge to laugh. Finally, their leader spoke. "The Sioux evil men, not like Omaha. Many years, they have driven us from hunting grounds. They not afraid of you guns. They buy guns from Mexicans, and their braves have many spears and fine bows. They will laugh at your guns. They will see your weakness and will hunt you."

By nightfall on the fifteenth, Eliza had made her decision.

There was no need to make dinner for the family. In Eliza's absence, Ann Howard had stepped in and cooked it, and then washed up the pans.

That left Eliza the sole task of nursing Isaac and Daniel, after which she took her husband for a walk along the river. She remained silent until they were well north of camp, where she scared up a blue heron that croaked once and then flapped heavily upriver. She saw an otter in the brown water, watching them curiously, dividing its attention between them and a fish. The mosquitoes seemed to be on the warpath that night.

"I've come to my conclusion," Eliza told Samuel. "I've weighed the pros and cons, considered several scenarios, and I've done the math. I think that we should leave here and head east to Saint Louis, Missouri. Sister Campkin tells me that many Mormons live there, and they are held in some esteem. It is the only safe place to be a Mormon within the boundaries of the United States. The temperature is moderate, so the winter won't be too harsh, and we should be able to find employment. Between you, me, Jane, and the boys, with a little hard work we should make out fine during the winter, and then we can resume our journey to Salt Lake in the spring."

Samuel peered down at her. With a couple of days of rest under his belt, he seemed to have recovered from his cold, and his cough was all but gone. He smiled benevolently. "So," he said, "you've made your decision?"

She knew that he would argue, though he did not have an argumentative temperament. "I have," Eliza said in a tone that invited no debate.

"Ahhh," Samuel sighed. "Sam Junior will be so unhappy. Of all the children, he is most anxious to go to Zion."

"We can go another year," Eliza said.

But Samuel bit his lip. "Are you sure? There will be a presidential election in a few weeks. If the Republicans win, there will be a war between the United States and the Mormons. Do you really think that Saint Louis will be safe? It will be the first to fall. Will any place be safe?

"And the war won't just be with the Mormons. The latest news out of Kansas tells of mobs rioting in the streets. Kansas City, Missouri, so near to Kansas will be the staging grounds for the war.

"Make no mistake, a war is coming—not just a war against Mormons, but a war between all of the states in the Union. If a Republican wins the presidency, that war will start this winter—perhaps in as few as eight weeks."

"I know," Eliza said. "I don't like our choices, either. But I consider this to be the safest and the sanest choice. I'm not a Mormon. That should ensure you and the children some leniency."

Samuel halted in mid-stride, his face twisting in pain as if to hide some hidden injury. "It may be the safest choice," he said. "But it's not the choice that I would make. You need to know that while you were out gathering information, the children and I made up our own minds. We're going west. The oldest children all want to come with me. I want you to join us."

The words were a slap in the face. Against her better judgment, her husband was taking her children. They'd desert her, she suspected, if they had to.

What of the babies? Eliza wondered. Surely he had to leave the babies with her.

But maybe he wouldn't.

Samuel was a good man, and a decent provider. If she tried to leave him, he could sue for custody of the children. Eliza didn't know the laws here in Nebraska Territory. He might have the greater claim. Certainly, in England a woman could not take a man's children from him legally. Or maybe there were no laws. Maybe he could just take the children. He had five hundred Mormons to back his claim to the young ones. If she tried to sneak out with the babies, she did not doubt that the Mormons would stop her. Eliza might be free to go, but Samuel would insist that the children stay with their father, to be raised in his church.

She would be left alone in this wretched, uncivilized country.

She looked into Samuel's face. The setting sun was a soft orange, the dusty air hanging overhead like smoke. Samuel's eyes glistened with tears, and his jaw had begun to quiver. "Please, please, for God's sake, come with me," Samuel begged. "For the sake of the children, and of me. I love you. I don't think I could stay sane without you. But don't try to hold us back and make us stay here among our enemies."

Eliza stood transfixed, her heart breaking.

We're both trying to save our children, she realized, *the best way that we know how. We're just trying to figure out what's best.* There were a million arguments that she could make, a million doubts weighing upon her mind. But of one thing she was sure: she loved her husband and her children.

"I'll come," she said.

7

ZION OR BUST

Captain Willie pulled out of Winter Quarters on the afternoon of the seventeenth of August, leading the first two hundred handcarts up an old road that passed the cemetery, then tramping over the rolling hills, lush and golden with grass.

Drawing the handcarts was hard. The grass grew to shoulder height on the open prairie, and near the rivers some varieties grew taller. Joseph Elder had ridden along the Missouri yesterday and chased up a couple of white-tail deer. He reported, "The grass was up to my shoulders even when I was riding on my mule, and though I spotted the flash of a tail as the deer bounded off, the grass was so high that I never could get a decent look at it, much less pull off a shot."

There was no proper road. The handcarts were forced to follow trails away from the rivers, up where the prairie grasses thinned along the tops of the hills. Thus they constantly were toiling up and down.

Worse, each handcart had at least an extra hundred pounds of flour on it. Captain Willie had tried to buy a couple more wagons back in Iowa. The company needed two more at the very least, but none could be had.

In part, it may have been that the townsfolk in Council Bluffs were still angry about the brawl that had taken place. Or maybe it was that Dane stirring up trouble. Or maybe . . . there just weren't any wagons to spare in that bustling city.

But he'd been forced to contend with the fact that he didn't have enough wagons to carry supplies, so he had to resort to begging the saints to carry some of their own wheat. Every handcart had to bear a sack of flour.

Some folks whined, but most didn't. As promised, James Hurren took five hundred pounds of flour so that some of those who were carrying cripples in their carts didn't have to bear the weight. Other men carried extra so that widows who had to pull children would have an easier time of it. Samuel Gadd put three hundred pounds of flour on his cart, and a couple of other men did likewise.

There was no horseplay when the group left Winter Quarters, as there had been four weeks earlier. Back in Iowa, on the first morning, the saints had decorated their handcarts, painting slogans like "Utah or Bust" or "Bound for Zion." The men had raced each other, jostling and even breaking handcarts, while women and children had to skip to keep up. Now, the folks were more sober. They knew that they were in for a long haul. Still the mood remained upbeat.

Captain Willie didn't know how many of the saints would follow him. Most, he hoped, but he wasn't going to stay any longer and try to convince them. He believed that a leader should lead by example, and that is what he did. He led, and if the rest of the saints wished to follow, he would be glad of it.

He did not pull a handcart himself, and though the church had provided him a fine mule to ride, he refused it. He didn't want to be seen riding about like some fine lord while women and children broke their hearts and their backs pulling handcarts. So he left the mule for some elderly folks to ride, whoever was in the greatest need, and Captain Willie spent the day helping others push their own handcarts, particularly the widows and the old folks.

He did not travel far that afternoon. It was only five miles through the gently rolling hills to the Little Papillion Creek, where the saints found good water and timber. It wasn't a great distance from town, but the emotional distance was enormous, for out here there was no roof over their heads but God's blue heaven, and there was no sign of a house or a road. The only sounds were the cawing of crows and the wind whispering through dry grasses. Even the ceaseless buzz of mosquitoes was gone. They were in the wilderness now.

Captain Willie brought only two hundred saints that

afternoon—his own hundred and those that belonged to Levi Savage. He wasn't about to let Savage remain alone with the rest of the company where he could poison their minds with his doubts and advocate his devilish doctrine. There was an old saying from the Italians, "Keep your friends close, and your enemies closer." Captain Willie was about ready to hog-tie Savage and throw him over his shoulder.

Most of all, Captain Willie worried about how Savage's murmuring might affect folks like Eliza Gadd. He felt sure that Eliza would witness miracles on this journey, and the time would come when the scales of doubt would shed from her eyes and she would be forced to see the truth. But that wouldn't happen if Savage kept spreading doubt.

In addition to the first two hundred saints, a small company of wagons came with him—wealthier saints from Europe, rich enough to buy wagons. There were twenty-two people in the small group, under the direction of a Captain Siler.

At the Little Papillion, Captain Willie met up with Colonel Babbitt's small wagon train. There were only four wagons, with a little freight, and a young woman named Wilson and her infant child.

They camped that night with the moon still nearly full while stars blazed like ice crystals in the heavens. Ten tents were pitched in a large circle, and the songs of Zion rang through the camp. There was a girl in camp, Rhoda Rebecca Oakey, whom Captain Willie suspected had the sweetest soprano voice in the world. As the camp was laid to rest, Rhoda Rebecca stood in the center of it and sang "A Poor, Wayfaring Man of Grief." The girl's mother was heartbroken and grieving, for Joseph Oakey had run off; so far the family's attempts to find him had been futile.

But oh, Captain Willie thought, *how Rhoda's voice is a balm for the heart.*

Her song was part lullaby for her mother and part prayer.

In the darkness, Captain Willie walked among the sweet hay and led Colonel Babbitt out of earshot from the tents. Captain Willie didn't want the saints that were under his protection to overhear any talk about Indians. He knew that he had to be cautious when traveling through Indian territory, but most of these English and Danes would go wild-eyed and hysterical if they heard about Indian troubles. For right now, Captain Willie needed to keep the problem quiet. Wind was sweeping through the hills in gentle waves, stroking the buffalo grass.

As they walked, they talked about safe subjects. "It appears that I need to go back to Council Bluffs," Babbitt said. "Some Dane has sworn out a complaint against the church, demanding the return of his property."

"There's nothing to it," Captain Willie said. "Hansen is nothing short of a beggar. He came here on church funds and still owes us for passage. He borrowed money from other saints to buy some pans. He never paid a penny for them, so we gave them to Jens Nielsen, the man who leant the money."

"Would it be so hard," Colonel Babbitt asked, "to just let the man have the pans?"

"Too late," Captain Willie said. "Nielsen has already turned them into some fine-looking hubcaps, trying to keep the dust out of his handcart wheels."

"Well," Colonel Babbitt sighed, exasperated. "I'll go handle the suit then." He obviously didn't relish the idea of getting stuck in Council Bluffs. "The circuit judge won't be in town for a few days, and if I don't go, he just might send a posse out and have them drag you back for trial. You don't need that kind of trouble."

"This Hansen," Captain Willie said, "he's a low sort of man. It sounds to me like he's out for all he can get."

"Well," Babbitt conceded, "when you've got nothing, you've got nothing to lose."

When they were out of earshot of the camp and its guards, Captain Willie asked, "So do you intend to have your men strike ahead tomorrow without you?"

"I do," Colonel Babbitt said.

Captain Willie didn't know why that choice made him so uneasy. "Even with the Sioux threatening?"

"I have little to fear," Colonel Babbitt said. "I've made gifts to every chieftain between here and Salt Lake this spring. I'm safer out here than I am on a sidewalk in Council Bluffs."

"I reckon," Captain Willie said. He wished that he had some kind of relationship with the Indians himself. Sure, Brigham Young paid bribes to keep the Mormons safe, but Indians had a strange way of looking at things. Brigham had a relationship with the chiefs, and the saints had a relationship with Brigham. Captain Willie's relationship to the chiefs wasn't a personal one, and as far as the Indians were concerned, the more distant one's relationship was with a chief, the more tenuous a hold it had on them.

Captain Willie searched his feelings. He wasn't asking Babbitt to ride with him out of fear for his own safety. No, Captain Willie felt genuinely worried for Babbitt. Babbitt's four wagons, heavily loaded with baggage, would make an easy target. Having a woman along made the wagon train that much more tempting.

"I'm begging you," Captain Willie said at last, "have your teams ride along with us."

But Babbitt stood firm. "We'll make better time on our own. My teamsters are more experienced than yours, and with a smaller company we'll make faster time. I do thank you for your offer, though."

Captain Willie had no hold on the man. Colonel Babbitt was his superior in every way. Back when Captain Willie had been a young man, Babbitt had been Joseph Smith's personal lawyer, and even now Babbitt could count Brigham Young and most of the apostles of the church as close personal friends.

Captain Willie couldn't blame the man for turning him down. Babbitt knew that the handcart company was short on wagons. Captain Willie had even tried to buy a couple of Babbitt's or, failing that, to hire Babbitt to carry some of the company's excess food for the first two hundred miles. But Babbitt wasn't falling for it. Doubtless, he saw Captain Willie as a beggar and thought that instead of offering protection, Captain Willie would regale him with pleas to haul baggage.

"Well, I'll be sorry to see you leave," Captain Willie said frankly.

But in the morning, Captain Willie didn't see Babbitt leave. Colonel Babbitt's men crept out of camp soundlessly well before dawn.

Shortly after breakfast, the wind began to be boisterous, gusting through the fields, wet and warm, a sure sign of storm. Clouds were massing on the horizon.

Within two hours, the rest of the saints came trudging into camp, the last "three hundred." But Captain Willie could tell that there were no longer five hundred people in his camp. The numbers were down significantly. Not a single one of the eighty Scottish saints had turned back, and only a couple of Danes were gone. As for the few Germans, French, Swiss, and the one princess from India, Sister Tait, all of them had come.

It was the English who had betrayed him. Over a hundred and twenty had turned back. The loss saddened him deeply, for among those who left were more than one family that Captain Willie had converted back in England.

As the last of the saints dragged their tails into camp, Captain Willie hunted down Levi Savage.

"Brother Savage, I've got a job for you," Captain Willie said. "We were supposed to have some milk cows, and some cattle for beef, but it appears that they've been left behind. Will you run back to Winter Quarters and fetch them?"

Levi Savage looked dumbfounded and peered off at the horizon and the gathering clouds. "They were left behind?"

The enormity of this "blunder" was not lost on Brother Savage. Captain Willie couldn't have just forgotten to bring their main source of meat and milk for the journey. He had left them on purpose, and he was going to force Levi to go fetch forty head of wild Texas cattle at the end of the day—then drive them here through a thunderstorm.

You're the one who said that "No man will work harder than I will to bring these people to Zion," Captain Willie thought. *I'm just helping you keep your promise. While I'm at it, I'm going to make sure that you're not around to poison the minds of the rest of these good folks.*

Savage did not grit his teeth or glare; Captain Willie had fully expected the man to belt him. But Savage just shook his head woefully, as if astonished that anyone could be so ignorant as to forget the cattle, and said softly, "I'd be honored to help you out."

Captain Willie felt blood rushing to his face, mingled embarrassment and shame. *He thinks I'm a fool,* Captain Willie realized, *and he's eager to help cover up my mistake.*

Savage and six other men had walked well out of sight when suddenly the boisterous winds began to blow a cloud of grasshoppers into camp, dismaying the saints. The grasshoppers blackened the sky, and soon grasshoppers covered the tents, got caught in children's hair, and sent the women screaming. Captain Willie had seldom seen anything like it. It was almost like some plague from the Bible, the locusts blowing into the pharaoh's court. Or more like the plagues of Mormon crickets that infested Utah.

So Captain Willie had the camp pack up and head west; they trudged for an hour more, making three miles, until they reached the Big Papillion Creek, where there was more water and more trees to shelter the company's tents from the coming storm. Most importantly, there were no grasshoppers.

As an added bonus, Captain Willie realized, it would keep Levi Savage out of camp that much longer.

Enormous gray thunderheads continued to build all during the day, until the day was as dark as night; finally the heavens grumbled as if in protest, and the clouds broke, unleashing waves of rain. Lightning seared the sky, and contrary winds screamed through the trees and knocked over one of the tents.

Brother McGaw, the church agent from Winter Quarters, came into camp that evening, riding a spooked horse, and took a short meeting in Captain Willie's tent where he confirmed the eight "independent wagons" as part of the Willie Handcart Company. But they were not put under the direction of Captain Willie. Instead, Captain Siler was left in charge of his twenty-two immigrants.

Levi Savage and his men drove the cattle in late at night, all of the men soaked to the bone, and ate a cold supper well after the rest of the camp was abed. Captain Willie saw the drovers there, hunched and weary after the storm, slumped like vultures around the smoking ruins of a campfire. Savage looked little worse for the wear.

But Captain Willie decided that the best way to keep Savage quiet was to keep him busy. Hours before dawn, Captain Willie blew the bugle, waking the camp. It was 4:00 a.m. by his watch.

"Out of bed, brothers and sisters," Captain Willie shouted. "It's going to be a fearsome hot day, with a long walk before we're through."

Some folks were slow to get out of bed, and Captain Willie decided that tonight at prayer meeting he'd give a fiery sermon on slothfulness.

The camp roused and cooked a hasty breakfast, and as the sun came striding up the horizon in a glorious display of rose-colored clouds, the saints set off. The camp moved well, except for one minor drawback. One of the cows that Levi had brought in last night was bawling for its calf, and no calf could be found. Perhaps it had wandered off in the night, but more likely, Captain Willie thought, Savage and his men had lost it in the dark along the way.

Well, Captain Willie thought. *We'll just leave that cow for the day and see if its calf can find her. At the end of the day, I'm sure that brother Savage will be glad for the chance to rouse himself for a one-man cattle drive.*

The company walked eighteen miles, stopping once to take lunch during the afternoon heat, and finally reached the river just before sundown.

To the north and the south, the hills continued to roll in gentle dunes, and dividing them was the mighty Platte, one of the world's most disappointing rivers. The land here spread in a broad plain, almost as flat as a well-made floor, and amid this, the river sprawled wide. In some places, the Platte was as much as a dozen miles wide but only four inches deep. Few fish could survive its muddy, unwholesome water, filled as it was with buffalo dung and piss, and one dared not drink from it except in the greatest extremity.

The locals declared that the Platte was "too thick to drink, and too thin to plow."

The river's course changed with each passing winter. Sandbars and islands sprouted up all across it. Most of these might survive one winter, only to wash away the next. But on some islands, a bit of timber grew, along with grape vines and plums, pea vines, hemp, and other valuable plants. Wildfires might rage across the rest of the plains, but these islands remained sheltered from year to year, creating small oases in the bland prairie.

The only problem was getting to these islands. In the winter, the raging waters sometimes carved deep channels that soon filled with silt. Thus the shallow Platte concealed many a patch of quicksand. One dared not risk crossing the Platte often, and it was sometimes better to stare longingly at a bit of firewood than to risk the trip to get it.

So the company camped that night for the first time on the Platte, a river whose course they would follow for the next four hundred miles.

There were heaps of driftwood on the banks here, and the white logs made an eerie sight at night as the bonfires reflected from them. It was as if the bones of the earth were exposed, red and glowing.

At dawn, Captain Willie sent one of the saints back to find the cow and the calf. He was a nearsighted little Welshman, terrified of Indians and wolves.

Then the camp moved on for the day. Over the past weeks, sand had blown up from the riverbanks, covering the trail, and the sand was wet from rain; the heavy carts often sank, sometimes up to the hubs. The added weight of the wheat only made the burden worse, forcing the saints to wear themselves to a frazzle.

Willie and the other captains spent their day going from handcart to handcart, lifting the carts and pulling them out of sinkholes, or else helping some of the sisters and the old folk pull the carts through the worst stretches of sand. He was going back and forth to help so much that Captain Willie figured that for every mile that one of the saints walked, he was walking three.

After they stopped, sometime after six in the evening, the camp had made only twelve miles, yet everyone was exhausted. The nervous little Welsh fellow returned with neither the cow nor calf—as Captain Willie had expected.

Captain Willie found Levi Savage and once again tapped him for the arduous journey. "Brother Savage, that cow and her calf are still missing."

Savage, who hadn't yet had a chance to eat dinner—he had been helping some of the sisters pitch their tents—shot Captain Willie a tired glance. "Always happy to oblige," he answered as he nearly staggered to saddle his mule. There was no anger in Savage's demeanor, no hesitation, even though Savage was so worn out that it looked like he might fall over.

As Captain Willie watched Savage ride out of camp, a woman spoke at Willie's back.

"That Levi Savage is a good man," Eliza Gadd said.

Captain Willie turned to face her. "You think he's good?"

"I think," Eliza said, "that he loves the folk in this company at least as much as you do. But you two have different ways of showing it."

Captain Willie paused. He could see that Eliza was right. But even if Savage loved his people, he had a bad way of showing it. He might stop them from coming out of love, but they'd suffer for his choice nonetheless. He was like a doting father who gave his children all that they wanted, hoping to please them, when they would have been better served by learning how to suffer a little.

Eliza folded her arms, kept peering off at Levi's back. "So, are you going to kill him? If that's what you're after, you could just shoot him. That would be a lot kinder than what you're doing."

She must think that I'm some kind of devil! Captain Willie realized.

He didn't have a clue how to begin to answer. "I'm only trying to keep that fool out of camp, so that he won't sow the seeds of discontent."

"Are you sure that's all that you're after?" Eliza demanded.

A verse from the Book of Mormon came to mind: "It is better that one man should die than that a whole nation should dwindle and perish in unbelief." Was it the Holy Spirit speaking or just a random thought?

This was hard doctrine, the kind that Captain Willie didn't expect Eliza to understand. God had commanded murder before. He told Moses to warn his people not to commit murder, yet within a month he ordered the genocide of dozens of tribes, hundreds of thousands of people—the Amorites, the Jebusites, the Perezites and the Philistines. God had not only ordered his people to kill the men in these tribes, but he also ordered the Israelites to murder the enemy's wives, their babes, and even to slaughter their sheep and their cattle, and to grind down their golden idols and throw the gold back into the rivers. Men like Saul, David, and Solomon were praised in the Bible for their capacity to murder. Certainly, even Christ's apostles had avenged Jesus' death, for they never could agree about how Judas Iscariot had died. Had he hanged himself, or stabbed himself, or fallen on the rocks and dashed his guts out? Captain Willie suspected that the apostles had done all three things to him—and worse.

But the question now was, "Did Levi Savage need to die?" Captain Willie hadn't considered that possibility. He wondered, and immediately felt that it was wrong. Captain Willie's bosom filled with a sweet sense of peace, and he knew the answer.

"No, I don't want to harm him," Captain Willie said, his voice growing soft and soulful. He needed to convince Eliza of this. He couldn't let her go on thinking that he was capable of such evil. "Savage errs in his doctrine, of that I'm convinced, but he's as innocent as a child. Still, sometimes a man who errs can be more dangerous than a drunken gunslinger, and you have to keep him in line. But as you said, Brother Savage loves these folks, and he wouldn't hurt a hair on their heads."

"Then be careful of what you do to that good man," Eliza said. "We haven't got enough men in the camp as it is. He's guileless; he doesn't even know that you're furious with him. He hasn't figured out that you're giving him make-work. He thinks that you're asking him to do these jobs because he is the best man in camp.

"And of that I'm convinced—he is the best man in camp."

8

Horny Toads

Dawn came hazy and cool after the storm. For the saints, it was a relief, and that morning, Baline rose early to cries of catbirds in the rushes beside the Platte. She felt invigorated and looked forward to today's adventure.

There was always something new and wondrous to discover on the journey. Yesterday she had found some flowers, like giant white lilies, whose petals were as big as handkerchiefs and as soft as clouds. Bright stones and pebbles could be discovered along the river, and lizards hid in the sand at the water's edge. One of the Rowley boys had caught a strange creature called a horny toad yesterday. It had rested in the palm of his hand as if it were tame; the Rowley boy was keeping it in his shirt pocket as a pet. Baline wanted a pet, too. Back in Denmark, she had had her own kitten, and now she missed it terribly.

So she threw on her clothes in the tent, nearly panting with excitement.

"Where are you going in such a hurry?" Jens asked, rubbing the sleep from his eyes.

"Father Jens," Baline begged, "vould it be evil if I prayed to God to find a horn toad?"

"What is a 'horn toad'?" Jens asked, and she explained that it was the most wonderful kind of lizard in the world.

Jens considered. "I don't know," he said at last. "It seems to me that while you are praying to catch this lizard, it will be praying to escape. Who will God listen to?"

Else ventured her opinion, "It is wrong to ask God for trivial things. If you pray, you must pray intently, asking God for things that you need."

The answers were like a slap in the face, and Baline peered down at Jens, saddened.

He seemed to look inside himself, then said, "You will find a horn toad today. I feel certain of this."

"That can't be right!" Else objected.

But Jens said, "God wants her to have a horn toad. I feel it. Though it may not be important to you, it is important to him. So he will give it to her, if she will treat it well."

"I vill!" Baline said.

She said a silent prayer as she rushed to the Hurren tent and found Mary still in her nightdress. Having just turned eight, Mary was two years younger then Baline, and Mary followed Baline around like a puppy.

Mary's little legs could hardly carry her through the tall grass, and often when they were walking, Mary would grow tired, then fall down and cry, wanting to rest.

Baline, being older and having the strength of the Danes, had decided to help Mary get to Zion, and so every day since they'd left Winter Quarters, they had begun walking together. Baline would try to cheer Mary on the long walks, and would hold her hand if need be, or stay with her when she got so tired that she had to sit and rest. Then, when the rest was over, they would run together and try to catch up with the handcarts. Agnes Caldwell had joined in, and now the three girls were inseparable. As they walked along, they often talked about how, when they got to Zion, they would insist that their parents all buy houses right next to each other, and they swore that no matter what, they would be friends for life.

So Baline helped rouse Mary from under her blanket, and then helped her shuck off her nightclothes and pull on a dress in the shadows of the tent.

"What are you two girls going to do today?" It was Mary's sister-in-law, Caroline Reeder, who was sixteen. Caroline was as slim as a willow frond, with dark brown hair. She always had a big smile and sparkle in her blue eyes.

"Ve are going to catch der horny toads," Baline offered. "You vant to come?"

"Sure," Caroline said, "but not until after a game of tag." She lunged for Baline, tagged her on the back, shouted, "You're it!" and then lunged out the door. Mary shrieked in delight and followed on her heels.

Baline followed, perplexed, as always, by this strange game. 'You're it!' they always said. But what did it mean? Anything could be an it—a cow, an elephant, a loaf of bread. And an it could be nothing at all. The English would say, "It is dark," and in that case they meant that the sky is dark or the whole world is dark. Or they might say, "It is late." In that case, trying to figure out what it was gave Baline a headache.

So when Caroline Reeder told Baline that she was it, Baline wanted to shout, "Vat? Vat am I supposed to be? A fencepost? A pollyvog? Vat do you mean, 'it'?"

This game, it was most annoying. Still, Baline shrieked with delight and rushed from the tent, chasing Mary.

For the most part, the mothers didn't want littler girls and boys in their way while they tried to fix breakfast over the campfires, and so the young ones scampered out of the camp, into the piles of driftwood that skirted the river, until "breakfast" was done. The breakfast was more than just one meal. Each man got a pound of wheat per day, while the women got twelve ounces, and the children Baline's age got ten. The wheat was self-rising, and once water was added to it, along with a little salt, it could be cooked into biscuits or small loaves of bread. Some people just mixed it with warm water and made a kind of cereal they called "skilly."

Each morning, the women would get out their fry pans or Dutch ovens and cook up the wheat. Most of the time, the women would cook all of the bread for the day at once; after breakfast, extra biscuits or loaves would stay hidden in their aprons, and the mothers would pass them out to the children if they showed signs of fatigue along the trail.

So it was that Baline raced among the fallen driftwood that golden morning, until all too soon Captain Willie got his walking stick out, thumped it against the side of a handcart, and announced that it was time to leave.

Baline, Mary, and Agnes were full of energy and decided to race ahead of the handcarts, reasoning that the carts would scare away any horny toads. Caroline came with them in order to make certain that the girls stayed safe.

The air was cool that morning, and the dew on the grass sparkled like diamonds and washed Baline's bare feet as she walked. She felt invigorated.

Other wagons had passed through here this summer, leaving something of a trail where the grass was trampled and cropped short by oxen. The girls rushed along it.

The trail soon left the bank of the Platte and rose a bit on the side of a gentle hill. They passed a bald patch of ground where prairie dogs lived, and the small squirrels sat up on their back legs and barked as the girls approached, then scampered for their burrows when the girls got too near.

There in the prairie dog town, they spotted a ball of half-digested fur, something that a wolf had shatted, and ahead they saw a patch of sand that the winter floods had deposited.

They hurried up to the patch of sand, hoping for horny toads, and Agnes let out a blood-curdling cry.

A big snake was lying on the ground in front of them. It had to be four feet long, and its belly was as thick as a log. It was light tan in color, like the sand, with darker diamond patterns along its back. The snake was so long that it blocked the whole width of the narrow wagon trail, occupying the space from one patch of grass to the other.

Baline did not know much about the snakes in America. This did not look like the vipers found in Denmark, which were brown with a black zigzag pattern on the back. But Father Jens had warned her that some of the snakes in America were poisonous. He said that she would recognize them by a buzzing sound that they made. This snake just rested, sluggish in the cool morning air. It was half asleep.

"What do we do?" Mary Hurren cried. She was terrified of snakes.

The girls looked back down the trail a hundred yards, where Caroline Reeder was walking toward them in that languid way that she had, seeming almost to float above the grass.

"There's a snake!" Mary shouted. "What do we do?"

"Jump over it," Caroline suggested.

The girls considered a moment, and Baline recalled a promise from the scriptures for those who had enough faith, "And if you handle any poisonous serpent, it shall not harm you." She recalled Captain Willie's promise. They were on the Lord's errand, and He would help them.

She looked to Agnes Caldwell, who smiled wickedly, showing her crooked teeth. She was always making up little rhymes, and now she invented a new one. She reached out and took Mary Hurren's right hand, and Baline took her left, and Agnes sang—

"Don't you shiver!
Don't you shake!
Just jump over that mean old snake!"

Agnes repeated the rhyme and crouched a little, ready to pounce, but Baline couldn't twist her mouth around the words fast enough to keep up with the other girls, and so she just repeated the last part of each line. "Shiver . . . shake . . . mean old snake!"

Then the girls leapt as high as they could. When their feet hit the ground on the other side, the vibration caused the snake to suddenly rear its head and a buzzing noise issued from the tail.

"Oh, it's a rattlesnake!" Agnes cried. Apparently she had been warned, too.

The girls screamed in glee and terror and leapt away from the snake, rushing past with a backward glance. But they had not gotten ten feet when Mary gave a cry and pointed to another rattlesnake on the trail. This one was much smaller, and its stomach was distended. Baline could almost see the prairie dog inside.

"Again!" Agnes called, and the girls held hands. This time the rhyme changed—

"Don't you shiver!
Don't you shake!
Just jump over that rattlesnake!"

The girls leapt high over the small snake and danced ahead a few yards, then spotted a third snake, almost as large as the first.

"This is getting creepy," Mary Hurren said. "Are we going to have to jump over rattlesnakes all the way to Zion?"

Baline wondered, and somehow she thought they just might have to. "Maybe we should turn back. I want to go home."

But Agnes urged them all forward, and they sang their rhyme and leapt over the third snake. Baline looked down the long path and suddenly realized that every few feet, for as far as she could see, a rattlesnake lay in the trail, dazed from the morning cold. She was barefoot and realized that if one of the snakes struck, her pink toes would make a tempting target.

Baline had shoes of course—a pair of brand-new leather shoes. She had gotten them two weeks ago but didn't have the heart to put them on. The shoes had been a gift. Not everyone in Iowa had been cruel to the Mormons. There were women who had passed out apples and plums from their trees, and one who had brought out a pail of milk, giving each child a drink.

Then there had been the man with the shoes. People said that his name was Charles Good, but Baline knew better. The Danish children had all recognized him instantly by his great white beard and the huge red sack that he carried on his back. It was Kris Kringle, and he had brought shoes! It could not be a coincidence that he brought shoes and candy, for back in Denmark, Kris had been making his way down chimneys and leaving gifts of candy and toys in children's shoes for nearly two thousand years.

Still, the stupid English refused to believe. They said that he was just a good man who wanted to help the Mormon children. But Baline felt quite sure that it was Kris, traveling in disguise. Everyone had forgotten her birthday back then except for Kris Kringle, but it was too late to go back to the handcarts for shoes now. Together the three girls gripped each other's hands, sang their rhyme, and for nearly a mile made a game out of jumping over rattlesnakes.

Baline had no fear. God was with her.

It wasn't until an hour later, when the sight of so many snakes had long ago driven the memory of her prayer from her mind that Baline caught her horny toad.

9

MIRACLES

As they traveled that day over sandy ground, the sun soon grew to be blazing hot and burned the haze away, until the sand beneath the travelers' bare feet sizzled.

It was quickly discovered that the whole trail was infested with poisonous serpents, and Eliza Gadd urged her children to stay on the trail, away from the deep grass. What's more, she stopped the cart and forced all of her children to put on their shoes. This wasn't necessarily an easy task. The shoes were bulky, and many children, and even Eliza herself, had discovered that walking over the sandy soil was much easier to do barefoot.

Young men went to the front of the trail with sticks to drive the snakes from the path, and this included two of Eliza's oldest. Captain Willie warned the boys not to hit the snakes, for according to Joseph Smith, one was not to harm wild animals.

So the boys were to pound on the ground, making thumping noises to drive the snakes away.

Still, Eliza wasn't taking any chances. She kept her eyes out on the margin of the trail, especially where the grass grew tall, and watched for snakes.

Ann Howard walked a little ahead, keeping extra close watch, holding five-year-old Sarah's hand with her left and seven-year-old Mary Ann's hand in her right. Sister Howard's gray dress was drab, but at that moment Eliza thought that she looked like an angel there, with her black hair flowing like a silken waterfall down her back.

That woman is an angel, Eliza thought. *Who needs heaven with women like her around?*

The company appeared to make it through the infested area in good order, no one receiving a harmful bite. But folks stayed on the alert all day. It wasn't until early in the afternoon that there was a shout from the back of the handcart train.

"Eliza," someone called. "Eliza Gadd. Help. You're needed!"

Eliza steeled her nerves. She handed off baby Daniel to Sister Howard and went racing back.

Eliza wasn't the only nurse in camp, but she had the best training. As she ran, she worried about who was bit, and where. For a young child, a snake bite could kill almost instantly. A serpent might strike the child's torso, or even its neck and face, and the venom would then spread through the victim quickly. An adult was more likely to get struck on a leg or arm, where a tourniquet could be applied, slowing the spread of the poison until Eliza could suck out the venom.

She hoped it wasn't a child.

Eliza raced to the back of the handcart train, but people kept urging her back even farther—back to the wagons that were following the trail. There she saw a woman lying on the ground, crumpled beside a wagon. A toddler, a young girl who was sitting in the back of the wagon, was peering down at her mother, crying.

It was Sophia Geary, a young woman from England. Eliza knew her by name, though Sophia was not a close friend. Sophia was only twenty-six, much younger than Eliza.

"It's her foot!" one of the teamsters shouted at Eliza. "She fainted, and the wagon ran over it."

Eliza ran to Sophia, who was shaking with pain and crying, lying in a fetal position.

"Let's get that boot off," Eliza said, reaching down, but Sophia pulled her foot away at the slightest touch.

"We can't leave it on," Eliza explained as she began to untie the shoe. "Your foot will swell inside it, and that will hurt even more."

The shoe went up above the ankle and had a dozen hooks on

each side. As gingerly as she could, Eliza untied the laces and began loosening the shoe.

"How did this happen?" Eliza asked. She wanted to know the whole story so that she could get some estimate of the damage.

"She was hanging onto the wagon, trying to steal a rest," the teamster said, "and the clumsy girl fell under the wheel."

Eliza steeled herself. It was likely to be a horrible wound. The supply wagon had thick iron rims around the wheels, and it carried two tons of flour, along with other baggage.

"It wasn't my fault," Sophia cried. "I wasn't clumsy. I fainted."

When some of the older children grew tired, they would hang onto the back of a handcart or one of the supply wagons in order to let others pull them along. Even some of the elderly saints resorted to this.

Of course, hitching a ride this way caused problems. If a man was pulling a handcart, it just made it that much harder to pull, and if you were hanging onto the side of a wagon, it was only a matter of time until you tripped and fell under a wheel.

But Eliza felt for Sister Geary. She was a young mother burdened with a three-year-old daughter. Her husband could not pull the wagon through the heavy sands with a child on board, not while carrying an extra bag of wheat or two, and the child could not walk, so Sophia was forced to carry her daughter, just as Eliza was forced to constantly be hauling one of her twins. Apparently, the blistering heat and her own weariness had combined in such a fashion that Sophia fell into a swoon.

Now Sophia lay on the ground in a heap, wracked by great sobs. Eliza tenderly tried to pull the boot off, but Sophia shrieked in pain.

Beneath the boot, beneath the stocking, Eliza could see that the foot was badly crushed, a blackened mess, bruised and bleeding.

Eliza hardly dared to touch it. It was swelling rapidly, and within minutes it tripled its normal size. Under such circumstances, Eliza feared that the swelling might cause Sister Geary's skin to split, leading to an infection.

"Do you have any salves in your belongings?" Eliza asked. It wasn't uncommon for a young mother to carry some petroleum salve, especially if she was nursing.

"No," Sophia whimpered.

Eliza had some of her own in the handcart, but she was nearly out. It would last only a few days. During the rest at Winter Quarters, Eliza's breast milk had begun to flow more normally, but now that they were on the march, she had begun to lose it again. She feared that in a few days, it would be gone altogether, and she would need what little balm that she had for herself.

What to do for bruising? Eliza wondered. When she'd worked for Doctor Boyle, he had always carried his own medicinal supplies, all bought in London. But Eliza had studied old books of herbal lore. There were plants that had been used to heal bruises going back as far as Roman times.

Eliza left Sophia's foot to the sunlight. It was bleeding just a bit, and she figured that letting it bleed out wouldn't hurt. Then she went down closer to the riverbank and picked some yellow flowers. The plant that they came from was a common one, with leaves shaped like clover. The old books called it melilot.

"It's good for healing bruises," Eliza explained as she wrapped the flowers—leaf, stem, and all—around the bruise. Then she put a layer of cloth over that, and Sister Geary sat on the ground, rocking back and forth, moaning from the pain.

"That foot is broken for sure," Eliza said when she was done. "You're going to have to ride from here to Salt Lake."

By now, Captain Willie had come to the back of the train. "You mean we've got another cripple?"

That was bad news, for there were already too many cripples riding in the relief wagon. Old Peder Mortensen and his daughter Lena were there, along with several elderly saints and a few others who were sick. Eliza knew that the company didn't have enough wagons to carry their food, much less passengers.

"I'm afraid so," Eliza said. "She won't be able to walk for months."

Captain Willie sighed, then knelt next to Sophia and peered hard into her eyes. "Sophia, we need to get you up into that wagon if we can. There's no water ahead for miles, so we can't just sit here and wait for you to feel better. Do you think you can handle the pain if we try to get you on the wagon?"

Sophia nodded bravely, but Eliza knew that she was lying. That swollen foot was filling with blood and fluid. It would hurt like the devil to move it at all.

"Perhaps we should give her something for the pain," Eliza suggested. "Does anyone have any whiskey?"

There wasn't much to be had on a Mormon handcart train. Joseph Smith's "Word of Wisdom" forbade the drinking of alcohol. But Eliza had seen more than one brother fortify himself while standing guard at night.

"I'd rather die than drink demon liquor!" Sophia cried.

Eliza bit back her first response. She was tempted to say, "Fine by me. Go ahead and suffer, if you're that stupid."

Instead she asked Captain Willie, "Is there any laudanum in camp?" Laudanum was a more powerful anesthetic than alcohol, but more expensive and harder to come by.

"I think that Brother Jeppson has some," Captain Willie said and took off. Moments later he returned with a bottle of snake-oil, a mixture of laudanum, whiskey, and who-knows-what-else. Genuine snake skin could be seen floating inside. It wasn't proper medicine by Eliza's book, but it would have to do.

In twenty minutes, Sophia gave off her weeping and her eyes took on a glazed, disinterested quality. Her husband came and picked her up, lifting the brunt of her weight, while Captain Willie gingerly hefted her foot up onto the relief wagon. Eliza followed alongside the wagon for awhile. Sophia lay in pain, crying out each time that the wagon hit a heavy bump or jostled.

That evening, when camp was set, Eliza unwrapped Sophia's foot and checked her wound. This act drew a small crowd of curious onlookers, the kind who always come to see a terrible injury. The ankle was swollen like a gourd. There wasn't much that Eliza could do for a crushed foot. It wasn't like a leg or an arm, which could be re-set. Eliza could only shake her head.

"Cold water will take down the swelling," one woman suggested.

But it was late summer, and the muddy water flowing down the Platte wasn't cold. It wasn't even cool.

"Let's try giving her a blessing," Captain Willie suggested as he peered over Eliza's shoulder.

A blessing was a ceremony performed by Mormon men who held the priesthood. Just as Christ had healed the sick and raised the dead in his day, men who held the priesthood would lay their hands upon the head of the sick and call upon God to heal the person.

Grunts of agreement rose from the group, and Captain Willie asked Captain Siler to do the honor, along with a friend to the Geary family, Brother Cantwell, who was said to have the gift of healing, and of course Sophia's husband.

Eliza backed away from the group as the men laid their hands upon Sister Geary's head and prayed. Such nonsense, in her estimation, was no more effective than dancing naked under the moonlight. But neither could it hurt, and it might keep the woman calm and fortify her spirits.

But Eliza could not help but cringe as she heard Brother Cantwell pronounce solemnly during the blessing, "I seal upon you a gift of strength and healing, and if thou hast faith, thy wound shall recover speedily, and tomorrow thou shalt walk."

Eliza was so offended by the mumbo jumbo that after the prayer, she hurried to her tent.

The next day, the company rolled out at eight in the morning and at noon stopped to ferry across the Loup River, where Captain Willie had a cow and a calf killed, giving the company its first meat in a week.

The Loup River was little more than a mud hole at this time of year. The rapidly sinking waters had left a series of stagnant sloughs, often too shallow to ford. So the first step in crossing was for some of the men from camp to go out in a canoe with poles and try to find a navigable path for the ferry.

There was a cabin near the ferry, the first in a future "city." The owner of the cabin, an obnoxious German, had plotted out the entire city with little pegs and felt sure that by next year this spot would be as bustling as Chicago. Doubtless, he lived in an imaginary city filled with fine shops and cathedrals, where he was the mayor, and every night was spent at the opera. By Eliza's estimation, all of the land-grabbers in Nebraska seemed as daft as the Mormons.

So the camp waited while the men found a path across the treacherous river, and then spent hours rafting the party over.

On the far side of the river, the ground became more sandy, less fertile, and the deep grass gave way to shorter varieties of "buffalo grass" that grew only two or three feet tall.

By day's end the company had traveled only eleven miles; Sophia Geary walked the last five of that, much to Eliza's dismay, hobbling along with the aid of a walking stick.

Most likely, Eliza imagined, that woman's foot is going to swell up as big as a watermelon tonight, and she'll be dead by morning. Won't Captain Willie be cursing himself then!

The wind kicked up in the evening, and more gray clouds began to crowd the heavens at sunset, threatening a major storm.

In camp that night, as Sophia limped about, Eliza sat massaging her husband's shoulders. They'd grown tight from pulling the handcart day after day.

As she did, she watched the young Sophia holding her three-year-old daughter on one hip, cooking dinner. Eliza could not hide the disapproval on her face.

Captain Willie wandered past Eliza and stood for a moment, inviting comment.

"Evening, Captain," Samuel said. Captain Willie nodded cordially.

He's always around me lately, Eliza realized. *This isn't a chance meeting. He's seeking me out. But why?*

"That woman should be in bed," Eliza said. "Sister Geary's broken foot is likely to set funny. She could end up a cripple."

"She'll be fine," Captain Willie said. "She has been healed. There is no power greater than the power of the priesthood. It was by the power of his priesthood that God created the heavens and the earth. Now he has given that very power to his disciples."

Eliza gritted her teeth and looked up at Captain Willie. "How do you know that it isn't my nursing that helped her to walk? I'm the one who made the poultice of herbs. I'm the one who has been giving her laudanum." Enough laudanum so that she could be dancing if she wanted to, a little voice in the back of Eliza's mind whispered.

"You said that her foot was broken," Captain Willie said in his own defense. "And now, she walks."

"I thought it was broken. Perhaps it's not. The ground is sandy here. The wheel probably pushed her foot into the ground, rather than crush it completely."

Captain Willie peered up into the darkening sky for a long moment. Clouds hid the heavens, dashing in from the east, massive and gray. It was as if a blanket were being drawn across the heavens, and the wind was kicking up, blowing this way and that. This didn't feel like just another summer thundershower. The wind was growing chill and damp. Eliza frowned just as one of the Danish boys began playing his violin.

"You disapprove of the violin?" Captain Willie asked. "You think it of the devil?"

It was a common sentiment. Many of the more Puritanical religions decried the violin and considered dancing to be a sin so wicked that it bordered on adultery.

"Not at all," Eliza said. "I heard Paganini play when he toured England in '32. The music was so beautiful, I cried. If ever I were to believe in God, it would come from his playing, not some man's preaching."

Captain Willie shook his head sadly. "Eliza, Eliza, what will it take before you believe?"

"Show me a miracle, Captain Willie," Eliza said with a sour expression, "and I will believe."

Ann Howard drew near and set a tin teapot into the coals. "Anyone like some tea?" she asked, glancing first to Eliza, then to Samuel and the others.

Several grunted their assent.

"'It is a wicked and perverse generation that seeketh after a sign,'" Captain Willie quoted some scripture to Eliza. Whether it was from the Bible or the Book of Mormon, Eliza didn't know.

"Eliza is neither wicked nor perverse," Ann spoke up in Eliza's defense. "She just doesn't see yet."

Eliza felt grateful for that, and a little surprised. *Samuel is the one who should have spoken in my defense,* she thought.

Captain Willie smiled as if he'd just thought of something, and whispered, "Okay, then, I'll see what I can do."

Eliza stopped massaging Samuel's shoulders and crossed her arms. *Is he planning to pull off a miracle?* Eliza wondered, both incredulous at such pomposity and amused by it at the same time.

Back in the tent behind her, she could hear Bill and Sam Junior wrestling. She'd have to go calm them down. "Whatever trick you conjure up," Eliza said, climbing to her feet, "I'm warning you, it had better be good!"

10

The Storm

Captain Willie did not come up with a miracle the next day. He found it hard even to get by. The day grew hot on the twenty-fourth of August. The ground became sandy, and a gale blew the sand into the faces of the immigrants mercilessly as they trudged beside the Platte. There was no cover from the wind. Trees were growing scarce along the river, and the ground ahead had become as flat as a table for as far as the eye could see.

The strength of the saints was beginning to falter. The muddy Platte River was much to blame, for there was no other water to drink, and those who drank it got bellyaches if they were lucky or dysentery if they weren't.

Many of the older saints looked parched and ragged, and even the younger ones began falling by the wayside. Sister Geary had fainted two days ago, and today it was Joseph Wall, a stout young man of eighteen, who fell. He'd been as strong as a bear when the journey started, but today after the party had double-teamed the handcarts to get them up a steep, sandy hill, Joseph's strength had failed. He fainted dead away, and no amount of water or prayer would rouse him. He was too frail to move, and they couldn't afford to sit at his side.

After waiting for a couple of hours, having the camp take an early dinner, the captains held a council and voted to abandon him. They decided to give him a flask of water and a little bread so that if by chance he did recover, the Martin Handcart Company or a wagon train might come by in a few days and rescue him—if the wolves didn't take him.

The only problem with that plan was that Joseph had a young sister, Emily. The Wall family back in England was an impoverished one, and the parents had only been able to afford to send the two children this year. But when Emily heard that her older brother was to be left behind, she stubbornly refused.

"We got a blessing from Orson Hyde before we left," Emily raved. She was a broad-faced girl with curly brown hair and red cheeks that colored up nicely when she got angry. "He's an apostle, in case you don't know! He promised that we'd both live to see Zion."

Captain Willie didn't like to argue with apostles, but as far as he could tell, Joseph wasn't breathing. The only thing that was keeping him warm was the sun shining on his inert form.

"Well, if you must stay," Captain Willie had told her, "then you must."

He'd ordered the handcart company to press on, figuring that as soon as the wagons got out of sight, Emily would grow frightened and come running. There were plenty of wolves here about, and they weren't shy about taking what they wanted. Indeed, last night, three calves had gone missing. Captain Willie sent Brother Griffiths back to get them, and he found all three. But he didn't have a gun, and when the wolves came and took down two of the calves, he could do nothing more than curse at them and hurl stones. He swore that he barely made it home alive.

Certainly, Emily would think about this. The wolves were following the company now, waiting for men and animals to die. When Emily heard them howling, she would know that it was time to leave.

But as the company stopped to rest for a few moments that afternoon, Captain Willie couldn't remain easy. He found himself pacing about, worrying about whether Emily would make it back to camp alive.

It was a child that changed his mind, a little blonde barefoot Danish girl. She came up behind him and tugged on his shirt.

"Captain Villie," Baline said earnestly. "I have been praying, and

I thought of something. This girl, Emily, and her brother, they need help vit their handcart, yes?"

"Yes," Captain Willie said.

"I can help."

Captain Willie reached down and patted her head. "You're too young to pull. You have to be thirteen."

"But I am strong," Baline objected. "And I am big for my age. There are many full-grown women in camp who are not as tall as me."

That was true. Among the poor, where starvation was so rampant, many of the women were stunted. Dozens of women in the company weighed less than a hundred pounds; Baline looked as if she weighed a little more than that.

"Also," Baline whispered conspiratorially, "I am Danish. That means I am stronger than the English, yes?"

Captain Willie hooted. Yet he suspected that she was right. He was an accomplished judge of horseflesh, and if Baline were a horse, he'd have said that she was a thoroughbred. She had thick arms, broad shoulders, good bones. She looked as if she had been bred for hard labor, and that counted for a lot in this world. He'd seen newborn foals so well bred that they could outrace a grown mare.

"All right," Captain Willie agreed. "I'll send Captain Chislett back for Emily and Joseph. But if he lives, you'll have to help pull their handcart every day until Joseph is well enough to walk."

So Baline went back with Captain Chislett, and that evening she came into camp with Emily and Joseph. He lived through the night and was able to take a little skilly for breakfast. After that, Captain Willie was willing to up the odds to 50/50 that he might live, and he swore that he would never again doubt the inspired words of an apostle.

August 25 dawned surprisingly cold, and clouds of low fog drifted across the prairie like smoke, obscuring everything. The wind nipped at Captain Willie's shirt tails. A storm was in the air, and Captain Willie didn't like it.

Too many people in his camp were sick already. Some had taken fevers back at Winter Quarters, or even as far back as Council Bluffs, and never gotten rid of them. Others had contracted dysentery.

Camp arose at 4:00 a.m., breakfasted, and then broke by eight. They traveled for two hours, the clouds growing thicker and the weather cooler.

At ten in the morning, a regular gale began cutting across the plains, blowing sand. Thunderheads rolled through the sky, as if to overwhelm the little group. Lightning flashed and thunder boomed, shaking the ground beneath the people's feet.

Ahead, sheets of rain could be seen falling from clouds as black as basalt, and a few wind-driven droplets began to pelt Captain Willie in the face.

Thunder roared louder and lightning flashed. The oxen bawled and lowered their heads, unwilling to pull the wagons further, obeying an ancient instinct to turn their backs to the coming storm.

There was no place to camp that offered shelter from the wind. There was no place to camp with clean water for fourteen miles. It looked as if they'd either have to forge through the coming storm, or turn back to last night's camp, among that grove of trees.

The cattle backed away, frightened, and even the shouts and whistles of the drovers could not get them to move. It looked as if they'd turn and stampede at any moment.

Captain Willie got an idea. He strode to the front of the handcart train, then simply knelt, removed his hat, and bowed, leaving his balding head naked to the wind and rain. As the handcarts drew up at his back, each man in camp followed suit, kneeling to the ground and removing his hat.

It took twenty minutes for the camp to gather at his side. By then, the rain was falling only a half mile ahead, and the winds were screaming through the grass.

When the camp had gathered, Captain Willie prayed fervently, softly, as if God were standing in their midst. "Lord, you know the needs of your saints, and you know the love we have for thee and for thy church. You know that we have faith in thee, and at this time, we wish to unite our faith for the benefit of those who are sick and weary among us. Father, thou who created the earth, who gave life to Adam and light to the sun, we beg thee, turn this fierce storm from us. We have put our faith in the words of your prophet, Brigham Young, and in his promise that the elements would be tempered for our sake. So now, we plead with thee, in the name of thy beloved son, even our master, Jesus Christ, amen."

Then Captain Willie did something that few men dared. He climbed up off of his knees, faced the coming storm, and raised his right arm. He called out in a loud voice, "By the power of the Holy Priesthood that I bear, and in the name of Jesus Christ whom I serve, I command this storm to part, that we may walk through upon dry ground."

The storm did not abate or turn back in its course. The wind continued to whistle and whine through the prairie grasses. The dark clouds rushed toward them, the rain descending in gray sheets.

But it did not fall upon them. Not a hundred yards ahead, the rain stopped, and though clouds passed by to their right and to their left, and drenching rain could be seen in both directions, the party walked through the afternoon without getting wet. They marched fourteen more miles over rough and sandy trails, until they reached a pleasant spot to camp on the edge of one of the lagoons that so often formed along the Platte.

No sooner were the tents pitched and dinner cooked and eaten than the storm broke, drenching all of those who ventured out from their tents.

As Captain Willie lay beneath his blanket that night, he thought about Eliza Gadd. *Let's see Eliza explain this miracle away*, he thought.

"It wasn't a miracle," Eliza said the next morning. The sun had risen bright and beautiful, and the birds were singing alongside the river as they will do after a rain. Captain Willie heard a gun discharge then some mallards began quacking loudly and flew from the rushes up the river. Apparently old man James was up early, doing some hunting.

"A miracle," Eliza explained, "is something that is impossible, inexplicable. What happened yesterday was not impossible."

"Not impossible?" Captain Willie demanded. "You heard our prayers. The storm parted. We walked for hours, with the rains falling to either side of us. You don't think our prayers were answered."

"It was improbable, I will admit," Eliza said. "Even remarkably improbable, but such things happen. There were times back in England when summer showers would hit the gardens of my neighbors and leave mine as dry as a bone."

Captain Willie gritted his teeth. *Is the woman stupid, evil, or blind?* he wondered. *Blind*, he decided at last. *Willfully blind.*

"If God or an angel were to stand before you," Captain Willie demanded, "and declare the gospel to you, would you believe then?"

"I suppose," Eliza said.

"When Jesus was resurrected, he appeared to the apostles weeks afterward in a closed room. One of them, Thomas, had doubted that Christ had risen from the dead, and so Christ commanded him to touch the prints of the nails in his hands and in his feet, and to thrust his hand into the wound in Christ's side, so that Thomas might know for a surety that Christ had risen. Thomas did so and praised the Lord. But do you know what Christ told him?"

Eliza scrunched her brow. Captain Willie figured that any six-year-old should know the answer. "I don't know," she admitted.

"Because thou hast seen me, thou hast believed. More blessed are those who have not seen, and yet believe."

"More blessed?" Eliza asked. "Funny, aren't I as dry as you are this morning?"

Captain Willie shook his head in consternation. *There's nothing I can do with her, Lord*, he said in silent prayer. *Some mules you can saddle, but others you have just got to shoot. Maybe you've got a miracle up your sleeve to show her, but I'm fresh out of ideas.*

11

The Trade

Baline pulled a handcart beside Emily Wall, the two of them toiling side by side as they waded through patches of sand. No one really ever "pulled" a handcart, Baline had realized long ago. The handcart had a handle, and you got behind the handle and lifted, then leaned forward and walked. In reality you "pushed" the handcart. But the English, she'd discovered, were not always accurate in their use of words.

The cart was not too heavy, Baline thought. It only weighed sixty pounds, and loaded with the Wall's belongings it only weighed a hundred. Joseph's added weight was the real problem, and the miles were taking their toll. It had been four days, and in that time they had pulled the cart nearly eighty miles, with Joseph lying sick and moaning in the back, hardly able to even crawl to his tent at night.

Last night, an old man, Brother Haley, had fallen behind the company and been lost. Men went out with lanterns to search for him, but he couldn't be found. The storm last night had drenched everything. So this morning a larger search party went to find Brother Haley, and they brought the old man into camp. He was shivering from the cold, and his teeth chattered so badly that he could not speak. He only managed to whisper in a croaking voice as he explained that he had seen the lanterns in the dark, but was too weak to call out.

Everyone said that he was going to die.

In the back of the handcart, Joseph Wall was making a slow

recovery. He could barely sit up to eat. He spent the days with a blanket pulled up over him.

Baline didn't mind pulling him. In fact, over these past days, she had felt happier than ever before.

Father Jens had said last night, "It is because you are serving others; and when you serve others, you are serving God."

"But I'm missing out on everything," Baline had said. Her legs had felt as if they were made out of anvils, and she was too tired to play tag with Caroline Reeder anymore.

"No," Jens had replied, "you are only missing out on selfish pursuits. You will find that when you are seeking happiness for yourself, God doesn't give you much help. He's slow to tell you what man to marry, or where to find a good job. But if you help others, miracles become as common as weeds, and the happiness that you thought you were giving away comes back to you a thousand-fold."

Jens was right about that, Baline realized. As she dragged the handcart across the prairie, her bosom seemed to burn with holy fire, and she felt that peace and contentment were radiating from her, as if she were filled with light.

Though she could not play or hunt for pretty stones and flowers, still she enjoyed the countryside. The rolling, tumultuous hills gave way to flatter lands once they had crossed the Elk Horn River. They had dropped down into flat lands where the going was more pleasant. The last four days had been sunny and warm, but a brisk wind had scooted across the river, cooling them.

The forage for the cattle each night was still good. The frequent summer storms left the grasses green at their roots, though their heads nodded with ripening grain in the colors of gold or ruddy red.

Trees were few to nonexistent here. An occasional cottonwood graced the riversides when they stopped at night, but most of them were old and dead, the white husks showing where lightning had taken the bark in ages past. Beautiful wild sunflowers rose up everywhere along the trail, taller than Baline, while butterflies in the colors of pale gold or orange with white darted among the wild purple thistle at her feet. Stalks of Indian tobacco raised their chocolate heads by the riversides, where mud turtles basked on driftwood out in the water.

Each night, Baline could hear the prairie wolves howling when they crawled from under their burrows. The moon had been dark the last few nights, and once the cooking fires were put out (so that they would not attract Indians), Baline had never imagined as many stars as she saw then. Heaven had never felt so close.

So Baline and Emily strained at their handcart that afternoon. The company had gotten a late start, not pulling out until one. The morning had been spent fixing carts and hunting for poor Brother Haley.

Now, as Baline walked, she saw signs of buffalo everywhere. For several days, she'd been finding tufts of dark brown wool hanging from branches or lying on the ground, and she imagined using it to knit a scarf or stuff a mattress, so she and the other girls had begun collecting it.

Yesterday Baline had spotted four buffaloes, great dark brutes, hulking in the distance. Captain Savage and Captain Siler rode out after them, and there was much shooting, but the muzzle-loaders had not been powerful enough to bring down the animals. Jens had explained that it would take a very lucky shot.

But the signs of buffalo were multiplying. The beasts' hoofprints along the river were deep in the mud, and in many places the grass had been crushed where the buffalo slept. Wolf tracks could be seen in the sand, too, for wolves were following the herds in great numbers.

Two days before, the group had found sign of Indians. Mary Hurren and Agnes Caldwell had found an anthill in the evening, where bits of sand and pebbles were raised in a mound, and among the stones they found some pretty beads made of agate. Captain Savage had said, "I reckon you stumbled on an old Indian burial ground."

"Imagine," Mary had said, "real dead Indians just beneath our feet!"

Baline wished that she had some beads. She'd promised herself that when she had free time, she'd go poke around some anthills, but on this muggy afternoon, all she did was trudge, her eyes fixed in the grass ahead of her, watching for stickers and bumblebees and snakes, so that she might spare her bare feet.

Suddenly someone shrieked ahead, shouting "Indians! Indians!" A shot rang in the air. Baline peered to the head of the handcart train. Brother Cunningham had fired a warning with his muzzle-loader. Smoke from the gunpowder hung in the air above him, a blue-gray cloud. Women began screaming in terror, pointing north.

Baline saw that indeed some Indians were riding up over a low rise. At first she thought it was a small band, but dozens rode over the hill, then hundreds. They came on stout little ponies unlike any that she'd ever seen. Some were brown with white markings, and Indian symbols were painted in white along their rumps and necks. Others were appaloosas, grey or red, with white spots upon them. The Indians rode bareback, and warriors carried bows and lances, war clubs and shields made of leather. A few even carried long-bore guns. Some had painted faces and wore bonnets of eagle fathers.

The Indians began to whoop, and their horses charged down the long, gentle hill. Baline could see scalps decorating the lances and some of the war shields. Women shrieked in terror, and many folks began to throw their carts over to form a barrier, while others just grabbed their children and ran. Those few men who had guns brought them to bear, while others grabbed axes, hatchets, sabers, knives—anything with which to fight.

Baline and Emily merely stood where they were, legs trembling, eyes wild with terror.

Captain Willie, up near the front of the column, was shouting something, trying to calm the people, but Baline had heard too many tales about these savages, and it was obvious that the camp was vastly outnumbered and outgunned.

Captain Willie called out from the head of the column, "Keep moving. Keep the handcarts rolling." There was an uneasy moment as men grabbed their handcarts and began walking again. "They're friendlies!" Captain Willie said, trying to calm the group. "Just ignore them. Don't let them see that you're scared."

"Come on," Emily told Baline, and together they started pulling.

But Baline's legs were shaking so badly, it was all she could do to walk. Her stomach was nervous, and she wanted to throw up.

The two hundred warriors raced toward the handcarts, and then with a whoop from a war chief, their horses suddenly stopped in a long line, as if for battle.

"My word," Emily said, her voice quavering, "if these are friendlies, I'd hate to see enemies."

The Indians sat on their horses and just stared at the handcart pioneers for a long moment. The men were wild-looking, and fierce. Baline saw scalps on the lances that were blonde and red, and the hair was long. The scalps could only have come from white women.

"Keep an eye on your baggage," Emily warned. "They're notorious thieves."

But it wasn't her baggage that Baline was worried about.

For long moments, the Indians just watched them, and Baline pulled the handcart as steadily as she could. Some of the Indians laughed and pointed, for they had never seen handcarts before.

They are as mystified by us as we are by them, Baline realized, and she laughed a little nervously, too, at the thought. It made them more human.

The handcarts just kept going, and suddenly the Indians turned and spurred their horses, began trailing alongside the handcart train, as if both parties had just happened to be traveling the same direction.

Baline had seen wolves trailing the handcart company that way.

Like the wolves, the Indians kept glancing Baline's way. Sometimes the braves joked together. For nearly twenty minutes the Indians kept this up, and Baline's jangled nerves began to ease.

Then suddenly one of the warriors gave a whoop, then cried "Yi, yi, yi," as he urged his horse and charged straight toward Baline.

He was forty feet from the handcart when he gave a mighty leap from his horse and crashed down near the rear of the cart.

Baline ducked, afraid that he would pull out his hatchet and take her scalp, for she had heard that her blonde hair was coveted by the Indians.

But instead the warrior leapt to the back of the handcart and gave it a hard shove. The box of the wagon hit her from behind, knocking her forward, and the Indian laughed in glee, and suddenly he was pushing the cart as fast he could, running. Both Emily and Baline had to duck under the handles and scoot away to avoid being run over.

Then the Indian went racing off with the cart.

"He's stealing our things!" Emily shouted. "He's stealing my brother!"

Joseph was still lying sick in the back of the cart.

Suddenly, all along the line, other Indians followed suit—racing into the midst of the pioneers, laughing gleefully, and absconding with carts, many that were loaded with children.

Twenty or thirty carts were taken in all, and the saints just stood there, dumbfounded. Brother Cunningham watched the Indians take off with his daughter, while he peered back and forth between the Indians and his leaders, trying to decide whether to discharge his muzzle-loader.

"For God's sake, don't shoot!" Levi Savage began shouting. "These are Omahas! They're friendly. They're taking us to their camp, to do a little trading and have a powwow!"

Baline just stood, watching the Indians make off with the handcart, and the relief she felt was so intense, and her fear so great, that she began to sob.

Shaking, she followed the Indians up over the hill, about a mile across the prairie, into their camp.

Trading with the Indians that night was an adventure that Baline would never forget.

Eight hundred Omaha Indians were camped along the edge of a creek, a place without trees for wood or shade. Many slept in houses, made of sod and sticks, that looked like earthen igloos. Others stayed in teepees. The hunt was on in earnest. Fires had been lit in long pits on the side of a hill, and strips of buffalo meat that hung on sticks were curing in the smoke, while Omaha children kept the camp dogs away from the food. Everywhere, old women were busy scraping buffalo hides.

The coming of the saints was cause for celebration. The Omahas brought out wares to trade—fancy moccasins made of deer hide and decorated with beads; necklaces made with beads carved from bone or agate, or with colorful glass beads supplied by trappers. They brought out beaded vests and blankets, but Captain Willie warned the folks against the blankets, for they had a reputation for carrying lice.

Baline had nothing to trade. Each person in camp was allowed seventeen pounds of personal goods. Between her coat, her shoes, her bedding, a change of clothes, and a bolt of blue cotton that she was supposed to give to her sister Margrethe to make a dress when she reached Salt Lake City, Baline had nothing more that she could carry.

So she watched Captain Willie and the other leaders of the handcart company disappear into the chief's sod hut to smoke peace pipes and exchange gifts; then Baline went into camp and watched others make trades.

The Omahas brought out their goods and laid them on buffalo hides. When a man found what he wanted, he would point at it, and the Omaha would go into a "trading circle," where dozens of spectators watched the bargains being made, often accompanied by catcalls and advice from the crowd.

Captain Willie had warned folks three days before not to shoot buffalo except on his orders. "We're on Indian land, and they depend on these buffalo. We can take what we need, but no more, and not without their permission."

So Baline watched as one of the Danish men, Ole Madsen, bartered with one of the lesser chiefs to buy the right to hunt a buffalo. Ole brought out a horde of treasures—a silk handkerchief, some beads that included a real pearl, silver coins from Denmark, a fine tea cup. The chief sorted through everything, a look of bored disgust on his face, until he found an old plug of chewing tobacco.

With great delight, the deal was sealed.

One woman traded her spare bloomers for dried buffalo, while

Else Nielsen bought some buffalo meat with a cup of old buttons. The Peder Mortensen family traded a fine knife for some beautiful beaded moccasins.

After awhile, Baline got bored and went to the blankets. She didn't want much. But for two days now she had been hoping to find some beads, and now she found a small necklace made by real-live Omahas. The beads on it were mostly carved from agate, though it had two silver beads and a piece of bright blue turquoise.

When Baline thought that no one was looking, she reached out and touched it, then picked it up. She liked it better than the necklaces made of bright glass trade beads, for with the stone beads each little bead had to be drilled by hand. She imagined that the necklace would make a fine gift for her sister Margrethe.

She was lost in thought when an Omaha brave grabbed her hand and gave a mighty whoop. Baline looked up at him, terrified. The Indians at the trading circle all gave a whoop in reply, and against her will, Baline found herself being dragged into the circle, still clutching the necklace.

"I vasn't trying to steal it," Baline shouted. "I promise. I vas just looking at it."

The brave pulled her down onto a mat made of buffalo hide, then squatted, staring at her.

"I don't have any-ting to trade," Baline said, feeling embarrassed and foolish. She tried to get up, but the big brave pushed her back down and then sat peering at her. Baline's heart pounded so hard, she could hear it in her ears, and her face went crimson. She didn't want these Indians to see how poor she was.

She sat there, feeling stupid, and looked to Father Jens for help. He squatted on the outside of the trading circle, grinning. She could tell that he thought her predicament was funny.

"Tell him I don't have any-ting to trade," Baline said, and one of the Omaha women translated her words for the brave.

Baline tried to turn and crawl away, but Jens called out to her, "Look at that fellow. He wants to trade. You have something he wants."

My shoes, Baline realized. She still had the new shoes that Kris

Kringle had given her, and she suddenly wondered if this would be a proper trade. *Maybe I can walk across the desert without shoes*, she thought. She'd imagined walking most of the way, until they got in the mountains. Now she wondered if she would really need them at all.

She turned and peered at the brave. He grunted at her, then hit the ground with both palms and nodded his head, as if begging her to come into the trading circle. Behind the man, a squaw stood holding a baby, while a young boy, perhaps five, whispered excitedly at the brave's back.

That's his son, Baline realized, *and his family*. She saw kindness in the man's face, a gentle smile on his lips, and suddenly she found that the brave who had terrified her a moment ago didn't scare her at all. *He's a family man, and a kind one.*

I'll give him my shoes, Baline decided.

She turned and knelt in front of him, letting her heart still. The brave placed the necklace between them.

"I have some shoes to trade," Baline said.

The interpreter spoke to the brave, and from the trading circle, Jens whispered, "No, Baline, you will need those!"

But it was too late to take back the offer.

The brave listened, thought for a long moment, then shook his head no.

"But I have nothing else to trade," Baline objected.

The interpreter spoke, and the Brave reached to his side, drew out a knife. He leaned close to Baline and raised the blade to her scalp.

"He wants your hair, Baline!" Father Jens warned.

Baline's heart pounded furiously and tears of fear welled up in her eyes. She'd seen the scalps that decorated the spears. Would he take hers, too?

But the Brave simply leaned close, gingerly took a lock of her hair, and looked at her questioningly.

Just a bit of my hair, she realized. *That's all he wants.* She remembered the stories about how the Indians prized yellow hair.

It will grow back, she thought. *I won't even miss it.*

Gladly, she nodded, and in a couple of seconds the brave whacked off a lock of her hair, then raised his prize up and whooped in delight.

The man's son began dancing around, and together they went racing for one of the sod houses. Moments later, she saw them tying her blonde hair to a child's toy spear.

Baline had her beads, and that night she felt like the richest girl in camp. The Omahas fed the pioneers and stayed up late playing flutes and drums. They were joined by the Danes. Brother Peder Mortensen, the cripple, brought out his clarinet while his son Lars played the violin. The Omahas danced merrily to the music, their feet pounding the ground with anklets that rattled, prancing around like buffalo or soaring like eagles.

That night, when Baline went to bed, there were more stars in the moonless skies than she had ever seen. She lay for a moment, thinking. Her mother had told her if she wanted to remember something forever, that before she went to bed, she should call the memory to mind and think about it, relive it, over and over.

Baline recalled her trade, committing it to memory, reliving it over and over so that she would be able to tell her sister all about it. Then she brought out other memories of the journey, fresh and shiny—the day that the ship Thornton passed through the icy fog, bells ringing every thirty seconds as the captains listened to hear if the sound echoed from an iceberg, and they passed a ship that was wrecked and burnt.

Next she recalled the day that the thousands of "sea horses," or dolphins, came leaping alongside the ship.

Then there was the day that Kris Kringle brought the shoes. Now this.

Among the happy memories, she heard the thunk of five-year-old Thomas Pederson as he fell from the upper deck of the Thornton, two stories, down into the hold. That sound would never leave her mind, she feared. The boy had crushed his head, and despite all of the prayers of the Danes, and all of the ministrations, he'd died after two grueling days.

Fiercely, Baline shoved the dark memory from her and filled her head with images of stone beads and prairie flowers, until the ugly recollection dimmed and faded.

The Omaha's drums kept pounding through the night, and as Baline lay her head down, it sounded as if the heart of the earth was beating, beating, never to be still.

12

The First Massacre

The saints did not have a prayer meeting the night of the Indian trade, Eliza noted, and that was sad. Eliza wasn't overly fond of the nightly instruction that came with prayer meeting, the sermons delivered by the various captains. Nor did she much care for the prayers themselves. But each night after prayer meeting, there was singing, sometimes with music and a dance or two. Sometimes members of the company were called upon to offer entertainment: some children were learning tap dance and ballet. Others could sing. Some of the men and women would tell jokes or stories.

But mostly the folks would just sit together in small groups, talking with friends. In Eliza's world back in Wimpole, she'd looked forward to visiting other ladies in her circle of friends once a week, where they would gossip over their tea and play parlor games.

Here, the visits came every night, and though Eliza had not known most of these women for more than three months, their close proximity allowed Eliza to grow fond of some of them quite quickly. Indeed, she felt a surprising sense of loss when she did not get to sit and visit with her friends that night.

Instead, she dragged herself back to camp after sundown, taking the youngest children to bed, and left her husband and the teenagers to their own devices.

Captain Willie and the others might stay out late, but doubtless the company would rise at 4:00 a.m., as usual. Fall was setting in, the days growing short, and as the changing seasons pared away a few minutes of light from each passing day, it grew hard for the saints to meet their goal of seventeen miles of travel. Rising early was becoming more important, Captain Willie warned, though as the journey grew harder, the pioneers found it more difficult to roll out of their comfortable beds.

Eliza felt exhausted. She tried never to carry more than one of the babies at a time, but at twenty-four months, the twins were getting to be a bit of a handful. After twenty miles of walking in a day, she felt worn through. The only blessing was that the pain in her back was enough so that she hardly noticed the ache in her legs.

As she tried to sleep that night, she found that she couldn't. She lay listening to the drums and the howls of wolves out on the prairie. Even though the children slept peacefully beside her, she felt that something was wrong. She'd seen Captain Willie's face as he'd come out of his meeting with the chieftain. His forehead had been furrowed by a frown, and he'd been silent. Bad news.

She lay worrying while others slept around her—the children, Sister Linford and her children.

Samuel came in an hour after dusk, when Sister Linford and the children were asleep.

"Are you awake, Eliza?" he asked.

"Yes."

"Can't sleep?"

"No."

"Oh, did you hear the news?" He sounded timid—as if he wasn't sure he wanted to say anything.

"What news?"

"The chief gave Captain Willie a letter from the commander of Fort Kearney, which is a few days ahead. Colonel Babbitt's wagon train was wiped out by Cheyennes. Two teamsters were killed, and that Wilson woman got taken captive. The savages killed her baby."

Eliza lay there, heart racing faster than the beat of the tom-toms. She recalled seeing the Wilson woman in her fine carriage. Eliza recalled being jealous of her, seeing how this woman would ride while Eliza was forced to walk. "When did all of this happen?"

"Two days ago, just up the trail a few miles from this village. The pony soldiers have gone after the Cheyennes. They're going to hunt them down and kill them."

Eliza wondered. The cavalry killed the Indians, so the Indians struck back, and thus more Indians would have to die. The cycle continued. What had Captain Willie said about how the Book of Mormon warned against military escalation?

"What about Colonel Babbitt?" Eliza asked. "Did the Cheyenne get him?"

"He wasn't there," Samuel whispered. "He's off in Council Bluffs. He doesn't even know what's happened."

Well, that's something to be thankful for, Eliza thought. She wondered what had happened to the Wilson woman, if she had been raped, or was even alive tonight. She wondered how it would feel to have a baby ripped from your arms and murdered.

She shuddered and Samuel crawled into bed and slid his arm around her. His arm comforted her, and it wasn't long before he kissed her. She returned the kiss roughly, needing his affection tonight more than she had in a long time. The children were all sleeping peacefully, and many of the adults in the tent were still out.

Samuel reached down and stroked her cheek with his hand. She wanted his love. It had been months since she'd had a private moment with him, and it might be months before they had another. Some couples, she knew, would lag behind the company so that they could steal some time alone, but ever the gentleman, Samuel had foregone such pleasures. He wouldn't risk embarrassing her.

Tonight, she wanted him to risk it. She knew how he ached for it. *Men are no different from bulls, after all. They have the same fire in their veins, the same rutting instinct.* But all too soon Samuel cuddled up with his cheek hugging hers and fell asleep, his arm serving to pillow her head.

The tom-toms kept drumming, and hours later, the rest of the adults came creeping in.

Eliza tried to sleep, but failed miserably.

At 4:00 a.m., the company horn blew, and the saints arose. Eliza found that she had gone dry. It had been hard work for these past weeks to retain her milk, and she'd tried valiantly to hold on. Even when she was aboard ship, during the rough storms when she got seasick, she'd struggled to keep nursing. The twins were so small; they needed the nourishment. So she rose, and tried to ignore the twins as they cried and pulled at her blouse.

She went to work with the other women, cooking bread for the day while the men tore down the tents and packed each one into a supply wagon, then carried the cripples to the relief wagon or a handcart. She knew now that she should have gotten some sleep. She could only hope that as the day drew on, her milk would come back in.

But her breasts, which had so often been gorged and swollen the past few months, felt empty and flaccid. There was a sense of finality to it this time; Eliza mourned, for holding her children and nursing them gave her a sense of attachment that she knew she could never regain.

Daniel and Isaac, the twins, spent most of the morning wracked with sobs, crying to be nursed; the boys wailed until their eyes grew red and snot ran down their noses. They threw themselves into the dust, hoping that their mother would take pity on them, all to no avail.

There was no milk to be found in camp. Some supplies were just hard to come by. The handcart company had brought along twenty head of milk cows, but most of the cows were still nursing calves, and they gave little milk. The ration was half a cup per family, per week.

Just after dawn, a few Omahas came to camp to trade, so the handcarts did not leave until seven.

As often happened, when Eliza was near her wit's end, Ann Howard stepped in. She saw what was going on with the boys and didn't even ask if Eliza had gone dry. She just took both boys and said, "Let's let them ride in my cart this morning. I'll make sure that we keep you out of sight."

Eliza wept with gratitude and gave her children over to Ann.

Each day, a different hundred was asked to lead the way, breaking the trail for those behind. By rotating companies it insured that no one group was forced to do the hard work of clearing the road ahead day after day. Nor would anyone be forced to eat the trail dust raised by other companies day after day.

This morning, Levi Savage's hundred took the lead out over the flatlands alongside the Platte.

They had not gone three miles from the Omaha camp when they came upon the remains of Almon Babbitt's wagon train. A couple of burned-out wagons and some bloody rags were all that could be seen from a distance, there in the deep grass.

But as the handcart company drew near, the stench of dead bodies grew thick. Three graves had been dug beside the wagons, and crosses affixed. But wolves had gotten to the graves, and the two dead teamsters were halfway out of the dirt, their blackened hands curled like claws, their bellies bloated, the ragged flesh oozing where they had been scalped.

Some sisters dropped their scarves over their noses to mask the stench, even as they wept. The children stared at the site of the massacre, eyes wide, faces leeched of blood and frozen in horror.

Eliza could hardly believe that the Cheyennes had attacked the wagon train so close to the Omaha camp.

Levi Savage stood beside the graves, as if waiting for the company to gather around him.

"Captain Savage," Samuel ventured, "shouldn't we cover the bodies? There are children about."

Captain Savage shook his head sadly. "Nope, I want you all to see this. Men, women, children. These poor folks were murdered in their sleep. These people were not vigilant, and they paid the price. We're going into hostile territory. You all need to know the price."

As the handcarts gathered, some folks milled about. Brother Cantwell kicked over a bloody shirt with his shoe and picked up part of a man's scalp, with greasy red hair. He held it up for others to see and, after a long moment of thought, pulled out his pocket Bible and laid it between the pages, as if he were pressing an autumn leaf.

When everyone had gathered, Captain Savage called out, "These folks were murdered just a few days ago. Captain Willie begged them not to go off by themselves, but they didn't heed his warnings, and so the Cheyennes killed them in their sleep. These are the lucky ones. The redskins carried off one woman, and there's no telling what kind of abuse she has been called to endure."

"Were there any other survivors?" one emigrant asked.

"A couple of men were able to run off and hide in the dark," Captain Savage said. "They got shot up some, but they're alive, recouping down at Fort Kearny.

"Now, the Cheyennes that did this are mostly dead. According to the letter we got, the cavalry chased them down and caught them in a cornfield. They shot sixteen redskins. But a handful of them escaped, and they might still stir up some trouble."

Eliza had to wonder about frontier justice. From her conversation with Colonel Babbitt, it sounded as if the military here was too quick on the trigger, and it didn't seem likely that the cavalry would find these bloodthirsty savages out picking corn. "Are they certain that they got the right men? I mean, how can we know that the army hasn't just made matters worse?"

Savage gave her a look that was both appreciative and reproving, as if to say, "You're smarter than I thought," then changed the subject. "I'll want some men to re-bury these bodies. We need to put them down deep, six feet at least, and lay some rocks over them, or the wolves will just dig them up again. Also, the baby has been dug out of its grave. Now, maybe the wolves got it, or maybe they just carried it away and buried it again to eat later. But I'd like some of you folks to look around, follow any trail you see, and try to find that baby."

Eliza stood, silently mourning. It was bad enough that this Wilson woman had been kidnapped. How much worse would it be to have your child murdered in front of you? Now, she might never be able to mourn properly, might never be able to see her child at rest.

"You men," Captain Savage continued, "I want you to see what happens when you don't keep a good watch. We'll be doubling our guard from here to Fort Laramie. You children, you need to remember to stick close to the handcart train from here on out. No playing hide-n-seek outside of camp, no playing cat-after-mouse away from earshot of the guards. If you see a redskin, what do you do?"

"Scream," a few children answered in unison. Eliza saw that they had been well trained.

"That's right," Captain Savage said. "Don't go trusting some Injun just because he looks friendly. More than one child has disappeared from a wagon train, only to end up a slave in some Injun camp."

With that, Brother Hurren gathered a burial detail and went to work on the graves. Captain Savage wandered around the campsite, studying wolf tracks.

Eliza and several other women fanned out and began searching the tall grass a hundred yards away, closer to the river, looking for the dead child. They had not gone far when Julia Hill cried out so startled that Eliza was afraid that she'd been bitten by a snake.

But after a moment, she burst into tears and said, "I found it. I found the baby."

Fighting back a rising sense of horror, Eliza went to the spot and saw not just the baby, but a dead woman. She recognized the woman's dirty blonde hair. It was Mrs. Wilson, lying in the grass as if she were asleep. The morning dew misted her pale skin, as white as ivory, and drops of water matted her dress. She was lying in a fetal position, clutching her dead baby tight against her chest. The baby's skull was misshapen. It looked as if the Cheyenne had kicked it in. But Mrs. Wilson had cleaned the wound the best that she could.

For a long moment Eliza stood frozen, studying the scene. Mrs. Wilson's fingernails were filthy, with dirt under them, and grave dirt was smeared over her dead baby. She had opened her dress and given her nipple to the child, as if trying to nurse it back to life.

It wasn't wolves that dug up the graves, Eliza realized, *it was a mother looking for her child.*

Eliza kept expecting Mrs. Wilson to wake up, to rouse from her slumber and turn her face toward them. There were no marks on her, no bullet holes in her back, no knife wound to the scalp. For all the world she looked as if she were just asleep.

"She starved to death," Julia suggested, "or died for want of water."

But the Platte River was not more than twenty yards away. The woman could have gotten a drink whenever she wanted. A person does not starve to death in only five days.

Another woman came up behind them and suggested, "The cold took her."

But Mrs. Wilson could have taken clothes from the dead men if she wanted. She could have fled to the camp of the Omahas.

No, Eliza decided, *it was none of those.* The poor woman died of fear and grief.

The camp had been attacked in the dark, Eliza imagined, and perhaps as the other teamsters fled, Mrs. Wilson had run off with them, fading into the grass, leaving her child behind. In a blind panic, she might have run for hours before circling back, only to find her child dead.

After that, she would not have wanted to live. So she curled up with her baby and let her life ebb away.

That is how Eliza imagined that it happened.

There but for the grace of God, Eliza thought, *go I.*

13

The Wild Cow

I've got problems with more than one kind of savage, Captain Willie thought as they rolled into camp that night.

Indians had been in his thoughts all day.

It's funny how the mind works. He hadn't seen an Omaha in five years, and now he couldn't get an image out of his mind.

It was a nightmare from his past. It came in his dreams last night: Wild Bill Hickman stood beneath a tree on the prairie, with the bodies of the three Omaha Indians hanging above him. He was bustling around the bodies, pushing them to watch them twirl, smiling with excitement. He was like a butcher displaying his prize geese in the market.

Captain Willie blinked the image away. It wasn't just a dream, it was a memory. When the Mormons had come through ten years past, in 1846, some Indians had stolen a couple of mules. Wild Bill Hickman had gone to hunt them down. It took a day or two, but he caught three young bucks, tied them up, tortured them nearly to death, and then hanged them upside down, cut their throats, and let them bleed out. They'd been Omahas, all young men between the ages of sixteen and nineteen.

When Captain Willie had happened upon the murder site, Wild Bill had grinned and asked, "Well, what do you think of my handiwork?"

One of the dead Omahas jerked, his lifeless muscles spasming, and for a horrifying instant Captain Willie had thought he was still alive, just waiting to be released from his misery.

The sight had sickened Captain Willie. For months he had tried to block it from his mind. Now, with the deaths of the folks in Babbitt's wagon train, the memory kept passing before Captain Willie's eyes.

As it turned out, Wild Bill Hickman had murdered the wrong men. It wasn't Omahas that had stolen the mules, but some Sioux.

One thing Captain Willie was certain of, the Indians had a strong sense of justice. It had been ten years since that tragic murder, but there would yet be hell to pay.

Captain Willie had thought that Wild Bill should be hung for his butchery. Wild Bill was a dangerous man. Take a rabid bulldog and poke him with a stick until he's mad as the devil, and that was Wild Bill all over.

But Wild Bill had too many friends in high places. He'd been a bodyguard to Joseph Smith and had served as a sheriff in frontier towns in Missouri, where mobocrats reigned supreme and lynching Mormons seemed to be the favorite sport of the locals. It took a man like Wild Bill to stand up to such folk, and many in the church were grateful to him. Brigham Young had even praised Wild Bill from the pulpit.

But Wild Bill had finally got himself excommunicated. After exacting such a heavy toll on some alleged horse thieves, it seemed ironic to Captain Willie that three years ago Wild Bill had been excommunicated for exactly that—running a ring of horse thieves up in Logan, Utah.

So there was more than one kind of savage to worry about. There were red ones, and white. Then there was Levi Savage, the fool. He'd left a hundred women and children mortified to the core of their souls by letting them see the victims of the massacre, and when Captain Willie had tried to have a word with him about it, Savage had nodded in a placating manner and then had gone off on a diatribe about how Captain Siler shouldn't be driving the independent wagons between the handcart company and the relief wagons. It made it too hard and too dangerous for old folks and the lame to get to the relief wagons when they needed to. One little girl had tried to carry some water back to her sickly dad in the wagons and nearly got trampled by one of Siler's ox teams.

Normally, Captain Willie would have agreed with Savage's logic, but he wasn't going to mollify Savage now, not after this latest debacle.

Captain Willie stomped about the camp, looking to the campfires. "Cook your dinner quickly," he told the folks. "The fires all have to be out before dark."

We don't want to attract more savages, he told himself. He wasn't very worried about the Cheyennes that had attacked the Babbitt train. According to the letter he'd gotten, the cavalry was trying to run them down hundreds of miles away from here.

No, it wasn't the Cheyennes—it was the Sioux that he was really worried about. The government had massacred their people for the past two years, and even though the Cheyennes were the ones who had attacked, Captain Willie suspected that they had done it at the prodding of the Sioux.

Most Sioux, Captain Willie knew, were good law-abiding folks. But their chiefs had no more control over them than the governor of Kansas had over his own people. The whole United States was going to hell in a handbasket, falling into anarchy. *Of course*, Captain Willie figured, *we can't expect any better from the Sioux*.

So he was worried about Indians. It wasn't a small worry, either. His stomach was winding up in knots over it, and he felt a chill running down the back of his spine. He'd felt that way only once before, when a grizzly had been trailing him up Echo Canyon. He'd heard its heavy footsteps, the cracking of brush, its grunts and sniffing. When he did, he took comfort, for he knew exactly where the danger lay. It was when the grizzly went silent that Captain Willie worried, for the bear could easily lope up the trail for an ambush, or suddenly come lunging from the nearest thicket.

He felt that way now. The evening seemed restful. The sun hovered on the horizon, a brilliant red, like a disk of molten copper. Wood doves cooed in the cottonwood trees here along the river. Buffalo grazed in the tall grass to the north in a large herd, a brown splotch along the horizon. The buffalo had muddied the water that flowed down the stream, which normally was as clear and pure as snow melt in the spring. But otherwise everything was perfect.

Everything seemed so right, yet everything felt so terribly wrong.

As Captain Willie went to his own fire, preparing to cook up a warm muffin, three little girls scampered up behind.

"Captain Villie," one of them called. "Can ve get some milk?"

It was that Baline Mortensen. Agnes Caldwell and Mary Hurren flanked her on either side, as thick as thieves.

"Have you had your rations for the week?" Captain Willie asked.

Getting milk wasn't a simple proposition. The cows were more than half wild, and their calves tended to drink most of the milk on the run. With all of the travel, the cows were hard-pressed to give any milk at all.

"I have not had any milk in veeks," Baline said.

"You're traveling with Jens Nielsen, though, aren't you?" Captain Willie asked. "Has anyone else in the family been drinking the rations? That boy of theirs?"

"I am traveling vith them," Baline clarified, "but they are not my real family. So, is only right that I get my own ration for my family: me."

Captain Willie sighed. He wasn't buying that argument. But he wasn't about to deny a child a drink of milk, either.

"All right," he said, "you can have your two-week's ration: one cup of milk."

"Thank you," Baline said.

Captain Willie turned to go, and Baline cleared her throat loudly.

"Yes?"

"Also, I vas thinking," Baline said. "The milk, it is for the babies, yes?"

"Yes?"

"Vell, most families, they have only the one baby. But Sister Gadd, she has two. So should she not get two rations?"

Captain Willie considered. If it were any other family, he might be inclined to argue, but he didn't dare offend Sister Gadd. He still had high hopes of converting her to the church.

"I suppose that you're right. You may have another cup of milk for the Gadd family."

"Good," Baline said. "Can ve get it from Brother Griffiths?"

Brother Griffiths was in charge of the commissary. He was a young Welshman with bad eyes and a fear of Indians that had seemed irrational ten days ago but made perfect sense now. It was his job to weigh out the rations every couple of days and then turn them over to the family.

"The cows are milked in the morning," Captain Willie said. "I'll make sure that he gets some for you then."

"But," Baline said, "the babies, they cry now."

Captain Willie sighed and looked about helplessly. He'd demanded a double guard for the night. Every available man was busy either fixing wagons or standing guard or else was already sleeping and would be roused at midnight to take up a guard post.

"I know how to milk der cow," Baline suggested.

"It's not milking it that I'm worried about," Captain Willie said. "It's catching it. Those cows are about half crazy."

"Me big brother can rope a cow," Agnes suggested in her thick Scottish accent.

"Well, you may have two cups of milk, if you can get them."

Captain Willie dismissed the girls by turning his back. He sat down by the fire, weary to the bone, and began cooking a sort of pancake in a small cast-iron skillet.

It was only halfway cooked when Agnes Caldwell let out a shriek of "Help! Help!" and the other girls joined in with their cries. A cow began to bawl and Captain Willie didn't even need to turn his head to see what had happened.

The cow came stampeding through the camp, right past his fire. It was an old red Texas longhorn with a rope lassoed around its neck. The cow bucked and bawled as she ran, and on the far end of the rope was Agnes's older brother, Thomas. The rope had tangled around his leg, and now the cow was dragging the boy about at will, raising a cloud of dust and knocking over carts.

A couple of the sisters began shouting, and one jumped in front of the cow, waving her hands, trying to get it to stop. But the cow lowered her head and charged. The sister dodged, putting a handcart between herself and the cow's horns. The cow slammed into the handcart, knocking it over, and then stood triumphantly beside it as dust rose from the ground and a wheel spun, squeaking.

Joseph Elder, a Mormon missionary returning to Utah, grabbed the rope and pulled it tight. The cow lowered her head but stood beside the vanquished handcart. Joseph eased down to the ground, making himself a smaller target, and made soft cooing noises to soothe the cow as he untangled Thomas Caldwell. Some other folks grabbed Thomas and pulled him away, then Joseph quietly led the cow to a tree and tied her up, giving her a short lead.

Captain Willie hurried over to check on Thomas. He was a thin lad, still more a boy than a man.

A vicious red swelling beside his neck suggested a broken collarbone. Captain Willie prodded the spot, and the pain of the wound left Thomas reeling.

Eliza Gadd came up behind Captain Willie and peered down at Thomas, taking it all in.

"You let children try to milk that wild cow?" Eliza demanded of Captain Willie. "What in the world were you thinking?"

"I . . ." Captain Willie came up short. *I was thinking of how tired the men were from pulling handcarts all day. I was thinking about how much work you women will have to do tonight. I was thinking about how good that warm milk would taste to your babies.*

But he knew that none of those answers would suffice. It wasn't what he'd thought. It was his lack of thought that she was condemning him for.

"I guess I wasn't really thinking at all," he said by way of apology.

"You Mormons," Eliza said. "You claim that God talks to you. You've got your prophets and apostles. But if God is so warm to talk to you, why didn't he warn you that this was coming?"

"Don't blame this on God, Eliza," Captain Willie said. "Sometimes he talks, and we just don't listen well. I was tired. I wasn't thinking things through. I'm sorry."

Captain Willie gave the Caldwell boy a blessing, hoping to heal him, but it wasn't to be. Captain Willie didn't feel impressed that the

Lord wanted an instant healing. It was much as it had been with the storm the other day. Captain Willie had been able to calm it, to split the clouds, but not turn the storm back completely. It was as if the Lord wanted to test his people.

So Captain Willie offered up a prayer and blessed Thomas that he might be comforted during his affliction.

But under his breath, Captain Willie wanted to curse. He'd just lost another man, one to help pull handcarts and set up tents. For the rest of this trip, Thomas would have to get pulled in a handcart or be relegated to one of the relief wagons.

I don't need any more cripples, he thought. *This company is crippled enough.*

Wearily, after giving the blessing, he turned away from the crowd.

"Where are you going?" Eliza demanded, her voice still tinged with anger.

"I'm going to milk a cow," Captain Willie said.

He got a tin pan and went to the cow, then knelt, as in prayer, and took her dirty teats in his hand. A few practiced squeezes brought some milk, but the stream was weak. He wouldn't get much.

The milk streamed and splashed into the tin pan.

Eliza came up at his back. "I'm sorry for getting angry at you. You're doing the best you can."

She stood there, tentatively. Night was coming, and he could feel her more than see her, nervously shifting from one foot to the other.

Or maybe she's not nervous, he thought. *Maybe she's comforting one of the babies.* He turned just enough to see that it was true. She had a sleeping baby in her arms.

"Sometimes a man's best isn't good enough," Captain Willie said. "You fall out of a boat, out in the middle of the sea, and you can swim all you want and never reach shore."

"Is that how you feel now?" Eliza asked.

It is, Captain Willie thought. He felt as if he were failing, despite all that he could do. Yet he had no reason to feel this way. The weather was good, the roads were clear, the provisions sufficient. He should have felt more at peace. But his mind was clouded with worry.

"You know what bothers me most of all?" he asked.

"What?"

"That I might do something to offend you," Captain Willie said. "This job—taking you folks out West—is the hardest thing I've ever done. I have to ask a lot of you folks. If I'm going to get you there alive, I'll keep asking and asking, and I'm afraid that sometime, I'm going to have to ask you to do something so hard that it will break your heart, and then you'll hate the church because of me, because of my weakness. I don't want to break anyone's heart."

"I know that."

"Then, can I ask a favor?"

"Yes."

"Promise me that you won't hate the church for anything that I do. You look at us leaders, and we're all imperfect men, trying to live up to some impossible standard."

"I won't take offense at you," Eliza said, "in the future."

"Eliza," Captain Willie asked, "why aren't you a Mormon? Your husband has been one for ten years, hasn't he? Your oldest children are all in the church. Is it because you believe in something else? Are you an Anglican?"

"I was born one," Eliza said. "But I've never had faith in it. The Church of England is a church of convenience. Old King Henry, a murdering adulterer, created it so that he could satisfy his lust for progeny, nothing more. With that as a foundation, what good can come from it?"

"So," Captain Willie said. "You realize that Henry didn't have authority from God to start a church. Is that what you're saying?"

"I don't know if I buy the argument that one has to have authority," Eliza said. "I suppose that one would need a firm belief, even inspiration. If I did buy the argument that one needs authority, then maybe I'd lean toward Catholicism. They claim to have it. But if they ever had authority, I can't imagine that they still do, what with the Star Chambers and the selling of indulgences, and syphilitic pontiffs proclaiming themselves to be infallible. So much murder and vileness has been committed in their name, how could I believe in that?"

Captain Willie sighed. "I know a lot of good folks who are Catholic, and Anglicans, too," he pointed out.

"But are they good folks because of their religion, or in spite of it?" Eliza asked. "I'm sure that there are fine and noble red men among the Cheyennes, too, and that there are saintly Jews. There might even be Moslems that will take their place in heaven on the right hand of God before your Joseph Smith ever gets there."

That was a bit uncomfortable. Captain Willie believed a man had to be baptized by one having authority from God before he could enter the kingdom of heaven, and that authority had been taken from the earth more than a thousand years ago, due to the great apostasy. The authority to perform priesthood ordinances had been given back to Joseph Smith by angels.

"You don't sound sure of yourself," Captain Willie said. "What do you really believe?"

"I believe that the current interest in piousness all started with the French Revolution," Eliza said. "Lords in Europe and even as far away as America heard the clank of the guillotines and feared that the killing would spread. So they hid their sins deep and began to feign piousness, doing good works in public, hoping that they would not be lined up against the wall should a revolution come.

"Historically, Captain Willie, the passionate interest that people like you show toward your faith is a cultural anomaly. Traditionally, men are far more passionate about money, mating, and winning glory. Traditionally, men are pigs.

"Your religion is nonsense," she continued. "It's all hopeful thinking and delusion, wrapped up in self-righteousness. The teachings of the heathen Egyptians make as much sense as Christianity. You ask what I believe, and I will tell you: I believe that when you die, your body will rot and turn to dust, and all of the light will go out of your eyes, and all of your memories and hopes and dreams will be turned to dust with them."

"It's a hopeless world you live in," Captain Willie said, "lonely and comfortless."

"I take what joy I can find," Eliza said. "I take joy in my children's smiles, and in the beauty of a sunrise, or the warmth of a fire. I try to hold onto those, and that is enough."

"Maybe it's enough for now," Captain Willie said. "But will it always be enough? When the storms come and life looks bleak, will you find comfort in empty memories? In my experience, not many folks can sustain such a hopeless view," Captain Willie said. "Even the Eskimos believe in more than you do."

"My father was a spiritualist, always trying to make contact with someone from beyond the grave—his beloved aunt, or his mother. He hired shamans and gurus and fakirs to contact the dead. They told him comforting lies that confirmed his faith. But I saw through their parlor tricks, and I'm afraid that I can have faith no more."

"So you don't believe in an afterlife?" Captain Willie confirmed.

"Not one whit."

Captain Willie thought for a moment. There were instances in the scriptures where angels had appeared to nonbelievers, and Captain Willie suspected that Eliza would never be baptized until she had some kind of witness from beyond the grave.

He fell silent and began to pray that Eliza might be granted such a witness. As he did, he found that the cow's teats had all gone dry.

The cow stamped her rear foot perilously close to the tin pail, nearly tipping it, and Captain Willie pulled it away, then turned and presented it to Eliza.

"Milk for your babies, madam," he said.

It was after sunset when Captain Willie got back to eating dinner. He ordered the fires to be scattered, and in the growing gloom, a carriage approached from the east, racing fast.

As it drew into camp, Colonel Babbitt leapt out. He'd just heard about the loss of his wagon train a few hours ago, at the camp of the Omahas.

"You can say it," Colonel Babbitt told Captain Willie. "You told me so."

Captain Willie sighed heavily. "Sometimes, you just don't get any joy from being right. I wish to heaven that I had been wrong."

"I saw what you did for my people," Colonel Babbitt said,

"covering over the graves. Were any belongings recovered? There was a great deal of money on those wagons."

"The cavalry stripped the bodies pretty good. They got your men's watches and papers, and took the load to Fort Kearney. There were some muddy clothes strewn about, so maybe the Indians got the rest. I imagine you'll find their personals all at Fort Kearney. We recovered a couple of your oxen. Found them yoked together just a few miles back up the trail. I imagine that you'll want them sent back to Winter Quarters? I figure I can drop them off with just about any train heading back to the states."

"That would be fine," Babbitt said. He stood for a moment, as if deep in thought. "You know, you may have saved my life in spite of me. If not for that little lawsuit, I would have been with the wagon train. You might even say that my life was saved by a couple of tin pans."

"Don't thank me," Captain Willie said. "Thank Jens Nielsen. Or better yet, thank the fool that sued him. You did win the case?"

"Oh, handily," Babbitt said.

That was cause for congratulations, but Captain Willie stood for a moment, deep in thought. He didn't feel like celebrating. In fact, his nerves had rarely felt so jangled. It was as if a cloud loomed over the camp, and over Almon Babbitt, too.

The Doctrine and Covenants said that the Holy Ghost would testify when a man heard the truth. Normally, the man would feel a burning sensation in his bosom, and his mind would seem quickened and decisive. But Captain Willie believed that the Holy Ghost worked in other ways, too. He had once had a woman try to seduce him and had suddenly felt so stupid and bumbling that he could hardly say his name.

He felt sure that that was God's way of protecting him so that he didn't fall into transgression.

At other times, he'd felt vague warnings, similar to the thrill that one feels when a huge storm is brewing. Right now, there was a nervous thrill in the air, and he found that his hands were shaking.

"Do you feel that?" Captain Willie asked. "There's a tension in the air."

"I feel it," Babbitt agreed.

Back at the camp, an old woman cried out in terror, "Indians! Indians!"

Both Captain Willie and Colonel Babbitt turned to see the danger, but there was no sign of Indians. "Sister Ingra," Captain Willie said. "She's been out of her mind for weeks, and she's getting worse. We practically have to tie her down to keep her from running off."

"The trail will take that one soon," Babbitt said. "Folks that old, they seldom make the crossing."

"This matter with the Cheyennes," Captain Willie hazarded, "it's not over, is it?"

Babbitt shook his head. "I don't think so. Not by a far piece."

The next morning, Almon Babbitt drove off in his carriage. He'd had a passenger with him, a Scottish woman heading for Salt Lake, but on hearing of all the Indian troubles she begged to be let off with the handcart folk, so Babbitt booked passage for her on one of the Independent wagons. Then he was off.

Captain Willie watched him go for a long while, his carriage receding through the golden grass, out over the prairie, where a herd of buffalo darkened the horizon like a coming storm.

For the next three days, Captain Willie's sense of danger grew. August died and
was born, and Captain Willie felt as if he'd passed through some invisible danger. September was here, a month where summer would linger on the plains, even as winter stalked them like a lion.

The Caldwell boy who had broken his collarbone, Thomas, seemed to worsen with each day. Despite the fact that there was little outward sign of a break, the boy went into a high fever and began fading in and out of consciousness. Eliza Gadd and Sister Crook both agreed that gangrene had set into the boy's wound, and both worried that he would die.

With each passing day, the numbers of buffalo grew. The buffalo, like the geese and the starlings, were growing restless, heading south. They seemed to move with nervous energy, flanks twitching to keep off flies, tails slapping at mosquitoes. Often they would burst into a run. Mostly they stayed in small herds of a hundred or two, but by the second of September, the number of herds was growing, and they could be seen in every direction—twenty or thirty herds to the north, another dozen to the south, a few herds behind them to the east, and a dark line on the horizon that revealed an endless stream of buffalo, like a black river.

A man could get caught up in that dark tide and get trampled and swept away, Captain Willie thought, and he didn't want to move forward.

On the afternoon of September second, he rode to a small hill to the north, trying to gauge the danger. It wasn't much of a hill, merely a rise that was perhaps twenty feet higher than the plains around him. But it gave him a little elevation, and what he saw disturbed him to the core of his soul.

Ahead to the west was a herd of buffalo that darkened the horizon. He could see no end to it. The herd spanned at least twelve to fifteen miles across—as far as the eye could see.

They raised clouds of dust as they plodded toward the south, and the grass ahead had been trampled so much, the earth seemed all but bare. Other buffalo wallowed in the dust, coating themselves with it so that the mosquitoes and biting flies couldn't get to their skin so easily, and the rising dust clouds coming from the herds darkened the skies, creating a gold-gray haze.

Millions of them, he realized, *there are millions of buffalo.* It would be foolish to try to drive through that herd.

If I had a choice, he thought, *I'd camp here, give the buffalo time to pass.* But the herd extended so far to the north, he couldn't see where it ended. It might take a week for the herd to pass, or more than a week.

He didn't have that much time. He said a silent prayer and prepared to move the camp in among the buffalo.

14

BUFFALO

Baline rose early the next morning, wakened by the deep grunts of buffalo and the bawling of their calves, a crude and demanding sound.

The air had a chill in it, and it was so thick with moisture that it left heavy dew everywhere. The scent of water mingled with the odor of buffalo, leaving a sharp bite. Baline crept outside the tent and saw buffalo all around, huge black shadows moving in the gray pre-dawn.

The men stood guard around the camp, guns and sabers drawn, trying to keep the beasts at bay.

The sun rose in a ball of red so bright it looked almost as if a huge fire was sweeping across the prairie from the east.

But soon there were the glad sounds of cooking pans rattling, and the campfires were set, and the comforting scent of cooking bread sweetened the air.

Baline was trying to live by the spirit now, trying to listen the way Father Jens did when he walked in the fields at night. Sometimes, if she listened hard enough, she felt inspired to do things. So now she walked through camp and felt prompted to move an ax before a child tripped on it or cut himself; then she went to the creek and brought water for some of the old folks who were getting too weak to care for themselves. She felt as if a fire were burning in her chest as she did it.

Sometimes lately she could go for an hour or more quietly doing good, averting little tragedies before they happened. But it was hard.

Eventually, when her work was done, the warm feeling would leave her, and it was almost as if she felt let down. She didn't want to have to come back to the real world. She wished she could have the Spirit to guide her forever.

The tents began to come down shortly after breakfast, though some were delayed. There were so many single women in camp that two of the tents had been set aside just for them. The young women refused to rise, until finally Captain Atwood began banging on a tin pan, driving the sleeping women from their tent.

As the last few tents were coming down, someone shouted that there was a dead woman in one. Baline ran to see who had died, but it was just an old woman, Elizabeth Ingra. Baline didn't feel sorry for her, even though she knew that she should have. Sister Ingra had been ranting for days. She couldn't walk very well, and so her ancient husband had been pulling her on a handcart. But Sister Ingra felt lost and often called out for help, claiming that she was being kidnapped, sometimes complaining that pirates had taken her captive. Other times, she would run about camp, half-clothed, dazed, as if in a dream, dodging from anyone who came near, but begging, "Please, how do I get home?"

Now Sister Ingra was at peace.

The camp stayed late in the morning as men dug a deep grave to bury her in. The Platte River was wide here, nearly fifteen miles across and only inches deep. When the hole was five feet deep, water began to seep into it, and they put the body in.

After the funeral service, Captain Willie went out into the water with his cart and came back with a huge slab of stone that he'd cut from the ground. The men made a crude marker for Sister Ingra.

It wasn't until ten that Captain Willie signaled for the camp to move forward. Baline helped Emily Wall pull her sick brother in the handcart, and the going was fairly easy. But they traveled only six miles before a halt was called. A herd of buffalo ahead was too thick to travel through, and Captain Willie told folks that they'd have to wait until the herd thinned.

So the men circled the handcarts, and the people took a rest. Baline ran off to find her friends. With all of the buffalo around,

Baline, Agnes, and Mary were forced to stay in a handcart. They couldn't go out straying, looking for wildflowers or birds or pretty stones.

Everything was ruined anyway. The buffalo had trampled the flowers and pooped all over them, so the girls just sang silly songs and sat in the back of a covered handcart, one with a little canvas over the top to keep out the sun. There were only a few like it in all of the camp.

As the sun rose high, the day stayed ominously dark. The buffalo herds were raising dust clouds that blocked out the light, creating a golden nimbus that floated in the air like mist. The buffalo milled about in the glow, huge dark creatures forever streaming south.

The sound of their hoofbeats was a constant rumble, gently shaking the earth.

"I wish I could put memories in my hope chest," Agnes Caldwell said. "If I could, I'd put this memory in."

"You have an hope chest?" Baline asked. "Is this like a dowry chest?"

"It's a chest that we put nice things in," Agnes said, "our best linens and tea cups, to save for when we get married."

In the old days, Baline knew, back in Denmark, such chests were filled with a young girl's treasures, and often with money, both to help support her family when she married and to pay to the family of the husband that took her. "I have such a chest," Baline said proudly. "It is carved from a special vood and smells very nice. The good vood keeps out der vat you call them . . . der butterflies that come at night?"

"Moths," Agnes said. Baline tried the word on her tongue.

"What do you have in your chest?" Mary asked.

"Oh, lots of things. I have China doll," Baline answered, "that is very pretty. I have cloth that I embroidered to go on chair, and picture of tulips. Oh, and I have some blue cloth that I vanted to make dress from, but mother didn't have time for to help me before I left. She said that they vill bring my chest ven come next spring, and then ve vill make dress for me, and one for my sister."

"What does the material look like?" Agnes said. Blue was Agnes's favorite color, Baline knew.

"Is like the color of robin's egg," Baline said, "but mother is going to help me embroider pansies on it."

"Oh," Agnes said, her eyes going wide in wonder. "That sounds beautiful."

Baline felt a pang. She suddenly missed her mother very much and wondered what she was doing back in Denmark. It was early autumn there. Mother might be working in the yard today thinning the tulip bulbs, or maybe if it was misty and raining, she would sit by the fire to knit.

Suddenly there was shouting up at the head of the handcart train, and a herd of buffalo came running beside the handcarts, not an arm's length away.

Several men pulled out their handguns, little derringers and pistols that went pop, pop, pop as they fired. The huge buffalo didn't even slow. They thundered past the startled pioneers, grunting and snorting, their eyes rolling back in fear. Baline spotted blood on one, dripping from its neck. Pop, pop, bang! The guns sounded like firecrackers going off, with the occasional bang as a genuine long-barreled muzzle-loader fired.

"I got one!" Ole Madsen shouted in Danish. He was leaping about the back of his handcart, waving his muzzle-loader in the air. A huge bull had run past his cart a few yards, staggered to its front knees, and just stood for a long moment, bleeding.

Pop, pop, pop! More handguns went off, until Brother Savage shouted, "Stop shooting, you idiots! Stop shooting."

The last of the buffalo raced away, perhaps a hundred yards from the handcarts, going out of the range of the settlers' guns.

Baline looked about, wide eyed. Over forty shots had been fired, but for all of their effort, the settlers had managed to kill only two buffalo. Ole Madsen had shot an enormous bull that finally keeled over and lay struggling for breath, while one of the English settlers managed to kill a calf.

It was a pitiful showing for so many hunters, with so many

buffalo to shoot at such a close range. The little guns just couldn't bring the buffalo down.

Brother Madsen raced out to his buffalo and cut out its tongue, then turned to leave the rest.

But Captain Willie came stalking down the line and demanded, "Aren't you going to butcher that animal?"

"No," Ole said. "This old bull, he not good for meat."

"The Prophet Joseph taught that we should never kill one of God's creatures without a cause," Captain Willie said. "He said that on the Day of Judgment, we'll be held accountable for every life that we've taken, down to the least toad or sparrow."

"I have its tongue," Ole said. "I vill have its hide, too, for keepsake. But the meat, it vill not be good. The bull, he stinks."

"Look at these buffalo," Captain Willie said, waving into the distance. "The herds look like they go on forever, but they don't. Once there were herds like this all across the land, from California to New York. Now there's none left in most of the country. If we take the lives of God's creatures needlessly, the day will come when we'll want their meat and find none. You're going to eat that old bull, and you're going to butcher it yourself!"

Ole Madsen's face turned red with rage. He wasn't about to butcher that disgusting old bull.

But Captain Willie called a halt, and several men cut the bull's carcass up, and Ole himself was made to stand there dispensing meat to the settlers. Baline's portion from the kills was two pounds, more meat than she'd seen at once in the last six months, and she longed to cook it, but there was no wood to do so. The last tree she had seen was six miles back, along the creek.

So Else Nielsen took all of the meat and put it in a pot so that the flies could not get at it, then Baline went back to pull the Wall's handcart, and the camp moved forward amid the herds of buffalo.

All afternoon the skies continued to darken, and soon a cold wind came streaming strong and steadily from the west. In part it seemed that the wind was blowing dust up from the hooves of the buffalo, and the dust storm grew so fierce that the settlers could not see a hundred yards. The dust and grit got in their eyes. But soon

Baline realized that the dust couldn't account for all of the darkness. Clouds were rushing in overhead, too, with the smell of coming rain. The odor of moisture grew thick in her nostrils, and the cloud kept growing darker.

Ahead, herds of buffalo raced in front of the handcarts, half hidden in dust, their shaggy heads and bodies becoming dark shadows against the gray. The pounding of their hooves upon the hardpan was like the sound of rising thunder, and with each beat of a hoof, more dust rose.

Baline squinted to see them. The great bulls kept to the outside of the herd while the calves and cows remained protected. But blowing dust stung Baline's eyes, and she had to put her arm in front of her face and forge on.

Suddenly, a gust of wind struck with terrific force, and all around her, dust devils sprang up, some of them just little twists of wind, others rising up in great plumes for hundreds of feet. It all looked so strange, as if they were forging through a wasteland of ash, and suddenly Baline realized that it was ash. The ground here had been burned bare within the past few weeks.

Baline fought ahead, pulling the handcart, while Emily struggled beside her.

Captain Willie walked down the line calling, "You kids pick up some buffalo chips. Ten each. Everyone will need buffalo chips tonight. We're going to have to call a halt as soon as we get clear of this ash."

"You vant me to get the chips too?" Baline asked. She was pulling a handcart now. It wasn't like she was a child anymore.

Captain Willie frowned as he thought. "Yes, you too."

So I am still a child, she thought, *in his eyes.*

Baline had seen the Indians cooking with dried buffalo dung, so she knew what Captain Willie wanted, but she could not shake a feeling of disgust as she stopped awhile later and picked up her first chip. The buffalo dung had flattened out like a pancake, but though the top was dry, the underside was moist and icky, and maggots crawled through it.

Baline tugged her handcart along, keeping her eyes out lest a buffalo get too close, and then picked up the largest and driest buffalo pies that she could find, some of them more than two feet across.

When she had all ten neatly stacked up and wrapped in her apron, she went to put them in the handcart, but Joseph looked at her weakly. "I don't want them creepy things in here."

So Baline had to carry the creepy things in her apron with one hand while she pushed the handcart with the other.

She trudged on. She felt so tired today that she wanted to fall down on the sandy ground and cry.

If I am *tired*, Baline realized, *how will my friends feel? Agnes always gets tired before I do.*

Baline couldn't do two things at once. She couldn't go help Agnes and push the handcart at the same time. The air felt heavy and pressed on Baline's eardrums so much that Baline almost felt as if she were submerged underwater.

It was as she was noticing this that she heard Captain Willie up at the front of the handcart company, calling. His voice was lost in the buffeting wind, but someone up ahead called out, "We'll camp here for the night!" She could not see far enough ahead to hear who was speaking, but Baline trundled forward until she found that the company had reached a small stream that wound over the plains. Here, the fire had not been able to burn off all the grass, and though the buffalo had trampled and eaten most of it, there was enough for the livestock to feed on.

It seemed a terrible place to camp. There was no shelter from the wind, no trees for shade. They were out upon a flat plain with hardly a blade of grass to slow the wind, which gusted this way and that, as if uncertain where to go, blowing ash into people's eyes.

A storm was coming, Baline felt certain. She'd seen enough summer storms.

Emily Wall jutted her head to the west. "See that?" she said. There was little to see—clouds of dust and ash rose up from the ground where herds of buffalo raced with frantic energy across the plain.

"What?" Baline asked, not sure what she was supposed to be looking for.

"The sky on the horizon," Emily said. "It is bruised. A storm is coming, a bad one. Not like the ones before."

Baline had seen plenty of bad storms in the past few weeks, storms so bad that they killed the folks who got caught in them.

During these storms, Baline had marveled as lightning blazed from horizon to horizon, bolts flying so quickly that the heavens were never silent. Torrential rains and hailstones had beat down upon the settlers like bullets.

The storms had thrown down tents more than once, leaving the settlers cold and wet. That was how Caroline Reeder had lost her niece, Selena Hurren. The babe got soaked in a storm the night it was born and quickly became ill. All of the prayers in the world, all of the love and warmth that the family gave afterward, couldn't save it. Nor could they save the old folks that died after each such storm.

Emily was right. The skies to the west were a deep gray green, and if Baline listened, she could hear the distant roll of thunder.

"Circle the handcarts," Captain Willie called. "Make a corral out of them. Get the cattle inside."

The settlers raced to get camp set up. Baline left the Walls and went back to the camp of the Danes. Tents were pitched in a frenzy. It was not hard to drive the pegs into the ground, for here beside the river, the soil was loose and sandy.

No sooner had the tents gone up, than the women set fire to the buffalo chips and began cooking. Dozens of handcarts were arranged in a circle, forming a corral for the cattle, while other handcarts were placed strategically between the tents, so that buffalo wouldn't wander through camp during the night.

In the distance, the booming drew closer and closer, and soon Baline could see a towering mountain of cloud rolling toward them, as if the clouds would sweep the little camp away. It trundled toward them like an elephant, the distant rumble of thunder giving way to trumpeting roars. Wind began to gust and scream through the camp, whistling as it tore through the desert grasses.

No sooner had the settlers eaten dinner than Captain Willie herded everyone to their tents, which were already lurching and straining under the onslaught of the coming storm. Three of the tents toppled, and men ran to them quickly, raising them up and shoving the tent pegs back into the sand. But the pegs would not hold, and so the men sat there helplessly, holding the pegs in, lest the tents take flight like kites.

"Women and children get inside," Captain Willie shouted. "Any boys over the age of twelve, we're going to need you to hold down tent pegs."

Every tent held twenty people. But in Baline's tent, there were only two boys old enough to hold down pegs, and at least five or six would be needed.

Baline uttered a silent prayer, asking God if she should go help. She felt good about it, as if her aid would be needed. So Baline went outside. She was bigger than some of the twelve-year-old boys anyway.

Thus she knelt outside the tent, using her knee to hold the peg in, as the storm engulfed them.

It came with the night. The sun dropped behind it, lost in the thunderheads, which soon sealed the plains like the lid to a kettle, blocking out all light. The only luminescence at all came from forks of lightning that split the sky, much of the light lost among the clouds, pealing and booming so that the earth shuddered.

Captain Willie came rushing past Baline just before the storm hit in force.

"Keep a keen eye out," he warned, shouting to be heard above the rising storm. "This is tornado weather."

"Vat is torn . . . tor-do?" Baline asked.

"It's like a dust devil that goes up a mile into the sky," Captain Willie said. "It can carry off children, tents, even buffalo. If you see one coming, get out of its way."

Baline had hardly ever seen a dust devil back in Denmark. "I vill do this."

She knelt down on the tent peg, using her knee to brace it, keeping all of her weight on the peg. For long minutes she sat there, feeling very alone. The wind beat against the tent like an old woman cleaning a dirty rug.

She worried about the storm. The wind was cold and blustery, smelling almost of snow. All through the summer, the storms had been warm and wet. But this one had the first bite of winter to it. Baline imagined catching cold from the wet, growing sick, and dying. It seemed like such a romantic way to go.

I would do that, she thought. *I would do that for my friends.*

"Do you need any help?" someone asked.

She looked up. Young Samuel Gadd stood over her. He was a large boy for a ten-year-old, at least when compared to the other stunted children in the camp. He had dark hair, piercing eyes, and a nervous smile.

"That vould be nice," Baline said, nodding. She thought that he would go around the tent, kneel and hold it down, but Samuel knelt down behind her and held the rope to her peg.

As he did, his hands brushed hers, and Baline felt an unfamiliar thrill. Her heart began pounding fiercely and she blushed, afraid that someone would see them so close together and at the same time afraid that Samuel might leave.

A gust of wind suddenly screamed through camp, and the whole tent leaned to the east. Baline threw her weight onto the rope, but it pulled so hard, she felt as if some monster had grabbed the tent, as if the wind itself were alive and malicious. The rope jerked in her hand, straining.

"Hold on," Samuel said. He pulled hard, steadying the tent, and Baline felt comforted by his sturdy presence.

On the far side of the camp, a tent toppled, and Baline saw two full-grown men racing to grab the ropes, pull the center pole upright.

Then the gust was gone, and in the lull, Baline found Samuel staring into her eyes, not blinking, not looking away. "You're pretty," he said. "You're about the most beautiful girl I've ever seen."

Baline didn't know what to say, except to be honest. "I'm not."

He nodded slightly, as if he'd caught her in a lie. "Beauty is in the eye of the beholder," Samuel said. "At least, I think that's what it says in the Bible. And you're pretty to me."

Baline couldn't argue with that, so she merely blushed.

"Nice, too," Samuel added. "You're about the best girl in this whole camp."

Baline wasn't sure what he meant by that. "Vell, who is the best then?"

"Ann Howard," Samuel said, "or maybe Caroline Reeder. Ann's nice to me and my family, but Caroline's nice to everyone. She's always helping old folks with their carts, and cooking for folks, and hunting for firewood. She's real nice."

Caroline Reeder was seventeen. She was a pretty girl with long brown hair and a smile so bright that you could light a candle with it. She often played with the children, tag or hide-n-go-seek or ring-around-the-rosy. In part, she really seemed to like children. But Baline had seen how she watched over them, too, always taking care that none of them strayed too far from camp or fell behind on the long march.

Caroline Reeder had Baline beat as far as goodness went. And she was more mature. Obviously, Samuel would like her better. But she was too old for him.

"You're nice, too," Baline said.

"When we get to Zion, you want to live next door to us?"

Baline frowned. She had no idea where her parents might choose to live. They were good friends with the Nielsens and had talked about moving to the same town. There were whole towns in Utah where just Danes settled. It didn't seem likely that she would live close to the Gadds.

"Sure, I vould like that," Baline said. But it was just a hope.

"Me too," Samuel said. He looked away and gripped the rope tight, for another gust of wind slapped at it, and for long minutes it became a fight to hold the tent upright.

Lightning grumbled in the distance, and soon it snarled overhead, arcing through the skies. The whole earth seemed to rumble, and hail pelted the back of Baline's neck, stinging her like a slap.

The sky grew green and gray, and the darkness deepened as if it were full night, though the sun would not dip below the horizon for another hour. Wisps of cloud plummeted to the ground in the distance, like a ghostly finger pointing toward the grave.

There were shouts all around as others fought to hold their tents, and suddenly the rope jerked out from under Baline. She held it as tightly as she could, but the rope pulled both her and Samuel a dozen feet.

For a moment, Baline had a vision of herself holding the rope as the wind picked up the tent and blew it away like a hot air balloon.. She clung tightly, resigned to her fate. The tent pitched over, and people inside screamed.

She and Samuel pulled on the rope, trying to keep the tent upright, but it just leaned. Several pegs had broken free from the sandy ground, and there was nothing holding the tent up. Some men came and wrestled the tent pole upright, shoved the pegs back into the ground, and hurried off to take care of the next emergency. The hail turned to rain, cold and miserable. Baline's summer clothes were ill-prepared to fend off such weather.

"Here," Samuel said. "Wear my hat." He shoved the broad-rimmed hat onto her head, and immediately the rain stopped pelting her neck and back.

"No," she said, for it was well known that out here in the West, no article of clothing was more needful than a hat.

"It's all right," Samuel said. "My hair is as thick as a beaver's."

Baline kept the hat on, for it held off the wind and water and it really did feel good.

Yet she worried about Samuel. She worried that he would take sick and die from the wet and cold.

An angel wouldn't wear someone else's hat, she decided.

She put it back on him. "Thank you," she said. "I'm all warm now."

Would an angel lie? she wondered.

Overhead, the thunder snarled, and the distant grumbling grew louder and louder. The ground beneath Baline shook from it, and the rope in her hands thrummed like the string of a guitar. Still the rumbling intensified, and Baline's heart began to race in fear. The father of all storms was coming.

"Stampede!" one of the men shouted. "Buffalo!"

He was racing out into the midst of the camp, pointing north. Baline squinted into the gloom and driving rain, and a streak of lightning burst overhead, revealing a dark herd of buffalo racing toward the camp. Their huge shaggy heads were low to the ground, and their black horns gleamed in the glare of lightning.

"Turn the wagons!" Captain Chislett shouted. He fired a pistol to get people's attention.

Men and boys suddenly abandoned the tent ropes and raced to the handcarts. Samuel Gadd took off with them.

The carts had been arranged in a large circle around the camp, creating a stockade so that the cattle couldn't wander. But now the buffalo were thundering straight toward them, and Baline could imagine the handcarts getting dashed to splinters.

The rumbling grew louder and more intense, even as lightning arced through the sky.

A young man who was supposed to be watching the cattle, Brother Caldwell, raced past Baline shouting, "Indians! I saw some Indians, just beyond that hill!"

No one listened. The men were pulling the handcarts, opening a space for the buffalo to pass through, and Baline wondered what to do. Should she stay here and hold the tent pegs? The wind shrilled through the ropes, which strained in her hand.

The ground shook beneath her feet now, and Baline could see the buffalo only a few hundred yards out.

The tent flap opened on the south side, and Sister Madsen poked her head out. "Get in here, child!" she called.

Baline held the peg, unsure. She wasn't worried about the tent falling too much. The people inside should be able to hold the center pole up, if they worked together, and to the buffalo, the tent would look as solid as stone.

No, she was worried about Samuel.

She saw him leap into the back of a handcart with Captain Chislett as the first few buffalo raced into camp, and the buffalo parted around them as if they were an island in a stream of fur.

As the buffalo neared her, Baline leapt through the flap of the tent. The ground continued to rumble, and she could hear the buffalo snorting and grunting as they raced past.

The women in the tent all huddled around the center pole, holding it upright in the gloom. Each woman held her precious babes close, hoping to shield them with their own bodies if worse came to worst. Children screamed in terror, and Baline's heart beat so hard that she was afraid it would break.

The stink of buffalo filled the air, a bitter scent of dirty hair, dust, and dried dung.

Some men began firing their guns, hoping to frighten off the beasts, but the pop and crackle of gunfire was lost in the snarl of lightning and the rumbling stampede.

For long minutes the herd thundered through camp. Sister Madsen led the inmates of the tent in fervent prayer, begging the Lord to "scatter the shaggy brutes of the earth." Four or five times, buffalo tangled their feet in the tent ropes, and the tent jerked violently as beasts tried to pull free.

After what seemed an eternity, the rumbling began to fade. The buffalo had passed, and men cheered all through camp, even though the wind still buffeted the tents and lightning snarled overhead.

Baline stayed inside the tent, soaked to the bone, as women and children stood shivering with terror and weeping in relief.

Then Captain Willie shouted, "The cattle are gone! They've run off in a stampede. Every able-bodied man come out of the tents! We must get them back!"

15

The Flood

Eliza Gadd begged her husband not to go out into the storm. Samuel had taken sick a month before in just such a storm, and though his cough had begun to lag, he looked gray and haggard, and she knew that he hadn't completely recovered.

"I have to go," he told her. "We need those cows. The babies need them."

He held Eliza for a long minute, hugged her close. Then he lit a lantern to ward off the darkness and raced into the gloom. It was as dark as night outside. The thunderheads rose up like mountains, sealing out all light. The sky grumbled and lights flashed high in the clouds, which released such a deluge that within minutes water began to seep under the tent.

The women quickly picked up their bedding, rolled up the blankets, and put them on top of the cooking pans to keep them from getting soaked.

Within an hour, the women found that they were standing in a puddle two inches deep, and the water was rising. It swirled about their feet in the darkness and flowed through the tent.

Eliza poked her head through the tent flap. Outside, all of the other tents glowed white from the inside, each lit by another lantern. All that Eliza could see was rain streaking past the tent flap and an endless pool all about. Ann Howard risked a peek.

"We're too close to the river," Eliza said. "I think that it's rising right under our feet."

"We shall be swept away," Grandmother Funnel cried.

"Not if we keep our wits about us," Eliza said. "If the water gets much deeper, we need only head to higher ground." But that was easier said than done.

There will be no sleeping here tonight, Eliza realized. She cast her mind about, trying to create a mental image of the area.

The Platte River was some fifteen miles wide at this point, but had been no more than a foot deep. The land seemed to be as flat and level as a floor. A few clear, deep streams meandered north of camp and then entered the river to the west. If the whole land was covered in water, the settlers wouldn't be able to head either north or west to search for high ground, lest they founder into those creeks. That meant that they could only backtrack, hoping to find some small swell to camp on. Higher ground might be as much as a mile off.

"What if our tents get swept away?" Grandmother Funnel fretted. "What if our carts float off?"

Then good riddance, Eliza thought. She had grown tired of handcarts and never wanted to see one again—unless it was being used as fuel for a nice cheery bonfire.

"We'll be all right," Ann Howard said as if she held some secret source of knowledge.

She thinks she's had a revelation, Eliza realized.

But Grandmother Funnel began to whimper in fear. Eliza's nearly six-year-old daughter, Sarah, clung to Eliza's skirt, pulling it down, begging to be lifted up like a toddler. Eliza already had her hands full with the twins, one in each arm. She cuddled them close, trying to keep them quiet, but the children were all distraught. It was Grandmother Funnel's fault.

Eliza held in her mounting anger at Grandmother Funnel, but the silly old woman just sobbed all the louder. Eliza finally blurted, "Shut your mouth. You're frightening the children!"

There was a shocked silence. In all of the camp of the saints, Eliza had never heard anyone speak as she had just done. Words of praise and comfort were far more commonly spoken than harsh sentiments.

The silence drew out to nearly a minute.

"Sister Gadd," Mary Ann, Grandmother Funnel's daughter, whispered at last, "I think you owe my mother an apology."

Eliza held her tongue. This pretense at being sisters was silly. There was a time when harsh words needed to be spoken, and now was the time.

"I'm sure that Eliza feels badly," Ann Howard said, "but she's right. For the children's sake, we all need to keep our heads."

So Eliza stood for a long hour, balancing the children on her hips, angry and ashamed.

Captain Willie came by, his presence outside the tent announced by the light of a dim yellow lantern. "Is everyone all right in there?"

"We're fine," Ann called back. "But the water keeps rising."

"We'll move camp when the men get back," Captain Willie announced, and he was gone.

The rain kept falling. After an hour the thunder faded away in the east, but heavy pellets of rain still pummeled down, and water swirled at their ankles.

By ten at night, all of the women and children felt faint from standing so long. They had to move their feet to keep blood flowing. The younger children wandered about in a daze, seeking a dry place to sleep. After walking fifteen miles during the day, followed by the excitement of the stampede, they were worn through.

"The men aren't coming back tonight," Eliza finally said. "The cattle are running with the buffalo. Who knows when they'll stop. We'll have to move the tent ourselves."

Eliza would have gone to look for higher ground, but she had to hold the twins. Both had fallen asleep in her arms, balanced precariously. She looked to Jane. At seventeen, she was the oldest of the children and the most responsible. *She should go*, Eliza thought.

But Jane wasn't dressed for the rain. Young Sam was already soaked to the skin, and he still wore his broad-brimmed hat. "Sam, can you take the lantern out and find some higher ground?"

"Me?"

"Yes, you. It's a dangerous thing I'm asking, for a boy to go out in the night and risk getting swept away in the flood. Can you do it?"

"All right," he said, bravely taking the lantern from its peg on the center pole. He slogged out into the storm.

Ann nervously watched him go, and then said, "I'm going with him." She hurried out into the storm.

After they left, Eliza fretted. *Why did I send him alone?*

The answer came slowly. Because of all her children, he most wanted to go to Zion. He wanted to help build the New Jerusalem and talked in awe of how Christ would someday come there to his temple.

Silly superstitious nonsense.

But Eliza was beginning to wonder. Sam was a good boy, the best of the family in her opinion. If anyone deserved God's favor, he did. If there were really angels protecting this camp, she imagined that they would be walking right beside him, guiding his every step.

A few minutes later Sam and Ann splashed back. Sam called excitedly, "There's a little rise, Mother, a couple hundred yards to the north!"

So the women moved the tent. They didn't take it down properly. Instead, Sam Junior stayed outside and pulled up all the stakes. Then Eliza and Sister Linford carried the babes, the children carried cooking pots and bedding, Ann led the younger women in lifting the center pole and thus the tent. Each person in the tent took his or her steps in unison, all choreographed to Grandmother Funnel's frantic cries.

Sam kept pulling the skirts of the tent until they were out of the flood. Then the women made their beds. Ann laid a wet tarp over the wet ground and threw their bedding over it all. The children climbed on top of the blankets and soon fell asleep, huddling together for warmth, and the women followed suit.

Eliza clung to young Samuel, keeping his body warm. Sister Funnel did the same for her mother. But Sister Marian Miller curled up in a blanket by herself, leaving Ann all alone. Ann was chilled through and through. She lay in a corner of the tent, teeth chattering, struggling to get warm, until Eliza offered, "Come, Ann, and lie beside me to get warm."

Ann scooted over in the dark and spooned up against Eliza's back, trembling from cold. Eliza worried for her, so she turned and hugged her like a sister.

"Thank you," Ann said. "I'm so cold, I do feel as if you might be saving my life."

"You'd do the same for me, Sister Howard," Eliza said.

At that, Ann smiled, and the low flame from the lantern reflected in her eyes. "Yes, sisters," Ann said, as if rejoicing at the thought. "I'd like you to think of me as your sister."

Eliza lay for a long time, holding Ann until the chills passed and Eliza fell asleep, just listening to the steady hiss of rain outside, the intermittent grumbling of thunder in the distance.

It was after two in the morning when her husband, Samuel, came in with Brother Linford. The lantern had been turned low, but Eliza saw that Sam was wet and chilled to the bone, shaking. He and Brother Linford went to a corner of the tent, and in the darkness they stripped off their sopping clothes, mopped the moisture from their bodies with their wet duds, and then put on dry.

Eliza worried that some of the other hens in the tent might be watching. She knew that the sound of the men returning had wakened Ann. She'd heard Ann's breathing quicken, and Ann had surreptitiously scooted away, leaving Samuel to fill her spot.

Will she try to peek at my husband's naked form? Eliza wondered.

She opened her eyes to a mere slit. Ann had her eyes squinted too tightly to be asleep.

What a modest creature she is, Eliza thought, *as sweet and saintly as the person she aspires to become—and I'm not.*

Samuel turned out the lantern and came to bed. He spooned against Eliza's back, cuddling for warmth. His whole body trembled and shook, and she realized that he was perilously cold.

She pulled his arms around her chest and then put her own arms over his, trying her best to share her body warmth. Almost, she wished that Ann would move close, share her warmth. But that would be too much like claiming him, as if Ann were also his wife.

"We got some of the cows," Samuel whispered in Eliza's ear.

"Only some?" Eliza asked.

"About half of them," he said. "We lost the oxen. We kept calling them, but they went off too far, and we couldn't find them in the dark. It will have to wait until morning."

Eliza fretted. The oxen were used to pull the supply wagons. Without them, the settlers would be stranded. There were cows and calves to be used for milk and meat, but they were too small to pull the wagons. The settlers needed the big steers.

"Should I go out and look for them, with some of the other women?"

"No," Samuel said. "The river is rising. In places where there were dry gullies last night, streams are flowing. It's too dangerous to move in the dark. Besides, Brother Caldwell said that he saw Indians driving that stampede toward us. We'll need to watch out for them."

Eliza's first thought was that the Indians intended to steal the oxen. But that didn't make sense. The camp was right in the midst of a sea of buffalo, and the buffalo meat that they'd gotten yesterday was far better than beef. The buffalo had been foraging on sweet grass since last spring, whereas the cattle that the settlers had been slaughtering were quickly becoming tough and stringy.

Maybe the Indians meant to kill us, Eliza decided. The Cheyenne had wiped out at least one wagon train in the past week. A few dozen warriors couldn't take on this many settlers. So she wondered, perhaps they had hoped to make the buffalo do their bloody work.

If so, they've failed, Eliza thought. *We're still here.*

At her back, Samuel coughed again, a sickly hacking sound that made his whole body shudder.

Another fear took her. "Is this the way that it will be," she asked, "you trading your life for your children's? Was it worth getting sick for a little milk for the twins?"

"Yes, I'll trade my life if I must," Samuel said. His body was still trembling from the cold. "If my children make it alive to Zion, I'll die happy."

"Don't you do it," Eliza said angrily. She knew the pain of losing a child. She'd lost one years ago. But she didn't want to be like Martha Campkin, acting as strong as a bull during the day, stifling her sobs at night when she thought that the children wouldn't hear. "Don't you leave me!"

"I won't," Samuel assured her. "I won't."

16

Tribulations

The morning after the stampede came wet and drear, with the taste of water so thick in the tents that Captain Willie felt that he could almost carve it into chunks with a Bowie knife and pass it out to his tent mates for breakfast. The rain kept falling for hours, huge droplets pummeling down, and when he finally did stick his head out of the tent, the land had been magically transformed overnight: puddles and pools and entire lagoons had formed, and the lazy Platte River that had been just a trickle the day before now was a raging torrent, muddy waters churning with a deafening roar. Even when the rain did let up, every so often, a phalanx of thunderheads would rush over and hurl a little more on the weary travelers, adding insult to injury.

At least the ash and dust that had been such a curse the day before had settled. The plains were all as black as night, except for a few patches by the creek. But Captain Willie could not see too far. A low mist rolled off the river, creating a haze over the blackened plains, and in the distance, torrents of rain fell in gray curtains.

The buffalo were gone, too, for the most part. It was as if, realizing that they had fulfilled their purpose in disrupting the handcart company, they had decided to disband.

Oh, little bands could be spied in every direction, but the vast, innumerable herd had wandered off. With only ash to feed on, they'd gone in search of sweet grass.

Things happen for a reason, Captain Willie told himself, *even things that we can't understand*. There were laws in the universe—the law of gravity, for example, that could not be contravened. There were spiritual laws that held equal force, that were equally incontrovertible. A man could not sin and hope to live in the presence of God.

As he stalked about the camp, trying to think of what to do next, Captain Willie worried that the stampede was a sign. He often found that God spoke to men through metaphors. Christ taught about life in parables, extracting powerful lessons from simple everyday things. So acute were his observations that sometimes it sounded as if one could learn as much about God by watching a seed grow and ripen as one could learn by reading the Bible.

Joseph Smith saw the world as a metaphor, too. Like Jesus, he taught that God was the literal father of all mankind, just as Captain Willie was the father of his family. Joseph also taught that just as a son will grow to be like his father, a man can grow spiritually until he becomes like God in every way—even to the point of creating his own worlds and populating them with his own offspring.

To Captain Willie, when he had first heard that concept, it seemed to be the most startling revelation in the world. As a youth he had been taught that men were base by nature, carnal and devilish and fallen—no better than some old fat sow waiting for the slaughter, and so fundamentally different from God that he was incomprehensible to mankind, a mysterious spirit that was somehow three Gods in one, without body, parts, or passions—despite all biblical accounts to the contrary.

But Joseph's teachings were far simpler and more sublime. God wasn't just floating around on some cloud in heaven anymore. In an instant, Captain Willie suddenly saw God as he was—a loving father, not much different from James Grey Willie himself, who was giving all that he had to rescue his children.

Knowing this made Captain Willie want to be a better man, to become virtuous and perfect as God was perfect. It made him appreciate his family and gave meaning to his role as a father.

But it seemed to Captain Willie that God's plan could be seen through all of nature. It was as if the whole world was a vast scroll with his word written upon it, if one could only decipher the text.

The great lessons of life were there to be understood, if one watched for them.

Captain Willie figured that it was God's way of making sure that even the heathen got a proper portion of the gospel, if they would only watch for the signs in heaven and in the earth, and listen to God's spirit.

Right now, the stampede seemed a warning.

Captain Willie sent men to the east, the west, and the south to hunt for the oxen.

But the land around the Platte was an unnavigable swamp, and early in the afternoon, two search parties came back with the news that no cattle were in sight. Buffalo were everywhere, and often the men would walk a mile or two, circling lagoons, wading through waters hip deep, thinking that they saw an ox, only to find some old buffalo that had wallowed in the red mud, leaving its dark hide the color of an ox.

He sent Captain Savage and Joseph Elder to the south on their mules, asking them to cross the river if need be. After all, the buffalo had been stampeding south.

They returned well after nightfall. The men were sopping wet, and the mules were caked in mud from hoof to neck. The mules had obviously gotten mired while trying to cross the Platte, and the men had been forced to swim for it. The only part of Savage that wasn't wet was his hat, which had a few sweat stains on the brim but was otherwise dry.

Captain Willie worried that Savage might be angry at being sent on such a nasty job, but Savage showed no sign of anger, just a weariness that went as deep as the bone.

Well, Captain Willie thought, *he swore that he'd work harder than any man on this trek, and I'm giving him every opportunity.* Yesterday, Captain Willie had sent him out buffalo hunting. Tomorrow, he'd be hunting cattle again.

"No sign of them cattle," Levi said mournfully, ashamed that he had failed. "We spent most of the day trying to find a way to ford the Platte, but the whole river is flooded. In places where the water was a foot deep yesterday, now it's twenty."

"Did you see the tracks of any cattle?" Captain Willie asked. A buffalo's track is wider than a cow's, and the crescent is foreshortened.

Levi shook his head. "Not that we could be sure of. Maybe some partials, but the buffalo were running behind them."

"What about Indian ponies?" Captain Willie asked.

"Nothing. Even if there were Indians driving them buffalo, the rain washed everything out. You think it was Cheyennes?"

"The Caldwell boy said that he saw them."

"No one else did," Savage said.

"Yes, but he was the one guarding the cattle, so he was the only one watching. I'm inclined to trust his word on this."

"Even if he did see Indians," Savage suggested, "it doesn't mean they were Cheyennes. Could have just been a hunting party driving them buffalo toward the river, hoping to corner 'em—Sioux or Omaha."

"Perhaps," Captain Willie said, but he felt uneasy. He dismissed Levi Savage and went to the campfire, a fire that he'd been able to start only because he kept a little dry kindling in a box in one of the supply wagons. Tonight, there was only one fire in camp, and folks had gathered around it to sing the songs of Zion, dry out their wet clothes, and take what cheer they could.

The Mortensen boy played his violin, but tonight the notes sounded sharp and brittle and gave no peace.

Captain Willie just sat at the fire for a bit, lost in thought. If the water was twenty feet deep in the Platte, Captain Willie knew they were in for trouble. The buffalo had stampeded just as the storm began. They might well have crossed the Platte before it rose, and be miles away on the far side. Or perhaps they stopped on some small sandbar in the river, only to be caught in the rising flood and washed out to sea.

He considered the predicament they were in. The trail was too muddy for them to travel tomorrow, even if they had a way to pull the wagons. The rain had stopped near midday, and once the clouds cleared out, the afternoon sun began to burn off the rain, raising a mist all along the river course, but pools of standing water up to three feet deep surrounded them on every side. They couldn't pull their wagons through the mud without the oxen. Half of the cattle were gone, more than thirty head. Some were just cows that had been brought along for milk and meat, but the missing cattle included the best of their oxen, the big old steers bred and trained to pull heavy loads.

The camp wouldn't be able to move without them.

The only thing that he could do was send men out again tomorrow and hope that the river fell enough so that the searchers could cross.

But that plan didn't satisfy Captain Willie.

God could bless a man, he knew. It was within God's grasp to turn aside a buffalo stampede, even if Indians were driving the buffalo. Such things had happened before.

Why, just a few months back, that old Dane, Peder Mortensen, had had his home attacked by an angry mob. Peder, being a cripple, couldn't defend himself, and so he prayed. But as the leader of the mob rushed through the gate to Peder's house, the thug suddenly collapsed, clutching at his heart. The astonished mob, seeing the man drop as if from a curse, had picked up their fallen comrade and fled in terror.

So God could bless a man, even in his most dire extremity. Why, Captain Willie figured that if God willed it, the whole camp could go leap on the backs of some wild buffalo and simply ride to Salt Lake!

But God wasn't blessing the camp. He was cursing it. Why? Captain Willie tried to read the signs.

Maybe it was because they had tried to waste buffalo meat. Ole Madsen had treated the lives of the animals with contempt, so maybe God was using the buffalo to humble him. That felt plausible, but it didn't feel right.

Captain Willie stamped around the camp, searching for a better answer. The Caldwell lad, Thomas, had never healed in his shoulder. It was still red and swollen after his tussle with the milk cow. Sister Gadd, a practiced nurse, said that the bone was infected with gangrene, and Captain Willie suspected that she was right.

Maybe there is *an infection in camp*, he thought. *Maybe there are evils hidden beneath the surface, needing to be attended.* It never ceased to amaze him how even some of the best saints could be so duplicitous. Back in Iowa, some of his men had sneaked out at night to milk farmers' cows. Another had stolen a pig.

The settlers' small rations didn't satisfy their hunger. It was hard work pulling handcarts through mud and sand, over rough trails; the work required more energy than the meager rations provided.

Back in Iowa, it had seemed that a pound of flour per day was more than ample for a man. These settlers were poor folk for the most part, starvelings unused to eating their fill.

Now he was beginning to see that even a starveling couldn't do hard work on an unfilled stomach. All of his life, Captain Willie had heard sermons against the sin of idleness, mostly from men who proclaimed that the poor were poor because they were lazy. Now he saw that the poor were lazy because they were ill fed. They couldn't find the vigor to work.

He knew that a plow-horse fed on grain could travel forty miles in a day, but even a thoroughbred fed on straw could not make ten. Apparently, the same was true of men.

Captain Willie peered up at the faces of the men and women sitting around the fire. They perched on the beds of their handcarts, for there were no dry rocks or logs to sit upon, and they huddled under blankets. Here and there, children peeked out, making a game of it.

Because of my stupidity, my people suffer, Captain Willie thought. *If they turn to theft, will God hold me accountable?*

There were times, Captain Willie knew, when God held one man accountable for the sins of another. A father who didn't teach his child to live in righteousness would have to suffer in the child's punishment, according to Joseph's teachings. A bishop who didn't hold his congregation accountable for their sins might suffer for it in the hereafter.

But Captain Willie was teaching his people to the best of his ability.

There was a little pilfering going on in camp. Sister Isaacs had had a loaf of bread stolen two days ago. A bowl of blackberries that Sister Jones had picked on an island yesterday disappeared before the evening meal.

Kids' handiwork, Captain Willie figured. You couldn't expect a five-year-old who has walked fifteen miles in a day to show self-restraint when he sees food.

There's only one thing to do, Captain Willie decided. *I'll have to exhort the camp to greater righteousness.*

He stood and clapped his hands. "Brothers and Sisters, may I have your ear," he called. "We're going to start prayer meeting early tonight."

Then he explained the difficulties they were about to face and the need for all of them to do their utmost to face the challenges ahead, whatever they might be. He called upon each captain to address the crowd and bear testimony. To his satisfaction, each captain exhorted folks to pray that the oxen might be found. Some exhorted the saints to rededicate themselves to the Lord and strive for greater righteousness.

In his own brief sermon, Captain Willie reminded his people that it was already September, and the camp had nearly a thousand miles still to travel. Winter was coming, and they didn't have enough rations so that they could waste an hour more looking for cattle, much less a whole day. He warned that the days were growing shorter. Two months ago, they'd had as much as eighteen hours of daylight to travel. Two months from now, they might get only eight. So he'd have to keep asking the saints to rise early, so that they might be prepared to strike out at the crack of dawn.

He repeated the request that each of them pray earnestly for the return of the cattle, and wondered if he should exhort some of these men and women who were already starving to fast, but he felt that the Spirit forbade him from doing so. So he exhorted them all to keep the commandments of God so that they might earn his blessings and sent them all to bed.

September fifth dawned warm and clear. The puddles were dwindling, and the waters in the Platte were lower. Captain Willie sent search parties out in each direction once again and then sat down to wait for the cattle.

The sun had not been up for two hours when he saw a familiar carriage driving from the west, its team of mules racing in fury, throwing mud from their hooves with every step. It was Colonel Babbitt, coming back from Fort Kearney.

He hopped down from the wagon and doffed his cap, looking sober. "I met some of your men out hunting oxen," Colonel Babbitt said, peering hard at the camp, as if searching for something, almost as if he expected the missing cattle to come popping out of a tent.

"Yes," Captain Willie said, "we've lost our cattle, and we're a bit mired down here."

Babbitt whispered low under his breath. "You're in a damn sight of trouble." His face was pale, and he was shaking. "You can't afford to sit here. You've got to get going."

"Our best oxen are gone. All I've got are milk cows."

Babbitt was a seasoned teamster. Captain Willie would follow his lead, even if Babbitt suggested that he take a shortcut through hell. But he couldn't help but recognize that something was being left unsaid.

A small crowd had gathered around the two men, folks eager for news.

"Is something wrong?" Captain Willie asked.

Babbitt looked around nervously, as if unsure whether to speak in public. "Let's talk in your tent," Babbitt said, and Captain Willie led the way.

Inside the tent, Babbitt took off his hat, as was proper when talking about the deceased, and put it against his breast. He said, "Another wagon train got wiped out a couple of nights ago, a group coming from California. The Cheyennes did it. I spoke to the commander at Fort Kearney, and he's sent more men to fight the Cheyennes. As you know, they caught some in a cornfield last week and killed thirteen of them, but the rest are on the run. The problems is, now the whole Cheyenne nation is going to war! The army had a huge battle with hundreds of war chiefs down in Kansas last week, leading more than two thousand braves. They were about a hundred and fifty miles south of here. Due to the fragile politics of the region, the army is forced to leave those troops in Kansas, so now many of the Cheyenne troublemakers are running north. They seem to be concentrating their forces along the trail up ahead at Ash Hollow."

Captain Willie bit his lower lip. The Platte River trail would lead them right into Ash Hollow. It was up in the high country, up on the

North Platte, a rugged region of steep hills. Ash Hollow itself was a region where a number of well-wooded, winding canyons all met into one long valley. It was the kind of place where Cheyenne war parties might hide for weeks without being found. It was the perfect spot to ambush the handcart train.

Babbitt reached into a letter pouch at his belt and pulled out a wrinkled piece of yellow paper. "I talked to two of my teamsters at Fort Kearney. One of them is shot in the leg and will be laid up for the rest of the winter. The other is just scared half to death.

"They said that their men got divided. Some of their cattle apparently 'wandered' from camp, and the men went out the next morning to search for them. They found the cattle some eighteen miles away and got back to camp late at night. They had just put the cattle to bed and crawled in themselves when the Cheyennes opened fire. The first shot took out the guard, and the captain hid behind a wagon wheel and opened fire with his revolver. He fired off all chambers before he got killed. My teamsters fired back, but they were vastly outnumbered and barely escaped with their lives.

"Hmmmm . . . ," Captain Willie said, now deep in thought.

"An ox that has pulled a wagon for twenty miles during the day will not 'wander' twenty miles in a single night," Babbitt said. "Those cattle were driven off.

"The Cheyennes knew that the teamsters had to go hunting for them, making it easy to come in at night, take out the guards, and then get to the woman and whatever else they wanted. It was just the braves' poor luck that my men got back with the cattle before they could carry out their attack."

Captain Willie suspected that he was right. He also knew where Babbitt's thoughts were heading. Willie's own oxen were gone, apparently driven off by Indians—which meant that the Cheyenne could be preparing to attack his company.

We aren't just dealing with a band of rogue warriors anymore, either, Captain Willie realized. *There could be hundreds, thousands of them.*

Babbitt handed Captain Willie the wrinkled parchment. "The soldiers found this at the attack site."

Captain Willie sat and squinted, trying to read in the gloom of the tent. The letter was from Mrs. Wilson, written in a florid, elegant hand, and was addressed, "Dear Cousin." It went on to describe how she had left Iowa on August 21 under a cloud of apprehension that had been growing daily, until on the 25 it turned to near panic when their cattle disappeared. She spoke of her love for her cousin and her gratitude for her friendship. The letter ended mid-sentence. Apparently, the attack occurred while she was writing.

Captain Willie handed it back to Babbitt.

"Mrs. Wilson hasn't been found yet," Babbitt said. "There is some uncertainty as to whether she is dead or alive. The army has taken some Cheyennes hostage, hoping for a trade, but they caught one wounded Cheyenne who said that she was beaten and left for dead soon after the attack, since she couldn't ride a horse well enough to suit the braves. But if that's true, the army scouts haven't been able to find her body."

"She's dead," Captain Willie confirmed. "Our people found her near the attack site and buried her." He couldn't bring himself to tell how she had been found, cuddling the corpse of her slaughtered child.

Babbitt groaned softly, as if he'd been hoping for better news. He shook his head. "Keep your men in camp, armed and ready. You'll need a heavy guard. Send men out to hunt for cattle, but only a few at a time. If you've got Cheyenne troubles, you might try looking on the south side of the river for help."

"The army? I thought the commander at Fort Kearney said we're not allowed to camp within ten miles."

"You'll get no help from the army," Colonel Babbitt said. "What you need is an angel, and I know where to find one—south of the Platte."

17

The Dark Angel

When Baline heard from some other children that an angel was in camp that night, she raced back with her load of buffalo chips as fast as she could.

She'd been tending the chips all day, carefully lifting them with a stick and then turning them so that the bottoms would dry in the sun. She'd realized at dawn that they would be needed, that the children would be sent to hunt for dry chips, and with the ground still being sopping wet, they wouldn't find any. So she had spent hours turning them so that others would also be able to use them; now, in the evening gloom, she dropped a dozen fairly dry chips by the fire, then peered about looking for the angel.

She'd never seen an angel before, and she expected a glorious being in white whose skin shone like lightning.

What she saw was a forty-five-year-old man with a receding hairline that nearly left him bald on top. But the rest of his thick brown hair was so long and greasy that it hung almost to his waist; his beard was even longer, and he had eyes so pale blue that they were practically devoid of color.

The whole camp had gathered around him, as if he was the main attraction at the circus, but she heard people whispering in awe, and there was a reverence to the group that she had felt only when the Apostle Lorenzo Snow visited her small church in Denmark.

The man before her was a living legend.

Baline heard Mrs. Cantwell whisper something about an angel, but she used unfamiliar words. Brother Amundsen, who spoke Danish with a thick Norwegian accent, was explaining in a whisper. "He is gunfighter, blessed by Joseph Smith himself so that he can never be killed in battle. But he himself has killed many men."

He smells bad, Baline thought. *He smells like a cow.*

"He is driving a team west, on the south side of the river," someone else whispered.

Now I know why he smells like cows, Baline thought.

"He wears the long hair like Samson," another Danish woman said, as if she was an authority, "and he must never cut it."

There were many others speaking. One boy said, "I heard that he can walk through walls and tread through dry leaves without making so much as a rustling sound."

Another girl whispered in Danish, "The Indians are terrified of him. They won't attack us so long as he is in camp."

Baline drew near, for the angel was speaking to Captain Willie. He spoke with a strange American accent, in a soft voice, and Baline had a hard time understanding him. So she wormed her way to the front of the crowd.

"Use buffalo chips for your fires from now on," the angel was saying. "Good dry ones won't give off as much smoke as wet wood will." He nodded approvingly at the chips that Baline had brought. "And make sure that your fires are all out well before sundown. A fire lighting up the prairie will call any Indian for miles.

"Most likely, these Cheyennes will attack by night. There aren't many of them, so they won't chance it by day.

"They'll watch your camp from a couple of miles off, and then wait for you all to go to sleep. They won't want to attack by the light of a full moon, neither.

"With such a large camp, they'll try to take the guards out with knives. You've got to watch out for that. These Cheyennes are good knife fighters, almost as good as me! I been nicked a couple of times."

He laughed, then continued. "Tell your guards to find high ground and then lie down on their bellies at night. A man walking around like he is guarding a castle wall, well, he's just begging for someone to slit him open."

"Mr. Rockwell, is there any way to stop them from attacking?" Captain Willie asked. "Should we offer them gifts?"

So, the angel has a name, Baline thought.

Rockwell thought for a long minute, then spit on the ground. "Call me Port. Naw, them Cheyennes don't want nothing except to raise a little hell. I hear that one of them young bucks, a fellow named Broken Tooth, swore to kill every settler who tries to cross the prairie this fall. That's a tall boast, but he and his boys will look like fools if they don't at least take a run at it."

But then he got an odd look on his face, as if an idea struck him. "These Cheyennes, they're a superstitious bunch. You can never tell what might turn them in a battle. We met an army patrol two days ago, and I heard a story. Down in Kansas last week, one of their war chiefs had a dream. He dreamt that if his men bathed in this one river, the soldiers' bullets couldn't pierce his men. Well, the general hears about this rumor, so when the Cheyenne warriors charge, he orders his men to draw their sabers! Seeing that their magic was defeated, the Cheyennes were so shocked, they nearly fell of their horses. From what I hear, you never seen such a slaughter. The Cheyenne couldn't turn their ponies and retreat fast enough." To drive the point home, Porter Rockwell said, "I'd do my best to make sure that my guards were all armed with sabers."

Captain Willie nodded to the other captains and made it so. There were a couple of old military men in camp who had sabers.

"Anything else?" Captain Willie asked.

"I don't know," Port said, casting his mind about. "Indians see a rainbow on their way to a battle, it's a sign that things go well. If they see a flock of starlings chasing a crow, it means they'd best watch out. Oh, and an owl flying across their paths—that's the worst. They think that owls are the spirits of their ancestors. If one crosses your path, it means that someone in your family is going to die. So if an owl flies across their paths, they'll turn around and head straight home. I heard about a feller down in Missouri once who could make a convincing hoot owl, and when some Indians came sneaking up on his camp, he gave a couple of hoots that sent them all shrieking in fear."

Baline had heard lots of owls since coming to America. Back in Iowa, she had heard the hoot of the great horned owls as they sat in the cottonwoods at night. But more often, she would hear the cries of the screech owls as they flew low over the fields, using their loud cries to startle mice from their burrows.

Baline got up enough courage to ask a burning question. "Are you real angel?"

Rockwell hesitated to answer.

"Everyone says you are," Baline assured him.

One English sister corrected her, used that unfamiliar word again.

"I am," Rockwell said. He said it firmly, looking into her eyes, and Baline did not doubt that he was telling the truth. But it was only a half-truth.

"So, vat is a venging angel?" Baline asked, for the English kept using that strange word.

"Uh-venging angel," Captain Willie said, and there was a silence provided for Rockwell to speak.

Rockwell seemed to think for a moment, and Baline offered, "Brother Nielsen says that ven ve serve God, it is the same as if ve vere angels."

"That's right," Rockwell said softly. "The thing is, God asks folks to serve in different ways. He might ask you to help a neighbor find a lost cow or take a kettle of soup to an old lady. But there's times when God needs someone with special talents. Now, God would never ask me to sing in church, but let's say that there's a gunslinger comes to town and shoots a sheriff down like he was nothing but a dog. God wouldn't ask you to do anything about it, would he?"

Baline shook her head. She'd never imagined such a terrifying situation. "I don't think so."

"Well, that's when God comes talking to me," Rockwell said.

Baline looked into his eyes, and he gazed steadily back at her with such deadly sincerity, she felt as if she were staring into the eyes of the devil himself.

"Oh," she said in a voice so small it came out as a squeak. She wanted to tell him that she was trying to be like an angel, too. She had felt inspired to turn over the buffalo chips today.

But the only words that escaped from Baline's mouth was a question that she would normally not dared to have asked anyone. "How many men have you killed?"

"I don't count 'em, Sugar Dumplin'," Rockwell said. "I just kill 'em. But you don't have to be afraid of me, unless of course you take to robbing banks. Every man or woman I ever kil't deserved to die. Bank robbers, assassins, thieves—I put holes in 'em all." He reached up to an old weathered vest and pulled it aside. The light from the campfire at his feet made the silver star pinned to his shirt shine like ruddy gold. He was a sheriff.

That comforted Baline, to know that he was a lawman. Then he looked right in her eyes, and his voice sounded soft and solemn. "You're an angel, too, aren't you? I can feel it in you. You're one of those folks that goes around doin' good."

Baline did not want to boast, so she did not answer yes. But every day she was learning to feel the Spirit a little better, becoming more and more of an angel.

Suddenly she became aware of the crowd around them, listening. She remembered her manners. As the English taught, "Children are to be seen, not heard."

Baline looked up at the crowd, her face flushed with embarrassment. Someone chuckled. Now they all knew her secret. They knew that she thought she was an angel.

She fled to her tent and hid.

18

The Broken Law

Orrin Porter Rockwell stayed the night, which gave great comfort to the saints, even to Eliza. She didn't believe that one man could fight off the whole Cheyenne nation, but she knew that the Indians were every bit as superstitious in their way as the Mormons, and Rockwell was purported to have "big medicine."

Eliza didn't speak to the man. She listened to his advice carefully and then shelved it away in a dark corner of her mind.

The next morning, Rockwell left for his camp on the south side of the river, some fifteen miles distant. The river was still swollen, and Rockwell had offered to carry some of the company's wheat, if they could just figure out how to get it across the river, but with the current flood, it was too dangerous to try. The wagons would simply wash away and the wheat would be lost, and the situation would only become more dire.

The best alternate plan that the captains could come up with was to move the camp with only half the wagons at a time. So on the morning of September 6, the leaders gave a rousing sermon. Brother Siler, the captain of the independent wagons, spoke at length and warned his people that great tribulations were about to come upon them. Then the first three hundred rolled out of camp. They traveled five miles to the banks of a small, clear creek, and set a new camp. The cows were given a couple of hours to feed and rest, then sent back to pick up the other half of the wagons, along with the rest of the handcart pioneers.

It made for a tedious trek. The last of the saints didn't make it to camp until after dark.

"This is a great plan," Eliza told her husband as the last two hundred began pitching tents in the dark, "if we want to make it to Utah in time for spring planting."

"At least we got our cattle and wagons into camp safely," Samuel said brightly.

"This time," Eliza agreed. But there were flaws in the plan. "I half suspect that at some future time, the Cheyennes will realize that the best way to attack the company will be to hit the drovers while they're taking the cattle back to pick the second load of wagons. That's when there will be the fewest men to guard them."

Sam looked around, checking to make sure that no one was listening. "It will be all right," he said. "I'm sure of it."

But Eliza wasn't sure. Samuel had lost his color again. The dust and rain and cold had all taken their toll. His cough would not leave him now, and worse, baby Daniel was getting it too. The child's voice was hoarse from crying for his mother's breast.

"Did you notice how small a distance we covered today—four or five miles? Captain Willie is afraid to go farther. He's trying to make sure that the drovers stay in sight of one of the main parties."

"I guess you're right," Sam said as if mystified by her powers of observation.

"If he keeps this up, we'll never cover more than six miles in a day. That puts us to Salt Lake in February."

"It will be all right," Samuel said. "There are men out looking for our cattle right now. Even if they don't find them, we may be able to buy some oxen at Fort Laramie. Or maybe one of the wagon companies will be able to haul our supplies."

She knew what he was trying to do. The leaders kept warning the saints against "murmuring," as if they didn't have the right to criticize their leaders. Right now, Eliza was perilously close to murmuring. Hell, she was about to swear out loud, screaming curses at the top of her lungs.

So she determined to make the best of the time that they had. It was true that they hadn't covered five miles in the past three days. But it was equally true that they needed this rest, even if it was forced upon them.

That afternoon, Eliza had taken time to wash all of the women's clothes in some clean creek water, then put them out in the wind to dry. Now by the campfire, she set to work mending every little tear. Ann Howard brought by a friend, a young Welsh woman named Mary Griffiths, and Ann played with the twins, keeping them distracted from Eliza's flaccid breasts, while Mary helped sew.

Mary was a fair-haired woman with eyes so pale blue they looked white, a shade that Eliza had seen only in the Welsh, and her hair was a honey blonde. She could have been strikingly beautiful if not for her rough skin. Yet she had a certain charm about her. She spoke with a soft comforting accent, languorous and musical.

She worked quickly with her sewing, betraying a wealth of practice, her needle dodging in and out of Samuel's worn shirt almost faster than the eye could see, and Eliza felt grateful. Mary was obviously an accomplished seamstress.

While the saints began singing hymns softly in the background, Mary looked down where Ann was playing peekaboo with the twins on the ground and said, "Gol," in such a gentle way that it sounded like the cooing of a wood dove, "don't you just love the tots?"

"Yes," Eliza admitted.

"They're so sweet and innocent at that age. Sometimes I look at them, and I think, 'He could grow up to be someone I'd fear to meet in a dark alley.' " She chuckled sweetly at the joke. "Or they could grow up to be great men, the kind who save entire nations, and their names could be revered. . . . All it takes is for us to help shape them, like a tree as it grows, pruning them back, giving them proper light and soil."

Eliza knew what Mary was leading to. She obviously thought that Eliza was raising her children wrong. Eliza wasn't giving them "proper light." She wasn't teaching her children the gospel according to the Mormons.

"I think that a child should be given his freedom," Eliza said. "I think that he should be free to choose what he becomes."

"Och, to be sure," Mary agreed. "But we have to give them some direction. A rose needs an arbor to climb. We can't just let it grow wild like a weed."

"My children are not weeds, and I do not let them grow wild," Eliza said.

Mary set her sewing down in her lap and stared at Eliza in surprise. "What are we talking about? I . . . meant no insult."

"You're criticizing me because I can't keep up with my own sewing and because I'm not a Mormon."

Mary Griffiths' mouth fell open in shock. "You're not a Mormon?"

Suddenly Eliza saw her mistake. Mary was camping with Woodward's hundred, and so she didn't know Eliza well. Eliza felt as if she stuck out like a sore thumb, but the truth was, you couldn't tell a Mormon from a non-Mormon just by looking.

Ann tried to cover for her. "Eliza's not a Mormon yet," she said. "But Sister Gadd is a dear friend."

"Oh, I see . . . ," Mary said. "You thought I was talking about your children, when I was just dreaming about how I'd raise my own little tots. I meant no disrespect."

Tears welled up in Mary's eyes, and she gazed at Eliza, begging forgiveness.

"Only a fool would take offense when none was intended," Eliza said, "and I'm not a fool. I'm the one who should apologize. I'm sure that no offense was meant."

"Thank you," Mary said. But it was obvious that she felt uncomfortable. In a few moments she finished with the shirt and announced, "My eyes are growing weary. You need the good light of day for proper sewing."

She folded the shirt and offered it to Eliza for her inspection in a very professional manner. Eliza took it, studied the holes in the elbows.

The stitching was marvelous. Mary hadn't just patched the worn-out elbows, she'd used her thread to weave the cloth back together to form a perfect whole. The new thread wasn't quite the same color as the old, and the new would be stronger, but the effect almost looked like magic.

"I can't believe it," Eliza said, wishing that she had enough money to hire Mary to do all of her stitching. "It looks as good as new."

Mary chuckled. "That's what the queen used to say."

Eliza did a double take. "You were a seamstress for the queen?"

"At Windsor Castle, until I left for better parts," Mary said.

There was a time when Eliza would have sought someone like Mary as an ally, when she would have courted her favor in order to gain a connection. As the queen's seamstress, Mary would have had the royal ear on nearly a daily basis. But out here in the wilderness, a royal connection was worthless. It would be better to know someone who was friends with the Cheyenne—or a wizardess with thread and needle.

"Thank you so much," Eliza said, and she rose up and hugged the woman.

"It was nothing, Sister Gadd," Mary said. "I see the way of it. I'm all alone in the world, but you've got your beautiful children to carry, and it's bound to weary you down to the bone. I'll come back in the morning and help you fix up the clothes for the small ones."

Late that night, Eliza stayed up with cranky babies. Isaac and Daniel were both developing the croup. Eliza felt sure that it was from want of proper nourishment. Her breasts had gone dry. She was getting to the end of her childbearing years, and she suspected that they would never be full again.

The camp didn't move that day. The plot to double-team the oxen had failed. So Eliza searched through the camp for some woman that she might hire as a wet nurse, but that proved problematic. Eliza had no money to pay anyone with. The best that she might offer was a promise.

But as she searched the camp, she found that that was the least of her problems. Most of the women leant sympathetic ears. Many of them wept to hear of her concern. But with so much walking, nearly all of the women had gone as dry as Eliza. There were only two women who could still give milk at all, and they didn't have enough to spare for a pair of boys who were just shy of two years old. There were newborn babes in greater need.

She could see her boys failing in health. It had been only a few days since she'd lost her milk, but both boys had begun to lose weight. The small rations provided for infants—six ounces of flour per day—wasn't enough to sate their hunger. Both boys were becoming congested and developing a croup, like their father.

So Eliza did what she could. Mary came and helped sew that morning, and afterward Eliza left the boys with Jane and went out to forage with Ann and Mary. In some places along the Platte, wild grapes and plums could be found, but the river was still so swollen that the women could only look longingly out toward the islands. Eliza searched in vain for wild strawberries during the day. She only hoped once the camp got underway again, better provisions might be found.

Eliza stripped some grains off of wild buffalo grass. The kernels were hard enough to break a tooth, but Eliza imagined that if she let them soak a couple of days, they might provide some nourishing sprouts.

Mary used a spoon to dig up a pile of bulbs of wild garlic that she found by a stream, and when she got back to camp, she passed out the excess to other families. That night Ann gave Eliza a little buffalo jerky that she'd bought from the Omahas. Eliza mixed in a little salt and made a special broth with it for her babies. Garlic was supposed to be good for the croup.

She made enough for everyone, and it was the best dinner they'd had in days. Eliza sat beside the fire that night, listening to the Oakey girl sing, gazing up at the stars, and she could not quite recall when she'd ever felt so content.

She'd had friends in England, women who sometimes came to tea. But this wasn't the same. They were mostly gossips, middle-class women who hoped to be thought of as upper-crust, and the tea parties always felt more like a duel for one's life instead of a pleasant afternoon with friends.

But here in the camp, as each passing hour seemed a little darker, a little more desperate, Eliza found that the folks around her were pulling together in a way that she'd never seen before. For the first time in her life, she had friends.

So many of these people were the poorest of the poor, stunted and uneducated, but Eliza found that she was liking them more than if they had been born to the gentry.

I'm becoming one of them, she thought. It was a disturbing realization, so she told herself, *I must fight against it.*

That night, Daniel awakened, crying from hunger and general distress; Eliza took him outside the tent so he wouldn't wake the others, and she bounced him on her hip and tried to sing him to sleep.

The skies above the prairie were as clear as could be, and in the cold high air, for she was at a much higher elevation than she'd ever been in England, the stars shone with a fury that Eliza had never seen. The River of Heaven lingered above her like a net of diamonds. The moon was not yet up.

She heard deep voices and went to the campfire. Willie and the other captains spoke in hushed voices, plotting how to get the handcart company moving.

The only other sound was the chirp of night birds and the distant howls of wolves.

Eliza listened to the captains for awhile but didn't hear their plan, only the comforting sound of their voices. With eyes gritty from sleep, she at last went to bed herself.

In the morning, the captains sprung their plan.

Prayer meeting was held at eight, and after singing "How Firm a Foundation," Captain Atwood had each captain speak. The captains reminded the saints of the terrible predicament that they were in and the need that they now had for every man, woman, child, and animal to focus their energies upon the task of moving as quickly as possible. They explained that the Lord would be willing to help them, but said that in order to receive God's blessings they had to purge themselves of their weaknesses. They urged the saints to greater righteousness, begging them to put aside their grumbling, their complaints, their contentions and hard feelings toward one another, and their pilfering, and to try to let their own good feelings toward one another increase and more properly align with the spirit of God.

Each of the captains—Chislett, Savage, Siler, and Woodward—expanded upon the thoughts of the other, each becoming louder, more fervent, and more emphatic.

Eliza had never been to a meeting that felt more scripted. She sat waiting for the punch line, fearing that she might be it, for certainly she had been one to grumble.

Brother Atwood spoke fifth, exhorting the saints with great force to repent and begging everyone to attend to their duties and to take whatever direction the captains might feel inspired to give them. He asked for each person to sustain their captains as they had done when the captains were first called to the position, by the raising of the right hand. He then asked that each person keep his hand raised so that they might get an accurate count. Of course, everyone voted to sustain the church leaders.

Eliza knew that the hook had been set.

As soon as the vote was over, Captain Atwood began talking of the need for sacrifice among the people. He pointed out how Christ showed the way by sacrificing his own life for his people. He said, "Now, if we are to become like him, we must be willing to surrender all that we have to help sustain Captain Willie in his calling.

"We may ask hard things of you. We don't have the oxen we need to pull our wagons. That means that, as we did in Iowa, we will have to ask you to carry wheat on your carts again. We'll ask some of you to carry a hundred pounds, but others may need to put four or five hundred pounds back upon their carts, or to add tents or other provisions. We would ask that you bear it gladly and without murmuring."

Among the crowd, Eliza heard gasps from some folks at the thought of bearing such a load.

"The savior promised us that he can lighten our loads," Captain

Atwood said. "He said, 'Take my yoke upon you, for my load is easy, and my burden is light.' "

He then turned to Captain Siler's people, those who belonged to the independent wagon train, and said, "I call upon you now at this time to consecrate all that you have toward the building up of Zion, and to the benefit of the church in general. This means that you will need to give up your wagons and your teams, to help haul provisions for the camp. It means that we may need to take your extra belongings and dump them on the plains. It means that many of you who have been riding in wagons or merely been walking beside them will now need to help pull handcarts, if possible. Or you may be asked to give up your seat on the wagons altogether, for the benefit of the sick or elderly.

"Will you do it?" he begged, his voice rising, encouraging them to meet his challenge. "Will you help become saviors upon mount Zion, saviors to these your brothers and sisters? Will you help the children, the infirm, and those dear old folks whose gray heads are bowed with age?"

Almost, Eliza thought that they would rise up and shout in chorus, "Yes, we will do it!" I'm not even a Mormon, she realized, and I would do it.

But not one of the folk in the independent wagons said yes. Instead, they stared down at the ground or off into the distance, avoiding the eyes of their leaders. Their faces were stony and pale.

One old woman said, "We didn't spend everything we own to buy these wagons just so that we could walk."

Several others in the independent wagons said, "Yes," or "Amen" or merely grunted in agreement.

Eliza knew what they were really saying. "We aren't dumb enough to die for your mistakes."

19

The Crossing

In the end, Captain Willie got no consideration from the independent wagon company.

He made his own plea, after Captain Atwood had failed. Willie started out with a joke. "You know," he said, "for the past four years, while I was laboring on my mission in England, I tried to follow the scriptural admonition to 'Waste and wear yourself out in the service of the Lord.' I was hoping that when I got released from my service, I could take a fine holiday at last. . . ." Then he just looked at a handcart and shook his head as if struggling to refrain from cursing, and the crowd laughed.

He preached and pleaded. He felt the Holy Ghost in the meeting, like a clear fire burning in his bosom. He knew that the power of his testimony was carried to the spirits of those who heard him speak.

But not one man, woman, or child in the independent wagon company volunteered the use of an ox or offered to help pull a handcart a dozen feet. Not one worn-out sock was discarded to make way for bags of flour for the handcart pioneers.

It was a good plan. If a mule can no longer pull a plow through rocky ground, you find a fresh mule. Those in the wagon company were the only fresh mules to be had.

Such preaching had worked before. At the beginning of the journey, Peder and Lena Mortensen had had their own wagon, but seeing the needs of the saints, the cripple had given up his comfortable ride and was now letting his sons pull him and his daughter in handcarts. He was setting a fine example.

Captain Willie tried not to develop any hard feelings for the rest of the folks in the wagon train. Several handcart pioneers had already passed away from hardship. Captain Willie was asking the rest of the independent wagon company to put themselves in a precarious position. *If I were in their shoes,* he thought, *and I knew that I was risking the life of my wife and children, I'm not sure that I could follow my own admonition.*

The problem was that Captain Willie couldn't not feel badly.

Christ had told his disciples that by losing their lives in the service of others, they would find life eternal. But those who sought to save their own lives would lose them. *What does that say about these folks in the independent wagons?* he wondered.

It means that not one of them is a true saint. It means that I'm doing a disservice to the church to bring them west. I might as well be carting in gamblers and fornicators and dancing girls from New Orleans as these folks. I'd be better off carrying sacks of dung across the prairie, for at least dung would nourish our gardens.

But I dare not give up on them yet, he thought. *The scriptures don't allow us to give up on a man. Perhaps if I only knew the right words to soften their hearts I could change their minds. Or maybe at the right moment they'll repent. Perhaps when they see enough suffering, these folks will get down off their fine wagons and lend a hand.*

Oh that I were an angel, he thought, *and could have the wish of my heart, to cry repentance to every people.* He wondered if perhaps he just wasn't eloquent enough to turn their hearts; or perhaps he lacked the charm needed or was not strong enough in the spirit.

What I need, he reasoned, *is someone who can act as a proper mouthpiece for the Lord.* Captain Willie knelt and prayed.

Atwood was the best speaker in camp, Willie knew. The people loved him. But they didn't love him more than their own lives. They'd proved that yesterday.

So for now, he could only go to his backup plan. He asked each family to carry another hundred pounds of flour on their carts. Some carried two hundred or more. Brother James Hurren put another five hundred pounds on his cart and offered to carry two sick children who couldn't walk. For that, Captain Willie prayed for God's blessing on the good man.

So the day was spent unloading flour and preparing for the rest of the journey. Many of the handcarts were in poor shape, and these had to be repaired. Tin cups were flattened and nailed over the hubs to keep out dust, or bound around failing axles to lend them strength. Bootstraps were cut into lengths and used to tie the iron wheel rims to the wheels. Precious slabs of bacon, bars of soap, and cow balm were used to lubricate the wheels.

Afterward, Captain Willie went himself and tried yoking up some of the wild cattle to the wagons. Breaking a wild cow was similar to breaking a horse. It was a task that should be handled slowly, in days or weeks. But they would need to get the animals broken in a day.

The task proved to be nearly impossible. Cattle don't learn as fast as a horse does. Normally, a wild ox would begin training for the yoke as a calf and at first would be put with a team of more experienced animals that would remain calm even if the calf became excited or angry.

But when he yoked the wild cows together, they only excited one another. A cow that might have just fought the yoke would see another bucking and suddenly would begin bawling and kicking in a frenzy. Some young cattle seemed determined to split the axletrees on the wagons, or break their own necks trying.

Many calves were still bulls. A proper ox would be allowed to grow for two or three years, then be castrated, in order to make it tame. But these bull calves seemed to have pure fire running through their veins.

The day grew hot and humid, and Captain Willie found that trying to break the wild cattle was fruitless. He had only two trained oxen that could be put to each team, and he needed six.

But the next day, the camp got up early, and by noon the cattle were yoked and the handcarts moved forward.

It was by far the hardest day that the group had yet endured. They were heading into the sand hills of Nebraska, an area of endless rolling dunes where the sparse grass barely held to the soil. With every footfall, a man would sink four inches into the ground, ripping out the grass, so that the road soon turned sandy. Both the handcarts and the wagons were too heavy to travel easily over such a bad road, and when the company came to a halt that night, after traveling only ten miles, he found that many a hard man had fainted in his tracks during the day.

But camp was set, and guards posted, and after dinner Captain Willie's spirits lifted a little. The handcart company was on the move now, though the road ahead might prove torturous.

At dawn a man rode from the West, hell-bent for leather. The guards spotted him five miles out. His horse foamed at the mouth, and the fellow's eyes were wide with fear. He kept a Colt revolver in one hand. He wore a faded army shirt in blue and leather pants, and he spent as much time looking behind him as he did ahead.

"Injuns!" he began shouting when he was a mile off. "Injuns! Injuns." When he was close enough to the camp, he cried, "They wiped out a wagon train, just up the trail!"

When he reached camp, Captain Willie went out to meet him. The man, a fellow in his late twenties, pulled off his hat to reveal unkempt hair and gasping, kept saying, "Injuns—just up the trail! They wiped out a wagon train!"

Captain Willie steeled himself. He knew of a couple of wagon trains that might be ahead of him. According to Porter Rockwell, Bishop Reed Smoot's train was a couple of days ahead, and Porter Rockwell's folks were traveling with him. "What wagon train?"

"I don't rightly know," the fellow said. "Just a couple of wagons. The leader was a fellow named Margetts, Thomas Margetts."

There were gasps from the crowd. Captain Willie had known the Margetts intimately. Just about all of the saints in England had known them.

Thomas had once been a missionary serving under Captain Willie. When he was released from his call, he had immigrated to America.

But last December Captain Willie began to learn of certain infidelities. He'd sent a letter to church headquarters detailing Thomas's sins.

"Thomas Margetts?" Sister Gadd asked. "Of the Oxford Margetts? Susannah too?"

The soldier looked down to the ground. "I'm sorry, ma'am. She got taken by the redskins."

"And her children," Eliza demanded, "Ann, Thomas, Lorenzo?"

"They didn't have no children with 'em," the soldier said. "They left them in Utah. The other folks, the Cowdys, they had a baby, but she's dead by now," the soldier said. "The Cheyenne cut her belly open. She was covered with blood, whimpering just a little, when last I saw her.

Wasn't nothin' I could do. I could see that she wasn't long for this world. So I left her."

Sister Gadd's face went white, and she turned away with tears in her eyes and stumbled blindly, as if looking for someplace to run.

One of the older men from England asked, "What in the devil were the Margetts doing out here? They just immigrated to Utah a little over a year ago."

"They . . . got booted out of their church," the soldier said. "Didn't say why. I didn't know them well." He cast his eyes about, desperately, and said, "I haven't had but my own fears to gnaw on in the past two days. I'd be much obliged for a mouthful of food."

"Certainly," Captain Willie said, and he led the man into his tent to speak privately, followed by the other sub-captains.

Captain Willie didn't tell anyone that it was his testimony that had most likely gotten the Margetts kicked out of the church—which indirectly led to Thomas's death.

The soldier's name turned out to be Henry Boutcher. He had been discharged from service in Laramie only a few days before and met the Margetts traveling in company with the Cowdy family, heading back from Salt Lake City.

Boutcher now explained in private the details of how the Margetts had reaped their terrible fate. He told how he'd joined up with the train, heading for Saint Louis. He'd gone out with Thomas to hunt buffalo, and they made a kill. Thomas had filled a pot with fat, which he hoped to use to grease the wheels of his wagon. He took it back, thinking to melt it down, and return with more buckets, while Boutcher finished butchering the buffalo.

When Boutcher returned to camp, he saw immediately that a wagon was on fire, its back half completely engulfed in flames. The horses and mules were gone, and a large group of riders was racing off into the distance. The camp was a mess. Clothing and goods had been pulled from the wagon, shirts and bloomers left scattered on the prairie. Thomas Margetts was dead on the ground, laid out beside Cowdy and the baby. There were no bullet holes in the men, though Thomas had an arrow in his thigh. Instead, it looked as if the men's heads had been cracked open by a war club. The baby lay crying in its own blood by her father's side.

The Cowdy woman was propped up against a little ridge nearby. Her dress had been torn open, exposing her breasts, and the lower portion of her dress was gone, leaving her bare legs splayed wide. She'd been beaten before she was raped, and by the way her tongue lolled out, it appeared that she'd been strangled at the end.

"She's the lucky one," Captain Savage said when he heard it. "Susannah Margetts is going to wish that she could trade places with her."

Captain Willie bit his lip. With his whole soul, he wished that he could find a way to save her.

"How far ahead are they?" he asked.

"Maybe sixty miles," Boutcher said.

"I thought the cavalry was hunting these butchers down," Captain Atwood said. "They're supposed to be two hundred miles west of here."

Captain Willie worried. It sounded as if their enemies were multiplying. The Caldwell boy had said that Indians were driving the buffalo that stampeded through camp. With every passing moment, his tale sounded more and more likely. Captain Willie desperately wanted some counsel.

For the second time in as many days, Captain Willie went to his tent and prayed for the Lord to send him help.

The handcart company set off that day with heavy hearts, trudging through the sand, as Henry Boutcher rode hard toward Fort Kearney to warn the commander of the latest atrocities on the plains.

There was no end of the sand. It seemed to grow heavier and deeper with each step. The sun glared off of it, and many a man groaned in pain and frustration. Some folks, blinded by fatigue and hunger, began to wander astray, walking aimlessly, so weary that they did not hear the cries of those who called for them to return to the safety of the trail.

Sweat drenched Captain Willie's clothes by the time he called a halt that night. But for the first time in days, there was wood for the fires. Several men waded through the Platte for nearly half a mile to reach it, there on a sandbar far out in the river.

Captain Willie watched a dozen women head off after the men, the Hill sisters leading Eliza and several others to hunt for wild fruit. He thought of calling them back for fear of Indians, but didn't have the heart to. The women were just foraging in an effort to feed their babies.

For three more days the company traveled over sand hills, each night dropping off to sleep more tired than the night before, each day, rising later.

On the twelfth of September, Captain Atwood finally put a halt to it. Captain Willie tried letting people sleep until five, instead of the normal 4:00 a.m. But on this morning, nearly two hours after bugle call, the folks in one tent were still abed. So Captain Atwood pulled the tent pegs out, hitched the ties to the back of his mule, and gave it a slap on the rump. The mule took off running, dragging the tent behind it, accompanied by the astonished screams of the tents' inhabitants.

Suddenly there were twenty angry women squatting on the ground in their night clothes, clutching blankets over their breasts to hide their scanty attire.

"Hear ye, hear ye!" Captain Atwood cried. "Come one, come all.

See the women, beautiful women, from far corners of the world, all confessed to the vulgar gaze!"

The camp rang with peals of laughter, for Atwood sounded just like a hawker down on Holywell Street in London, where prostitutes handed out lurid etchings to reveal the unholy acts that they would perform.

"Please," one sister cried. "Show some decency. Put the tent back up!"

But Captain Willie had to shake his head. "Bugle call will be starting at four again from now on. The sun is up, and we should have been on the trail an hour ago. I can't give you any leeway. The lives of our children depend on you getting out of bed."

He turned and left, but Captain Willie fretted all day. Try as he might, he couldn't get the people to pull the handcarts more than a dozen miles through the sand. If there'd been enough oxen to haul the provisions, they'd have made eighteen or twenty miles easily, but it seemed that a man could not get the strength to pull these carts.

In part this was caused by a lack of food. But there was another problem: they were climbing toward the Rockies, and the air was growing thinner with every mile. These folks from England and Denmark had spent their lives at sea level. More and more, they were left gasping like fish out of water.

They drew near North Bluff Creek, where the Margetts and Cowdys had been attacked. Captain Willie suspected that no one else had found the bodies yet. He didn't want the women and children seeing the horrific scene that Boutcher had described, so he asked Joseph Elder to take a couple of men ahead and bury the remains.

Late that afternoon Joseph Elder came back and reported that the job was done—the bodies buried, the wagon pushed off into a small gully.

"The wolves and the buzzards didn't leave much to see," Joseph said. Yet horror showed plainly in his face.

When the camp passed the massacre site, Joseph Elder made sure that handcart train swung wide, and none of the immigrants noticed anything amiss.

The worry and the work combined to drain Captain Willie.

When they camped that night, he was so weary that he just wanted to lie down and die. But before he had a chance to do so, a guard shouted, "We've got visitors!"

He turned east and saw what he had been praying for: a "mouthpiece of the Lord" riding in a convoy of fine carriages.

Franklin D. Richards was young to be an apostle. He was a first cousin to Brigham Young and his family had been among the first that Brigham converted to the church—but his family ties had nothing to do with the reason he was called to the high position of apostle. At the age of thirty-five, he was a genuine phenomenon, a fireball. For several years he had presided over the church's missionary efforts in England, constantly publishing pamphlets and books, speaking to congregations, and arranging for the immigration of tens of thousands of new converts.

It was in this context that Captain Willie and Franklin D. Richards had developed a deep and abiding friendship.

Richards was one of the most handsome men that Captain Willie had ever seen, with thick wavy blond locks that looked as if they should have hung upon Zeus or Apollo, and blue eyes so piercing that they were almost mesmerizing. His fine bearing could have made him a legend on the stages in London or New York, and many a woman, upon seeing him, would grow flushed and light-headed. His easy manner of speech, his graciousness, his self-assurance and gentle voice inspired confidence in all who met him. When it came to swaying crowds or softening the hearts of evil men, the church had no equal.

More than that, Captain Willie accounted Richards as a close friend. Captain Willie had worked under the apostle's direction as a missionary in England.

God has sent me a David, Captain Willie thought, *just when I need to face my Goliath.*

The carriage that led the way was an ebony black with stallions chosen to match. In its wake came half a dozen older carriages and a pair of light wagons, each pulled by four fine horses or sturdy mules.

Richards had a host of missionaries with him, about twenty strong men returning from their labors in Europe, all dressed in suits.

"Brothers and Sisters, I congratulate you on making it this far on your journey," Franklin D. Richards said that night. He stood on the back of a wagon, with the half moon floating overhead in a sea of stars, while campfires lit him from underneath. "More importantly," he teased, "I congratulate you on the loss of your cattle."

The audience laughed tentatively to hear him make light of such a huge defeat.

"Many of you are a good deal thinner than when I last saw you in England. Though pound for pound you are less than you were, I don't think there's a man here who doesn't look twice the man that he was. Hard work, sunshine, pure water, and fresh air seem to be a tonic for a man. You're all getting your fill of these things.

"I know that you're worried about the road ahead. I want to put your minds at ease. I'll be hurrying on ahead to carry word of your plight to Salt Lake City, and I'll do all that I can to smooth the path before you.

"You're worried about food, and I can promise you that you can be at ease. I'll make sure to purchase what flour and bedding I can find at Fort Laramie, so that you may replenish your stock. It has been the practice with the handcart pioneers that we send wagons out to help on the last bit of the way, and so you will find food again at Fort Bridger.

"When you reach the Great Salt Lake, the prophet will come out to greet you himself, with open arms.

"But food is the easy part. You're also worried about the lateness of the season and the possibility of snow.

"But let me say this on the matter: this setback of yours, this loss of your cattle, will prove your salvation if you but hearken to and diligently obey the counsel we give you this day. Now, Captain Willie here has been placed in charge over you, and you are to listen to him . . ."

At this he paused and looked to the folk of the independent wagons, for as yet they had not agreed to consecrate their belongings to the benefit of their brethren. They cared far more for their grandmother's china and lace than for the lives of their brethren.

"If you will hearken to Willie's counsel, I promise you in the name of Israel's God and by the authority of the holy priesthood that no obstacle whatever shall come in the way of this camp. By your united faith and good works, with God being your helper, you can overcome all obstacles, whether it be the heat of the sun, the cold of snow, or hostile Indians that bar your way. The weather will be moderated for your benefit, and even if the Red Sea should interpose, you shall by your union of heart and mind and hand, walk through it like Israel of old, stepping through the watery deep and coming out dry-shod.

"The Lord will protect you, and not only will your children come through this alive, but also the old and frail, those whose white heads are bowed down with age."

At Richards's words, Captain Willie felt the spirit of the Lord ignite a fire in his heart, and he understood by the spirit things that Franklin D. Richards had not put to words. The very purpose of life, as the scriptures said, was to prove the souls of men, to see if they would do as the Lord commanded in the face of all obstacles. Certainly this journey would give these folks a chance to prove themselves as never before. If only his people would unite, become one in heart, living as the people of Zion should, nothing could stop them, for God would be with them. He looked about the camp, the fires of revelation burning in his bosom, and he saw many a man and woman weeping openly, tears streaming down their cheeks.

Richards continued, "By the spirit of the Lord, I feel assured that there will be some few trials ahead that will test your faith, trials that would test the faith of even the most stalwart prophets of old. You shall face challenges even like unto Abraham, and you must endure them as proof to God and the brethren that you have true grit. But if you hold true, you shall partake of God's blessings, even the blessings of Abraham.

"There are many who scoff at the handcart system. Nevertheless, it is the Lord's plan. Your journey, when people will hear of it, will first puzzle, and then astonish the nations, and the time will come when your very faithfulness will strike terror into the hearts of those who hear of it.

"So worry no more. I encourage you to live the principles of your religion, not only openly before the world, but privately in your own hearts, in your families, and in your intercourse with each other. I enjoin you to scorn all the trials and difficulties which might block your way and assure you that, as a result of such a course, you shall find favor with God and have the confidence of the brethren—things which are, in all events, of far more worth than all the gold, silver, and precious stones in the universe.

"Do as Captain Willie has asked you. Remember the covenants that you made at baptism, to live as Christ lived. Some men dream of having faith that will move a mountain, but they don't have the faith to draw a handcart. Some men dream of giving their lives in some grand sacrifice that will astonish the world, but they don't have the faith to give of their time little by little, day by day, in a way that only God would notice.

"Don't just dream of Zion. Make it a reality now. Keep the commandments. Give your lives, and you shall find life eternal."

The Holy Ghost was felt in its almighty and renovating power during the speech, and the people seconded his sentiments by a hearty "Amen" from time to time.

When Richards fell silent, he sat down and let his counselors speak, Daniel Spencer and Cyrus Wheelock. Each admonished the people to humble themselves and keep the commandments, and each bore fervent testimony to the truthfulness of the gospel and God's promises. Daniel Spencer reminded them of the blessing that they would receive if they did so and went so far as to promise that storms would part along the way. Wheelock went even further and promised that if they were faithful, not only would the elements be tempered, but "winter would turn to summer" for their benefit.

The apostle's every word, and every word of his counselors, was like a hammer blow, chipping away at the flinty hearts of the people, encouraging them to try God's plan, to divest themselves of their worldly goods and spend their energy helping one another. Their words had the tendency to build up, strengthen, and encourage the people and seemed to electrify their hearers.

Yet Captain Willie wondered if they had really heard, if the "Amens" would be followed by deeds. What would the independent wagons do? Would they toss out their riches and use their wagons to carry supplies? Would they get off their lazy behinds and walk, letting the sick and feeble take their seats?

Or was the apostle merely preaching to the stones?

That night, after the speeches, when the only sounds on the prairie were the gentle snores of the pioneers and the burble of the Platte as the river flowed past, Franklin D. Richards sat in a circle with Captain Willie and the missionaries around a dying campfire, where coals glowed a ruddy orange as they cast off the last of their warmth.

"I'd advise you to move your people to the south side of the river first thing in the morning," the apostle said, staring into the fire as if in vision. "It sounds as if all of the Cheyenne's attacks are centered here on the north bank. At the very least, you'll be closer to the Smoot and Rockwell trains."

It was sound thinking, Captain Willie knew. The south side of the river had a trail that was seldom used, for it was harder on the animals. Even farther south, on the South Fork of the Platte River, was a trail that led from the States out to California and Oregon. Normally, the Mormons took the north side of the river to avoid confrontations with the "gentiles" heading for California, many of whom might be hostile. The army often patrolled the California trail, but the patrols generally ignored the trails on the North Platte River. Captain Willie figured that they did so mainly because they felt more sympathy for the gentiles. But it might also have had to do with practicality. The truth was that the Mormons tended to have good relations with the Indians, or "Lamanites" as many preferred to call them, for the Mormons believed that the Indians hailed from a noble lineage and that the time would come when the Lamanites would find favor with the Lord.

"I'll be happy to take the south trail," Captain Willie said, "as soon as I can find a safe place to ford. The river is still fairly high after last week's flood."

"We can cross right here," Richards said.

"We'll have to check for quicksand," Captain Willie said.

"I feel quite confident that you won't encounter quicksand," Richards said. "The Lord is with us in this. But if it makes you feel easier, I'll cross with my missionaries first, to prove the trail."

Captain Willie nodded in approval.

"We're in a hurry," the apostle said. "We'll be racing back to Salt Lake in order to make certain that you get your needed supplies. I would be grateful if you could have a calf slaughtered for us, so that we won't have to hunt along the trail."

Captain Willie considered. Giving away a calf was a hard thing, but then he recalled how in the Bible, when the poor widow fed the prophet, her own small stores of food were multiplied day after day. Surely, if he gave the apostle a calf, the Lord would repay him sevenfold. "I'll have the fattest one in the herd slaughtered for you first thing in the morning."

"Thank you," Richards said. "That would be greatly appreciated."

"You know," a young missionary named Joseph Young said, "we could probably give these folks a couple of our wagons and double up in the carriages. It would take a huge load off of them."

"And it would slow us down," Richards argued.

"Not if some of us missionaries stayed behind," Joseph suggested. "Half of us could help pull the handcarts. I'd be willing to stay."

Richards shot him a patronizing smile. Joseph Young was nobody, a young Welsh convert to the church, only twenty-three years old. His only claim to fame was that he happened to have the same last name as the prophet. "I've thought about that, but the Cheyenne are on the war path, and they're taking out every small wagon train they come across. If we drop any wagons from our train, cut down on the number of men in our group, we'll invite attack."

"Then just leave me and a couple of other strong men behind to help pull handcarts. You can take a few cripples with you, if you just need warm bodies."

Richards stared hard at Young, the anger rising plainly in his face. He looked as if he would shoot back a retort, but thought better of it. Instead, he turned his full attention to Captain Willie.

"These people don't need our help," he said, his eyes riveted on Willie, though he was obviously answering Joseph. "They have the means that they need to save themselves and must be given every opportunity to do so."

Thus he dismissed Joseph, and asked Captain Willie, "Tell me, you said that there was a great deal of murmuring in the camp of late. Is there someone that you see as the source of the trouble?"

The finest calf in the herd was butchered at dawn. The apostle and missionaries had a fine breakfast of steak, and then the excess meat was loaded into one of the wagons.

A prayer meeting was held at 7:00 a.m., but it was not the normal meeting. First of all, rather than meeting at the center of the circle of tents, Franklin D. Richards insisted that it be moved outside of camp, about a hundred yards to the west. There the saints congregated, and Richards delivered a powerful sermon about the need for the immigrants to support their leaders. He spoke about the great evils of murmuring against the church, of spreading dissension, of challenging their leaders' every word.

Then he turned, eyes blazing like the barrels of a Colt, and said, "Levi Savage, step forward."

Savage's face drained of its color, and he stumbled toward the center of the circle.

Richards said, "I've heard that you don't approve of the handcart system and that you've been preaching against it. I've heard that you've publicly warned these folks to turn back. You, sir, are a malcontent, and the deed was heinously done. I propose to put you on trial for your membership in the Lord's church."

Savage was totally unprepared. Captain Willie almost felt sorry for him. He looked like a child being spanked for something he didn't know that he'd done wrong.

"I beg your pardon, Elder Richards," Savage said. "It's not that I'm against the handcart system. It was initiated by the Lord's anointed, by the prophet himself, and from what I've seen, I believe it is superior in just about every way. I spoke against coming, but not because I'm against the system. The lateness of the season was my only concern."

Richards looked to Captain Willie. "Have I been misinformed?"

Captain Willie stood. He hadn't meant for it to go this far. Savage was a good man. Captain Willie felt that Richards was being a bit harsh. "No, you haven't. He spoke against coming, and later on he railed on me for letting Captain Siler drive his teams among the handcarts."

"I never meant no harm!" Savage said, tears springing to his eyes. "I swear to God, I meant no harm."

"Yet you've done harm," the apostle said. "You've done great harm. You spoke against your leader; you did it in a public forum; and in doing so you undermined his authority and the faith that others had entrusted in him. It is because of you that this camp has come under condemnation by the Lord."

The apostle stared hard at Levi Savage, then glanced toward Joseph Young. Captain Willie suddenly understood what this was about. His own argument with Savage roughly paralleled the apostle's problems with Joseph. Savage was a frontiersman, one of the best on the plains. He was also completely without guile and believed that speaking the truth was a virtue even when another man might recognize the value in holding his tongue. In short, he was just like Joseph, who felt that he too had some right to question his leaders.

So, Willie realized, the apostle was going to make an example of Savage.

"There are others who have questioned the virtue of leaving so late in the season," Richards said. "I spoke with John Taylor on this very matter," Richards cited another of the apostles, "and told him that I would take full responsibility for it and that he could wash his hands of it, if he wished." He said this with a tone of pride, for it was

Richards who had published the pamphlets throughout Europe that encouraged the saints to come to Zion by handcart; up to this point, the experiment had been a rousing success. "But you, Mr. Savage, are in error. There is a time for stating your opinions, in the appropriate meetings, when offering counsel to your leaders. But once a decision has been made by aid of the spirit of the Lord, the time for giving counsel is at an end! The hand of the Lord lies heavy on this camp for its divisive spirit. Unless you repent in all sincerity . . ." He did not need to threaten further. By calling Levi Savage "Mr." instead of brother or captain or elder, he had symbolically stripped him of his membership.

Savage was already reduced to tears. He stood, trembling, hat in his hands, as if he stared spiritual oblivion in the face, a death more sure and final than the mere separation of the body from the spirit. He feared it more than death. Why should he not? If indeed The Church of Jesus Christ of Latter-day Saints was the true church, the only organization that held the authority of God to perform the ordinances necessary for salvation, then where else could Savage turn for hope?

Nowhere. He might cling to the remnants of his testimony for a time, might struggle to remain faithful, but if he was removed from the church, then like a coal taken from the heart of a fire, in time his testimony would cool, his faith dwindle and finally die.

"I'm sorry," he said, staring at the ground and shaking his head from side to side. "I'm so sorry."

For a long hour the apostle continued his admonitions, drilling the point home, making a public example of Savage, until his tearful confession was found acceptable.

At the end of the meeting, Richards told the group, "Now we will cross to the south side of the Platte," and he got into his carriage and drove it into the water, and the handcart pioneers grabbed their possessions and followed.

The brown flood of the Platte seethed, and at times the horses waded up to their bellies, walking tentatively lest they flounder in deep water or trip over a stone. But at last the carriages and wagons made it through without damage.

On the far shore, Franklin D. Richards stopped, and for the rest of the day he watched as the handcart pioneers tried to forge the river.

It was the custom that every child over the age of five walk beside the handcarts, but the water was swift and ran two to three feet in depth most of the way. Thus, the smaller children could easily get swept away. So the parents put the little ones into the handcarts, then struggled through themselves. At times, the flood came up above the boxes of the handcarts, and carts would begin to float away. Lest the family bedding get wet, the women carried it on their shoulders, while the men struggled to haul their bags of wheat on one shoulder while pulling their handcarts along.

The Platte was more than a mile wide at this point. The arduous crossing took the whole day, and some men and women, those with many children, had to make multiple trips.

As Joseph Young watched, his jaw grew tight, and he asked Richards, "Are you sure that we shouldn't go out there and help?"

"And ruin a thirty dollar suit in this muddy water?" Richards jested. Then he grew more serious. "No, this is a test of their faith to see if these people will follow the will of the Lord. In the days to come, these people will have to endure harder things than this."

20

The Birth of Despair

After slogging through mud for a mile and slipping barefoot on slimy stones, Baline climbed up out of the Platte, chilled to the bone, her dress nearly ruined from the mud. She was exhausted and sopping wet.

She had helped Emily Wall pull her brother through the raging flood. Twice she had lost her footing and found herself floating off, and twice Emily had reached out to save her. Emily told her to cling to the handcart's handle, and once Emily made a game of pulling her in the deepest water, saying "I'm a whale, and you're a whale rider," and then she made whale noises.

By the time the two girls reached the far shore, some folks were already setting up camp. Everyone would need to change clothes and let their shoes dry by the fire.

Baline and Emily dragged the handcart up onto the bank, and Joseph Wall tenderly climbed out. He had been sick for two weeks and still was running a fever. But at least he could feed himself now, and he could walk from the handcart to the tent.

Amid the commotion as the saints set camp, the apostle and the missionaries bade the handcart pioneers farewell, and the pioneers gave the Hosanna Shout, the men crying, "Hosanna! Hosanna! Hosanna!" and throwing their hats while the women waved bandannas and white kerchiefs in the air.

It was all very thrilling. Baline had almost never seen an apostle.

On previous occasions, she did not understand English well enough to decipher a word that they said, but this time she had understood almost everything that Franklin D. Richards had spoken. His words had stirred her and made her long to be a better person. She recalled the promises he'd made, and she longed to earn the reward promised by the Lord.

As she stood peering at the apostle, who waved out the back of his black carriage, a man harrumphed, "Well, don't they make a picture, riding off in their fine carriages!"

She looked up at the fellow. It was John Chislett, one of the captains of a hundred.

Then he turned to where the men pulled their handcarts, still struggling through the wide Platte, while women with babes in their arms walked along, their children nervously clutching onto their skirts. "And don't we make a fine picture."

It was hard not to see the disparity, but Baline kept her mouth shut. She did not want to murmur about a servant of the Lord.

But Chislett made her wonder.

She stood gazing out across the wide river and saw eagerness and despair in the eyes of people in equal measure.

Poor old Father Haley, for the English all called him "father," was splashing through the water, reeling from fatigue. He had dropped his hat, so that his white hair blazed in the sun. It had only been two weeks since he had spent a night lost in the storm, so blinded by hunger and fatigue that he had lost his way. He looked even worse now. He would head southeast a few steps, stare bleary eyed toward the shore, then turn southwest, cutting through the flood at a slant, tripping over every stone.

I should go help him, Baline thought, and she took a hesitant step toward the river, just as he reached the banks. He stumbled forward and fell facedown, half in the water. A woman behind him shouted for help, but by the time that Baline got there, she could see that old Father Haley had stopped breathing.

A couple of men each took an arm and dragged him up onto the riverbank. "He's cold as a fish," one man said. "Let's get him over to the fire."

They hoped to revive him, but Father Haley just lay, his face frozen into a grimace of pain, and squinted at the ground until Captain Willie threw a blanket over him, hiding his corpse.

Baline stared in horror. She had never watched a person die, never seen someone succumb to that final moment of death.

That evening as the sun was slowly setting, she went to Father Jens, who was taking his evening stroll outside camp. He walked along, contemplating the scriptures, exercising his mind more than his body. Baline asked, "Apostle Richards, he said that if we kept the commandments, even our aged folk would get through alive."

Jens could still not understand a word of English, so he asked, "Are you certain he said this? Maybe you misunderstood."

"I know what he said."

"Well, that old gentleman has been sick for weeks. Perhaps his death is the Lord's way of telling us that it was his time to go."

But that didn't satisfy Baline. The apostle had promised that even the aged would survive. Yet the apostle's carriage could still be seen on the horizon when Brother Haley expired. That seemed wrong.

But the apostle had also promised that the Lord would test them. Maybe Father Haley's death was part of that test.

Baline said, "I felt the spirit when the apostle spoke, burning in me like fire. Didn't you?"

"Yes," Brother Jens said thoughtfully. A mile in the distance, a condor soared through the sky, its black wings vast and majestic. It was only the second one that Baline had seen on the trek. *It has to be the king of all birds*, she thought. It dropped suddenly to the ground, as if to eat something that Baline could not see, and she lost sight of it in the tall golden grass.

"Then that means that his prophecy was true, right?" Baline said. "Yet Brother Haley is dead."

"Perhaps," Jens said, "we are the ones that are not true. The favor of the Lord can only be won by our righteousness."

Suddenly she recalled Captain Chislett's cutting remark. Surely the Lord could not condone such talk. Could it be that the Lord was angry because there were still those that murmured in the camp?

Or was it something else? Captain Willie had wanted the independent wagons to join the handcart company, and they had refused. Perhaps their selfishness was the problem.

If we do not have the favor of the Lord, Baline wondered, *what is to become of us?*

That night, a chill wind swept down from the west, colder than any wind that she'd felt all summer. Baline lay awake for a long time, shivering and worrying. The apostle had said that the Lord would temper the elements for their benefit, that winter would be turned to summer. But less than twelve hours later, Baline could feel winter in the air. It was as if the Lord was cursing them instead of blessing them.

Wolves were howling out on the plains, and every few minutes she would hear the shriek of a burrow owl as it hunted on the wing, trying to startle mice out of the tall grass. It was an odd sound, so high in pitch that it was almost like the squeaking of a bat.

The tent fluttered like sails in the cold wind and trembled.

Winter is coming.

Mice are dying, she thought as she heard the screech owls cry over and over again, and she tried to imagine what it would be like to be as small as a mouse, with death hunting you on the wing.

The next morning the camp would have left at first light, but they had to bury old Father Haley. The ground was so cold that it had the slightest touch of frost, and the wind kept battering them. A hole was dug, a service held, the wind carrying the words away from the speakers so that Baline could not hear, and the camp rolled out at eight thirty.

They had a long day of it, the cool dry wind in their faces, and began to travel through a land devoid of trees. Joseph Wall was still too sick to walk, and so Baline helped Emily pull the handcart. By the end of the day, her back ached and her calves felt like stone. She was far too tired to play. Too tired even to think.

That night there was no shelter from the wind, and it would not stop.

The following morning, they left camp at shortly after dawn but had not traveled a mile when another elderly saint died, an Englishman named Turner. They did not have time to stop, so they dumped his body into the sick wagon.

The road was rough and sandy. The brisk wind blasted sand into people's faces, and Baline's lips grew as rough as tree bark. By noon everyone was exhausted, so Captain Willie let them rest as they buried Brother Turner.

"Our old are beginning to die," Baline heard one grandmother say, but Baline hoped that it was not the "beginning" of anything.

The land was changing. A few days before, the prairie had been flat for as far as the eye could see. But now there were rugged brown hills off to the west, and the ground was swelling up to meet them. Everywhere there were rocks, and the ground now had a crust upon it, so that when you walked, it sounded as brittle as dry bones.

The handcart company was forced to leave the river after the burial, for the riverbank became sheer cliffs dropping down into the water. The saints had to pull their carts up a steep hill. The supply wagons had to be double-teamed. Four cattle were harnessed to wagons normally pulled by two, and then they dragged the wagons for several miles up the steep trail. When they finished, the same cattle were herded back down the trail to bring the rest of the wagons. Since the best of the oxen had been lost, the going was particularly slow.

While the men worked to get the wagons up the cliff, some Indians came walking up from the brush down beside the river. Baline joined the crowd as the Indians conversed with Joseph Elder, using a combination of sign language and broken Omaha. The Indians looked much like others that she had seen. They wore loincloths made of deer hide to cover their bottoms and had simple brown moccasins. Their chests and faces were painted with bits of tan and white. It wasn't war paint, Baline decided, but hunting paint that would make them blend in with the trees and grass.

"They say that they're Arapahos," Joseph Elder told Captain

Willie. The three Indians flashed their hands and pointed east, uttering a few words. "They say that the Sioux and the Cheyenne have a large war party to the east and that they attacked a big wagon train five days ago. They say that the Cheyenne will kill us all if we are not careful."

"What do you think?" Captain Willie asked Joseph Elder.

"These men look like Sioux to me. I think that they're trying to pull one over on us."

"Ask them what happened at this big attack," Captain Willie suggested. "How many whites were wounded? How many killed?"

The Indians spoke among themselves for a bit. They could not answer the question, so they suggested, "You come to sleep next to our camp. We will protect you."

Captain Willie looked skeptical, scratched his chin. "Where is your camp?"

"On the far side of the river," the men answered.

Captain Willie spoke softly with his leaders. Even if he had trusted these Indians, Baline knew he wasn't willing to risk another crossing of the Platte. The river narrowed here between the hills. The water was swift and deep. He told the Indians, "That is too far out of our way."

"But the Sioux and the Cheyenne will kill you!"

Captain Willie said calmly. "We have many guns and much powder, and we have sabers. If the Cheyenne come, we will kill them all."

The three Indians shook their heads in dismay, as if Captain Willie was a fool.

Captain Willie made a gift of some tobacco to the three, brought just for this purpose, and then sent them on their way.

The pioneers traveled another dozen miles before dark, climbing through narrow canyons. Hills rose high above them, and for the first time in days, the wind abated just a little. Joseph Elder rode ahead of the camp and killed two buffalo. The immigrants dragged themselves to the kill and pitched their tents near an old buffalo wallow that had filled with water, but it was foul and stale, unfit for man or beast.

Finally the wind stopped altogether.

When everyone got to camp, Captain Willie said, "These two buffalo, I feel confident, are a blessing from the Lord. We gave the apostle a little meat yesterday, and the Lord has repaid us four-fold today." It was true that they had made only two kills, but two large buffalo far outweighed one calf, so the Lord truly had blessed them four-fold. The settlers feasted that night, with each person in camp getting nearly two pounds of meat.

But not all was well. The fear of a Cheyenne attack was strong. Captain Willie ordered the men to set a triple guard and then made sure that all of the cattle were hobbled together in the midst of the camp, encircled by handcarts and wagons, and then tied to the wagons. There was no feed for the animals to eat, no water for them to drink. The camp was set on a flat where there would be no bushes or rocks for the Cheyenne to hide behind while they crept close.

It was obvious that Captain Willie was preparing for battle, and the camp was subdued. They did not sing hymns for fear that their voices might carry over the prairie and reveal their location.

They ate early in the evening, and Captain Willie had the fires out well before nightfall. Then a prayer meeting was held in the deepening gloom. "We'll keep it short tonight, folks. We're all tired and need our rest. But I've got to warn you. I feel uneasy. The horn will blow at three, and we'll depart within the hour thereafter, with no stops for breakfast."

One English settler asked, "Why are you so uneasy? There were only three Indians."

"We're getting near Blue Water," Captain Willie said. "The army murdered nearly three hundred Sioux here last year at this time. With the weather changing, you can bet that it will stir up bad memories. There's some among the Sioux that will be looking for vengeance."

The full moon rose shortly after sunset, huge and golden at first, then fading to silver as it climbed in the sky. The stars shone by the thousands, and out over the fields, where the summer grass had been burned to white, it seemed that it was as clear as day.

Dinner didn't satisfy Baline that night. She'd used too much energy pulling the handcarts up the steep hills. Even with a belly full of buffalo, she felt that she must be as hungry as the cattle. After prayer she lay in her bedroll, snuggling next to little Niels.

What was it that Porter Rockwell had told them? Baline tried to recall. The Cheyennes wouldn't want to attack under a full moon. It would be too easy for the saints to see them coming, too easy to shoot back. That knowledge gave her some comfort.

Baline laid in her tent for a long time, listening to Brother Madsen snore, the wind flapping the door of the tent. Out on the prairie she heard a lone wolf howl and wondered if it was a real wolf or one of the Cheyennes. A night bird shrieked.

She had just dozed off when she heard the cry of "Indians! Indians!"

The bugle sounded; someone fired a gun.

There were cries of terror within the tent as women grabbed their babies and tried to hide in corners.

Father Jens leapt up and rushed out the tent flap with nothing more than a hatchet, wearing his cotton nightshirt and a sleeping cap.

For some reason that Baline could not fathom, she thought it would be safer outside with him rather than hiding in the tent. Some animal instinct drove her to bolt out in Jens's shadow, but by the time she got outside, she could not see where he'd gone.

"I saw an Indian," one Danish saint was shouting off to her left, and there was a great deal of commotion in that direction.

For a full second Baline stood at the mouth of the tent. Inside, Brother Madsen was crying, "Where are my shoes? Where, ugh, where are they?"

"Over here!" his wife cried.

Baline stared out across the field of grass, almost as white as snow. Wherever the dry grass still stood, it was white, and where it had been crushed, there were shadows like footprints.

The full moon slanted overhead, approaching its zenith. As she gazed, an Indian slowly rose from the grass, only a hundred yards away. She knew it was an Indian by the way that the moonlight reflected from his naked shoulders, and she could see a cord of black hair snaking down around his neck, across his bare chest. His face was painted with white slashes on the chin and white dots on the forehead. He had a muzzle-loader in his right hand, and he began to level it, taking aim at some settler.

Baline did not plan what happened next. She shrieked, once, loud, like a screech owl. It was not a sound that a man could make. The pitch was too high. Even a woman could not have made it, only a little girl. She had not practiced it, hadn't even thought of it. But she had heard it over and over again last night.

The Indian fell back a pace, looking to his right and left, as if seeking for an owl.

Baline dropped to her knees, keeping her eyes just high enough so that she could watch him over the tops of the grass, and she shrieked once more. She did it even better this time.

The Indian raised his rifle, shouting and waving to someone unseen, "Hiyaah! Huh!"

Then he whirled and crouched low, racing through the tall grass. Others repeated the cry, and suddenly Baline saw a dozen hunched shadows rise up from the grass and begin racing away. She could hear one of the redskin's camp dogs yipping in excitement.

The Cheyenne fled.

21

The Night March

The cry of "Indians" stirred the camp like a hornet's nest. It was not yet two o'clock in the morning, but since the saints were not likely to go back to sleep anyway, and with the moon being full under crystal clear skies, Captain Willie called for the saints to rise and begin travel immediately, lest the redskins return in greater number.

Eliza shoved the two boys in the back of the handcart under a blanket and walked as if in a dream through the silver moon-glow.

The banks of the river narrowed here, and it flowed through a canyon that grew increasingly deep. In order to keep the saints from being spotted by enemies, Captain Willie had them go back down the bluff and follow the Platte.

The journey was hard. The settlers hadn't gotten much sleep that night. The men had been called upon to pitch the tents, carry the invalids to the tents, stand guard through the night, pull tents down, get the invalids to the carts, and move again. It was as if this long march was just an extension of the day before.

The settlers kept watch, and every now and again, some child would point up to a rocky bluff and cry "Indians!" But whenever Eliza would look, she'd see nothing.

"It's just a bag of moonshine," her husband Samuel said, trying to comfort her. His cough was not yet gone, and Eliza worried about him working so hard. But he seemed calm tonight, strong and stalwart, tireless and fearless. He seemed more than a man—a monolith, unmoved by the scrawny fears that tore at the breasts of the rest of the immigrants.

The company moved through an eerie landscape of moonlight and moon shadow. They had crossed some hills yesterday afternoon, and now they were back beside the river. The recent floods had cast huge piles of sand upon the banks of the Platte, in some places three and four feet deep, covering the grass, so that the riverbanks were otherworldly drifts of ivory sands with the occasional island of rock thrusting up through it.

Pulling the handcarts, so heavily laden with bags of flour and sleeping children, proved to be difficult, and Eliza found herself floundering, lifting the wagon each time a wheel got stuck, shoving with all her might, only to have the wagon get stuck again.

Wolves followed the settlers, howling in the distance, though some thought that it was Indians only pretending to howl like wolves.

They toiled long through the night, and when the moon set, the sun was just a pink ball on the horizon.

Eliza kept walking and must have blacked out for awhile, for it seemed to her that the sun suddenly rushed into the sky. One moment, it was just a speck at her back, and the next the whole world filled with light.

The settlers kept traveling through the narrow canyon, with mountainous hills rising up a thousand feet on either side. These were much taller than the gentle green downs of England, and Eliza peered up at them in wonder. They rose up, great rolling blocks of sandstone as smooth as the shoulders of the world.

I am like a snail in their shadow, she thought, *puny and insignificant. My march means nothing to them. The end of it means nothing; the beginning is nothing; our most desperate prayer is beneath their notice.*

"Have you ever seen such mountains?" little Sam Junior asked at last, stumbling from exhaustion. His small head swiveled up to gaze at the slopes.

Captain Savage was walking past, looking for folks in need of help. He pushed the handcart over a sand drift.

"Aw, these aren't mountains," he said. "They hardly count as foothills. They're nothing compared to the Rockies."

Eliza's daughter Jane was floundering from weariness. "Captain Savage, when are we going to stop to rest?"

"I don't know," Captain Savage said. "This is intolerable country. Captain Willie wants to get through it in a hurry. He hopes to make Ash Hollow by dusk."

Eliza faltered. The name Ash Hollow seemed a portent. That is where the great massacres had occurred in the past two years, and the army had said that the Cheyenne that had wiped out the wagon trains were congregating there. In the past two weeks, Captain Willie had not even mentioned the place.

Yet we'll be there by nightfall, Eliza realized.

Captain Willie called a halt at ten, after marching for eight hours straight. He didn't stop because he wanted to camp. Indians had been spotted on the bluffs above.

So Captain Willie sent scouts ahead to make certain the trail was secure, and he sent men up over the bluffs to ascertain that the Cheyenne weren't preparing an ambush.

The women used driftwood to build a campfire to cook lunch, and afterward everyone fell asleep, nearly fainting from exhaustion.

Eliza's head was spinning. She put the children to sleep and was about to lie down for a nap herself when Captain Savage returned.

He went to Samuel and called softly, "Brother Gadd, time to wake up. We need you to stand guard."

Samuel snored, using nothing but a mound of sun-drenched sand for his bed. He was too worn-out to hear. Captain Savage was about to give him a soft kick to the ribs when Eliza called out, "Leave him be. I'll stand his watch."

Captain Savage studied her. It was the custom in camp that only men stood watch. "You sure, Sister Gadd?"

They were killing her husband, working him to death. Couldn't they see that?

"Very sure," Eliza said.

Ann Howard had been carrying Sarah half the night in her own handcart. She stumbled as she drew it into camp and saw the fuss. "Go, Eliza," she said. "I'll watch the children for you."

Captain Savage handed her a pistol, and Eliza studied the

weapon. She knew that she was supposed to make sure that the cap was secure and the powder dry. She peered down the barrel to make sure that a ball was inside.

"Whoa, ma'am," Savage said. "Begging your pardon, but don't hold a gun that way unless you're fixing to blow your pretty little head off." Gently, he pushed the barrel from her eye.

"I doubt that this pea shooter could do much harm," Eliza said. "My head is harder than that. Besides, it doesn't even scare the buffalo."

"Well," Captain Savage said, "it scares me."

He nodded toward a bluff up above, a climb of perhaps eight hundred feet. "Your watch is on top of that rock. If you see an Indian, scream at the top of your lungs, but hold your fire. Wait until he's ten, twelve feet away, and then aim for his chest. Think you can do that?"

"I believe so," Eliza said.

"Good," Savage said. He began to walk away.

"Uh," Eliza asked, "is there any trick to it—shooting the gun, I mean?"

Captain Savage turned, gave her an odd look, part unbelieving and a bit dismayed. But certainly he knew that any proper woman in Eliza's social class wouldn't know how to handle a firearm.

He came back, flipped a switch down by the trigger guard. "There," he said. "The safety is off. Now all you have to do is point the gun, hold your hand steady, and pull the trigger."

"Got it," Eliza said.

Savage gave her a quizzical look and said, "Maybe you should wait until the Indian is five feet away, so's you can't miss."

Eliza left the camp and climbed the hill. Its sides, brown with dry grass, had reminded her of bare shoulders. But they were steep, and the climb was exhausting. The grasses turned out not to be all brown. She found wildflowers as she walked, great trumpets of white, like lilies except that they came from a creeping plant, and golden balls that looked like cotton, and stalks of vibrant red flowers called Indian paintbrush. The grasses were strange, various breeds of needle-grass rising up in purple-brown clumps, their long thin blades turning to silver at the tips.

When she reached her lookout, she realized that she was fully exposed. The valleys below her on every side were vast, and the hills rolled on ahead in seemingly endless undulations. She could see a wide canyon on the far side of the bluff, with a silver stream winding through it. There were no trees for a Cheyenne to hide behind for at least five miles in any direction.

So Eliza stood with her pistol in hand, feeling very masterful. She figured that if an Indian came charging over the nearest hill intent on doing her harm, she'd have a good half an hour to steel her nerves before taking her shot.

Some of Captain Willie's scouts could be seen marching through a valley to the west, coming toward her. For an hour she watched as they returned, scaring up a pair of antelope that raced away, until the three men, beaten and dog-tired, trudged up her hill, sweat streaming down from the brims of their hats, their breathing ragged.

"We saw about twenty Indians up ahead," one of the men, Joseph Elder, reported, "but they took off running to the west. We followed them maybe five miles, until they got well out of sight."

"Mmmm," Eliza said, glad that the Indians were gone. "Cheyenne?"

"Hard to say," Elder replied.

"I found some of their droppings on the trail," a nasty little Welshman said. "Looked like Cheyenne poop to me." He burst out laughing at his poor joke. Eliza didn't crack a smile.

The men descended to camp, and Eliza stood on the hill for long hours. The afternoon breeze kicked up, and she spent some time watching golden butterflies flitter about among the wildflowers. A cottontail rabbit hopped through the purple-gray sagebrush nearby. She almost hoped that the Indians would return, just for some excitement.

She watched the camp to be sure that her children were all right. They were all inside sleeping, and Samuel was climbing up to her. She tried to wave him back. She wanted him to rest. But he ignored her. It took a long time for him to reach the top; when he did, he was wheezing. He had to squat a moment with his head between his legs to try to get his wind.

"You should have stayed down," Eliza told him.

"What, and miss a chance to survey the land from this proud

eminence with my handsome wife?" He looked up, and Eliza saw lines of worry and wisdom etched in his face that she had never noticed before.

We're growing old, she thought. *This trip is taking its toll.*

"What have you been doing up here?" he asked.

"Thinking," she said.

"About what?"

Eliza considered how to answer. "About something Doctor Boyle once told me," she said. Doctor Boyle was the physician she had worked with back home in Wimpole. "As you may know, he had a fondness for mathematics, and before we left, he explained some papers that he was reading, the works of a German scientist in the field of thermodynamical transfer of energy."

Samuel gave her a puzzled look. He didn't have a scientific mind and lacked any training in the field. In fact, though he spent his days calculating rents on properties and trying to figure out how to increase his monies as an investor, the truth was that he wasn't very good at math, at least not at the higher maths. He spent more time tilling his own rented fields than he should, and thus had the physique of a common laborer.

So she tried to explain. "You see, our body is a physical system. We are constantly converting energy from our food and using it to work. It is simple mathematics, and the mathematics . . . tell me that we're in trouble, more trouble than you seem to know."

Samuel frowned. "How so?"

"Look at it this way: from the time we got off the train in Iowa, we have been eating a constant diet of flour baked into bread, with almost nothing else. For each man in our group, you get one pound of flour per day. That sounds like a lot. That's a whole loaf of bread. But it isn't enough, it isn't enough by far."

Samuel objected, "Most of the folks in the handcart company have never had this much to eat in their lives."

"True," Eliza said, "but neither have they had to work so hard. You're dragging the handcarts through mud and sand and rivers for ten hours a day. You're climbing hills. Even when we stop, you get no rest. You have to put up the tents and carry the cripples to their tents, then stand guard all night, watching for Indians in the middle of a storm. In the morning you bear the cripples to their wagons, take down the tents, and start all over again. All of this requires energy, far more energy than you get from a pound of bread. That's why you're growing thin. That's why you've had to put four new notches in that belt of yours so that your pants won't fall off. That's why you're hungry all of the time, even when you've finished eating. You're starving to death. We're all starving. You can see it in the faces of the children. A healthy baby should have a nice fat face, but our children are beginning to look as if their skin is just stretched over their skulls. Their fat is almost all gone, and when that happens, starvation sets in, and the body begins to use muscle to get energy. Lose enough muscle, and you die."

Samuel stood for a moment, thinking. Surely he had to see what she was getting at.

"It will only happen faster as the cold weather sets in. The body needs more energy to heat it in the cold."

"What shall we do?"

"Eat more, work less," Eliza said. "I've seen some of the men at camp, sacrificing themselves for their children. Brother Linford, he doesn't want to see his children go hungry, so at breakfast he always finds some reason to leave camp, to go chop wood or tend to the livestock, so that his children are eating his share.

"Yesterday you followed his bad example. You think that the children will thank you someday, but what thanks will they give you when you're dead?"

Samuel looked as if she had slapped him. He'd gone off to "hunt for firewood" with Brother Linford yesterday at breakfast.

"More thanks than they could give me if they were dead." The comeback hurt Eliza so badly that she grunted as if in pain. In apology, Samuel begged, "What, what would you have me do?"

"Eat your fair share," Eliza said. "Eat more than your fair share if you have to. Eat some of mine, and some of Jane's and Bill's and Sam Junior's, and Mary Ann's, and Sarah's, and some of the twins' shares."

"And put the children at risk?"

"If you must," Eliza said. "It's better that one of them dies than you. I have plenty of babies. I lost one before, and it didn't kill me. But I have only one husband."

Samuel shook his head. They'd lost Susannah to smallpox ten years before, when she was still just a toddler. Losing a child was the hardest thing that Eliza had ever done. Samuel asked, "You could live with that choice?"

"We may have no choice in the matter," Eliza said. "Nature makes the choice for us." She stared him down.

"We needn't worry about food," Samuel said. "Elder Richards said that he'd get more provisions at Laramie."

"He said that he'd get them if he could," Eliza corrected. "The army wouldn't let us within ten miles of Fort Kearney. Winter is coming on. What makes you think that they'll sell wheat to a bunch of travelers too foolish to set off at the right time of year? What makes you think your enemies—men who wish that we were dead—will give you the time of day?"

Samuel seemed shaken. He peered about, as if trying to come up with some grand argument that would convince Eliza that she was wrong. But Eliza knew that he wasn't her equal in some ways. He was her better when it came to goodness, to sweetness and gentleness, but her sharp wits far out-mastered his.

So she threw him a bone. "Maybe it won't come to that. Maybe if we all starve a little, all of us will live through this. Just eat your fair share from now on."

She'd been trying to bring him to this point.

"All right," Samuel said. "I will." He swallowed, and Eliza saw that it was a hard choice for him to make. "If we're lucky, maybe no one will die."

"It's too late for that. Look at old man Turner and Father Haley. The dying has begun."

22

Hidden Serpents

Captain Willie couldn't have pushed his people any harder. He had them break camp early that afternoon and take off again, making another four miles, before stopping for the night.

It wasn't only that he was worried about the Cheyennes. The water was bad, and with bad water came sickness. He could feel a constant ache in his stomach. Bad water could lead to loose bowels, which would soon leave folks dehydrated and hasten their demise. He'd seen too much of it ten years earlier, when so many died on the journey west.

The problem was that the Platte was so muddy that you shouldn't drink the water at all. Drinking from a buffalo wallow was a little better, for at least the buffalo dung had a chance to settle to the bottom. But even that was not advisable.

So he'd tried to camp each night at the mouth of some clear stream that fed into the Platte. Thirty miles back, such streams had been common. Now there were none. There was no good water ahead until you reached Ash Hollow.

Once he reached it, he worried that he'd have to fight the Sioux for it.

So he drove his people forward until both the oxen and some of the handcarts began to give out; he found himself on a broad plain beside the river and hunkered down for the night.

The going had been rough all day, climbing up and down ridges, wading through drifts of sand. A dozen handcarts broke their axles as their pullers climbed down a rocky ridge. There were no trees to fix them with, Captain Willie knew, until they reached Ash Hollow.

So they camped, and men went to work cutting leather from worn shoes and strapping it around the broken axles, hoping that they would hold. Others had to clean the sand out of their wheel hubs.

The camp that night was bleak, and folks made do with bad water as best they could. Captain Willie warned them against it, but after a hard day's pull he saw men, women, and children all creep down to the river to furtively dip their hands in the muddy water, sipping as little as they dared.

That night, the weather began to turn. A terrific wind came howling downriver just before dawn, and the temperature dropped perhaps as much as forty degrees in less than an hour.

When the settlers got up, they found a hard frost on the ground. Captain Willie put them to work mending their handcarts some more, hoping that the wind would cease. As the folks were mending their carts, one of the Cantwell children, seven-year-old Ellen, began to play in a sand drift. She had no sooner put her hand in when she latched onto a giant rattlesnake.

The thing struck her hand, and soon the whole camp was in commotion. Captain Willie rushed to hear what the fuss was about and saw the biggest rattler he'd ever encountered. Though he had often preached about how one ought not to treat God's creatures roughly, he pulled out his pistol and blew the monster's head off, muttering a prayer as he did, asking for God's forgiveness. He picked up the huge snake with a stick for fear that it might strike even after its death. It had sixteen buds on its rattle and must have weighed ten pounds. He tossed it off the trail, where it could do no more harm.

Captain Siler, who led the independent wagons, immediately began sucking the blood from Ellen's wound, and she fought him for a bit and then fell into a swoon. When he was done sucking the wound, he made a plaster from some buffalo grease and mixed it with gunpowder, then smeared it over Ellen's hand, to help draw out the poison.

By then Ellen's fingers had turned black. The poison was having its way with her. Little Ellen began to rant from a fever dream, and cried in pain, so Captain Siler poured a good dose of whiskey down her throat. When she passed out, Captain Willie gave her a blessing, he being the mouthpiece for the prayer while Captain Siler and Brother Cantwell attended. It was the most uncertain prayer that Captain Willie had ever given. He stood waiting for a long time for the spirit of the Lord to direct him, but all that he felt was sick inside, and cold and clammy outside.

The wind practically screamed downriver, tearing at their clothes and hair; he just stood for a long time wondering what to say.

Captain Siler was in charge of the independent wagons, and Brother Cantwell was a wagon owner. For days now, Captain Willie had been trying to get Cantwell and the other wagon drivers to see that they needed to give their wagons to the church, surrender them for the good of all the pioneers.

Surely they had to see that the Lord was angered. Already two men had died from starvation. The water had turned bad, the Cheyennes were hounding the camp, an icy wind was blowing with a devilish fury, and now an innocent child lay at the verge of death. Brother Cantwell had to see that his own selfishness, and the selfishness of others like him, had brought the wrath of God down upon the camp.

Captain Willie longed to find the words to express these thoughts, but when he tried to speak, his tongue was bound. The Lord would not allow Captain Willie to rebuke the Cantwells.

After long minutes of silent prayer, he simply said, "Ellen Cantwell, by the power of the holy priesthood that I bear, and in the name of my master, Jesus Christ, I lay my hands upon your head and bless you that you shall live, and you shall be healed. Amen."

When he was done, he stood looking down at the feverish little girl, and he felt empty inside. The Lord had wanted no remonstrations, no blame heaped upon the Cantwells. All that He wanted was for one little girl to know that he loved her, despite the horrors to come.

So Captain Willie called for the handcarts to move, and they traveled on. The icy wind howled all through the day, lifting sand from the drifts beside the Platte and hurling it into the pilgrims' faces. Men lowered their heads so that their hats shielded their eyes, and they trudged through the sand drifts, pulling their carts, while the women and children shielded their eyes with their arms. The sand and dust in the air became so thick that Captain Willie could not see three hundred feet ahead.

The icy wind drew the heat from exposed limbs, turning knuckles and faces red. Some of the women began to faint, and others became too tired to pull their handcarts.

Captain Willie checked on Emily Wall and Baline Mortensen. The two girls were having a tough time of it, both of them weeping as they trudged, heads bent to the ground as they fought the stinging wind, pulling Joseph as best they could. Captain Willie urged them on, pushing the cart for a mile to give them some rest.

The oxen began to balk, and by early afternoon, the drivers had to resort to the whip.

Progress slowed, and many gave up altogether; some men just fainted, dropping in their tracks.

As daylight turned to darkness, Captain Willie ordered the men to pitch their tents; he had to give up the march. Many women and children were strung out on the trail behind, and Willie had to send his captains back to retrieve those who had collapsed by the wayside. The whole camp did not get in until ten o'clock. By far, this had been the most arduous day of the trek.

His people were cold and miserable, looking half dead.

As they shivered through the short prayer meeting that night, then went to their beds to collapse from exhaustion, he thought, *If I were a Cheyenne, I would choose tonight to attack.*

23

Ash Hollow

For Baline the next few days became a nightmare. She pushed the handcart each day, and when she did, she could not put her arm up to shelter her from the icy winds. That left her with a sore right ear. The ear itself turned red and swollen, and a knot rose up behind her earlobe. Her nose became so clogged that when she walked, she often found herself with her mouth wide, gaping like one of the big old buffalo fish down in the Platte as she gasped for air.

At night the pain left her ear pounding like a drum, and she could not sleep lying down. But when she tried to sit up, she could not sleep either.

Father Jens administered to her, pouring olive oil upon her head lavishly, olive oil that had been consecrated for use of the sick. Then he poured some oil in her ear and afterward laid his hands upon her head and blessed her by the power of the priesthood. But he did not heal her. Instead, in the blessing, God only confirmed his love for her and told her that though her trials would be great, she would overcome them.

Still she helped pull Joseph during the days as best she could. It had been more than two weeks since he'd fainted, and now he sometimes would get up and walk for an hour, giving the girls a rest. But he could not walk for a full day. The fact that he was alive at all was a blessing from the Lord, and Emily would sometimes look at her brother and weep with gratitude. Baline felt humbled and grateful to be a part of this miracle.

Enormous hills now flanked each side of the river, and the

company could not follow the river's course any longer, for ahead it wound for miles through narrow canyons. They pulled the handcart up over a long steep set of hills, fourteen miles, without a drink of water.

Halfway up through the trek, Baline fainted, dropping in the traces.

When she woke, Emily and Joseph were standing over her, and her ear pounded like a drum. Cold sweat stood out on her forehead.

"Your cheeks are all flushed," Emily said. "You're sick with fever. Get in the wagon, and we'll pull you."

"No," Baline said. "I not vant to be burden."

"It's all right," Joseph said. "It's my turn to pull you for a little while."

So Baline got up and tried to stand well enough to get into the cart. But as she did, a thought took her. "I don't want to ride," she said stubbornly. "Someday, I want to tell my children that I valked all the way."

Joseph laughed, a merry sound that she had not heard from him before. "All right," he said. "Lean on me then, and I'll help."

So they walked, and it felt good to be able to just walk for awhile, without pulling Joseph's weight in the infernal handcart.

The handcart pioneers did not all travel at the same pace. Those who were strongest would move along swiftly, while those who were sick or had lots of children tended to lag behind.

Thus Baline and the Walls paused to rest often that day, until they were far behind.

Baline stopped to lie in some tall grass for awhile, her ear pounding. She was feeling sorry for herself until a rickety handcart drew even with her.

A woman called out, "Cristopher, is your sister dead yet?"

"I don't know, Mum," a small boy answered.

"Look in the cart," the mother answered.

Baline sat up on an elbow and peered over the top of the golden straw. Sister Panting was pulling a handcart all alone, sweat streaming down her face. Her eyes were puffy from tears. Sister Panting's young daughter, Jane, had taken sick from drinking bad water.

Six-year-old Christopher raced to the back of the cart, followed it a moment. "Not dead yet, Mum."

"Are you sure?" Sister Panting asked. She sounded so weary, Baline wondered if she just wanted to get rid of the child's weight. But then she realized that the babe had been crying for days now, growing more and more sick. Probably, in despair, her mother just hoped that the baby's suffering would end.

Yet Baline had great hope. An apostle had promised that the family would make it to Salt Lake alive, so Baline knew that the baby couldn't die.

She climbed up out of the grass, along with the Walls. Emily Wall came to Baline, hugged her, and together they traveled the rest of the way. Seven miles they tramped, until Joseph was nearly reeling from fatigue. But at last, the handcart reached the top of a tall hill, and the company descended a slope into Ash Hollow. The descent was so steep that the men had to tie ropes to the wagons and lower them down.

Even at first glance, there from the top of the hill, Ash Hollow seemed a wonder. Given its somber-sounding name and the fact that several massacres had occurred here in the past two years, Baline had imagined that it would be a hellish place. Somehow, she had thought that it would be devoid of life and that she would see the bones of the Sioux lying in piles.

But Ash Hollow was like the Garden of Eden.

For days now the grass on the plains had been growing thin, and there had been no buffalo along the river. In the past five hundred miles, Baline had seen so few trees that she could no longer close her eyes and imagine a forest. For the past hundred miles, she had had nothing but filthy water to drink.

Suddenly in the shelter of Ash Hollow she saw a network of valleys protected from the wind, where lush grass covered the valley floor. A clear stream meandered through it, and stately trees grew at the water's edge in abundance. These were not the pithy cottonwoods with rotten heartwood that grew along the Platte. These were stout alders, oaks, and even a few pines. The hillsides were covered with wildflowers in shades of white and yellow. Down in the valley,

Baline could hear wild turkeys gobbling. As other settlers descended the hill, the first group to reach the stream scared up a huge bull elk with enormous antlers. It trotted away majestically.

Baline thought that Ash Hollow must be the most beautiful place on earth. Certainly, it was the most beautiful place she had ever seen, and for a long time she stood on the side of the hill, unwilling to go in, as she tried to capture it in her memory forever.

It was only after several minutes that she realized how Ash Hollow had taken its name. The dirt on the sides of the canyons was all gray, for in some ancient time, volcanic ash had drifted from the skies in great heaps, and then the river cut its channel through the ash. In a few places, where the river had carved away the hills, the soil was the color of the ashes from a campfire.

When the settlers reached the valley floor, Captain Willie called the saints together in a splendid little meadow. After the bitter cold of the past three days, the day had suddenly grown very hot, and Captain Willie just stood there sweating and smiling.

He called out, "Ladies and gentlemen, we've now reached Ash Hollow, and there's no better place to recoup. We've got lots of folks with busted axles on their wagons, and we're going to spend the rest of tonight and tomorrow cutting down trees so that we can fix your handcarts. I want to congratulate all of you. We're now at the halfway mark on our pilgrimage. We've come halfway between the train depot in Iowa and Salt Lake City!"

There were shouts of "Hurrah," and the men threw their hats up. Captain Willie shot his pistol in the air, and others followed suit. Each blast sent Baline's ears thrumming with pain, so she put her hands to her ears and waited for it to quiet down.

Baline felt miserable, weak, and sickly. They'd reached the halfway point, and she wasn't sure that she could make it the rest of the way.

One woman complained loudly, "Captain Willie, please tell me that the rest of the trip will be easier than it has been."

Captain Willie scratched at his chin, thinking. "Well, you've eaten a lot of trail dust the past few weeks, walking them dirt roads through Iowa. We've made it over the sand hills, where I suspect that we've had the toughest pulling. From here on out, we move onto higher ground, where the soil is firm, the water is cleaner, and the pulling should get easier. I know that some of you are carrying more than your fair share of flour, but as we eat it down, the loads will get lighter. Once we reach Fort Laramie, we should be able to get some more oxen and resupply. So, yes, I think we've made it over the rough part."

"Vat about der mountains?" a Dane asked.

Worry flashed across his face, then Captain Willie's expression brightened. "Once we reach the Sweetwater, you'll be glad to be in the mountains," he confirmed. "The nights may get cold, but it will only make the day's march that much more comfortable!"

"But what about the mountains we must climb?" the woman asked.

"Crossing the Great Divide is child's play," Captain Willie said. "It's not like climbing a mountain. It's a long, gentle swell, more of a tall hill. The air is kind of thin, but the going isn't tough. Jesus had his hill to climb, and this will be ours." Captain Willie grinned broadly, and said, "Brother Mortensen, I think that we should celebrate tonight. Will you folks play for us?"

"Yah, I be happy to play!" Brother Mortensen said. "Ve all be happy to play for you."

The whole Mortensen family was musically inclined, and so a cheer arose; once again Baline found herself holding her ears.

So they reached Ash Hollow. Emily went to Captain Amundsen and demanded that Baline be enlisted among the sick. For the first time in three months, Baline got to sleep in a real house. Captain Amundsen took her to an abandoned trapper's cabin where the sickest of the sick were housed, and he built a fire in the hearth. Baline got to lie on the dry floor all afternoon with several other sick inmates.

But though Ash Hollow was beautiful, Baline could not enjoy it. She took a high fever, and in her fevered state she worried much for Ellen Cantwell, for the girl was lying beside her, suffering from her snakebite. Ellen was feverish, too, and her fingers had swollen up like a toad and grown so black that it looked as if they would fall off, despite the fact that Captain Willie had promised that Ellen would recover. Baline had played cat-after-mouse with Ellen many times, and now Baline had to worry that they would play no more.

That afternoon the infection in Baline's ear seemed to worsen despite all the care that had been taken. Captain Willie sent Sister Gadd to help nurse Baline and the others back to health.

Sister Gadd candled Baline's ear. Baline had to lie very still for the process. Sister Gadd took a piece of paper and rolled it up to make a trumpet shape, then set a candle outside the large end of the trumpet, while the small end was placed deep in Baline's ear canal. The heat from the candle entered Baline's ear and warmed it, melting the wax, which would dribble down the long end of the trumpet. As the candling began, the pounding in Baline's ears brought tears to her eyes.

Eliza stroked Baline's cheek as the ear drained. The drumming intensified, as did the pain, until Baline lay in a sweat, ears pounding as if thunderclaps sounded overhead.

Baline looked up at Sister Gadd. Everything seemed tinged with yellow, and Baline's fever sharpened her sight so that it seemed that Eliza's every hair, every wrinkle, was chiseled into Baline's memory.

"Sister Gadd," Baline said weakly and with sudden clarity. "I think I vill die tonight."

Eliza smiled dismissively, giving a little snort of laughter.

"You think I am stupid," Baline said, "don't you?"

"No," Eliza said. "I don't think you are stupid. I think you are just young. You have an earache. People don't often die from earaches. The eardrum will break instead, and release pus from the infection. It is like having a pimple."

"People can die from pimples," Baline said. "My father knew der man vat died." She felt so tired, she closed her eyes. "You think I am stupid. I see it in your eyes."

Eliza's hand froze for a moment, then she continued stroking

Baline's face. Eliza's fingers were covered with the girl's sweat. She thought, *How perceptive of the girl; I wouldn't have guessed it.*

"You think that all of us Mormons are stupid," Baline said softly, "just like the rest of our persecutors."

Eliza hesitated. "I'm not that way," she said. "Did Captain Siler give you some of his medicine?"

"For the pain, yah," Baline said, her voice a bit too thick.

"You're drunk," Eliza said. "That was whiskey he gave you."

"Oh," Baline said dismissively. "But is truth. People say ve are stupid and that people so stupid should not be allowed to live their own lives."

If the child is drunk, Eliza realized, *she's not very drunk—only enough to loosen her tongue.*

Eliza wanted to argue that she didn't feel that way, but in truth, she did. She was proud that her mind was sharper than her husband's or Captain Willie's. She could hardly believe that she had cast her lot with this company of fools. But Baline was oversimplifying things. Eliza didn't believe that just because she was smarter, the fools should lose their freedom. But she did believe that they needed to leave the deeper thinking to their superiors.

At last she said, "It's a bit more complex than that. It's not that I detest fools. It's just that I don't trust them. Who would want a fool for a doctor, or a lawyer, or even working as a simple clerk in a store? You Mormons seem to think that people should be allowed to rule their own fates and those of others because they are decent and compassionate. You hope that God will enlighten stupid men, make them equal to their tasks. But in the end, compassion doesn't make a difference.

"Back a few years ago, a foolish young neighbor of mine tried to heat his home on a cold winter's night by making a large fire. But he made the fire so huge, it leapt out of the hearth and burned down his home, killing his brothers and sisters, the same people he had hoped to warm.

"Now, I might lament his idiocy. I might mourn the loss of his family, and ache for him personally. I lament that he suffered such a horrible tragedy. But at the same time, I must be ever-vigilant against such stupidity. Compassion is a virtue, but compassion without wisdom is a terrible waste."

"You are proud," Baline accused. "You look down upon us."

"I simply worry about men like Captain Willie," Eliza objected. "He has tremendous compassion, and because of it, you love him and are eager to follow him. But he has no training for his job, and not enough experience. He hardly knows the trail, and he knows nothing at all of the Cheyennes."

"Who should lead us then?" Baline asked.

"I'd prefer someone with less compassion and more natural intelligence and training—someone like Almon Babbitt."

Baline shook her head sadly. "You lie to me," she said. "Maybe you lie to yourself. You say that you have good reason to distrust those who are foolish, but your distrust, it has grown to something more. You are proud to be smart. You look down on others and think you are better than der rest, so you give yourself the permission to take advantage."

Eliza was thrown for a second. She didn't see herself as one who tried to take advantage.

"The strong," Baline said, "they think that they should rule the vorld because they are strong. They crack the heads of those who will not bow down to them. They are barbarians, and ve scorn them. But those born to privilege think they should look down on others because, like you, they attend the fine schools."

Eliza shifted her weight, turning away from Baline just a bit. But she couldn't leave the child completely. She had to hold the candle near the trumpet in Baline's ear.

But now she saw Baline's point, and it horrified her. *Am I really a barbarian?* Eliza wondered.

Baline went on, "Those who go to fine schools call those who are unlearned fools, as if it vere great sin. Even ven they argue among themselves, they call each other 'fools' and treat each other vit contempt. They despise those who are veak in the mind ven they should be showing compassion on them. You, you are intellectual barbarian."

"Intellectual barbarian?" Eliza asked. "My, aren't you using big words today." She was impressed. This girl had not spoken a word of English four months ago.

I've underestimated her, Eliza thought. But it wasn't just the child's vocabulary that surprised her, it was the philosophy she expressed. "Where did you get such ideas?"

"Is something my father taught," Baline said. "Intellectual barbarism is German trait. The Germans, they teach that only those who get learning at university can be smart, and those who have no learning, they are nothing. Just as barbarous man will use gun to steal and kill, the intellectual uses his mind. He takes advantage of those whose minds are veaker than his and treats them like cattle yoked to plow, making them his tools. He thinks because he is smarter, is no sin to hurt them."

"So this concept of intellectual barbarism," Eliza said, "this is your father's notion. But tell me what you think."

"I think you are intellectual barbarian," Baline said. "That is vy you von't join us. You are afraid. You don't vant people to think you are stupid too."

Eliza realized that Baline was right, at least in part. "I don't believe in your God," she said. "I don't believe in magical thinking. It's ludicrous. It's nonsense."

"You don't vant to believe," Baline said. "You don't even vant to hope there is God. The Book of Mormon, it asks you to do experiment. It asks you to pray to God for self, to find out if he lives. If you do, he vill reveal himself. But you don't do experiment, because if you learn that he lives, you must change the vay you live."

Eliza had always believed that she was someone special. She saw through the gypsy tricks that had fooled her father, and she had always believed that his faith was a weakness. She'd always done well in school. Perhaps she wasn't at the head of her academy in math, but she was in letters and manners.

She believed that some societies, some ways of looking at the world, were superior to others.

Frequently it galled her to be in this company of . . . of misfits and fools, with its lunatic women like old Sister Ingra, and the children all stunted from hunger and covered with lice, and women who could carry on conversations only if they had to do with topics as mundane as the weather or yesterday's gossip.

Yes, Eliza was proud to be intelligent, to be educated and well-bred. She was proud to be an intellectual. But Eliza also knew that Baline had her. This little ten-year-old girl saw right through her to the very core.

"The truth is," Eliza said, "some people are better than others. I don't like admitting it in public, for I don't want to hurt any feelings. But some people are more intelligent than others. They form the core of an intellectual elite, people whose insights and discoveries are going to change this world, carry it into the future. I would like to think that I'm part of that group. I'm not part of its inner circle, but I sit on the outside, within hearing range.

"Baline, if ten thousand cripples try to race against just one man with real speed and stamina, they can never catch up. In the same way, the advice of ten thousand fools can never equal that of one really wise man.

"I think that you Mormons are listening to fools. Their belief in prophecies and healing and miracles is all nonsense, and listening to them will only get you in trouble.

"You may not like hearing this, but it's the truth. Some people really are better than others, not just by accident, but by breeding. Out in the wild, a dog will mate with whatever female he comes upon. Most people do the same, but some people take more care in selecting their mates. There really are people of good breeding who are wise, and strong and handsome and noble, and while every ill-bred mongrel out in the field might wish that he were the equal of such, he isn't. The Americans say that 'all men were created equal,' but we all know that that is only wishful thinking."

"You make mistake," Baline said. "Ve are all spirit children of God, vit the power to become Gods, like he is. Ven you look into the eyes of someone like me, you see yourself. If it vere not so, you vould not be sitting here, you nurse, trying to help."

That was true, too. Eliza might not want to be counted among these mongrels, but at the same time, she cared deeply for these people.

"My, you're a wise little one," Eliza said, "you with your big words and your piercing insights."

What else could she tell me about myself? Eliza wondered.

Baline stared up at her, and the child's eyes were so blue, it was as if the summer sky was caught in them. "You are good person," Baline said. She reached up and stroked Eliza's hand, the one that was touching Baline's cheek. "The people in the vagon train, they call themselves saints. Some even try to be saints, and fail. But I see your kindness, how you treat sick, and I think you are saint."

She's flattering me, Eliza thought. But though Eliza saw through it, she felt gratified. Since she had come among the Mormons, no one had cared enough about her opinion to try to flatter her.

"I didn't know that you'd developed such an extensive vocabulary," Eliza said. "It seems that you don't just ape big words, you have genuine thoughts to go with them." She mused on that a moment. *Someday*, she thought, *Baline will become a formidable woman.* "It will be nice to have someone in this camp who is my intellectual equal."

Sister Gadd finished the candling, but felt worried. "Well, your ear canal is clean, at least. But I'd hoped to get some pus out of it, and all I got was wax. That means the infection is still in there."

She petted Baline's head and said, "Get better soon. Little Samuel misses you, I'm sure."

Baline had to wonder at that. Sometimes when Baline had gone to the Gadd's tent to fetch Samuel, Sister Gadd had given her disapproving looks. Father Jens had explained, "The English, they feel that it is improper for a girl to call upon a boy. They think that it means she is forward. But us Danes, we know better. How else is a boy to know that a girl wants to marry him, if she does not bring him a few treats? Of course, it must end at that. She must never ask for kisses."

Baline had felt embarrassed. "I don't want to marry him!" she'd objected. "I just want to play."

But now the thought was planted in her head. Someday she had to marry someone. Why not Samuel Gadd Junior? He thought she was pretty, and he had touched her hand in a way that made her heart flutter.

Though the whole subject of marriage at Baline's age was taboo, and its rules and obligations were still shrouded in mystery, it was not far off. Baline had known of girls who married at the age of fourteen. That was only four short years from now.

Baline told Sister Gadd. "I vill try very hard to get better. Sam is good friend."

Sister Gadd smiled sadly, the small wrinkles in her face showing. As she left the old cabin, pushing the door open, Baline wondered when night had fallen. It seemed that only an hour ago they had reached Ash Hollow; sunset should have been a couple of hours away.

I must have fallen asleep, she thought.

Outside, she could hear someone hollering in the distance, a man's voice echoing off the canyon walls. A few minutes later, Sam Junior himself came into the cabin, in company with Agnes Caldwell and Mary Hurren. Hovering above the children was Caroline Reeder, the vivacious young woman who had so often led the children in games and quietly kept an eye on them.

A cozy fire was burning in the hearth, a fire so hot that it left Baline's forehead glazed with sweat, and the flames seemed to dance in Caroline's and Agnes's dark eyes. The children were grinning broadly from ear to ear, except for Mary, who was pouting just a little.

"Baline," Caroline said, "we brought you a present!"

Only then did Sam Junior hold up a large tin cup brimming with berries. "It was my idea!"

Baline's stomach rumbled at the sight of them. She had sometimes picked berries along the path, of course, as they made their way along the trail. But it had been weeks since she'd found any.

Nor had Baline had any meat for several days, and her stomach was constantly grumbling.

"Blackberries?" Baline asked.

"And raspberries!" Agnes Caldwell cried out with glee.

Baline felt as if it were Christmas. She hadn't seen so much fruit at once since—well, since she'd passed the orchards in Iowa. But then the fruit had been forbidden her. She hadn't seen so much fruit that she could eat in over a year.

"Thank you," she said, tears welling in her eyes. Raspberries were her favorite. She took the cup and grabbed several blackberries, leaving the raspberries to be savored last, then began to chew. Every berry seemed perfectly ripe. They were neither too tart, nor were they going soft and sweet, the way that they did before they began to mold. She realized that her friends hadn't just brought her a gift of berries. They'd been sure to give her only perfect berries, the best that they could find. "They are so good," Baline said. "I think they are the best I ever taste."

"There is a creek not far from here," Mary said. "The blackberries grow thick there."

"Veren't you afraid of Indians?" Baline asked.

"Not much," Caroline said. "The army came here hunting for Cheyennes just last week. I think they chased them all away. We should be able to sleep well tonight."

That was comforting news. But it had still been very brave to go hunt for berries with the Cheyennes about.

Someone opened the door, coming to visit one of the other sick folks in the cabin, and Baline heard that call again, the man's voice echoing through the canyons.

"Vat is he yelling about?" Baline asked. "Is someone hurt?"

"Nancy Stewart is lost," Caroline whispered in Baline's ear. "We got into camp tonight, and she was just gone. Captain Willie has sent search parties out to find her."

Nancy Stewart was the passenger that had joined the camp after Almon Babbitt's wagons were attacked. She'd bought passage on one of the independent wagons. In fact, Baline suddenly recalled that she had been riding with the Cantwell family. Now Baline realized why Caroline whispered. Sister Cantwell was only feet away, sitting with little Ellen.

"Oh," Baline said. She recalled how old Father Haley had wandered off the trail a couple of weeks ago in a weary stupor and had suffered through a storm. She felt sure that this had led to his death. "Ve must pray for her."

Caroline led them in prayer then, and afterward Baline ate a few more raspberries. She saw Mary Hurren's frown deepen.

Baline offered, "Vould you like some?"

Mary glanced back at Caroline, as if seeking permission. Caroline gave her a stern look, and Mary politely declined.

"I think it's time that we go," Caroline said. "It's getting late, and you need your rest."

Caroline leaned down and gave Baline a peck on the forehead, her lips feeling cool and sweet against Baline's skin. Mary and Agnes chimed in, "Good-bye!" and each of the girls knelt and squeezed her hand.

The girls all turned to go, but Samuel Gadd just stood staring at Baline, a look of fear on his pale face. He stumbled forward, knelt, and grabbed her hand, squeezing it as the girls had done. He glanced back to make sure that no one was watching and saw Mary, Agnes, and Caroline all staring at him. He started to rise, then gathered his nerve and suddenly dipped down and kissed Baline on the cheek!

"Get better soon," he said, his eyes looking all soulful, and then he jumped up and raced out the door.

Mary and Agnes giggled, and Caroline smiled her congratulations at Baline. But Sister Cantwell said in a huff, "How brazen!" Then she shouted at Samuel's fleeing back, "Your mother will hear about this."

That night, Baline's ear kept pounding. Several times she woke in a fever, believing that she heard Indian drums pounding in the distance. She cried through the pain silently, not wanting to wake the others in the cabin.

At last, late at night, Captain Siler came into the cabin to check on Ellen Cantwell, and seeing Baline's pain, he gave her a large draught of whiskey.

Baline lay down for a while and slept better. The whiskey took the teeth out of the pain, turning it into a dull throb, until finally she felt the pressure release, and a nasty fluid seeped from her ear.

Afterward, Baline slept, and her dreams of Indian drums were gone. She woke only once more in the night. Though her ear felt better, she was still having night sweats, and her clothes were fairly drenched.

When she woke this last time, Father Jens was kneeling on the floor beside her. He had a long stick and was stirring up the embers in the hearth.

Everything seemed so quiet and still. The other sick folk in the room breathed so softly. There were no more shouts in the distance.

"Did they find Nancy Stewart?" Baline asked in English.

Father Jens peered at her until she repeated the question in Danish and then answered, "Not yet."

"You look worried," Baline said. "What's wrong?"

"The search parties came back. They found her tracks heading south of here. There were Indian tracks beside hers. They think that maybe the Cheyenne took her."

Baline pushed herself up onto her elbows. Her ear was wet where it had been draining. She felt very weak. Jens picked up a rag and began wiping the foulness away from her ear.

She said, "I am feeling better. We should go look for Nancy."

Baline felt inside her. She had heard many testimonies in church where women talked of losing precious things—rings or coins. When they prayed, the holy spirit would lead them to the items right away. For weeks now, Baline had tried to live worthy to have the spirit's presence every moment. Right now, Baline could feel the warm, sweet burning in her bosom that signified the presence of the spirit. She felt sure that if she went searching for Nancy, the spirit would lead her.

"You stay down," Jens told her. He glanced at the cup of berries. "You are too sick to go out hunting for this woman in the cold night. I will go look for her in morning. It is almost light."

"Can I come?" Baline asked. "I feel sure that I can find her."

Jens chided her. "Sometimes the Spirit leads us to serve others.

But sometimes, it is God's will that others serve us. Right now, it is your job to let others earn a few blessings. Do you understand?"

Jens noticed the berries in her cup. Baline had left the raspberries. "Do you not want these?"

"I'm saving them, for later."

Jens knelt beside her. "Let me tell you a story: years ago, an old woman had a huge apple tree, and on it grew the largest, sweetest, and brightest red apples in all of Denmark.

"One year, she picked her apples and thought, I will save the best for later. So she took the apples, carefully wrapped them in paper, and laid them in her fruit cellar. A few weeks later, she went to bake a pie, and as she opened her apples, she found that some had begun to go bad. Little bruises were forming on them. So she thought, I will take these and put them in my pie and save the good ones for later.

"And this she did. She made a pie, a good pie, but not a great pie.

"At Christmas, she went downstairs, dreaming of apple strudel, and once again she found some apples going soft. So she used the old ones first.

"At the new year, she thought, it is time to eat my good apples!" and she went down to her fruit cellar. "But the time for fresh apples had passed, and there were no more good apples.

"She was old, and she told me, who was only a young boy, to always remember this lesson: 'Take good things in life while you can.' Some think that there is sin in this, but God made sweet apples for us to enjoy while we can.' It is just one way that he has of showing his love for us."

"So I should eat my raspberries now?"

"Yes," Jens said. "Also, I think it is time for you to start wearing those shoes that Kris Kringle gave you."

Baline had worn them only one day, the morning of the hard frost. By then the sun had warmed the ground enough so that she could take them off. "But I'm saving those for the cold."

"You're growing up fast," Jens warned. "Soon they will no longer fit you, and they'll be as worthless as rotten apples."

Baline felt inside and was sure that Father Jens was right—both about the raspberries and about her need to let others serve her. "But what about Nancy?"

"We'll find her, if it is God's will," Jens said, and he held out the raspberries.

She chewed them thoughtfully.

Lately, Baline felt as if she had been spending long days watching people get ill, waiting to learn if it was God's will whether they recover or die.

"The apostle said that we would make it to Zion safely," Baline said. "Do you think that he lied?"

Jens thought. "I don't know," he said. "I do not think he is an evil man. I don't think that he would lie on purpose. But a person can be mistaken, and bad advice can do as much harm as a lie."

"Even an apostle can make mistakes?" Baline asked.

"Even apostles," Jens said, his voice going low, for there were some who would consider such words to be blasphemy. "The Apostle Peter once forbade the disciples to preach the gospel to the gentiles, until God showed him in a dream what he must do. Paul once taught that men should not marry but should give their lives in service to God, until Peter corrected him. Even apostles make mistakes. Like us, they are growing, struggling to do what is right. That is why we must pray always to get our own answers, and not rely totally on others to receive inspiration for us."

"So maybe Apostle Richards was wrong?" Baline said. "Maybe on this journey we will all die?"

Jens gave her a comforting pat on the cheek. "No," Jens said. "The apostle is buying food and oxen at Fort Laramie. You'll see. The way is hard, but the Lord is with us still."

The next day was cold, and intermittent rainclouds dashed across the blue sky. Work parties went out to cut trees to make axles for the carts, while search parties hunted for Nancy Stewart.

A calf was killed at dawn, and Else Nielsen made a rich soup from its bones. After drinking some, Baline felt better than she had in days. She got up and went outside. The men were gone from camp, except for the old and sickly, and the women were washing clothes. Else took Baline's dress so that Baline was forced to wander around for awhile with only a blanket over her. Baline had no other clothes. Else warned Baline to go back and lie in the sick house.

Baline wanted to sneak out of camp, to go hunt for Nancy Stewart, but she couldn't do it naked, so she went back to her spot on the earthen floor by the fire.

That evening, just after dark, the men from the work party came into camp and carried Nancy straight to the sick house. She was delirious and moaning, and kept thrashing about, crying, "Wolves! Wolves!"

The men fed her some soup, and soon Nancy came out of her delirium enough to relate some of her tale. The day before, she had gone ahead of the handcarts as she entered Ash Hollow, and there she found that the trail split. One branch went north, and another south. She took the southern trail and walked for miles before she realized that she was all alone and lost.

"By then, it was growing dark," she whispered. "I lost my path in the darkness. At night, wolves circled me, and I kept trying to stare them down. Often, they would lunge at me, only inches away, and I would strike at them with my fists, but the wolves kept trying to circle behind me. I found a thick stick and swung at them, but no matter what I did, I could not drive them off. I finally climbed a tree for safety, but I could not rest there, or get any sleep.

"In the morning, I walked and walked until I heard the sounds of axes and men shouting as they felled the trees."

After relating her tale, Nancy fell into a deep slumber. She was chilled and shaking from her arduous journey, and Baline wanted to give the woman a blanket, but didn't have one to spare. The night sweats were still bothering Baline a little, so she crawled up beside Nancy and just lay there, sharing her body warmth. Nancy was so cold, Baline almost worried that she might drain away Baline's own body heat.

24

The Hunger of Dazed Birds

Eliza had to deal with a small embarrassment that evening. A Sister Danforth came and informed her that her son Samuel had been seen "kissing a Danish girl." The news, of course, would be all over camp.

Eliza knew immediately whom Sister Danforth was referring to, but asked, "Does the girl have a name?"

The woman drew back, flustered. "A name? You want a name? It was just some Danish girl."

Of course, that was the problem. Sam Junior kissing a Londoner might have merited a laugh and a wink. Sam kissing a Dane was a scandal.

All of these Mormons, Eliza thought, *calling each other brother and sister and acting as if a person's nationality doesn't matter. They're always so relentlessly liberal in their politics, on everything from the issues of slavery to women's rights. Well, for once I get to be the broad-minded one.*

Eliza pressed, "But certainly even those . . . those Danish creatures have names? I mean, people have names in Chipping Sodbury. I hear that even the lowly French have names, and they don't even know how to bathe! So this girl must have a name."

Sister Danforth seemed confused by Eliza's tone but finally leaned close and whispered conspiratorially, "It's that little girl that runs loose like a wild Indian: Baline Mortensen!"

Eliza affected complete indifference and said dryly, "Oh, her. Well, Sam has my express permission to kiss her. In fact, I was planning to give him permission to kiss any girl he wants. If he's going to grow up to be a good polygamist, he might as well start getting some practice!"

Sister Danforth, totally flummoxed, turned and fled, eager to relate Eliza's words to anyone silly enough to listen.

Eliza had to work hard to keep from grinning too much that morning. She found herself enjoying the stares and giggles that followed wherever she went.

She even took time to check in on Baline and found that her eardrum had burst and the girl was now well on the way to recovery. Eliza couldn't help but notice that the very same woman who had come to warn her about her son's unnatural affection found a reason to step into the sick house, obviously hoping for some sort of a screaming fight, so Eliza made sure to give Baline an extra-long hug as she said, "Now, Baline, do come by our tent for dinner this evening."

Samuel Gadd finished affixing a new axle to the handcart before the company rolled out of Ash Hollow at two in the afternoon. They skirted a broad swamp filled with cattail rushes, hugging a hillside lush with grass, until they reached the Platte River.

The day was cool, and during the afternoon march, a fine cold drizzle began to fall in a steady shower that soon had everyone drenched.

The company slogged on. September was rapidly fading away, and with the constant breakdowns of handcarts, the delays to care for the sick, and the delays to bury the dead, the saints were falling farther and farther behind schedule. Eliza calculated that they wouldn't make it to Salt Lake until November at their current rate.

Their food would run out well before then, and she hated to think about the possibility of snowstorms in the mountains.

Still, spirits were fairly high. Bill helped push the handcart without complaining, and Sam Junior, as usual, fulfilled his duties eagerly. Mary Ann, now eight years old, marched beside the handcart stoically, even in the rain, so that only the twins and six-year-old Sarah had to ride.

Eliza took a mental note each time that Samuel stopped pulling the handcart in order to cough.

The settlers made twelve miles before they set camp that night, then rose in the morning of the twenty-first and pushed on. The rain had not let up.

Today is the equinox, Eliza realized. *Equal days and equal nights. From now on, the nights will grow longer than the days.*

The rain became an icy deluge that day, and many folk, weary to the bone from trying to pull handcarts through sand and mud, finally staggered back to the sick wagon, begging to ride.

To Eliza's dismay, Samuel quit pulling shortly after noon and just stood, back hunched, with a hacking cough. "I'm sorry," he said at last. "I can't go on."

"We'll manage," Eliza said. So Jane and Eliza pulled the cart alone. The little ones all sat in the cart, using a tarp to keep the water off. Baby Daniel popped his head out from beneath the tarp and watched his father leave, calling, "Da?"

Eliza pushed the baby back under the shelter. "Da will be okay," she lied, and pulled the handcart, providing a comforting presence for the babies, while Jane pulled at her side.

But minutes later, Samuel returned. "The sick wagon is so full that the driver turned me back. Folks are slogging beside the wagon, holding on so that the oxen might pull them. But there was no room inside."

Eliza had been helping tend the sick. Most of those on the wagon were ill with dysentery, and often the wagon would have to stop so that someone could stagger into the nearest bushes to relieve themselves. It was a filthy disease. Samuel was better off away from the wagon.

Samuel's face looked gray and pasty; his eyes were haunted. Eliza wanted to put him on the handcart, but between the twins, little Sarah, and the flour, the handcart could hold no more.

"Grab the back of the handcart then," she said. "Jane and I can pull."

Between the mud, the rain, the sand, the weight of the flour in the cart, and Samuel hanging on in order to get a little rest, it made for a hard day.

That afternoon one of the children in camp, a little red-haired boy named William Leason, succumbed to death. He'd had a burning fever, along with dysentery.

As the men pitched tents in the rain, with a fine mist rising up from the ground, mournful wails from William's mother ascended above the camp, sounding eerily like the howl of a wolf.

The baby's death sent Ann Howard into a panic. As soon as the tent was up, Ann rushed them inside and put them under a pile of blankets to keep out the chill.

"Let them run around a bit," Eliza said. "They've been sitting in the handcart all day."

"Run around?" Ann said. "We've got to keep them warm!"

The woman has good protective instincts, Eliza thought. *She would have made a good mother.*

So Eliza got out some tin pans and put them under the blanket, letting the babies bang them with spoons, so that they could make a game out of getting warm.

Ann rounded on Mary Ann and Sam Junior, her voice shrill and desperate. "You get under the covers, too. Tomorrow, you ride on my handcart!"

Sam looked up at Eliza, hoping to get a reprieve. "Mother," Sam Junior said in a hurt tone, "I don't want to be treated like a baby. I can walk tomorrow."

Eliza considered the thermodynamics of the situation. Every bit of energy that Ann expended in the children's behalf spared the children a bit, increasing their chances of survival. Eliza glanced at her husband to see if he'd venture an opinion, but Samuel looked haggard and weak, and squatted like a dazed bird, unhearing.

"You can walk," Eliza told Sam Junior. "But when you grow tired, perhaps you'll welcome Ann's kind invitation."

Ann grinned at the victory. Outside in the evening gloom, a

light sprang up, and smoke filled the air, mingling with Sister Leason's wails. Despite the wet, Captain Willie had managed to start a fire with the kindling from the tinder box. The rain had fallen for two days straight, and Eliza knew that if it didn't stop soon, they'd run out of kindling. Tomorrow there'd be no fire.

"You all stay inside and dry off," Ann said. "I'll go cook your dinner." She bustled out, taking her own cooking pans.

Eliza crawled under the blanket and played with the twins, hugging them and cuddling to make sure that they were warm. Sarah crawled under the blanket, too, and Eliza peered up at her for a moment and was taken aback. Sarah's face looked so skeletal. There was hardly any flesh on it, and the girl had dark circles under her eyes. When she grinned at her mother, the effect was horrifying.

For days now, Eliza had watched helplessly as the twins starved. They were losing weight, an ounce or two per day, so that their ribs poked out more and more.

But she hadn't been watching Sarah and the other children as well.

Ann was right. Sarah and even the older children were in trouble. Eliza couldn't rely on the other women in the tent the way that she could on Ann.

The other women were all subdued, worn out, even though none of them worked half as hard as Eliza had to. The Linford children, being in their teens, were more of a help to their parents on the trek than a hindrance. But Brother Linford was as starved as Eliza's husband, and his wife, Maria, had a weak constitution. Grandmother Funnel had once run the mission home in Norfolk, taking care of missionaries but also keeping several boarders. One would have thought that she would be used to serving large numbers of people, but the long trip was taking its toll on her, leaving her haggard. Her daughter, Lizzie, took care of her, and Marian Miller specialized in just taking care of herself. With four women to pull one handcart, the women were all making out well.

Not like Eliza. She felt as if she was being stretched thin. Her husband was worn to a frazzle. The twins were in that exploring phase, always running about and putting things in their mouths, and one mother could barely manage the two of them, much less cook and clean and look after and entertain the rest of her brood.

She had to let something go, so she had been letting everything go, just a little. The children had runny noses. Her daughter Mary Ann was in charge of combing her sister Sarah's hair but hadn't done it in three days—a dangerous thing when half the camp was afflicted with lice. So Eliza was relying upon Ann.

Suddenly, Eliza came to a decision. She climbed up out of the tent and went outside, where Ann was at her handcart, mixing up bread dough.

"Ann," Eliza said, "I want to ask you a favor."

"Anything," Ann said.

"If I die, I want you to take care of my children."

There was a long silence. It was an eerie moment to ask, for almost as soon as the question was out of Eliza's mouth, Sister Leason began to wail again.

Can't anyone get that woman to shut up? Eliza wondered and then immediately regretted the thought, for she had lost a child once, a babe born just before her son William, who was now twelve, and she recalled how the cries had been torn from her throat and how her heart felt as if it might split open at any moment. It was because Susannah had died that Eliza had gone to work as a nurse, hoping to arm herself with as much knowledge as possible so that nothing like that ever happened to one of her children again.

Ann looked up at Eliza from the corner of her eye. Soberly she asked, "Are you feeling ill, Sister Gadd?"

Eliza felt inside, tried to explain herself. "Not yet. But I feel so weak, stretched so thin, I'm afraid of what might happen. We've got miles and miles to go. I think that we should all be afraid. I think that we should all be prepared for the very worst. We've had three deaths in camp this week, and if you look around, you can see how the old folks are failing. Now it's hitting the children. So I need to know, can I count on you to mother my children if I die?"

Of course such bargains were made between friends all of the time out here on the prairie. Sister Campkin's husband had asked a young man named Joseph Young to watch over her in the event of his death, and so when Brother Campkin did succumb to an illness, Joseph had brought the Campkin family from Kansas City to Iowa to get them started on the trek. Joseph was working the cattle drive with Eliza's oldest son, Albert.

"You know," Ann said, "I love your children as if they were my own, the babies especially. If anything should happen, I want you to know that you can rest easy. I'll be their mother."

"Thank you," Eliza said, feeling that the matter was settled. But apparently it was not, for Ann leapt up and hugged her close, clinging to her as tightly as could be, as if to seal the bargain.

The next morning dawned bright and fair, but a cold rain began to hiss through the air again at noon. An hour later, Brother Jesse Empey from England was slogging along, pulling his handcart through the mud, when he fell dead to the ground, still gripping the handles of his cart.

That night, after the funeral, Joseph Wall came to Baline's tent and announced, "You're done. No more pulling the handcart. From now on, I'm going to walk."

Baline had been pulling him for a solid month. It's true that in the past week, he had ridden less and less, but Baline had held to the daily ritual as if it were a sacred responsibility. The hard work had made her lean and strong. The muscles in her calves and in her back felt like cords of rope. But she was also exhausted every night.

"Good news, huh?" Father Jens said that night. "Now you can play with your friends tomorrow."

Baline had hardly played with them for a month. She was too tired tonight, and it was too rainy. But she knew that tomorrow would feel like a holiday because she had no cart to pull.

After that, the days began to blend into one for Baline. The rain broke that night, and so she had enough energy to play for half an hour the next afternoon, but she grew tired quickly. It was the same the next day, and the next.

The trail began to rise steadily. Gone were the sweet lush grasses of the plains. Instead, the grass thinned to nothing and the rocky hills became a desert, with only the sparsest sagebrush and smattering of cactuses. With the grass went the buffalo, antelope, deer, and the Indians and the wolves that fed on them.

One brother from England, William James, had a large family, and he was accustomed to going out each day with his shotgun and bringing back rabbits or maybe a goose for his children. Now, he came back empty-handed.

Beside the river, where one might expect lush grass at the water's edge, was the worst of all. Prairie dogs, a type of small squirrel, were constantly nibbling the grass down to its roots. Brother James went out one day and brought back only a pair of prairie dogs. His shotgun had blown each creature nearly in half. No one in his family would eat them, but others in camp were hungry enough to do so.

So Levi Savage and Joseph Elder quit hunting for big game. Instead, the women and children foraged for what the wilderness offered. Savage showed the immigrants how to cut down a prickly-pear cactus and scrape off the needles, then slice it up and fry it up for dinner. It tasted like a green bean, and though it offered little sustenance, Baline began to look forward to having a little cactus in her nightly "stew," a broth made with cactus, a little wheat, and water.

The settlers also learned how to make soap from yucca roots, but this required one to dig in ground as hard as cement, and though Baline tried it once, she found that she did not have the energy to try a second time.

No cattle were butchered after the saints left Ash Hollow. None of the cows gave milk.

Gone were the berries, the wild plums, and grapes. The only trees along the river were ancient cottonwoods, without bark or leaves. Their heartwood was as white as bone, and as the pioneers plodded through this empty land, among the dead forests, with the prairie dogs giving their little barks of warning, Baline felt as if she were wandering through some wasteland from her nightmares. In her imagination, the dead forest became giant bones, like backbones and cracked ribs, as if some vast beast had died.

There was no time to stop, no time to rest. The food was growing short, and each day Captain Willie would urge the people on with the call of "Fort Laramie is not far. Get up. Go on." With forced marches through these dead lands and the nights beginning to freeze, people began to weaken, to sicken, and to complain. The captains tried rousing them with speeches, but even the finest oration cannot fill an empty belly.

Baline found that Mary Hurren and Agnes Caldwell had grown too tired to play anymore. There were no nightly games, no hunting for pretty flowers or treasures. Nor, when the girls got tired, could Baline move them with stories about going to see the prophet or visiting Zion. Instead, the girls got together with Sam Junior, Bill, and the Linford boys and together they went on nightly hunts, roaming far to search for cactuses or rattlesnakes or songbirds, but always dreaming of bigger game.

In this time, Baline found something she hadn't expected. Despite the growing sense of desperation, despite the specter of death, she was content in a way that she'd never felt before. She was at peace.

The camp had begun to work like a well-oiled machine. A few weeks ago, Baline had gone about seeking to do good, to seek inspiration on how to help others. Suddenly she realized that all around her, others were doing the same.

When it was time to set camp, no one shouted or asked what needed to be done. If tent poles needed to be carried from the supply wagon, men and boys showed up to carry them. If a pot needed to be washed, someone would pick it up, wash it, and set it in its place.

In their morning scripture study, Jens was reading the Book of Mormon, where it talked about how the people of Nephi grew in spirit only when the Lord sent them tribulations to humble them.

Suddenly in every prayer, morning and night, Baline noticed how the saints began to praise the Lord—often with tears in their eyes, often sobbing—as they gave thanks for their constant hunger or expressed gratitude for the merciless cold, for their poverty, their thirst, for their sickness and their fatigue.

Baline hadn't known that a person could value such things, but she began to see how it humbled people and brought them closer to God, and as Jens once said, "We are so blessed to have so many needs."

So the saints plodded from sunrise to sundown, longer if the moon allowed, almost racing toward the safety of Fort Laramie. In the lonely march, it was not uncommon to hear some weary soul begin to sing a hymn in an effort to find strength or to see an old woman mumbling prayers almost ceaselessly.

As her fat wore away and her energy dwindled, sometimes Baline felt that the only thing that let her move forward from one stop to the next was the spirit of God which seemed to fill her like an inferno.

Not all of the people felt as Baline. Some fell away. There were a few who shirked their responsibilities—men who would abandon their guard posts at night; women who wished their own children dead so that they might have a few extra morsels of food.

Eliza, with her seven children, had to guard against those who would pilfer any food left unattended. She learned not to leave a loaf of bread to cool, or even so much as a cactus leaf unguarded.

Rock formations began to rise on either side of the river, towering structures of sandstone with names like Mastodon Lookout and Indian Fortress.

On September twenty-third they climbed a small hill and spotted a huge finger of stone pointing toward heaven, still far to the west, called Chimney Rock. The settlers staggered on, and on the twenty-fourth they camped in the shadow of Chimney Rock, a place so beautiful, with its striations of brown sandstone and gold- and gray-colored clays, that it was almost as if God had decided to erect his own temple here in the wilderness.

Here, Captain Willie and Captain Savage stood side by side and begged the people to stop their grumbling and seek a spirit of accord. It seemed to Eliza that the two men had reconciled, and whatever animosity Captain Willie had felt toward Savage, it was far in the past.

The next morning, they turned their backs to Chimney Rock and struggled on.

Eliza was called upon to minister to the sick on a daily basis. The people were failing quickly. Some women had begun to lose hair, and faces that had been fat when the journey began now looked as if they were but skulls. Eliza's hunger was more than a gnawing in the belly now. It was a consuming thing that she felt in every fiber of her body, leaving her constantly drained.

Now it was not just the old that begged to ride in the sick wagon. It was the children of six or seven who had grown too weak to walk. It was the pregnant women and those who had carried toddlers across the prairie. It was men who'd been asked to pull handcarts for too long and then stay up too late guarding against the Cheyenne. It was teenagers who began to suffer terrible cramps. It was everyone who wanted in the sick wagon.

Eliza now longed only to reach Fort Laramie, hoping that they might find some oxen to buy to help pull the wagons.

That day, Captain Savage was sent out to hunt for buffalo or deer but found only a half-starved horse, a bay mare. It was too weak to carry an adult, but it was valuable all the same. With time and proper feed, it could fatten up, become a fine animal. Savage let the children take turns riding it, giving many of them a relished break from the journey.

Eliza felt grateful for that. The company had several mules that the church had provided for the captains, and Captain Willie had refused to ride his, as had the others, except in emergencies. Some of the elderly were allowed to ride the mules, but not the children. Now, the young ones had a chance to ride, those who were ages five to nine, expending a little less energy than they would have otherwise.

Minute by minute, Eliza thought, *Savage is lengthening their lives.*

The twenty-fifth was the birthday of her twins, Isaac and Daniel, who turned two. Eliza had no presents to give them, so William, Sam Junior, and their ragtag friends ranged far and wide that day, hunting for prickly pear cactus so that the twins might eat their fill. Brother James heard of their need and went out that evening and shot the family a prairie hen, a plump bird that looked much like a black chicken.

Brother Chislett warned them against trying to eat it, for he said, "There's a reason that a starving coyote will chew his own tail off rather than eat one of them birds." He was right. Eliza had to hack the carcass with an ax just to gut it, so tough was its flesh. The meat turned out to be as chewy as gristle, and the fat was so putrid that the twins spat it out, far preferring to feast on cactus, of which they got their fill.

Still it left Eliza feeling melancholy. It was a far cry from the birthdays in England, where the children might get shortbread for a treat, along with some new clothes or a toy.

Samuel saw her mood, gave her a hug, and promised, "We'll make it up to them next year."

Eliza realized that she was being silly. The twins would never remember this birthday no matter what gifts they might receive. They were just too young.

The saints were too tired to sing around the campfire that night. The camp felt cold and miserable, and as Eliza looked from one haggard face to the next, each with the stamp of death upon it, she found herself wondering who would fall next.

Soon after prayer meeting, she took her sleeping Daniel to the tent.

She heard Lizzie Funnel and Marion Miller giggling inside, a sound that seemed odd, for she had heard so little laughter lately; Eliza stopped to listen.

Lizzie: "Surely you jest. Brother Hurren is large, but he's all bone. I'd much prefer Sister Greeley. She has very fine hams on her."

Marion, giggling: "It's not ham I'm hungry for, it's some nice greasy bacon, and with that belly of his—"

Eliza opened the tent flap, and both the young women covered their mouths with their hands. "How dare you!" Eliza said, her eyes flashing with anger. "Proper young ladies—talking about cannibalism? I should . . . I should . . ." Eliza huffed as if seeking a sufficient threat—"I should boil up both of your bones for soup!"

The girls squealed with laughter, and Eliza laid the toddler under his blankets.

But when Eliza got back outside, she heard a commotion. In the midst of dinner, one man grabbed the food from his three children and his wife and began to bolt it down greedily, mad with hunger. His wife screeched at him and tore at his eyes with her fingernails, and he tried to wrestle her off.

He was a lean man, so starved that it looked as if his eyes bugged out of his skull, and he barely had the strength to fight his wife. Because of his starved condition, Eliza suspected that he was plagued by stomach worms and that whatever he ate merely became food for the worms, but she had no wormwood to treat him.

It was commonly known that he was a thief and had stolen a farmer's piglet in Iowa. Now, as the food grew scarce, pilfering was becoming more of a problem. This starveling was considered the most likely suspect. So as he fought his wife for a bit of bread, some men dragged him off, kicking him for good measure, and thrust him out of the camp. He sat out in the desert all night, wailing and moaning like a madman as he begged forgiveness.

But the guards shouted, "You stay out there for the night. Try to come back, and we'll shoot."

Eliza worried for the wretch. She thought of going to Captain Willie to get permission to give the man a blanket, but worried that he might deny the request.

So Eliza took her own blanket out, along with the inedible prairie hen, and told the wretch, "Merry Christmas."

As the man fell upon the greasy bird, doing his best to rend some flesh from the bone, Eliza said her first prayer in many years: "God, I hope I'm never that hungry."

❦

On the next afternoon, the twenty-sixth of September, Anne Bryant, a dainty old woman, won Eliza's little contest, becoming the next to die. She'd been riding in the sick wagon for days, and Captain Willie had asked Eliza to check on her. The day was particularly grueling. The company left the side of the Platte and had to march fourteen miles over dry, rocky roads through Rubideaux's Pass.

The day was so cold and the road so hard that even the animals began to balk, staggering in their traces, stopping, refusing to go one step farther.

At day's end Eliza found Anne sitting in the sick wagon, apparently asleep, her skin grown cold and pale. After that, hunger and fatigue conspired to turn the next few days into a walking nightmare. Eliza marched each day, sometimes wandering in a daze, and felt as if she herself might be the next to go. *Each of us is dying a little every day*, she thought.

Near the last of September, as Captain Willie said they were nearing Fort Laramie, they met a wagon train heading back east. It consisted of about twenty families with perhaps a hundred people in all. Their leader stopped to talk to Captain Willie, and word came down the line, whispered from one handcart to the next, "They're apostates, leaving Utah." And a few moments later, "They say the Cheyennes killed Almon Babbitt, not too far ahead of here."

Eliza could hardly believe it. Almon Babbitt had seemed so sure and masterful. He'd made the trip over the plains forty times and befriended every chief. How could he be dead? She wondered, *Yet how is it that we, so unprepared for this journey, made it past the Cheyenne alive?*

As the wagon train passed, Eliza expected the apostates to hurl insults and taunts, but Eliza watched the faces of the women and children. They weren't angry at the saints and didn't curse their foolishness for coming. They just looked beat.

Much as we do, Eliza told herself.

Two hours later, the handcart company came upon a contingent of cavalry soldiers, also heading east. Captain Willie had fallen back with the sick wagon, and so Levi Savage spoke with the commanding officer, a stern little man with an astonishingly rough face. The officer, a sergeant, gave the handcart pioneers a look of studied contempt and peered at them as if trying to assess whether anyone in the group might be worth shooting.

"We heard that Almon Babbitt's dead," Levi Savage said cordially. "Any truth to that?"

"Deader than Jesus," the sergeant said, his eyes roving over the women in the group with undisguised lust. He never bothered to look Savage in the eyes.

"Can you tell us more?" Savage begged.

"He put up a good fight," the sergeant said. "Killed a whole passel of Cheyenne. Seven of 'em, some say, maybe eight. They 'et his liver for it."

Then he saw Levi Savage's half-starved bay mare. Eliza's daughter Mary Ann was taking her turn riding the horse.

"Where'd you get the mare?" the sergeant asked.

"I found it, four days back," Savage said.

The commander thought a moment, then announced, "That's my horse."

Savage's face darkened. "If that was an army horse, wouldn't it have an army brand on it?"

"It's my horse—my personal horse," the sergeant said, "and I'll be taking it back now."

Everything about it seemed wrong. Eliza knew the man was lying. He had no claim on the animal. But he was smart enough to know these Mormons couldn't afford horses.

Sam Junior offered, "Maybe you should talk to Captain Willie?" then asked Levi Savage, "Want me to get Captain Willie?"

The sergeant replied by drawing his Colt and aiming between Savage's eyes. All twenty soldiers immediately drew rifles from their scabbards, covering every man and woman within fifty yards. Eliza didn't know much about guns, but even at a glance, there was something odd about these. The barrels were too short, and each one had a cylinder on it, like a Colt revolver, to hold multiple rounds. These were the army's new experimental rifles, the 1855 Springfield models.

Eliza looked into the sergeant's eyes and saw only a hollow thing. There was no humanity, only a passionless beast. He'd killed before and would do so again. What had Babbitt said, "Steer clear of General Harney and his men?"

These men would murder us all for a half-starved horse, she realized, and then they'd laugh about it for the rest of their days.

As a soldier took the horse, Eliza knew that Savage would get no justice. He could lodge a complaint at Fort Laramie, but these soldiers were all in it together.

Surely the sergeant had to see what dire circumstances the settlers were in! Yet he stole the horse right out from under Eliza's daughter, leaving her to walk. *Minute by minute,* Eliza thought, *he'll be killing my daughter.*

That's when Eliza knew that there would be no food for the saints at Fort Laramie.

25

The Whoremonger of Laramie

Captain Willie had always tried to be the best man that he could be. He studied the scriptures diligently and meditated over the best books. But at times he wondered how much any of that really helped. *The world is so complex*, he thought, *that sometimes despite our best efforts, it seems almost impossible to know what is right.*

He found himself in such a dilemma on the day his company finally reached Fort Laramie. It was the twenty-ninth of September, and his people were failing quickly. He could look into their eyes at night and see their bleak condition. It was almost as if the only thing that held their spirits to their bodies was hope, the hope that food and warm clothing might be waiting for them at the fort.

So on the twenty-ninth they approached the fort, seeing the first signs of civilization in many weeks. About seven miles from the fort, they reached the Indian agent's office, run by a Mr. Tippets. It was a long building used as a storehouse, and outside it were several tee-pees, very clean and tidy. A few Indians sat listening as one played a wooden flute.

As the handcarts neared, the Indians rose up, dusted themselves off, and watched the saints with great gravity. Two of the dozen Indians wore huge war bonnets, decorated lavishly with beads and a hundred eagle feathers. It seemed to Captain Willie that the bonnets were larger than those worn by the Sioux, and one of men's shirts, red with white spots, was too colorful to be Pawnee.

The hair rose on the back of Captain Willie's neck.

Tippets himself came out and stood by the door, with his young Sioux squaw at his side, a shy creature of thirteen or fourteen.

Captain Willie strolled over and addressed him quietly, jutting his chin toward the Indians. "Are these Cheyennes?"

"Yep," Tippets said, speaking around a huge wad of tobacco.

"Are you aware of the attacks they've been making on settlers?"

"Yep," Tippets said again, then he spat on the ground beside the door. A brown spot in the grass showed where a spittoon should have been. "They've come to make amends."

"I heard that they took a woman captive, Susannah Margetts?"

Tippets nodded. "They've agreed to give her up. Major Hoffman has been holding some of their people hostage over at the fort. So they're bringing the Margetts woman in to trade. She ought to be here in no time."

A wave of relief washed over Captain Willie. He'd been vexed about the Cheyenne for weeks, his muscles knotting with worry. Now he felt the tension slowly begin to ease.

"I don't get it," he said. "What led to the hostilities in the first place?"

"A couple of young bucks tried to stop a mail coach back in August, wanting to get some tobacco. The driver got scared and pulled a gun, shot one of 'em. So the Cheyenne went and took revenge for his murder on the first trapper they come by.

"So Hoffman rounded up a dozen Cheyenne and tried to put 'em in jail. They figured he was out to hang them, so most of 'em took off running into the dark, and the army shot one of their chiefs.

"After that, they figured Hoffman was fixin' to wipe 'em out. The chiefs wanted to make peace, but some of the young ones went on a rampage."

"Hunh," Captain Willie said. He eyed the Cheyenne. Like the Sioux and the Cherokee, they were very civilized looking, a handsome people. But he'd seen their bloody handiwork, too.

"Any news out of Kansas?" Tippets asked.

"None fresh. You?"

"War's fixin' to break out," Tippets said. "The army run off Old John Brown, so a bunch of slavers been crossing the Missouri, tryin' to finish what he started. Been eight or ten battles just in August alone! Oh, and they freed the governor!"

Captain Willie shook his head sadly. He was out of touch with American politics. Joseph Smith had prophesied that the North and South would go to war, but that the opening shots would be fired in South Carolina. So Captain Willie believed that the war was coming. He just doubted that it would start in Kansas.

"Uh, you Mormons pro-slavery, or against?" Tippets asked. The question was hostile, and Tippets looked as if he'd throw a fist if Captain Willie answered wrong.

Considering the fact that Tippet's wife had been bought like a slave, Captain Willie figured that Tippets was pro-slave. Still, a man has to stand up for what he believes. He wasn't sure if he should tell Tippets that he believed that the main reason that the Prophet Joseph Smith was assassinated was because he had preached abolitionism in a pro-slavery state. Many of the same Missourians that were murdering folks in Kansas were probably leading the mob that shot the Prophet.

"Mormons are against it," Captain Willie said simply. "We believe that all men and women are children of God, created in his image, with the ability to become as he is."

Captain Willie waited for the man to throw his punch, but Tippets just grinned broadly and thrust out his hand, offering to shake. "Glad to hear it!"

Captain Willie said his good-byes and continued plodding up a dusty road, the first real road that he'd seen in five hundred miles, and he began to wonder. *What if I were to see Susannah Margetts at the fort? What would I say to her? Would she blame me for getting her husband kicked out of the church? Would she blame me for her husband's death? Surely she's been abused by the Cheyenne braves, probably dozens of times. Will she blame me?*

He felt guilty. Such a terrible price had been paid for Thomas's indiscretions. Captain Willie would not have wished such horrors on anyone.

He trudged on. The company was forced to make camp about four miles west of the fort. The land closer had all been grazed down to stubble, so that there was no feed for the cattle. Not that there'd been much feed lately. Summer was past, and the grass here in the high desert, which was never abundant, had all been blasted by the summer sun and turned to straw. The oxen might just as well have chewed dirt, for all the nourishment the straw gave.

The company camped on a small hill near a seeping spring that gave rise to copious small willow bushes and weeds. These were all that the oxen would have to eat.

Because they camped late that night, Captain Willie sent Captain Woodward to the fort to learn what provisions the apostle had been able to procure.

Woodward returned with nothing but a letter. While the saints huddled around a campfire, Captain Willie retired to his tent and read it by candlelight, unfolding the heavy yellow parchment and easily deciphering the flowing script. Franklin D. Richards said:

"My Gracious Friend and Dear Brother in the Gospel, Captain James G. Willie—

"I feel to praise the Lord and to congratulate you on making it thus far in your journey.

"But I fear that I have unpleasant news. I have spoken to the commander of the fort, Major William Hoffman, and explained the extremities that you suffer under. But I fear that he is no friend to the Mormons, and rather than offer his hand in brotherhood and take this opportunity to succor the Lord's people, he rather rejoices in our afflictions and sees it as an opportunity that he will turn to his benefit.

"Consequently, there is nothing much to be had at the fort. There will be no clothes, no blankets for your little ones, no teams or oxen to pull your wagons.

"A little food is available, but Major Hoffman will only sell it at prices so dear that one might as well pay in blood. He demands $20 per hundred pounds for flour when he should only get $2 or $3. Even then, he will not save your lives, but claims that he hasn't enough to provision your company or the others that follow. I have arranged a line of credit so that you can purchase what you may—a little beans, rice, salt, and bacon, and beg you to make good speed as fast as you can to the Sweetwater, where more supplies will await you.

"In an effort to hasten your journey, I ask that you leave the independent wagon company here at the fort for the next two weeks so that their oxen may rest and they do not slow your company.

"Do not let these trials distress you. We came to this earth to be tested, to see if we are worthy or not to stand at God's side in the world to come. It seems that God wishes to test your people a little further. But be of good cheer, brother, and know that God loves you, and that his prophet stands waiting to greet you with arms extended wide in the beloved valley of the saints . . ."

By the time Captain Willie had finished reading, his hands were trembling in fear.

What in the world was Richards thinking? Had he lost his mind? Had he ever even had a mind to lose? Captain Willie couldn't tell his people that there was no food, no clothing—that an apostle of the Lord had failed to keep his promise! He couldn't speak such words to mothers who already couldn't sleep at night because of the wailing of their hungry babes!

Leave the independent wagons behind? It was true that the folks on those wagons had refused to consecrate their goods to the benefit of the group, but it was also true that they were of some help. As the provisions failed, it left more room in the wagons for those who were too sick to travel. Without the wagons, a number of the aged and infirm would have to walk. Taking the wagons from them was practically murder.

Captain Willie made some calculations on the back of the letter. He had brought enough food to last for seventy days, but the company was far behind schedule. At the rate that his rations were dwindling, he might manage to make it to the Sweetwater, but there was a good chance that the supplies would run out. Captain Willie's blood boiled at the thought, and he tore the letter in outrage.

Damn you, Franklin D. Richards! he seethed. *You lied at every turn.*

He tried to calm himself. He stilled his breathing and wiped sweat from his brow. He got up and paced. He could not remain angry at an apostle of the Lord for long. To do so risked damnation.

Surely Richards knows what he is doing, Captain Willie thought. *Surely the Lord has told him something that I am not privy to. Can it be that the Martin Handcart Company, which is just a few weeks behind, has greater need of the oxen? Or has Apostle Richards divined the condition of the oxen and knows that they need a rest?*

It was true that the oxen that pulled the independent wagons had more weight to haul than those that pulled the food, for the food was nearly gone. Thus, the oxen that pulled the independent wagons were struggling to keep up.

So Captain Willie calmed himself, girded his loins, and obeyed the counsel of the apostle.

He went back out to the campfire and hurled the crumpled letter in, watching glowing worms of fire devour the paper, leaving little green lines of flame along its edges.

The next morning, he dressed himself and walked four miles to Fort Laramie. Dozens of his people did the same, strung out in a line in front of him, others behind.

The fort itself was an aging set of buildings made from adobe, as brown and sere as the prairie around it. The fort had originally been a trading post for trappers. Back then, its only real defense was a raised plateau that might slow a cavalry charge. But the army had recently purchased the buildings and turned it into a walled city complete with guard towers and expanded garrisons for the soldiers. Here in the wilderness, it served as a haven for travelers and traders.

Just a couple hundred yards outside the fort, two dozen teepees stood, the Cheyenne come to negotiate.

The soldiers in the towers seemed agitated, tense.

Captain Willie entered the fortress, which was not an elaborate affair. There were two separate barracks, one for the enlisted men who ran the fort, another for the cavalry. Officers and non-military personnel had some small homes on the property. Other than that, there was only a post office, a cantina, and the trading post.

Major Hoffman stood out in the harsh sunlight, surveying the Mormons as they entered the fort. He was an aging man of fifty, with silver hair and cold blue eyes. He wore his uniform well; his flesh was tanned, and he was firm of bearing. Yet somehow the very fact that he stood here reminded Captain Willie of a drunkard hanging onto a pole as he loitered outside a saloon, gawking at the passersby.

Captain Willie strode up to the major, doffed his hat like a humble petitioner, and introduced himself. "Sir," he said, "I've got four hundred people wanting supplies, and a long stretch of desert in front of us. One of my men came by last evening—"

"Mr. Woodward," Hoffman interjected, displaying his ability to recall names.

"Yes, and he was able to order a few supplies. But I need a week's more, at the very least. I figure about a ton of wheat might do it. But if you lack that, then Mexican beans or rice—anything will do. And I need some fresh oxen. I'm willing to trade out my tired ones. May I have them?"

Hoffman sighed and glanced away, obviously perturbed. "No you may not," he said. "This is a military fort, not a supply post, or a charitable establishment. In case it has escaped your attention, we've had hostilities with the Cheyenne since August. I've been ordered to reestablish the peace if I can. The Sioux, Cheyenne, Arapahoe, and Blackfoot are all converging on this fort. I'll need what little I have to host them and buy them off with gifts. If I don't succeed, I may need the supplies to hold off a siege. My apologies, sir," he said, without affecting a tone of regret. "Good day."

"I'll pay top dollar," Captain Willie offered.

Major Hoffman ground his teeth and rounded on Captain Willie. "Not on your church's credit! It's been like pulling teeth to get any money out of them as it is, and with winter coming, you're all going to freeze anyway. What will happen then? How eager will Brigham be to pay for food for a bunch of corpses?"

Captain Willie bit his lower lip, glanced away in embarrassment. *So,* he thought, *now we come to the real reason.*

The church's emigration fund had been operating at a loss for several years. Many were the saints who had sold the church horses or cattle or other goods on credit, knowing that they might never be repaid.

Or maybe it went even deeper than that. Major Hoffman might be one of those people who felt such contempt for Mormons that he would rather see them all dead, even their toddlers, than to feed one.

"I see," Captain Willie said. "Thank you for your time."

"I wish you well," Major Hoffman replied, dismissing him with a nod.

Captain Willie went into the trading post, a dark room with many nooks and corners, filled with blankets, knives, and axes, along with various kegs for beans and pickles, and bags to hold grain. A pot-bellied stove in one corner had belched enough smoke in the morning to leave the air thick and bitter, while the scent of bear fat—which was coated on leg traps to keep them from rusting—left a putrid odor hanging in the air. New woolen blankets and lamp oil rounded out the scents. Somewhere in the shadows, rats were squeaking.

Captain Willie went up to a bespectacled clerk. "I'd like to buy some provisions," Captain Willie said. "But I'm shy on cash." He had two dollars and ten cents to his name. "I do have this watch—" Captain Willie pulled a gold pocket watch from his vest, "from Switzerland. I bought it in London just last winter for sixty dollars."

He held it up so that the clerk could see the fine engraving on it. Pheasants and rabbits ran around the rim, while a swift hound chased after them.

"I can give you twenty for it," the clerk said.

Captain Willie unstrapped his pistol, held it up. With the cessation of hostilities with the Cheyenne, he hoped that he wouldn't need it. "And this?"

"Six dollars," the clerk offered.

"Fine," Captain Willie said and gave up the only possessions he had that were of any value. He wandered among the bins, searching for food that he might buy in bulk. His watch would only buy a hundred pounds of flour, and that wouldn't last the company a day. Bacon, corn, beans, rice—all were out of the question.

He wondered if any of the immigrants might have a stash of money that they would offer, but he was quite sure that everyone else was at least as broke as he was.

As he searched, several Mormon women entered the trading post, talking gaily, until they saw the price tags. Few had enough money to buy anything. The widow Martha Campkin traded a fancy necklace for a few sweets for her children. Sister Caldwell traded some silver spoons and glass beads for five pounds of barley. The widow Rowley broke into tears as she traded her wedding ring for five pounds of bacon.

After she'd made her purchase Sister Caldwell came and whispered into Captain Willie's ear, "Did you hear? The commander of the fort is looking to buy himself a wife!"

Captain Willie raised a brow. "Major Hoffman?"

"I guess that's his name," Sister Caldwell said. "Christina came into town with me, and he spotted her on the street and called her into his office." She paused, as if waiting to relate something delicious. Christina McNeil was a strikingly beautiful young woman who was helping the Widow Caldwell drag her four children and her handcart across the plains. "So, he took her to his office and begged her to marry him. He said that she was far too pretty to starve on the plains, and he wanted to make a fine woman out of her. He showed her a bag of gold and bragged about how much money he makes, and he said that all our folks were so starved that they'd be a disappointment to any buzzard that landed on one of us looking for a meal. He warned that she would starve in the mountains if she continued on with the saints. She thanked him for his offer but told him sternly, 'I'd rather take my chances with the saints!' So he told her that there were no hard feelings and presented her with a nice ham! She's carrying it back to camp even now."

Captain Willie wasn't sure what to make of this. Major Hoffman was chasing girls that were young enough to be his daughters, if not his granddaughters.

"Has he made any other such offers?" Captain Willie asked.

He stepped to the door, saw the major opening a door for another young woman. Captain Willie squinted to see who it might be, but his eyesight was going, and he only saw that she was young.

"He seems rather desperate," Sister Caldwell said.

Captain Willie wondered at that. It was an unsavory deed. He wondered if any of the girls would accept. He wouldn't blame the one who did. After all, Hoffman might be saving her life.

But it galled him that Major Hoffman seemed to have ample food to bribe women into his bed, but none to feed a starving child.

Captain Willie gritted his teeth and vowed to move his people out of this accursed place as quickly as he could.

At last he found some barrels of hard biscuits that he could afford. They weren't much, but they were food, even if they were barely edible. With his gun, his watch, and all of the money he had, he bought three hundred pounds of hard bread—enough to hold his people for a day.

At a little after eleven, Captain Willie held a council meeting with his captains and relayed his bad news: there was almost nothing that the saints could buy in the fort. Franklin D. Richards had not been able to keep his promise, and as far as he could tell, there were no other provisions made.

Captain Willie knew that he could not delay telling his people openly. Rumors would soon spread. So he broke camp at two in the afternoon and traveled seven miles, passing the fort. Half of the independent wagon company pulled away from the handcarts and formed a little circle on a bluff overlooking the fort. The other half, having stronger oxen, remained with the company.

Captain Willie set camp in the early evening on the banks of the Platte River, not four miles from the fort. It was just as well that they stayed close. If any of his people had money, they would need to make sure to return and buy as many provisions as they could afford.

So he held a quick prayer meeting and warned the people about their dire predicament.

"What are we going to eat, if the provisions are gone?" one of the older men asked.

"We'll have to rely on the Lord to provide," Captain Willie said. "He can line up buffalo from here to Salt Lake City, if he so desires. But remember, it is up to you to do your part and find what you can to eat. Faith without works is dead. As the scriptures say, 'It is by grace that ye are saved—after all ye can do.'"

He closed the meeting, and almost immediately, half the company fled to the fort to buy goods.

At sundown the sky darkened slowly, fading from its piercing blue to a dark violet, a bruise in the heavens. A warm wind came rushing across the prairie, making the grasses rattle.

The immigrants rested for the night, and the sweet sound of violins stole through the camp. A few soldiers rode in from the fort, and Captain Willie worried that they would make trouble, but they only sat and chatted, making small talk, and one fine tenor served up a few songs before he left.

At ten that night, Captain Willie began to get some distressing news. William Woodward had been in town and had stopped to buy a meal in the cantina. He'd seen a man that he knew, an apostate named Steven Forsdick, walk into the cantina and peer across the room.

His eye caught hold of a young saint, a woman named Lucinda Davenport, who had been sitting at a table looking rather despondent. The two stared across the room at each other for all of thirty seconds, and then Forsdick boldly crossed the room and begged, "Marry me."

Lucinda said not a word. She took his hand, and together they went straight to Major Hoffman and were married.

Captain Willie knew the girl. She had been traveling with the independent wagons, with the Grant and Kimball wagon specifically, and thus she was not under his care. She was one of the weak-spirited creatures that had refused to consecrate her belongings to the church.

"We're better off without her," Captain Willie guessed.

But the news worried him. He told Woodward, "Go through the camp and find out how many other people are missing."

Half an hour later, Woodward returned with the news. "Christina Brown is gone, too." Christina, a young woman who had not been faring well, was nothing but skin and bones.

So, Captain Willie decided, Major Hoffman snagged himself a wife after all.

On the morning of October 1, the company rose to find that David Reeder, age 54, had died in the night. While the burial detail was at work, several men rode in from the west, missionaries heading to the states. They reported that the Apostle Parley P. Pratt was in their company, not far behind.

So services were held for Brother Reeder. Though Captain Willie felt an urgent need to get back on the trail, he dared not hurry the ceremony. Brother Reeder had several adult children in the camp, along with their husbands, wives, and children.

All morning long, Captain Willie felt tension building. He kept doing the math and feared that supplies would run out before he could reach the Sweetwater. So he asked the company clerk, Edward Griffiths, to give an accounting of the food on the wagons, hoping that there might somehow be enough. An hour later, Griffiths brought bad news. There was less wheat than Captain Willie had imagined—by three thousand pounds! Frantically, Captain Willie went with Griffiths and made his own count of the bags, confirming the news. Seven days' worth of supplies had vanished.

Major Hoffman had been willing to sell the company a little food, over a ton, but it wasn't even enough to make up for the loss.

"Are you sure that you've been measuring the wheat properly?" Captain Willie asked, and Griffiths showed him the one-pound scoop that was used for men, the twelve-ounce for women and older children, and the three-ounce scoop for toddlers.

Yet entire bags were gone, at least thirty of them.

Captain Willie wondered. Could Indians have crept into the camp by night and carried them off? He doubted it. Too much was gone. Besides, the Cheyenne would have stolen the mules and the women before they took the wheat.

No, it had to be thieves in camp, and there had to be more than one, for far too much food had been taken for a single man, or even a whole family. A ring of thieves, then. But who could have done such a thing?

There were several men that he might suspect. There was the wormy fellow who stole from his own children. Yet it couldn't be just one. It had to be several of them, men who stood guard at night, he imagined.

Captain Willie's mouth went dry and his heart pounded. He had always tried to be a good man, and now he feared that he was leading his people down the path of destruction.

By noon the company broke camp and traveled seven more miles until they reached the crossing for the Laramie River, which was both freezing cold and very deep this time of year.

The army had built a bridge over it, but when the saints reached the bridge, they found that it was guarded; a locked gate barred their way. A sign nearby said that the gate was to be open each day from eight until five, but though it was only four in the afternoon, the guards had the gate closed tight.

Captain Willie tried to persuade them to open it, but the men refused. One of them claimed, "We don't even have the key. It's at the fort, and we can't leave our post to go get it."

"If the gate is not to be opened today," Captain Willie asked, "when will it be opened?"

The guards looked at one another and finally answered, "Not for the next week, at least. The major wants this road sealed off, with all of the Indians about."

Captain Willie nodded. "Then we'll make camp here," he said. "Will you ask the major if we might have the gate opened in the morning, for just a few minutes, so that my women and children don't have to brave this water?"

The guards agreed, and Captain Willie set camp in the early

evening. As the sick wagons were unloaded, it was discovered that one of its passengers, William Reade, an elderly man, had passed on. Two deaths in one day. It seemed odd. William Reade had been a wealthy landowner back in England, and Brother Reeder, who had also died today, had worked in his employment. Master and servant both struck down in a single day. It seemed a portent.

The camp was set on the banks of the Laramie River, where the feed for the oxen was good. Captain Willie did not sleep that night. He set his guards as normal and then stayed up, hidden in his tent, and watched the food wagon, hoping to catch the thieves. It was the dark of the moon, with only stars shining violently in the heavens, and it was as good a chance for a thief to break into the wagons as ever. Yet no one did.

In the early morning, Captain Willie presided over another funeral service but didn't have the stomach to speak. His heart was heavy, and his eyes felt gritty and swollen, so he let Levi Savage do the honors.

A few missionaries rode into camp just after the service and announced that the apostle Parley P. Pratt was close behind. Captain Willie hoped that the apostle might bear some good news.

At eight in the morning, yesterday's guards rode in from the fort. Captain Willie asked if they had the key for the bridge, but the men only shook their heads. "Major Hoffman says you can swim it."

So the men waded across, carrying the women and children. Captain Willie made eight trips himself, until his legs were so numb that he feared that he would stumble on the slick round rocks beneath his feet.

Some men did falter. On his fifth trip across the river, Brother Gadd slipped underwater while carrying one of the two-year-old twins, then came bobbing up out of the water, stricken with fear. Another Dane slipped and floated a hundred yards downstream before he could get his footing.

When the saints reached the far shore, they sat shivering in blankets uncontrollably, struggling to warm themselves. But starvation was taking its toll, and Captain Willie seemed unable to recover.

Fortunately, the sun beat down strongly, and the saints nooned in its glare, wrapped in blankets, sunning themselves.

Parley P. Pratt rode up just as the last of the saints were climbing out of the water. Though he was nearly fifty, he was broad of chest and had a bold chin and dark hair that made him look more like some warrior of old than the mild preacher that he was. As Captain Willie and the others sat, steam vapors rising up as the hot sun smote their clothes, the apostle addressed the saints.

Parley was a good-natured man, one who often seemed to smile. He looked out over the company, appraising them, and inwardly Captain Willie wished for a blessing from the apostle or wished that Pratt would prophesy some good for the company.

"You're a tired-looking crew," Parley said. "You're as worn out as any company I've seen on these plains," he said gently, and it seemed to Captain Willie that that acknowledgment alone eased the weight from his shoulders. "You know, you're pulling these handcarts across the prairie at a snail's pace, but twenty years from now, there will be train tracks running over the ground here, and some of you will ride those rails and look out the window and see places you remember. You'll think back on how it took you a day to travel the distance the train goes in an hour, and you'll smile and think back at how hard it was, and how much stronger it made you, and how this journey blessed your lives, and you'll feel to praise the Lord for it.

"Fifty and a hundred years from now," Parley said, raising his voice, "your children will make machines that move even faster than those trains! They won't be satisfied to travel thirty miles an hour, or even fifty. They'll speed across the plains in little vehicles that travel farther in an hour than you can walk in a week! Eighty miles an hour, a hundred. They'll make other machines that fly through the air so fast, that they can cross the length of the plains in less than an hour. A thousand miles an hour they'll travel, two thousand, three, and more!"

Captain Willie peered around at the pioneers, worn faces with skin stretched too tightly and felt that Parley P. Pratt was losing them with his outrageous claims.

"It will happen!" Parley exclaimed. "I have seen it, and I know that it will be. Why must we do it? Because we are children of God; it is in our divine nature to scoff at boundaries, to overcome our limits, to grow and prevail as God has prevailed."

He gazed out over the crowd and turned his attention to speaking about Zion, about planting and building and creating a Godlike community in the West.

As he did, Captain Willie's mind wandered. All too soon, the apostle was done speaking, and he bade the saints good-bye. In the company of several missionaries, Captain Willie rode with him back to Fort Laramie and asked in private, "I got a letter from Franklin D. Richards. He said we can expect provisions at Pacific Springs. My people are in dire need. Do you have any good news for us?"

"Not the kind of news that you want or need," Parley answered. His tone was sober, thoughtful. "I saw him on the twenty-fourth of September. We camped at Independence Rock."

Captain Willie's heart froze, and his stomach tied into a knot. Independence Rock was only a couple of hundred miles north, up on the Sweetwater. Ten days ago, Franklin D. Richards was still more than three hundred miles from Salt Lake.

"So you saw no help for us?"

Parley stopped for a moment, thinking. "He told you that food would be waiting at the Sweetwater," he said, "because that was our original plan. When we contemplated trying the handcart method, we thought it prudent to provide outposts for the saints to resupply at. One was to have been built on the Sweetwater, another at Fort Bridger, and one near Fort Laramie. But Brother Brigham wasn't expecting so many handcart people to come. Two hundred, three hundred. That was our guess. So last winter, we began to wonder if it was worth the cost to build the outposts. It was decided that for this year, for the purpose of testing the handcart system, it made more sense to just send out supply wagons to meet the companies."

"But . . ." Captain Willie thought frantically.

"The supply post that Richards told you about doesn't exist," Parley said. "I'm sure that as soon as the prophet learns about your predicament, he will send food. But he had no forewarning that you were coming, that anyone was coming." Captain Willie thought furiously. "Elder Richards can't have made it to Salt Lake yet," Parley continued. "He asked me to tell you again to expect supplies at Pacific Springs. I bade him God speed and urged him to kill his horses if he had to. I can only hope that he is making good time. So far, it seems that the weather is holding."

It did indeed. Warm winds had blown in, and today it was hot, gruelingly so. After weeks of freezing weather along the Platte, it seemed as if summer had returned, and Captain Willie wondered if Richards's prophecy was indeed coming to pass and the elements were being tempered for his people's benefit. He hoped so. Heaven knew that his people could not take any more hardship.

"We don't have enough food to get us to Pacific Springs," Captain Willie said. "Someone has been plundering our flour at night. At least a ton is missing. I stayed up all night in an effort to find out who did it."

Elder Pratt's face hardened. He went from outrage one moment to acceptance the next. He was a frontiersman, well accustomed to dire circumstances. "Put guards on your supply wagons then, every night. If I guess right, you've been using the same men on each guard shift for weeks?" Captain Willie nodded. It was the best way to make sure that the men knew when they could rest. "Change the schedules. Make sure that you mix the men up."

"All right," Captain Willie said. "But that won't get the stolen flour back. I can't make it to Pacific Springs."

"Then reduce your rations," Elder Pratt advised, "and pray."

That night, as the company made camp, Captain Willie spoke beside Levi Savage and Captain Atwood and advised the saints that they needed to reduce rations by twenty-five percent, and at the same time lengthen their marches by five miles per day.

This meant that instead of getting a pound of flour, the men would get twelve ounces. Instead of getting twelve ounces of flour, the women would get nine. Instead of getting ten ounces of flour, the large children would get seven and a half. Instead of getting six ounces, the small children and toddlers would have four and a half.

"In the past three days," he said, "we've made but seven miles per day. We need to make twenty."

He saw strong men bow their heads and mothers reduced to tears. Children wept at the news and one man swore out loud, but what choice did they have?

When he asked for a sustaining vote of the plan, each person in the camp meekly raised his or her hand and voted to cut their rations.

That night, a tight guard was placed over the supply wagons. Captain Willie was nearly delirious from lack of sleep. He'd been awake for two days straight, and when he closed his eyes in his tent, he knew nothing until morning.

At dawn the handcarts set out, leaving the North Platte River and crossing some hills. There would be no feed for the cattle until they reached the river again, twenty-one miles distant, and no water for anyone. The temperature was a blistering 120 degrees, and Captain Willie had to keep his hat brim pulled low to save his tired eyes.

At noon the camp rested at the top of a bluff. During lunch, one of the Danes, Peder Larsen, expired. It seemed beyond comprehension. Peder was a strapping bear of a man, perhaps the strongest Dane in the camp, and like James Hurren, had carried hundreds of pounds of flour when others balked at lugging a single bag. To add to that, he often pulled his daughters, ten-year-old Anna Sophie and six-year-old Martine, along with an infant son in his cart. Yet he had lain down to rest at noon, very weary, and had asked his wife to give him a boot to use as a pillow. Now, the imprint of the boot was deeply imbedded in his white cheek.

Captain Willie didn't have time to bury him in the middle of the day, so he laid the body in the back of a sick wagon, and the company marched on.

They made twenty miles that day before darkness forced them to stop. They had not reached water. So they pitched their tents. There was no prayer meeting. Everyone was famished and exhausted.

They dug a hole by starlight and laid Peder Larsen in, while wolves sang a hymn in the background.

Captain Willie had never felt more exhausted in his life, but just before bed, Brother Gadd came to his tent. Brother Gadd looked haggard and worn to the bone. He covered his mouth as he coughed, and he was shivering despite the fact that the night was blistering.

"Captain Willie," he asked. "I need a blessing. Can you bring the consecrated oil to my tent?"

"You do look like you need a blessing," Captain Willie said. "I'll be along shortly."

"It's not for me," Sam said. "It's for our baby, Daniel. I dropped him into the river yesterday, and now he's down with a fever."

"I'll be right there," Captain Willie said. He went to his pack and fished around in the dark until his hands closed over a small silver flask with a golden eagle etched into it. Back in England, such a flask might have been used to conceal whiskey. But Captain Willie put it to better purpose.

He went to the Gadds' tent and found a miserable sight. Eliza sat holding the baby Daniel, who lay wheezing, unconscious, his eyes rolled back in his head. Eliza's oldest daughter, Jane, wept bitter tears, and the rest of the children hovered around their mother and the babe, crying also.

"He's been shivering and feverish since yesterday," Eliza explained, "but he quit shivering when the sun went down. It's like his body just gave out. We couldn't get him to eat, and I tried pouring a little tea down his throat, but it just went into his lungs and made him sputter."

Captain Willie looked at the babe, picked it up. He'd seldom seen a child so near to death's door. He wanted to offer words of comfort, so he felt inside himself, listening for the Holy Ghost to whisper something to his heart and heard nothing, or something that was worse than nothing.

Captain Willie fell silent. He wanted Eliza to see a miracle, something that would change her.

He recalled an incident from the scriptures where the disciples tried to cast a demon from a child, healing her, but they were unable.

So they took the child to Jesus, who healed her instantly, and afterward they asked, "Why could we not heal her?" Jesus answered, "This kind goeth not out but by fasting and prayer."

Captain Willie looked down at Daniel and felt in his heart, *This kind goeth not out but by fasting and prayer. But how can I ask this family to fast when they are all on the verge of starvation?*

I will fast, he promised himself.

He took Daniel in his hands, lifting him, and was surprised at how light he felt. At the beginning of the journey, he'd lifted one of the twins and thrown him in the air, playing. Whether it was Daniel or Isaac, he could not recall. But the child had to weigh close to thirty pounds back then. This boy was all skin and bones now and could not have weighed much more than fifteen pounds.

Samuel Gadd stood across from him and placed his own right hand under the child's head, as Captain Willie took out his flask and anointed the babe. The boy was clammy and sweaty. All through the anointing, Captain Willie prayed fervently for the child.

Afterward, Captain Willie sealed the anointing by the power of the holy priesthood and pronounced a blessing. He strained, listening with every fiber of his being, hoping that God would offer a miracle.

But Captain Willie's prayers seemed to rise up and echo back at him, as if the heavens were made of brass, and in the end, he could only offer a blessing of comfort for the family.

In the Book of Mormon, it said that "the continual, fervent prayer of a righteous man availeth much."

Captain Willie wouldn't have called himself righteous, but for years he had struggled to be the best that he could. He stumbled away from the tent, weary to the bone, and knelt in the dry grass under the stars. On a nearby hill, the wolves sang. *They're trailing the camp*, Captain Willie realized. *They smell death upon us.*

So he poured out his heart for long minutes as he begged the Lord to bless Eliza Gadd, to comfort the family, and to heal the child. Thus, he began his fast.

Eliza lay alone in the tent that night, a candle burning beside her. Her husband Samuel was feverish and should have been in bed. But he was needed to guard the food wagon, and so he went.

To Eliza's relief, at midnight Daniel roused a bit. His chest began to rise and fall more strongly, and he peered up at her, whimpering as if to beg for food. She tried to feed him a bit of bread, but he batted it away weakly. "Drink," he said. "Drink," and his little hand went to her blouse as he tried to pull it open. She had thought that he had forgotten by now. She hadn't had any milk for a month, so she gave him a little cold tea. He drank a couple of gulps and afterward shoved it out of her hand. "Drink, Mommy," he said weakly, then began to weep as he tried to nuzzle her breast.

She had nothing to give him but hoped that at least he would rest. So she opened her top and lay beside him as he took her nipple. He sucked at it only once, then seemed comforted and drifted to sleep.

"Rest now, and be strong," she said, and she pulled the blanket over them both.

The night was warmer than it had been since July, and she lay for a long time, relaxing.

Eliza didn't know when she had stopped believing in God. She supposed that it had happened when she was seven. Her father had invited a gypsy to the house for a séance, a woman named Madam Cravinski, and the old woman had come dressed in purple silks, wearing golden pendants and chains with pagan symbols on them—the eye of Isis, a cat, and the Star of David. Madam Cravinski lit perfumed candles that evening in preparation for summoning the spirits of the dead, and she asked questions about the woman that Eliza's father had wanted to contact, Eliza's deceased aunt Constance. She set Constance's portrait and some of her belongings upon the table, as if upon an altar.

The summoning was not to take place until midnight, and Eliza had wanted to stay up to see the ghosts. But her father sent her to bed.

Shortly afterward, Eliza sneaked downstairs from her room and hid under the big walnut table in the dining hall, with its ghostly white tablecloth draped all around her.

The candles burned all evening, and the moon glow streaming through the windows cast webs of silvery light everywhere. Just before midnight, Eliza's parents, the maid, and Eliza's uncle all entered the dining hall and took seats at one end of the table while the gypsy sat at the far end. Eliza had to scoot up to the middle of the table to avoid being discovered.

The séance began. Madam Cravinski asked everyone to hold the dead woman's image in their minds and call her name, explaining that the dead were often drawn to those who spoke of them. As the others called out, Madam Cravinski chanted in some ancient tongue and sometimes stopped to blow strange, nonmusical tones upon a flute. She called to Eliza's Aunt Constance for several minutes and then fell silent for a long time.

"Someone is here," the gypsy announced, and everyone stopped calling. The hair rose up on the back of Eliza's neck in anticipation.

"Spirit, announce thyself," Madam Cravinski commanded. "If thou be the spirit of Constance, knock three times."

Just then, something hit Eliza in the face. She was several feet from anyone and couldn't imagine what it would be, but she backed away by instinct. Just in front of her, something tapped the table. Once, twice, three times.

She peered into the shadows under the table, trying to figure out what it was and realized that it was a stick with a bit of bone on the end, perhaps a finger bone.

She studied it for long seconds, and she saw that Madam Cravinski was holding the long stick under the table. Eliza hadn't seen her with a walking stick earlier, and as Eliza peered at it she realized that this wasn't a walking stick at all. It was long and as thin as bamboo. Several sticks were hooked together in telescoping fashion, each fitted with a brass ring, so that they telescoped a good six feet. Thus, Madam Cravinski was able to sit at one end of the long table and pound on its middle.

She asked a few questions about life "on the other side" and answered each with a knock. But all too soon the spirit "grew weary" and the "connection" was broken. Madam Cravinski pulled in her little telescoping wand and stuffed it in a fold in her robe. Then she reached up and pulled something down off the table. Eliza realized that it was a fake arm with a ceramic hand, and that it had been sitting on the table all of the time while Madam Cravinski pounded from beneath. In the shadowy light of the candles, no one would have noticed. Madam Cravinski tucked the fake arm up under her scarves too and pulled her robe closed.

The séance ended and Madam Cravinski went home for the night, showered with gifts, and praise, and heartfelt thanks.

For days afterward, the household was abuzz with talk of the séance. Eliza dared not tell what she had seen, for fear that she would be punished for violating her father's rules.

But she had vowed to herself that she would never be fooled as her father had been. She refused to believe in anything again—spirits, ghosts, magic, Santa Claus, God—they were all the same. But as Eliza lay with Daniel, listening to his labored breathing, a part of her desperately needed some comfort. She prayed so softly that no words came out, only her breath. "Dear God, if you are there, save my son. He is innocent and deserves to live."

It wasn't a fancy prayer, like the written prayers chanted in the Anglican Church, where the priest and the choir and the congregation each took turns speaking words so sublime that they were poetry, echoing from the tall ceilings. Yet her prayer came from the heart.

Eliza slept easier for it, until the bugle roused her at five in the morning.

She lay there under the blanket for a long moment, feeling her husband warming her back. It was not a cold morning, but her stomach was knotted from hunger. The twenty-mile march of the day before had left her worn to the bone.

Little Daniel had inched away in the night, and she could feel his lips barely brushing her nipple. She pulled him tighter against her for a moment, and as she roused further from her slumber, pure horror coursed through her veins. She could feel his little lips, cold and rigid, ringing her nipple; his chest no longer rose and fell.

Eliza bundled the baby up in a comforter and quickly threw on her clothes before her fellow inmates in the tent could rise.

As she dressed, she rehearsed in her mind all of the bad choices that had brought her to this point. She could have stayed in England when her husband left, could have tried braving it with her little ones. Yet with her mother and father dead, she would have had no one that she could rely on. So she'd chosen to follow her husband, to join all of the other foolish Mormons in Utah.

By the time she dressed, she was so full of grief and rage that she was breathless. Her heart pounded so hard in its cage of flesh that she thought it might burst.

It had only been one day on reduced rations, and Daniel was gone.

The death of a child brings an unspeakable pain. It didn't matter whether the child was shot out of her arms by a cavalry soldier or crushed under the heel of a Cheyenne. The pain was the same. This child had been ripped out of her arms by God.

She carried Daniel out of the tent in the cool dawn. The sun had not crested the horizon. Only a thin red line, like a bloody wound, heralded the coming day. In the distance, some strange bird shrieked again and again.

Eliza carried Daniel over to Captain Willie, who knelt over a fire, stirring up the ashes as he prepared to throw on a little sagebrush as tinder.

"Daniel's dead," she said, the words coming out cold and harsh. She opened the blanket so that he could see the child's face.

Captain Willie's jaw dropped as if she had slapped him, and he rose up with a smoking stick in his hand, one end a cinder with glowing worms of light on it, like a magic wand.

"Oh, Eliza, what can I do?" he asked, opening his arms as if to hug her, comfort her, his magic wand raised in the air.

She looked at the cold dead babe in her hands and wondered, *What can be done?* Captain Willie had not been able to heal the child. Certainly he wouldn't be able to raise it from the dead.

Due to the macabre miracle of death, there was nothing left of Daniel in the cold body she held. The essence of life had all leeched away. He would never smile again, or look up at her with a twinkle in his eye. He would never hold her hand or warm her with his breath as he kissed her cheek. He was clay. Whatever was left of Daniel just didn't matter.

Captain Willie wishes to convert me, Eliza thought. *But I shall convert him.*

She hurled the cold lump of flesh at Captain Willie's feet.

"Do what you will," she said at last. "Throw Daniel into the fire. Eat the child yourself, if you want. No sense in letting all that meat go to waste."

Eliza whirled and stormed away.

Captain Willie picked up little Daniel Gadd and dusted off the babe's face, then wrapped him in his blanket, covering the child one last time.

It had not been five minutes since he had learned that Brother Ben Culley had passed away in his sleep. It was the third death in less than twenty-four hours.

He watched Eliza's back for a moment, then went and set the child in his handcart, and kissed Daniel good-bye on the forehead.

He had only begun his fast last night, but now he swore to maintain it. He would go without food and water this day, as he had promised the Lord, though he could not hope to gain the blessing he had desired.

The day looked as if it would be another hot one.

Slowly, Captain Willie trudged out onto the prairie a couple hundred yards from camp, until he was lost in the shadows. There he knelt and poured his heart out to the Lord in prayer, not for the babe, but for Eliza Gadd.

26

A Hot Bath

The morning of October fourth, two more graves were dug on the prairie, and Daniel Gadd was laid beside old Ben Culley. Eliza stood stoically, rage chiseled on her face, her eyes rimmed and red as she refused to cry.

Baline mourned for her. More than that, she watched Sam Junior during the service and saw the pain in her friend's eyes.

Terrible hunger knotted Baline's stomach as Brother Gadd spoke a few final words over Daniel. Brother Gadd's face was drawn and haggard. But there was hope in him still. He said, "The prophet Joseph taught that a child who dies before the age of accountability, before the age of eight, dies without sin, and as such is taken to the bosom of our Father in Heaven.

"God, who is perfect, loves all men perfectly. His love swells wider than our own. His wisdom and compassion are immeasurable. We cannot care for our children as he would. We cannot love them as he does. We cannot begin to comprehend the joy that they feel as all of their pain and hurts are swallowed up in his presence."

Brother Gadd choked back a sob, and Baline peered into Eliza's eyes to see what effect the words had on her, but Eliza peered off into some inner hell, and if she even heard, Baline could not tell.

"I thank God that he sent the Prophet Joseph Smith to bear witness of this truth," Samuel Gadd said. "Without it, I would be comfortless now, and lost."

You wife is lost, Baline thought.

"I know," Samuel Gadd said, "that though the skin worms eat

my flesh, I shall stand beside the throne of God someday, and he will hand my son into my arms, resurrected and perfect, restored to his flesh, and God will allow me to raise this child that we love so dear."

Ann Howard burst into tears now, water flowing freely down her cheeks, for she had loved Daniel almost as if he were her own.

"So we say 'good-bye' to Daniel for a little while, and not farewell. We need not mourn Daniel.

"As we trudge now to Zion, we can be comforted knowing that little Daniel has already reached the Zion of our God and dwells forever in that sweet place."

Samuel Gadd's testimony lit a flame in Baline's heart, a flame so powerful that she felt as if she would be consumed.

As his father quit speaking, Sam Junior looked to the west, as if peering into the heart of Zion itself. His eyes filled with tears. It had been ages since he'd spoken of his dream of seeing Zion. Almost Baline had forgotten her own dream. Now, Sam Junior stared off longingly, as if he would abandon the camp and run the rest of the way.

Only yesterday Baline had stood beside Anna Marie Larsen as she buried her own father, Peder. The Larsens were tent mates with Baline, and Peder was from the island of Lolland and was a longtime friend of Jens Nielsen.

So much pain in such a short amount of time.

She had imagined that in helping her friends reach Zion, she would only have to lift them up and urge them on when they were tired. Now they faced challenges that Baline had no experience with.

After the service, she went to Eliza Gadd and tried to think of some way to reach her, some way to heal her pain, but nothing came to mind.

I would give her food, if I had it, Baline thought. But she had nothing to give.

So while the men heaped dirt over Daniel's still form, Baline hugged Sister Gadd and offered the only words of comfort that she could think of. "I love you, Sister Gadd."

Eliza's eyes flickered, as if she barely heard, and she peered at Baline for a long moment, as if trying to make sense of her words, and then replied, “It doesn’t matter. Love doesn’t make a difference now, does it?”

Baline ate that morning, but it did not help. She had been starving slowly for months.

The company did not march far. They reached the river again and began to follow it north. They only got two miles when Brother Ingra, an old man nearly seventy, collapsed and died. He’d pulled his demented wife in his handcart across the plains for hundreds of miles until she died, and now he was dead too.

“We’ll stop here,” Captain Willie ordered. It was the fourth death in less than a day. “We’ll slaughter a calf and get some rest. It’s too hot to travel anyway.

“You women might want to wash your bedding and give everyone a turn at a bath. The lice are getting thick in camp bedrolls.”

Among the Danish saints, the deaths of so many were shocking, and as some of the women and infants went off to bathe and wash clothes, the elders held a meeting.

The heat was unbearable, and Captain Amundsen ventured a thought. “The apostle Franklin D. Richards promised that the weather would be tempered for our sakes, and his counselors said that winter would turn to summer. It is my opinion that this has come to pass, for it is October fourth now, and it is as hot as midsummer.

“Therefore,” he suggested, “I propose that we show our trust in the Lord. Let us take our excess bedding, those things that weigh down our carts, and get rid of them. Let us prove our faith!”

This show of faith was greeted by cries of “Amen,” and the Danes immediately went to work tossing out the extra blankets and coats that were no longer needed. This saved the women a great deal of washing.

Thus the afternoon was relatively relaxed as the men slaughtered a calf. As the cooking fires were set, Baline saw something unusual: the men butchered a half-starved calf, but there was nothing to go around. They cut out its liver, heart, testicles, and brains to fry. The women used its kidneys, tripe, hooves, and bones for soup.

But the bones had no meat on them, not a scrap of fat, and so there was almost no meat to go around.

In desperation, Captain Savage took the calf's hide and sliced it into long strips. Then he scraped the hair off the hide and threaded the hide onto a stick. He poked the stick into the fire and roasted the skin, then fed it to the children. It tasted wonderful. Aside from a hint of singed hair, it tasted like steak!

Baline and the other children grew excited. The hide tasted good and helped fill their bellies. But more importantly, several children discovered a new source of food: leather.

It was everywhere! Emma James, a girl of sixteen, had a pair of sandals that were falling apart. She washed them well in the river and then threw them in a cooking pot to boil that night.

Others found pairs of old boots to eat or had thick straps of leather bound around the axles of their handcarts to hold them together. Now that they no longer had wheat weighing down the carts, the leather straps were not needed. Every handcart had the wheel rims tied to the wheel with hundreds of little strips of leather, for the wooden wheels had shrunk as they dried, and the leather kept the rims from falling off. For days now these worn bits of leather had been shredding, so Baline went to work finding the pieces that looked most likely and tore them away from her own cart, then she picked the strips from the wheels like fruit, and the family placed the leather in a pot.

Since there was so little wood on the prairie, the children took the discarded bedding and made campfires, and Baline cooked her leather over it, letting it simmer all day.

That night, for the first time in weeks, Baline got enough food to fill her stomach.

27

The Death of Samuel

On the morning of October fifth, the handcart company rose before dawn and headed out.

Eliza was terrified to the core of her soul. Samuel had not slept well that night, tossing and turning. He tried not to worry her. But at night she heard him weeping for baby Daniel, and she knew how deep the hurt went. Eliza worried for his health. He'd been wasting away for months now.

So at breakfast, Eliza tried to feed him extra. Normally she made his bread for the day in a tin pan, then gave him the loaf so that he could carry it, feeding when the need took him. Today she had taken a couple of ounces of her own dough and added it to his loaf. But Samuel looked stricken when she offered him such a large loaf.

"No," he said. "I will not eat my fill and watch another of my children die." He stared at her accusingly for a long moment, licked his lips, and begged, "Have you been giving me extra all along? Is that it?"

She knew what he was asking. He wanted to know if she had stolen food from Daniel's mouth. He wanted to know if it was their fault that the baby had died.

"No, I swear—not a mouthful. The extra today, it's from my stores."

But Samuel stared at her, unbelieving.

I should never have suggested feeding him from the children's stores, she realized. Now he'll always wonder. Eliza had driven a wedge between them. It was as if, at that instant, her marriage broke. She could almost hear it, like a tree splitting in half.

Samuel looked stricken, turned away, and fumbled for something to say, anything to fill the silence.

At last he bit his lip. "Split my loaf between the children," he said. "I find that I have no appetite today."

Eliza wasn't about to give his food away.

So on an empty stomach he set off, pulling the handcart all day. The company traveled near the banks of the Platte again, for the land around the river was growing hilly, rugged and desolate and full of rocks. But down by the river there was still some grass and young willows for the cattle to forage on, and the trail was not so steep.

It was not a hard day, for the weather had cooled, but at its end, Samuel would still not eat. He was pale that night, exhausted and dreary as he sat beside the campfire. In the distance, wolves howled. They were trailing the camp, waiting for people to die, Eliza knew. She wondered briefly if they had dug up her baby, then pushed the ugly thought from her mind.

Eliza went to the campfire, produced the loaf of bread from the pocket of her apron, and forced it into Samuel's hand. "Eat this," she said. "Go ahead and eat. You can't go on without food. It's simple math. Pulling that handcart takes all of your energy."

She saw from his expression that he no longer cared.

Yesterday when he'd laid baby Daniel in his grave, Samuel had been so full of hope, so full of faith. He'd talked about raising the child in the life to come. Now, Samuel was a broken man.

What could have changed? she wondered.

Guilt. That was the only thing that had changed. Her husband had always been a good man. He had always followed the admonition from the scriptures, "Let not the sun go down upon your wrath." On those rare, rare occasions when he did have hard feelings against her, of if he worried that he might have offended her, he made sure that he worked the problem through quickly.

But now he'd lost his trust in her. "I didn't give you any of the baby's portion," she said. "We're all starving, a little at a time. He just took sick, that's all."

Yet she knew that he would wonder. It was that way when a child died; a parent would always wonder if the child might have survived if he had just done this or done that. But the truth was, too often death came to children despite all that their parents might do to hold it at bay.

Eliza left the bread on Samuel's lap, and he stared at the oversized loaf in disgust. At last he finally broke off a piece from the loaf, and a wave of relief washed through Eliza to see him eat.

But instead he just broke pieces from the loaf and fed them to the children, then went out for the night to stand guard duty.

Ann Howard saw what was happening and asked Eliza, "Is there anything that I can do?"

"Go talk some sense into him," Eliza suggested. "He won't listen to me."

So Ann went out under the starlight and talked to Samuel for a long hour. Eliza could see their silhouettes in the distance, Samuel at his post upriver. Ann stood close to him, as close as if she was a lover, and from the bobbing of her head, from her agitation, Ann could tell that she was pleading desperately.

At last she reached up and put her arms around him, hugging him long and sweetly, and then she returned. That's when Eliza knew that Ann had fallen in love with her husband.

Eliza went sleepless that night. Her stomach cramped painfully from the lack of food, but that was the least of her hurt. She mourned for her child. She mourned for her husband.

But most of all, she replayed every kind thing that Ann had ever done—the changing of baby's diapers, the cleaning of cooking pots, the straightening of beds, the help with washing and sewing. Ann had been everywhere for the past months, acting almost as if she were Eliza's servant. *Why?* Eliza had to ask. The answer was obvious.

Among the Mormons, a man had to get permission from his first wife before he could take a second. Ann would need that permission. She needed to seduce Eliza as much as she did Samuel.

Eliza lay awake for hours, tossing in her blankets, until at last she went back outside. The moon was but a sliver of cold platinum light.

Samuel was sitting on a rock, fading into sleep. There were other guards on duty, but most of them seemed to be congregated around the food wagons, trying to protect the meager stores.

Eliza touched Samuel on the shoulder, startling him awake. He blinked as if he'd wakened to discover that he was drowning, then peered up at Eliza. "What's wrong?" he sounded so frightened, as if he feared that another child had come down ill.

"Are you in love with Ann Howard?" Eliza demanded.

He hesitated. "No." But he'd held back a little too long.

"Is she in love with you?"

Now the silence drew out for tedious seconds. "Yes."

She wanted to shriek at him. She wanted to slap him. "How?" she asked. "How did it happen?" He said nothing, and into the silence she hurled headlong. "Did you do anything? Did you say anything to encourage her? Did you touch her?"

"No—nothing," he said. "I didn't even know of it until tonight. She didn't declare it until tonight. I just thought . . . she has become like part of the family."

Eliza considered and knew that he was right. He'd gotten sick with a terrible flu shortly after they were assigned to the tents, and for a week he'd been incapacitated. Ann had helped nurse him then, and Eliza realized that that was when it happened. There is something about serving a person that makes the heart vulnerable. You cannot long serve someone without falling in love with them. So Samuel had aroused her mothering instincts.

"Do you want to marry her?" Eliza said.

"No," Samuel said.

"Even if I gave my approval?" Eliza was testing him now, trying to determine whether he had fallen under the woman's spell to even the smallest degree.

"No," Samuel said. "I've only ever wanted one wife. I've only ever loved one woman—you."

"Then, if you love me," Eliza said, tears coming from her eyes, "eat what I put before you. I swear, I never gave you any of the baby's food. It was just unfortunate luck. I can't bear the thought of losing you. Eat what I put before you, even if I give you all of my food."

"I'll eat," Samuel finally agreed. "But I won't eat your share. Don't you see that I can't do it?"

Now she understood. He worried about her too much. If she were to die, he wouldn't be able to go on, knowing that she'd given her life for him. "I see."

Samuel kissed her then, and Eliza went back to bed, cuddling baby Isaac to get him warm, making sure that Sarah, Mary Ann, and Sam Junior all had the blanket snugly pulled over them.

She wondered what to do about Ann. She considered beating her with a stick in the morning, driving her from the tent. She considered talking to Captain Willie, having the woman removed from her premises. People would talk. Oh, the gossips would have a gay time with that.

Ann's voice came out of the darkness, soft and frightened. "So," she said, "now you know."

"Now I know," Eliza said, rage seething in her voice.

"He said that he doesn't love me," Ann said, "not the way that I love him." She sounded small and frightened. "I don't know how it happened. It's not just him that I love. It's you—the children. I just . . . I just want to be a part of your family."

The poor hen, Eliza thought. Ann was a thirty-three-year-old and had never married. She'd probably never have a child of her own. She'd die a spinster.

Eliza had always had the comfort of a family. She'd gone straight from her parents' home to Samuel's. But she could imagine how it must feel to grow old alone. She could imagine, but she could not sympathize.

"Poor hen," Eliza said. "You sad, stupid hen."

On October sixth, Samuel ate his breakfast, and Eliza finally rested a little easier.

The company kept to the North Platte River for the day. The water was only inches deep this late in the fall, and it was relatively clean and clear so far above Laramie. Rugged hills had begun to spring up everywhere, orange sandstone rocks blazing in the bright sun. Creosote bushes and cactus eked out a miserable existence in the cracks of the rocks, but there was nothing else. No trees, no rolling grasslands, no deer or antelope to eat.

Since the river was so shallow and offered the most level course, the company forded it often in order to avoid the rugged terrain—seven times in a single day.

Captain Willie did not urge the company to travel twenty miles that day. For on the reduced rations, he could no longer push them so far. He had to be satisfied with a march of sixteen.

Even if he had been able to convince his people to go on, he could not convince the oxen. They were lagging far behind the handcart company now.

In the shallow waters that day, the children found crayfish and a few minnows, and so that night Eliza had a little meat to fix with their bread. She boiled the crayfish and gave three to each child. Then she boiled the minnows whole. The children did not like the looks of the fish, but Baline and some of her Danish friends came by and peered at the boiled minnows, floating dead in the pan, longingly. Baline put a little salt on them and swallowed one whole, showing the children how to eat "Danish style." It did not take long for the starving children to each bolt down a couple of minnows.

Ann Howard crept around the camp as timid as a kitten. She tried to take Eliza's cooking pot to clean, but Eliza told her curtly, "That will no longer be necessary."

Ann slinked away and never bothered her again.

That night it grew cool. By dawn a heavy frost covered the ground. Many people had worn out their shoes and eaten the remains, so now they wrapped rags on their feet to keep out the morning frost. Others just gritted their teeth and bore the pain.

The company made only fifteen miles each day on the sixth and seventh. The children were starving, and each day they searched for new sources of food. For a couple of days, the children ate the leather off of the handcart wheels. On the sixth they'd discovered the crayfish, and now each time the company came to the river, the children descended en masse, making it almost pointless to hunt.

It was on the seventh that Eliza noticed Baline chewing her hand. She was gnawing the skin from her knuckles, as if it were leather. Not only that, she was showing Sarah how to do it, giving the six-year-old lessons.

"Stop that," Eliza told her. "Don't teach my children how to do that."

"But," Baline said, "I am just trying to help. Everyone is doing it."

She looked so plaintive, so sincere, Eliza could not be angry.

"I know you're trying to help," Eliza said. "But eating yourself is not the answer."

Once the camp was set that night, Eliza walked along the river looking for something, anything, to feed her children. Others had already gotten there ahead of her. Children were splashing out in the water, looking for crayfish. She saw some teenage boys stripping the bark off of bushes and then nibbling at it, and one little girl cutting down cattail rushes and tasting the stems. Another toddler was hunting under rocks, where he caught a lizard. He got so excited when he caught it that he cried out, eager to show the others, but then got a fearful expression on his face, as if worried that someone might steal his prize, and he scooted off with it.

It seemed that the whole camp was becoming manic, frenzied, in the search for something to fill their bellies.

Eliza saw a small rabbit up in some rocks, but it hopped away before she could get it.

That night, when Samuel came in from guard duty, he had a high fever and was shaking violently.

By dawn he was so ill that he could hardly speak when spoken to. Yet he dutifully pulled the handcart through the day, and that night Brother Linford volunteered to take his post at guard duty.

On the eighth the camp woke to find that their strongest ox had died in the night. Captain Willie declared that it should not be eaten, for he feared that the meat might carry some sort of sickness or poison. So the animal was skinned, and the dirty hide was cut into small squares. With these, Brother Hurren made makeshift sandals for some of the children.

The company tramped on all day. Bleak rocks rose up out of sterile ground. The cold sun bore down upon them, astonishingly bright, but as heartless as a winter storm.

On the afternoon of the eighth, Samuel was pulling the wagon when he suddenly stumbled. Eliza ran to him and begged him to get up, but he stared forward like an ox that has been struck with a sledgehammer, his eyes wide open but void of understanding. Young Samuel Junior and Jane raced to pick him up, but he staggered forward in a dream, unable to lift himself.

He began to hack and cough, and droplets of blood rained down on the ground. Samuel had pneumonia, and for that there was no cure. The only thing Eliza could recommend was food and rest, and she could not give him much of either. She urged the children to pray.

Eliza had the children help him onto the handcart, and she pulled him the last few miles to camp while the children crept along beside their father, weeping in fear, as they helped push the cart.

The days were fast growing short, and the nights too long. The night came brutally cold, too cold to sleep much, and in the morning Eliza roused from her bed as tired as when she'd lay down.

She felt guilty. She didn't have the energy to play with her children anymore, or even to clean them. She could barely manage to feed them their small rations.

And Ann knew that her aid was no longer welcome.

But the children did not seem to mind their mother's dereliction of duties. They were as weary as she. Samuel was too ill to speak much on the morning of the ninth.

As the children prepared to break camp, Eliza had him lie on the floor of the tent and listened to his heart, then each lung. His lungs were both congested and full of fluid. He had to gasp for each precious breath.

For a few moments they were alone in the tent, as all of their belongings were packed. Eliza gave him a long look and just held his hand, her fingers entwined around his. Samuel looked perpetually famished. He'd lost fifty pounds since the start of the trek.

"So," he said, gasping for air, "this is it, isn't it?"

Eliza studied his face and said gravely, "Do you want to say good-bye to the kids."

He shook his head. "No. What if . . . I make it? I'd put them through . . . that . . . for nothing."

Eliza nodded. She could see that it was for the best.

"They all know that you love them," she said. "They may not know much else, but they know that."

Samuel bit his lip, and tears of gratitude came to his eyes. He was struggling for each breath, and Eliza dared not ask him to speak more.

"My only regret . . . is," Samuel fought for a long moment to get some air, "that I'm leaving my family out here on the plains."

He broke down after that and began to weep.

"You almost got us there," she said. But there was no stopping him. Now that the tears had begun to flow, he could not hold them back.

Eliza found Captain Willie and asked permission to admit Samuel onto the sick wagon. Samuel leaned heavily on Eliza's shoulder as he staggered to the wagon. He couldn't quite make it, so Jane and William came. Eliza took one arm, Jane the other, and William took Sam's feet, and somehow they managed to get him to the sick wagon.

Then it was time to start the trek again. Eliza went to the handcart. The children had it all loaded. Little Isaac was bundled up in the back with the family's few belongings.

Young Sam Junior coughed. Eliza put the back of her hand to his forehead and found that he was burning with a fever.

For a long moment Eliza studied the handcart. Pulling it, she knew, was a death sentence. Whoever spent their energy that way was most likely to die. It was simple mathematics.

Jane must have seen Eliza's reticence. "Do you want me to pull today?"

"No," Eliza said. "I'll pull." She peered at young Samuel, saw that his face was flushed. "I want you to ride in the cart today. Keep Isaac company, all right?"

Samuel nodded and went to the cart, sat down gingerly, as if afraid that his weight might break it.

Eliza picked up the handles. The sun had just cleared the horizon when she began to pull. At nine in the morning the company stopped for a brief rest.

Eliza was more than exhausted by then. It seemed that her very bones ached from fatigue. She fell to the ground to take some rest and lay on her face as Jane went to check on her father. Moments later Jane came rushing back.

"Father's dead!" Jane screamed, still a hundred yards back down the line. "Father's dead!"

She sounded surprised, shocked, as if she'd never considered the possibility that her father might die. But to Eliza it seemed as natural as the sunrise.

Of course he's dead, Eliza thought. *With every footstep of this damned journey, he has been plodding toward it.* She had seen it coming for weeks, like a yellow rose back in her garden in England, taking days as the tiny bud formed and grew, then inexorably opened.

Eliza climbed to her knees, went and sat heavily on her handcart, head bowed in fatigue.

Still Jane stood at the back of the handcart shrieking, "Father's dead! He's not moving!" As if Eliza had the power to will him back to life.

"Quiet, you silly girl," Eliza said. "We all heard you."

Captain Willie had been up at the front of the column, but now he raced back and stood before Eliza, hat in hand. "Oh, Eliza," he said. "I am so sorry."

Eliza closed her eyes. She couldn't stand to look at him anymore. She didn't want to ever see his face again.

She searched her mind. "How far have we walked?"

Captain Willie hesitated, taken aback by the question. "Eight hundred miles, I suppose."

"Hunh," Eliza said. "We've walked all this way and still no sign of God."

She did not attend her husband's funeral that night, when Captain Savage and Brother Linford interred him in the stony ground.

28

Signs and Wonders

Baline felt terrible about Samuel Gadd's death. She went to the funeral that night, but neither Eliza nor Sam Junior was there.

Afterward, she asked Captain Willie why. Captain Willie took her hand, led her to an old wind-fallen tree whose bark was bleached whiter than bones, and invited Baline to sit beside him.

"Eliza . . . she's grieving too much," Captain Willie said. "Sam Junior, he's too sick."

"Sam is sick?" Baline asked.

Captain Willie fell silent and peered down at Baline. He was struggling with his own demons. In the sudden silence, the sound of shovels striking into the dirt came loud as the workmen filled in the grave.

It was my faith that drove us here, Captain Willie thought. I should have listened to Levi Savage. I should never have brought these people out here in the wilderness. I should never have listened to Franklin D. Richards when he counseled us to go on. I should have turned around and taken these people back to safety, back to Kansas City.

He wanted to give Baline some hope, some comfort, but now he realized that he needed to prepare her for the worst. "Samuel is sick," he explained, "with the same thing that killed his father and baby Daniel. I think that you should know that. He's been a good friend to you."

The import of those words was not lost on Baline. She took a deep breath and sat for a moment, trying to grasp the enormity of it.

"But he can get better," Baline begged. "God can heal him?"

"God cannot bless that family, I think," Captain Willie said. "A person must invite God into his life and put faith in him. But Eliza can't do that, so her own unbelief will undo her."

"I have faith," Baline said in a small voice, as if fearful that her own childish faith might not be enough.

"I do too," Captain Willie said. He put an arm around her and squeezed, but he wondered, *or do I?* He felt so tired, so empty inside.

I saw the Prophet Joseph Smith raise the dead, he told himself. *I saw cloven tongues of fire alight on the Kirtland Temple, and heard the rush of wind as angels entered through the windows and ministered to many*. But that all seemed so long ago, in another lifetime, and Captain Willie could no longer even recall the Prophet Joseph's face.

Did it really happen? Captain Willie wondered. *Was that man really dead when Joseph raised him, or was he like Joseph Wall, so close to death that you couldn't tell the difference?*

What of the fires that lit the Kirtland Temple? Captain Willie had seen the northern lights at times, green and gold flames flickering at the limit of vision on cold winter nights. *When I saw the fires above the temple*, he wondered, *could it have been the northern lights?*

That night, Baline talked with Father Jens about the Gadds. He suggested that Baline not just pray for Sam Junior, but that she also pray for food.

The morning dawned clear and cold, and so when she got up, Baline went to the handcart to get her shoes. But she searched all through it and could not find them.

At last, feet freezing, she went back into the tent and told Else, "I think I lost my shoes. They must have fallen on the ground." She wondered if she should run back down the trail to hunt for them.

"They were in the back of the handcart last night," Else said.

Baline wondered if she could have missed them. But no, that was impossible.

"Are you sure?" Baline asked.

"Someone must have stolen them," Jens suggested.

Baline hadn't thought of that. There had been some pilfering in camp last month, but no one had ever stolen anything from her.

"Maybe someone just borrowed them," Baline said hopefully. "Maybe someone got cold feet in the night and borrowed them."

Else gave her a pained look. "People are eating their shoes," she explained. "I think someone got hungry, and to them your new shoes looked like a loaf of bread."

Baline's mind had a hard time twisting around that thought. *Someone has eaten my new shoes*, she told herself, *my only shoes*. Tears of frustration leapt into her eyes, and Baline collapsed onto the ground, fighting the urge to wail in despair.

Jens came and sat next to her. "Here, here," he said, his eyes twinkling with delight. "There is a rule in my house, and you must obey it."

"What?" Baline asked, sure that he would tell her that it was against his rules to cry. But she was mad enough to break them.

"Here is the rule," Jens said. "If someone is hungry enough to eat your shoes, then you must let them."

Baline thought about it for a moment, then burst out laughing. Jens laughed too and threw a bundle of dirty clothes on her, and for a moment they wrestled.

Still Baline had to hope that some other child had just borrowed her shoes. If they had, she would find them soon enough.

So on October tenth, as the company trudged ahead, Baline kept her eyes open, but no one was wearing her shoes. As she tramped along on the cold ground, she realized that it had been weeks since she had thought much about others. Baline's own sickness, her own hunger, had driven her to distraction.

Today, I must be an angel, she thought.

So she began looking for food for Sam Gadd.

Food was everywhere, she decided, if you knew where to find it.

One boy in camp had found a rabbit two days ago. He had been climbing in the rocks and spotted a cottontail rabbit hiding in the grass. It was frozen with fear, inches from his hand, and so he had reached down and grabbed it, picking it up by the ears, and had brought it back to camp to eat.

Yesterday Sister Mortensen had suddenly remembered that she had a pincushion in her bags and that when she had made the pincushion, she had filled it with barley. So she had cut it open at the seams and used the barley to make a tiny loaf of bread.

Food could be found in the most unlikely places, Baline was beginning to realize.

As the handcart rolled along, Baline studied the pieces of leather on it that held the iron rim to the hub. She had collected some of the scraps a few days ago and boiled them for soup. Now she wondered if any more leather had worn away enough to harvest.

But as she strolled beside the handcart, peering at the scraps of leather, Else gave her a stern look. "Do not tempt yourself," she said. "You can't have it."

Forlorn, Baline went down to the river. She had eaten breakfast before leaving camp this morning, but already her hunger was a hard, gnawing thing.

In the cold morning air, wisps of steam rolled off the water, and Baline took a few moments and stepped inside. The water was warmer than the air, and it felt good on her cold feet. She tramped around, wading, searching for a big fish. But no one had found any big fish here in the shallows of the North Platte. Nor had they found mussels or turtles, as could sometimes be discovered a few hundred miles downstream. Here the river seemed dead. There were periwinkles on some of the rocks, and Baline bit through one, breaking the shell in hopes of getting some sweet meat inside, but it seemed that only a shell was her reward. An hour of hunting under rocks brought a harvest of three crawdads. It was not much to feed a starving friend. Baline put them in the pocket of her apron, then had to race the rest of the morning to catch up to the handcarts.

Every step today was hard. It was as if the air had congealed, and Baline had to struggle through it. It was only her own hunger that made her feel that way, she knew.

The company made six miles that morning, and at noon they reached a trading post, at a place where a large toll bridge had been placed across the Platte. A man named John Reeshards operated the bridge. He had a present for the Mormons: blankets made from buffalo hides. The apostle Franklin D. Richards had purchased thirty-seven of them for the Willie Handcart Company, and since Jens Nielsen had two children with him, one of the robes was given to the family.

"What?" Else asked when she saw the hide. "The apostle didn't buy any food?"

But obviously, Baline realized, Else was not thinking clearly. When I get hungry enough, Baline told herself, I will eat that buffalo skin.

So as the company rested that morning, Baline took her three crawdads and gave them to Sister Gadd. "For Sam Junior."

Eliza smiled down at them. "Fine crawdads," she said. "Are you sure that you don't want to eat them yourself?"

Baline was shocked at the idea. What could Eliza be thinking? Then Baline had it: she thinks that Sam will die. "Please give them to Samuel?" Baline asked.

"All right," Eliza said. "I'll cook them for him." She got her pot and Baline ran down to the river and put in a little water as Eliza struck up a small fire.

As they waited for the water to boil, Baline said, "I am very sorry about your husband. He vas a good man."

Eliza smiled strangely, a slight twist of her lips. "He was," she agreed. "That is what got him killed. He gave and gave and gave until he had nothing left to give, and then he fell over and died."

Baline didn't like her angry tone.

Eliza's eyes flashed, and she peered hard at Baline. "You should learn to be a bit more cunning, sweetheart. Look around. It's the greedy and selfish people who are doing the best—those that lift a loaf of bread off another man's table, those that are willing to sneak supplies from the wagon at night. People like my Samuel . . . they just die."

Baline didn't know what to say. She didn't want to argue, and she didn't agree. *God can bless me if I keep his commandments.* "Someone ate my shoes," she said, hoping for a little sympathy.

"Well, you see what I mean?" Eliza said. "Somebody else is growing fat off of other people's shoes." She chuckled sourly as if she had made some great joke. "You should have eaten them. I hear that they go down well with a little brown mustard." She cackled again.

"I vill go and see Samuel now," Baline said. The water had hardly had time to boil, but she had found that little crayfish cook up very fast.

She carried the pan back to the sick wagons and found Samuel Junior lying in the back of one, a glaze of sweat streaming down his face. She called his name, and he peered at her for a long time before he recognized her. Even then, he was too weak to speak. Instead, he just lay there wheezing, his chest heaving with every inhalation. He was occupied solely by the labor of breathing and did not have the energy to talk. Now Baline saw why his mother thought that he was as good as dead.

"I brought you treat," she said. "Ven I was sick, you fed me. Now I feed you."

With that, she tore the tail off of each boiled crawdad, peeled off the shell, and pulled off the nasty blue vein in the tail. Then she dropped the white meat into Sam's mouth. For each bite, he opened his mouth only the tiniest bit, into a small circle, and peered up at the morsel longingly, like a baby bird begging from its mother.

For the next few days, the company moved slowly, making only ten or twelve miles per day. They left the Platte River and began crossing over dry hills, where they hoped to strike the Sweetwater. The trail grew impossibly rough and rocky, and the cattle balked. Four of them gave out entirely and had to be left behind, and when some men returned for them, they found a pack of wolves gorging on the finest specimen. The men rushed in with sticks and tried to rescue the meat, but the wolves drove them off.

Baline found nothing to eat that day, and so on the next morning she shared some of her own rations with Samuel.

On the twelfth of October, two of the young men who had been driving the wagons abandoned the journey. Captain Willie gave them two day's rations so that they could walk back to Fort Laramie and enlist in the army.

After traveling twelve miles, the company stopped at a clear spring for the night, and the next morning they traveled on, passing through the Devil's Backbone, a strange formation of rocks that thrust up high on either side of the trail like bits of bone, forming a natural avenue. The sun on the stones on either side of the road cast cold shadows; a buffeting wind whistled through them and the hollows of some of the rocks let out a soft moan, like the voices of the damned.

That afternoon the trail descended down from the hills again into the swampy basin of Poison Spider Creek. Here, there were strange new plants, lush and green.

Baline went out to forage with a dozen other children. In the swampy water they found some green weeds with long yellow roots. One of the children said that it was a wild parsnip, and it did look much like a parsnip, so the children dug the tubers from the ground. The girls filled their aprons and took them back to camp. The women rejoiced and threw them into boiling water.

For the first time in weeks, there would be enough food to eat. They had just begun dining when Millen Atwood and Levi Savage came in from their nightly hunt. Millen took one look at the tubers and began kicking the pots over. "Don't eat those!" he shouted. "Don't eat those. There's enough poison in one of those to kill an ox!"

Baline had already eaten half of one of the wild parsnips, and she was loath to part with hers. But an hour later the roots felt like iron in her stomach.

Captain Willie told the camp that one of the cows was so starved that she would no longer move. There was no meat on her, but he said that anyone who wanted it could have some. Almost immediately one of the men in camp shot the animal, and the starving inmates raced to her with their knives, eager to get any food at all, and slashed her to pieces.

As they fought around the carcass, Baline watched them dully. *We have become wolves*, she thought.

Still she was able to get a rib bone. She had Eliza boil it up, and then Baline spooned the broth down Sam's throat.

The night was brutally cold, and when Baline got up on October 13, she felt so weak and dazed that she could hardly walk.

One of the older children that Baline sometimes played with, Elizabeth Cunningham was found dead that morning, and her parents buried her in a shallow grave.

After traveling a few miles, Elizabeth Cunningham's parents recalled that like the Walls, they too had been promised by an apostle that they would live to reach Utah, and so her tearful mother and father returned to her grave.

They dug her up and took her cold body to a campfire, where her mother boiled some water. Her father spilled some warm water on her face to clean it, and suddenly Elizabeth flinched. So her parents poured warm water all over her, to wash her, and when they were done they brought Elizabeth back to the handcart train.

Baline was delighted to see that her friend was raised from the dead, so she raced ahead in the handcart train to tell others the good news. But when Eliza Gadd heard of it, she just shook her head in disgust. "You foolish people! You keep burying the living and then calling it a 'miracle' when they refuse to stay in their graves!"

Baline saw that there would be no convincing Eliza.

One of the Danes, Paul Jacobsen had refused to stop eating the wild parsnips last night, and today he had to be hauled in the sick wagon. Brother Jacobsen died just after the company halted that night, twelve miles farther down the trail.

That night it was bitter cold, and the wolves were out in force, howling again. The full moon rose red on the horizon, and Baline stayed up to watch, for tonight the moon was eclipsed by the shadow of the earth. It was not much of an event. The shadow stole across the moon slowly for a long hour, but never blotted it out. Father Jens came out to watch with her.

"Remember the fireball?" he asked.

On August third, the company had been marching through Iowa when a huge ball of flame had shot across the horizon from west to east. It left a streaming trail of smoke, and huge red dots that smoked in the air. As it passed overhead, there was a sound like thunder, as if a hundred barrels of gunpowder had exploded all at once. The sound seemed to make the very ground jump.

"I remember," Baline said.

"Now that was a sign in the heavens," Jens said. "Not like this little shadow over the moon."

"If it was a sign," Baline said, "what did it mean?"

Jens bit his lip. "Maybe it was like an arrow, pointing the way we should go." The fireball had been heading east, back across the world, toward Denmark.

"You think we should have not come?" Baline asked.

Jens did not answer. He only stared into the sky thoughtfully.

"We are running out of wheat fast," Baline said. "I saw into the supply wagon today. There are only a few bags for the sick people to sit on. It won't last for another week."

"I know," Jens said.

"But we were supposed to have wheat for seventy days—and we bought extra supplies at Fort Laramie. We should not run out for at least three more weeks!"

"Captain Willie thinks that someone has been stealing the food," Jens said. "But I do not know how that could be. Someone would have seen."

Baline was horrified. Her friends were starving, and someone was stealing food? It was the same as murder.

The next morning, on the fourteenth, Sam looked worse when Baline called on him, offering to share her bread. He opened his mouth for her, but did not have the energy to chew his food, and so Baline was forced to just leave the bite in his mouth, and then leave after saying a prayer for him.

The morning grew bitter cold, and the company came down out of the stony hills, where they saw the Sweetwater River before them, a silver band winding through a relatively lush valley. It would be good to have clean water once again.

Yet on the western horizon, one could see the Wind River Mountains mantled from top to bottom with snow, and there could be no doubt that winter was in the air.

For the moment, the saints were all right. As they traveled near the Sweetwater, they began to find signs of buffalo again. There were buffalo chips on the ground, and brown wool caught in some of the bushes. Baline hoped that the hunters would go out and shoot one, but nowhere was a buffalo to be seen.

"They have all gone south for the winter," Jens told her.

When they reached the Sweetwater, they made their first crossing on a nice bridge. Baline could see trout gliding through the water, but the water was so crystal clear that you could not catch them. Still, she could see holes in the mud where the crawdads hid.

She went down and stepped into the clear water and found that it was as bitter cold as winter snow. She could not long endure it and came out of the water without a crayfish.

She had not found any food to give Samuel for two days running.

In the afternoon, the company reached a huge hill that seemed to be one enormous, strangely rounded boulder, the color of rusted steel. It was called Independence Rock.

The company stopped in its shadow, and a few boys climbed on the rock while Captain Willie went to an old buffalo skull lying at its base. He reached inside and pulled out an oilskin pouch. Inside was a letter. He read it, and Captain Savage asked, "What does it say."

"Elder Richards promises us that we will have supplies at Pacific Springs," Captain Willie said.

He peered off toward the Wind River Mountains, all clad with snow. There was nothing new in the message. Apostle Parley P. Pratt had said that he had camped here with Richards but that there would be no food at Pacific Springs.

Even if there is, Captain Willie thought, *we can't hold out that long. Richards has surely killed us.*

Captain Willie marched his people as far as he could before sunset.

That evening, at the end of a long day, Baline went out to hunt for buffalo chips for the fire. She was just returning to camp, and the sun was lingering on the horizon, when she heard a shout.

She looked behind her and saw Sister Panting holding out her apron, as if she carried something heavy in it. Sister Panting was the young woman who had left her husband in England. Her baby Jane had nearly died but was all better now.

"Children!" Sister Panting cried. "I have food! I have food from an angel!"

Instantly the children around Baline all dropped their buffalo chips and sprinted to Sister Panting. True to her word, she had an apron filled with perhaps fifty pounds of dried jerky.

"I went hunting for buffalo chips," Sister Panting said, alternating between laughter and tears, "and I came around a small hill. There was an old man there, and he asked me how the camp was doing. I told him that we were starving, and he took me to his home, a little cave. There were sacred books all along one wall, and a drying rack for buffalo meat on the others. He waved at the wall and said, 'Take all that you can carry, but remember to share it with those in need.' So I heaped the meat into my apron and left. Just as I got outside the door of the cave, I walked perhaps a hundred feet and realized that I had not thanked him. So I turned around, and he was gone. He was gone. The cave was gone. I walked back and could find no sign of it! I can only believe that he was an angel."

Each child grabbed a handful of jerky, and Baline took one for herself, then begged, "May I have some more for my friends?"

Sister Panting allowed another handful and then went prancing toward the camp with a dozen children following at her heel, leading them like the Pied Piper.

Baline stopped for a moment. She wondered, *If I go into the hills, will I find that angel?*

She imagined that he might give her more food, or, barring that, that she would at least be able to thank him in person.

She searched until she found Sister Panting's bare footprints, then followed them back into some rolling hills. She went for nearly a mile, until full darkness had fallen, and at last she found a dozen buffalo chips on the ground. She wandered about in the sagebrush for a bit, until it was too dark to see. She could find no sign of an old man, a cave, or any place where Sister Panting might have found the meat.

So Baline knelt and thanked God, then raced back to camp to feed Samuel. She was sure that the meat from an angel would be especially good at helping him regain his vigor.

29

Sweetwater

The journey up the Sweetwater had always been pleasant before. For the first time in months, the company had a constant supply of fresh clear water to drink, and with it came a release from the sense of infirmity and lethargy that plagued the company as they traveled over the Platte. Once again there was hope of fresh meat. The willow thickets along the river provided cover for mallards and cottontails, deer and elk.

So the journey should have been pleasant. But Captain Willie had never traveled here so late in the fall, when the dead straw carried no more nutritive value than a mouthful of ash.

The specter of the Wind River Mountains, always ahead, covered in sheets of ice, constantly reminded him of how soon the winter would come.

The people were slowing down, as were the oxen. It wasn't their fault. They were all nearly dead.

In camp that evening, the weather was brutally cold. One young woman, Caroline Reeder, was found by her brother-in-law, James Hurren, shortly after sundown. The young woman had gone out to hunt for sagebrush so that she could build a campfire and had succumbed to the cold. James had found her lying in a stupor. So the folks quickly boiled water and tried to warm her. But it was no use, Caroline died just after sundown, and the children mourned, for she had often spent the evenings leading them in games.

This seemed like a turning point to Captain Willie. Before,

it had only been the old and the babes that were dying. But now death's sickle lashed out and harvested even the best among them.

On that bitter night of October fourteenth, Captain Willie had to plead with the people once more. "We have to cut back on rations."

He had rarely seen such seething cold hatred on the faces of so many women. If he'd been a child molester caught in the act on the streets of London, he might have expected such glares.

But oh how they hated him. They raised their hands, sustaining him, even as many of them suspected that they were voting to die. The company had cut back on rations before and found that they didn't have the energy to travel very far. How far would they get per day on even less? The saints reluctantly agreed to smaller rations of flour. The men then would get 10½ ounces per day; women and large children, 9; smaller children, 6; and infants, 3.

So the company plodded along the Sweetwater. Marching through the tall grass, lost among the splendor of the Rockies, he felt as if they were no more significant than ants marching upon a table.

Surely, God had tired of hearing their prayers.

On that day, the company reached Devil's Gate, a stark canyon with sheer black stone walls where the river rushed through. They had to leave the river and march through the hills to avoid the canyons, a tough journey.

Wolves were tracking the company constantly now. Another calf gave out during the day, and the wolves got it before the men could.

Three people succumbed to death in the course of the first day after cutting rations, a portent of things to come.

The company had to cross the Sweetwater three times in order to avoid the sheer canyon walls, and though the water was not deep and the river was not wide, Captain Willie had seldom felt water so exceedingly cold. Setting foot in it stole a man's breath and drove all thoughts of decency from his mind, all hope and restraint, so that many a man swore openly in front of the women at the top of his lungs.

Captain Willie, along with the sub-captains, were forced to make many trips through the water as they carried the women and children and invalids over on their backs.

Once he got out of the water, it took an hour for the painful cramps in his legs to subside, and several hours to warm.

Thus the days became a painful blur. During the coming week, they plodded closer to the mountains every day, and as they did, the westerly winds became icy. Even the noonday sun could not penetrate the cold, so that even as his lips were chapped and his skin burned, he could not get warm. His shrunken belly nagged him constantly.

On the night of the seventeenth, another person died, and at last the man who had been stealing wheat was caught. Captain Woodward brought him in. It was Edward Griffiths, the chief of the commissary, the man who had been entrusted to give the wheat out.

"I saw him giving bigger scoops to his friends," Captain Woodward said. "It happened so fast, at first I thought I imagined it. He had the scoops in a bag, and he would dole out the wheat into a flour sack, never letting the scoop really out of the bag, so that you could see. But I caught him red-handed. He had the big scoop in there and was giving extra to his friends."

Edward Griffiths stood timidly, twitching and fidgeting, peering through his thick spectacles. His thick curly hair had grown long in the past few months.

Captain Willie didn't know what to say. He'd trusted this man, just as he'd trusted Franklin D. Richards. Only one word came to mind. "Why?"

"I didn't take much," Griffiths said. "And, and you'd do it, too—if someone put the power in your hands and let you choose who was to live and who was to die. You'd give a little extra to the decent folk and leave the rest to rot. They come begging for it, you know," Griffiths said. "Men who were as strong as steel when we left England, they come begging for food for their wives and babes. Who could say no to that? Who could turn them away?"

Captain Willie hung his head for a long moment, wondering. *Would I have done as he did?*

No, he decided. *I wouldn't have done that. I wouldn't have fed dishonest men and let folks like Caroline Reeder and Samuel Gadd starve. And the babies.* Griffiths said he did it for the babies, but how many of them had died on this trip? He could name at least half a dozen. Griffiths hadn't been saving them—he'd been killing them.

He looked down at Edward Griffiths. The man didn't have the haggard look of the other starvelings in camp. His paunch still had some fat to it. Obviously, he'd been doing quite well for himself.

Strange that I didn't notice that before, Captain Willie thought. But he realized that he would have just chalked it up to the fact that Griffiths was single. The single men and women were faring better than those with families, for they weren't wearing themselves out in the service of others.

"Who have you been feeding?" Captain Willie demanded. "I want their names." Griffiths named only three people. Three men that he'd trusted. He knew the families. Good women, good children. He would have had a hard time turning them away himself.

"Who else?" Captain Willie demanded. He wanted the names of the real blackguards.

"No one, I swear!" Griffiths said, sweat breaking out on his forehead.

Captain Willie was speechless. He'd done the math. The company was supposed to have had enough wheat to last for seventy days, but they'd run out after only sixty-four. Given the extra supplies that they'd taken on, and the fact that he'd cut the rations by a quarter three weeks ago, the company should have fared better. "You only gave out a little extra?" Captain Willie demanded. "By my calculations, I have nearly three tons missing, over ten percent!"

"No!" Griffiths cried. "I never took that much. I swear. Just a little here, a little there. It might add up to a couple hundred pounds, but not a ton. I swear! I-I-I know where it went! The wheat must have become compacted. All those tons of wheat on the wagons, they weighed down on the ones beneath, flattening the bags, so that when I measured out a scoop, there was a little more weight than there should have been. I knew it was happening, but people were already starving when we got to the bottom of the bags, and no matter how much we had to eat, it never satisfied our hunger!"

Captain Willie considered the possibility. He'd seen that the bottom sacks were flattened but had never considered the implications. Could they really have lost ten percent of their wheat that way? It meant that each man might have gotten an extra ounce and a half, each child a half ounce. That wasn't much, but over the course of months it would add up.

Griffiths was sweating profusely now. Surely he imagined that a beating was in store.

Captain Willie decided to loosen his tongue with a threat. "You can try to feed that bone to some other dog," Captain Willie said. "But I'm not buying it. If there was a tree within five miles of here, I'd hang you. If I were to waste a bullet on you now, no one would blame me."

Griffiths shot him a feral look, and suddenly his eyes flashed in the lantern light. "Such animosity," he clucked. "Yet I've seen to it that you captains were always well fed. You should show a little gratitude."

Captain Willie had never weighed his own flour to see if he'd gotten too much. Normally, he just asked one of the children in camp to fetch it for him. In fact, he didn't have the tools to actually weigh his own food. But he suddenly realized that of all the captains, none showed the extreme lassitude that others were developing, despite the fact that each of them had done the work of five men. Could it be that he'd been getting more than his fair share?

Yes. Not a lot more. He'd have noticed that. But an ounce here, another ounce there. It could have made all the difference.

I have found the thief, he told himself, *and I am he.*

Captain Willie had never hit a man before. It wasn't a saintly thing to do. But he threw all of his weight into the punch that floored Edward Griffiths.

Captain Willie put Levi Savage and William Woodward in charge of passing out the flour. It wasn't a hard job, and it wasn't one that they would have for long. The camp would run out the next day.

We're a hundred miles short of Pacific Springs, with no guarantee that we'll even have food there.

Captain Willie strode through the camp, listening to the wolves in the hills howl like madness on every side. The people had come out to the campfires to warm themselves. He'd decided to keep the fires alight so that his people would get warm. They'd seen no recent sign of Indian activity, and right now, he felt that he'd welcome a massacre over what the future held in store. What he saw broke his heart: men that he'd brought into the church, men who had been so strong that they could have wrestled bears for their dinner six months ago, now huddled under blankets, their faces as pale as ghosts, so weak that they were unable to feed themselves. He saw women and children so far gone in starvation that even if food came tomorrow, there could be no saving them. He knew that their gaunt features would haunt him for the rest of his life, their hollow cheeks, the women's hands so devoid of flesh that their frail fingers seemed to be but bones.

But I won't live for long, he told himself. It was a hundred miles over rough trails before they could reach Pacific Springs. The company had only been making eight or ten miles per day. Each time that he'd cut their rations, they'd slowed by five miles per day. How would a man, one of these starved ghouls, pull a handcart full of clothes and crippled children a hundred miles without food?

Even if they made it, he no longer believed that Richards could keep his promise. There would be no food.

Lord, he prayed, *if it be thy will that we die, at least let us die with some dignity. Don't let thy people go out as the Donner Party did. If we are to starve, let us not eat one another.*

He couldn't imagine that his own people would ever do such a thing six months ago. But the hunger was a terrible thing, eroding his sensibilities. He tried to sing hymns at times, to take his mind off of it. But it was always there, urging him on, and often he would look at the bark of some bit of sagebrush and in his madness he wondered if by gnawing it he could get some relief.

He felt like a cornered animal.

All that I can do, he told himself, *is my best.*

So he planned to work like one possessed until the very end.

At the beginning of this journey, his first night aboard the

Thornton, he'd knelt in prayer and consecrated his life to bringing these people across the world in safety. He'd pleaded, "Lord, I will do all within my power to bring these people across the ocean. I dedicate all of my time, my talents, and labor. I pray thee, Lord, to let them come through in safety. I pray that not one soul will be lost on this trip, not the oldest matron, not the sickliest babe."

He had not thought it a sin to try to make such a bargain with the Lord. The Mormons were a covenant people and know the value of making such commitments. More important, he thought that it was what the Lord would want. Surely he would want to prove to his people the wisdom of the handcart system. Surely he would want to encourage the poor of Europe and Asia to follow his commandment to gather to Zion.

Yet it hadn't taken a week aboard the ship before the first elderly woman vomited her guts out. Every death since had seemed like a slap in the face from the Lord, God's punishment to Captain Willie for making such a bargain.

He wondered why he had been unable to stop the dying. He'd plead with the Lord for endless hours. He and his men had labored ceaselessly to bring the saints across safely.

At first, he'd thought that God was punishing his people for their unrighteousness. But Captain Willie didn't believe that. There had been a spirit of peace and camaraderie during most of this trip that he'd seldom felt among a group of people. There were true saints in his camp, men like Levi Savage, Brother Hurren, and Joseph Elder that he would measure among the best in the church, and there were countless widows and humble poor in the camp who didn't have a mean bone in their bodies.

I'd gladly stand up to a firing squad and die for these people any day of the week, he thought.

Even the lowliest people in his company were no worse than folks you'd find on the streets of Chicago.

He had three men in camp who had taken food from Griffiths. He had Woodward talk to them, and all of their stories had matched. They'd gone to Griffiths in secret and begged for extra when their wives or children began to fail. None had been getting extra rations for more than three weeks.

Captain Willie could see their dilemma. *Do you beg for more or watch your loved ones die? Which is the greater sin?*

Watching your children die, he decided.

He forgave the men from the bottom of his heart.

The only one he wasn't sure of was that rascal Griffiths. Captain Willie didn't believe that he'd gotten to the bottom of the mess.

The story of the compacted wheat made perfect sense. They'd weighed out scoops of wheat back at Winter Quarters, and used the same scoops to measure with all along. If Griffiths was right, Captain Willie wondered if any harm had even been done. Yes, they'd given out the food a little too fast, but the people would have starved in either case.

Yet if Griffiths was covering up any darker sins, Captain Willie had no way to tell. Even if there were a couple more like him, would God destroy an entire city to get rid of a couple of rats?

No, Captain Willie felt that something more was going on. God in his heavens was trying to teach him a lesson.

Maybe he's trying to teach me to put on my coat when I go out into the rain, he thought, *instead of begging him to hold the rain back. It might be something that simple.*

Or it might be more complex. The rules of heaven could change from time to time. The Lord required more of his disciples as they grew in faith and strength. In the early days of Christ's ministry, he told his disciples, "He that is not against me is with me." In other words, Christ wanted his disciples to tolerate those whose views, while not in line with theirs, were not entirely antagonistic. But at the end of his ministry he demanded obedience from those who would call themselves his disciples. A time had come when there could be no lukewarm saints, and he told his disciples, "He that is not with me is against me."

Perhaps God has a similar lesson for me, Captain Willie thought. *Perhaps the time has come when he won't molly-coddle his people any longer. Maybe we can't expect flocks of quail to fall out of the sky every time we get hungry.*

Or maybe I was a fool to listen to Franklin D. Richards. He thought back on the promises that the apostle had made. He'd promised them food and aid, good weather and fair roads, protection from the Indians and disease. Any con man on the streets of Liverpool would have made the same offer, for enough money.

We accepted his words as if they were inspired. *Was I a fool to do so?*

He thought back. He believed that he'd felt the Holy Ghost that night. He'd felt sure that it bore witness to the truthfulness of the apostle's promises.

But Captain Willie wasn't so sure anymore.

Maybe I imagined it, because I wanted so badly for it to be true. So I took his word with the faith of a child, without fasting and praying myself for a true witness.

Richards had been so slick, so cocky. He'd strutted around as he spoke in the Lord's name, as if he carried God around in his back pocket. Captain Willie had thought that Richards spoke out of faith. But what if it was all a show? What if the apostle was nothing more than a charlatan who boasted in the Lord merely so that others would think well of him?

Perhaps God is smiting us for listening to his lies.

Yet he could not hold onto that thought for long. It was a wicked thing to doubt an apostle of the Lord.

Judas Iscariot was an apostle, a small voice whispered in the back of his mind. *Even the greatest man can fall. Even the finest man has his flaws. Put not thy faith in the arm of flesh, but only in the arm of the Lord.*

Wracked with doubt, Captain Willie worried. *Have I wasted my life? Have I been led astray by false teachers?* There had been times in his life when he was sure that he was following God's plan. But now he felt empty, so utterly hopeless, he wondered if he had been deceived.

Late that night, Captain Woodward came to him. "I've got a fellow in my hundred that wants to know if he can have the last of his rations. He wants to eat it all now and go to God with at least the memory of a full belly."

"Tell him he can have it," Captain Willie said. "It doesn't really matter now, does it? We're all going to die anyway."

"It's come down to that?" Woodward asked.

"It has," Captain Willie said soberly. "I think it's time that each of us make peace with God and man."

So after Woodward was gone, Captain Willie went out into the deep grass beside the river and knelt in prayer. He spoke few words. "Lord, I've done all that I can to save these people, and I've failed." He wanted to pray for them, to beg the Lord to spare them, but he'd offered that prayer so many times before and in so many ways, that he could no longer muster any hope for an answer. "Thank you for this life you've given me. Thank you for letting me know and serve these good people. If I've done wrong, I beg thy forgiveness. Now, I pray, let thy will be done. Smite us utterly if thou so desire. Strike me with lightning if you want. Let the Cheyennes dance around their fires with my scalp on their spears. Let the wolves tear my entrails out while I watch. Let all the children in the camp starve if that is what thou desirest. But I shall praise thee, whatever thy course. If in thy wisdom thou deemest it wise to thrust me down to hell, I will honor thy name. Amen."

As he climbed up from his knees, so weary that he could hardly stand, his head reeling from the labor, he wondered if perhaps that prayer was what the Lord sought him to learn.

So often in life it seemed, the saints prayed so fervently that the Lord would protect them. "Take away my suffering, Lord. Take away my trials. Take my pain and the consequences of my own laziness and stupidity." *Maybe the Lord has grown tired of such pleas*, Captain Willie thought. *Maybe by making them, we even thwart God's plan.*

There was a time, he knew, in the premortal existence, when God the Father laid out his plan for mankind, when he told the spirits of men that he would build a world where they could come and inhabit bodies, where they would have the opportunity to be tested, to see if they would do good or evil. The scriptures recalled that on that day, "the morning stars sang together, and the sons of God shouted for joy" at the news.

But what had God promised those premortal spirits that brought tears of joy to their eyes? Nothing more than trials, tribulation, and untold suffering. None of the things that people desire, but all of the experiences that are required for men to become like God himself.

Christ descended below all things—torment, pain, ridicule, Captain Willie thought. *Now it's my turn. Time to prepare to die.*

He realized that he needed to make amends. It was time to seek forgiveness from anyone that he might have offended.

One name came foremost to his mind—Eliza Gadd. He had never sought to offend her. But she hated him anyway. She blamed him for the death of her husband and son. The fires had gone out while he pondered and prayed, and the camp was dark. The only light came from the cold stars that winked above, veiled by a thin mist. He decided to speak to her tomorrow.

❦

The morning of the eighteenth dawned sunny but cruelly cold. There were so many sick in camp, that in one group of a hundred, there were only two men well enough to help pull down the tents.

The company followed the Sweetwater for eight miles, then forded the river and camped on the far side. It was a good day. Only one man died.

But Captain Willie knew that tomorrow would be hell. The company would have to travel sixteen miles through rugged hills without water. The last couple of times that they had done that, the people had died in droves.

Captain Willie had his men pass out the last of the wheat and then slaughtered two half-starved calves. The only supplies left in camp were the barrels of hard bread that Captain Willie had bought at the fort. That would have to suffice after tomorrow.

He made the rounds that night, visiting folks, offering what comfort he could. When he reached Eliza's camp, Eliza was talking cordially to Sister Rowley. Each of the women sat on logs near the fire, holding their youngest, all wrapped up in blankets.

They seemed an odd couple at first. Sister Rowley was the poorest of the poor, a woman of terribly humble circumstances. But then

Captain Willie recalled that like Eliza, she'd once been wealthy. Her husband had been a gentleman farmer. But when the apostle Wilford Woodruff was staying at Rowley's home, things went bad. Wilford Woodruff had converted hundreds of people in the local area, whole parishes, and some of the ministers were angry. Police were called to arrest him, but Woodruff converted them, too. So a mob formed, intent on killing the apostle. Several men had broken in the doors to the Rowley house, a mansion called Mars Hill. But Brother Rowley had stood in the doorway and heroically tried to fend them off so that Woodruff could escape out the back. The mob took out their wrath on Brother Rowley, beating him senseless, leaving him brain damaged and partly paralyzed. He'd tried to provide for his family but was frustrated in the attempt, and over the next three years he was forced to sell off his property just to pay his doctor bills.

He died shortly after that. Now Sister Rowley was a widow with seven children and was so destitute that Captain Willie hurt every time he looked at her. She'd been forced to send her six- and seven-year-old sons to work in the coal mines for fourteen hours a day. Often her boys had been so far down in the shafts, they were not allowed to come out for a week at a time. As a result of breathing coal dust, her boys had persistent coughs.

So Eliza and Sister Rowley sat by the fire, as close as two peas in a pod. Sister Rowley held her two-year-old daughter, Ann, who was softly wheezing.

Sister Rowley will be good for her, Captain Willie thought. *She'll teach Eliza everything that she needs to know to be a widow. Eliza will be good for her and help nurse that baby back to health.*

Captain Willie nodded cordially at the women, stared into Eliza's eyes. The sadness behind them fairly smote him.

"Are you well?" he asked. "Is there anything I can do?"

"Nothing," Eliza said.

"Your children, they're all right?"

"As well as starving orphans can be," Eliza said.

"Sam Junior?"

"He's recovering. Brother Linford has taken his place on the deathbed." Captain Willie was grateful to hear that Sam Junior was better, but if John Linford had taken ill, it meant that there was no man to help with the tent. No man to pull the handcarts in the company. No man to stand guard at night. It meant that the Linford boys and William Gadd would all have to pick up the slack.

"It must be hard, losing Samuel," Captain Willie said.

"Actually," Eliza said coolly, "it was quite a relief. I'd been worried about all of the other hens in my tent, afraid that one might try to take my husband, and now I'm fully reassured on that count."

"I suppose," he said, and he realized that no matter what he said or did, he would not be able to comfort her. He'd never had to handle the kind of pain that she was feeling. He hadn't had to watch his own spouse and child die because of someone else's errors in judgment.

"Eliza," he said, "I've come to ask your forgiveness for anything I might have done to offend you. I've done all that I can to bring you folks safely to Zion—"

"And now we're all going to die?" she finished.

He didn't rise to her bait.

Eliza bit her lower lip, seemed to change her mind. "You've done well," Eliza said. "I think that Colonel Babbitt himself would have done no better at bringing us across, considering his own current state. If it is any comfort to you, I don't blame you for what has happened. If you had not been leading this band, the church would have found someone else just like you, and the results would be the same. Nature will take its course, and I'll get to watch my babies die, and you'll watch us die, and then the wolves will have us all.

"I only hope that you've learned your lesson. There is no God in heaven, watching over us. There are no unseen forces that guide our destiny. There is only wind and sun, soil and ice."

Captain Willie did not want to argue. He didn't have the heart for it anymore. Eliza had once sworn to convert him. Captain Willie wanted to tell her that she had nearly succeeded. He'd been struggling with his own doubts, more than he could ever recall in recent years. It wasn't the starvation and hardships of the trail that were gnawing at him—it was the feeling that he had been lied to by an apostle of the Lord. "Almost," he said, "thou persuadest me to be a nonbeliever."

Eliza smiled and replied, "I would to God that not only thou, but that all men were nonbelievers."

Captain Willie laughed. Not only had Eliza recognized the scriptural quotation, she had also remembered Paul's response—and turned it into a jest. Clever woman.

"Unfortunately," Captain Willie said, "I can't *not* believe. When I look at the morning sun rising over the hills, or smell a wheat field, or hear the sound a newborn baby's cry, I feel compelled to acknowledge the existence of God, and thank him for all that he has given me. I only hope that someday you can say the same."

There was nothing more that he could say, and so he merely plodded off.

Around another fire he found dozens of saints gathered, teeth chattering. Some of the children were weeping from hunger, and a young man named George Cunningham, in his early teens, tried to comfort them.

"I dreamt last night that a wagon was coming today, a wagon filled with food, coming from the valley. I saw four men with it, two teamsters and two outriders. One of the outriders had a strange saddle, black with silver studs. I've never seen a saddle like that. But they're coming today. The food will be here today."

It was a good dream, but one old man in the circle guffawed. "There isn't anyone coming to help us. Don't give the children false hope. You'll only break their hearts. We have to help ourselves."

The Cunningham boy's mother cut in, "Don't be so hasty. George has the gift of prophecy. If he dreams that something is going to happen, it happens."

Captain Willie wasn't sure which side to take, so he said nothing.

The camp was soon cleared, and the handcarts prepared to rattle up into the winding hills. Captain Willie took a moment to give a short oration. "Brothers and sisters," he said. "I am reminded today of the blessings we receive from our tribulations.

"I remember when we started this journey, you folks were all so eager to get to Zion, you about busted your handcarts racing across the prairie. But you've suffered a little tribulation, and look how you've all grown. You've learned patience from it. Hang it all, you've all grown so patient, I about can't get you out of your bedrolls in the morning." There was a little light laughter.

"And you've grown in compassion. I been watching your kids, kids that three months ago were so eager to play that they couldn't be bothered to hunt for firewood. Now this camp could hardly run without them. It seems that when there's a job that needs to be done, there's half a dozen kids willing to do it. They've learned that lesson from the example of their mothers and fathers, and I must commend you one and all.

"I've seen you grow in faith. I know that some of you feel like you're broken. I know that the fires in your heart are burning dim. But I've seen you keep drawing your handcarts when the mud was up to your hubs and the sand was blowing in your faces, and that's faith. That's real faith at work.

"So often I've watched you, and I've felt to praise God and thank him for my association with you.

"The Prophet Joseph once said, 'I glory in tribulation. I delight in trials. I feel to praise the Lord when hell bars the way before me.'

"We've all grown so much, I only feel sorry that my dear wife isn't here to get her share of torment and disappointment." Again there was some laughter.

Captain Willie choked up. "We've got a long road ahead of us today, a long cold road—if my nose for weather is reading things right. Remember that its tribulation that turns a boy into a man. It's privation that turns a man into a saint. It is not until you suffer as Christ suffered, when you feel so much pain that you think you're about to bleed from every pore, that you can develop the kind of love and empathy that he bears toward us.

"So let us suffer today. Let our trials make us, not break us. Come what will, let us sing our praises to God for the experience."

He led the camp in singing, "Come, Come Ye Saints" and took up Eliza Gadd's handcart and began to lead the way.

The grass was sere and brown, and up in the rocks along the bluffs, a little sagebrush clung to the cracks. On a ridge he saw a huge buck antelope standing, just watching them, but it was nearly half a mile away, so far off that no bullet could catch it.

The day had already started out brutally cold, but they traveled only two miles when an icy wind began to howl, as sharp as a wolf cub's teeth, coming in from the northwest, carrying the cold down from the Wind River Mountains.

Clouds began to blow in ahead, blotting out the sky. They formed a great fist in the deepest shades of gray. A vortex formed in their center, like a cyclone pointed right at them, and Captain Willie knew that the company was in trouble.

They had just passed Ice Creek, a swampy little piece of ground where, if a man had a mind to, he could dig a couple of feet below the ground and harvest great blocks of ice even in midsummer.

Thunder rumbled in the heavens as the dark gray clouds roiled toward the saints. There were only a few cattle left, but they began to bawl and back away from the coming storm, their horns low to the ground.

Captain Willie marched forward and recalled how, back in August, he had parted such a tempest. Now he peered into the killer storm and whispered to himself, "Lord, let thy will be done."

He turned and gazed back at his followers. He could have told them to set up camp, seek some shelter from the storm, but he needed them to get to Pacific Springs. He pointed forward. "Our camp is fourteen miles to the west! Keep going. No matter what the Lord throws at us, don't you dare stop!"

The wind nearly stole the words from his mouth, but his people obeyed.

Cold rain slashed through the leaden skies, ripping into his face. Captain Willie lowered his head, grabbed onto his hat, and forged ahead. In five minutes, his clothing was soaked. In ten minutes he was shivering from chills. Lightning flashed all around, and balls of hail the size of marbles poured from the heavens. The women and children cried out in anguish, and Captain Willie shouted, "Keep going!" In ten more minutes, the hail stones quit bouncing off the rocks, and now the icy wind carried a blizzard.

Huge snowflakes struck the ground, sticking to the hail and forming a layer of ice over everything. Captain Willie saw icicles forming on the brim of his hat. He peered back, saw icicles taking shape on women's bonnets and skirts. The children kept trudging in his wake.

One Englishwoman, Eliza Smith, a woman only a little younger than Captain Willie, was plodding along, pulling her handcart, when she suddenly dropped, falling dead with a smacking sound, like a piece of meat slapping onto a butcher's block.

Other people were struggling through the blinding storm. Children in the back of handcarts peered at him with forlorn faces, as if begging him to stop.

Captain Willie trudged on. The blizzard dropped four inches of snow over the next half hour and then just as suddenly as the storm had hit, it quit. But lowering clouds raced on the raging winds, making noonday dark and gloaming.

He called a halt to the march, lit a bonfire, and gave the saints some time to dry out. "Beat the icicles off of your clothes," he warned them. "You don't want them turning back into water."

The saints drew in a circle around the fire and pulled blankets over their heads to hold in the heat. The only stores now consisted of the hard bread and a few pounds of dry apples, and Captain Willie wasn't about to give out any food, even though the children were weeping from hunger and some had dropped, insensate from the cold.

As they were standing beside the fire, George Cunningham let out a shout. "Look! They're here—the men from my dream!"

He pointed off to the horizon, a mile ahead, but there was no sign of anyone, no sound of creaking wheels or horses whinnying.

Yet Captain Willie felt hope leap in his breast, for the spirit of the Lord bore witness that help had come. Women began to cry out, "They're here!" "Here they come!" and every eye studied the horizon. But there was no sign of movement, and at last some folks said, "What do you see? There's no one there."

Atop a snow-covered hill on the horizon, he saw a pair of hats bouncing, and suddenly a pair of riders climbed into view, followed almost immediately by a lone wagon.

The saints let out a cheer. Women wept for joy and hugged one another, and men threw their hats in the air. One of the riders drew a pistol and fired in celebration, then spurred his horse into a gallop. He had a large buck strung over the front of the horse, and a smile plastered across his face. As he rode close, Captain Willie saw that it was Joseph Young.

He drew into camp, drew his buck knife, and cut a rope that held the deer to his saddlebags, then dumped the carcass into the snow. "Good thing you've got that fire going," he said. "This creature was just begging to be cooked. He threw himself right in front of my gun and demanded that I pull the trigger."

The camp rejoiced. It had been weeks since they'd bagged any fresh game.

Moments later, Cyrus Wheelock, who had served as a counselor to Franklin D. Richards, rode into camp on a black horse with a black saddle, with silver studs in it. It was a Spanish-style saddle. Young George Cunningham went to it and studied it closely, for it was the saddle he'd described from his dream.

The men dismounted, and widow and children took turns hugging them, weeping for joy.

Moments later the wagon reached the group, and men began throwing out pieces of clothing—fine gloves and shawls, shoes, stockings, jackets and even a few buffalo robes. "There's plenty more where that comes from," one man called out. "We've got forty wagons full of food on the trail behind us, compliments of Brigham Young."

"We're saved!" a cry went up, and people who Captain Willie thought would never smile again began to dance and weep for joy.

Cyrus Wheelock stood up on the buckboard of the wagon and

pointed to Joseph Young. "You can thank this young man here," he said. "When we got within sight of Salt Lake, while the rest of us were riding our carriages into the valley, he leaps out and runs five miles like his britches was on fire and barges straight into the prophet's house and warns him of your need.

"By the time I got there, Brother Brigham was so mad he was practically frothing at the mouth. He called an emergency meeting of the presiding bishopric right then and there, held an all-night meeting to calculate what you folks would need. That was on the night of October fourth."

Eliza Gadd stood listening, riveted to the tale. *Oh why*, she wondered, *could not Samuel be here to hear of it, or baby Daniel?* The date hit her like a slap in the face. October fourth was the day that Daniel had died. He was lying in her arms, struggling for breath, at the very moment that Brigham Young was holding his meeting.

"It was hot that day, hotter than I've ever seen in October," Cyrus continued, "but Brother Brigham told the brethren that a storm was coming and that the church needed to bend all of its efforts to save you folks. So he decides that he has to have someone lead this group, and he tells the bishopric, go and get me Ephraim Hanks." At that, Cyrus Wheelock peered around at the saints, as if noticing that something was wrong, and said, "You folks haven't seen Hanks, have you?"

"No," Captain Savage said. "Should we?"

"He's supposed to be riding up ahead of us," Young said. "We imagined that he was three or four days ahead, at least, maybe a week."

Captain Willie shook his head. There had been no sighting of him. But it wasn't unusual for two parties to miss each other on the trail. Hanks might have followed the river when they cut across land.

Ephraim Hanks was quickly becoming a legend in the Church. Even Eliza knew his name, for Captain Savage had served in the army with him and spoke of him fondly. Ephraim was as hardened a frontiersman as had ever walked the plains. He had worked for years as a mail carrier between Salt Lake and points east, often traveling alone through hostile Indian territories. He'd carried the mail over frozen mountain passes when the snow lay four feet deep and swam through raging rivers while carrying mail bags on his head. As a marksman, he was held to be the equal of Porter Rockwell. As a soldier in the Mexican War, he had been recognized as a man utterly without fear. But far more than Rockwell, Hanks was known to have a spiritual side.

Savage had once told a story of a widow down in southern Utah who grew so gravely ill that she could no longer take care of her children and fell into despair, fearing that all of them would die. She prayed for help, and several hours later, Ephraim Hanks came knocking at her door in the middle of the night. She made her way to the door, crawling, unable to stand. She unbolted it, surprised to see Hanks—for of all the men in the world, she had hoped to see him the most, for his gift of healing was well known.

"The Lord told me that you were sick," Hanks said, "and I've ridden forty miles in the last two days to heal you."

He then laid his hands upon her head and commanded the illness to depart.

The woman sat for a moment, stunned, for it seemed that a great weight had lifted from her shoulders, and to her astonishment, she said, "You know, I think I am healed!"

"Good," Hanks said. "Now can you get up and fix me some supper. I'm bone tired and haven't had a bite in two days."

So she did.

Captain Savage had told dozens of similar stories about Ephraim Hanks.

Cyrus Wheelock continued, "So Brother Brigham tells his secretary, 'Send a rider for Ephraim Hanks first thing in the morning.' Now Ephraim was down at Utah Lake, laying up some trout for the winter, and Brigham figures it will take a week to find him and fetch him.

"But Ephraim had an inkling of what was going on. He said that he had been worried about the handcart companies all throughout the fall, and as he was out paddling on the lake in his canoe that evening, he got a tremendous fear.

"So he put his trout in the smokehouse. As he lay in bed, he had hardly gone to sleep when he heard someone call his name, 'Ephraim!'

"He rose and called out, 'Who's there?' But no one answered. He went to the door, thinking that a stranger might be searching for him, and called out twice.

"At last, he realized that it was a dream, and he went back to bed.

"But a while later he heard someone calling his name again. He rose up in his bed, reached for his Colt, cocked it, and waited for someone to open the door. No one did. So he lay back down to sleep, but as he did, he heard someone calling his name a third time, so he pulled his gun and took aim at the noise, then thought better of it and answered, 'Yeah, Lord, thy servant heareth.'

"In the corner of the room, he saw a dim figure, the outline of a man."

Captain Savage laughed. "That's just like Ephraim Hanks—to draw iron on an angel of the Lord. That angel is lucky he didn't get his gut shot."

Cyrus Wheelock gave a deep belly laugh and continued, "So the angel says, 'Ephraim Hanks, those handcart people out on the plains are in trouble. Will you not go help them?'

"Ephraim looked steadily on the angel and answered, 'Yes.'

"Immediately the apparition disappeared, and Ephraim leapt from bed and pulled on his trousers. He packed his saddlebags and his gun, waited for the moon to come up, so he could ride in safety.

"He put his spurs to horseflesh and rode all night, so that by eight in the morning, just as he was entering the outskirts of Salt Lake City, he found Brother Brigham's messenger riding hell-bent for leather racing toward him—"

Cyrus Wheelock nodded to Joseph Young.

"Uh, that would have been me," Joseph admitted sheepishly.

"What did you say?"

"I almost didn't recognize him," Joseph said. "We'd only met once before. I asked if he was Ephraim Hanks, and he said yes. So I told him that the prophet needed his help, and he said, 'I know. We've got to go save them handcart people.' "

The crowd laughed to hear the story related, and Eliza realized that this was hugely important to these men, to fill her children's heads with stories about angels coming to their rescue.

Is there any truth in it? Eliza wondered. She didn't dare open herself to believe. She'd been hurt too many times before.

"So that's on Sunday morning, the fifth of October," Wheelock continued. "It's the first morning of October conference, and the whole church had gathered.

"Brother Brigham gets up to the pulpit, and he says, he says . . ." Cyrus Wheelock stopped for a moment and pulled out a piece of yellow newspaper from his jacket pocket. "I thought you might want to see what he said yourselves," and men hunkered close to get a look at the article.

Cyrus said, "The prophet stood at the pulpit, and he pounded on it with his cane to get everyone's attention, and then glared out over the audience and he said, 'I will now give this people the subject and the text of the Elders who may speak today and during the conference.

" 'It is this: On the fifth day of October, 1856, many of our brethren and sisters are on the plains with handcarts, and probably many are now seven hundred miles from this place, and they must be brought here. We must send assistance to them. The text will be, 'to get them here.' I want the brethren who may speak to understand that their text is the people on the plains. And the subject matter for this community is to send for them and bring them in before winter sets in.

" 'That is my religion; that is the dictation of the Holy Ghost that I possess. It is to save these people. This is the salvation I am now seeking for. To save our brethren that would be apt to perish, or suffer extremely, if we do not send them assistance.

" 'I shall call upon the bishops of the church this day. I shall not wait until tomorrow, nor until the next day, for sixty good mule teams and twelve or fifteen wagons. I do not want to send oxen. I want good horses and mules. They are in this territory, and we must have them. Also I want twelve tons of flour and forty good teamsters, besides those that drive the teams. This is dividing my texts into heads. First, forty good young men who know how to drive teams, who will take charge of the teams out on the prairie that are now managed by men, women, and children who know nothing about driving them. Second, we need sixty or sixty-five good spans of mules, or horses, with harness, whipple trees, neck-yokes, stretchers, lead chains, and so on. And thirdly, we need twenty-four thousand pounds of flour, which we have on hand . . .

"'I will tell you all that your faith, religion, and profession of religion will never save one soul of you in the Celestial Kingdom of our God unless you carry out just such principles as I am now teaching you. Go and bring in those people now on the plains. And attend strictly to those things which we call temporal, or temporal duties. Otherwise, your faith will be in vain. The preaching you hear will be in vain, and you will sink to Hell, unless you attend to the things we tell you.'

"Then the prophet calls for volunteers to drive the teams, and says that they must be ready to leave tomorrow, and Ephraim Hanks stands up and says 'Hell, Brother Brigham, I'm ready to go now.'"

The people laughed and rejoiced and Cyrus said, "You've never seen the prophet's jaw drop so far or so fast. It was a wonder.

"Then Brigham calls for clothing. He asks the women to give up their hats and gloves and shawls, and the men to give up their jackets and the children to give up their shoes and stockings—anything that they can take off which modestly allows, and he has the folks throw them in a pile at the foot of pulpit, and he and his wives throw in their own shawls—and that's the clothes you're wearing now!"

By now the crowd was overwhelmed by the good news, and even Eliza found herself weeping in relief.

Joseph Young said, "Cyrus, where is that navy blue scarf?"

Cyrus peered through the crowd until he spotted the dark blue scarf, and he pointed down to Eliza's son William. "You take good care of that scarf, sonny. That's the prophet's own scarf, and he just might want it back!"

William's mouth was agape, and he hugged the scarf to his chest as if it were some unimaginable treasure.

Suddenly the enormity of what was happening struck Eliza. Hundreds of men and wagons were coming into the wilderness to rescue them, driving their horses hundreds of miles, in an effort that was bound to take months to accomplish. In all of the history that she knew, from Rome to Greece to modern times, no rescue attempt had ever been mounted on such a grand scale.

As the company quickly butchered the deer and cooked the venison, their rescuers could not steel their emotions, seeing the saints' wasted condition. Many of those nearest the fire had been pulled from the sick wagons and could not stand. Others were just walking skeletons.

Joseph Young spotted one young lady, Emily Hill, and called out, "Emily, is that you?"

"Of course it's me," Emily said.

Joseph suddenly let out a deep, wracking sob, and looked as if he would sink to the ground.

"What's wrong?" Emily asked.

"You, you just look so starved," he said. "I almost didn't recognize you."

Emily gave a confused chuckle. "I can't look that bad. I mean, I haven't had a mirror to look into for three months, but I can't look that bad."

Joseph reached into his pocket, pulled out a small onion, and begged her, "Please, eat this."

As they stood talking, Captain Willie took Cyrus Wheelock aside to chat privately. It was obvious that this wagon couldn't stay. Wheelock needed to get to the Martin Handcart company, which was somewhere behind them, days or weeks away.

"How far back are the supply wagons?" Captain Willie asked.

"A day, maybe two. They're strung out all along the trail, each of them coming as fast as they can. Our wagon is light, so we took the advance."

Captain Willie considered this. He had only one day's worth of supplies left—the almost inedible hard bread that he'd bought at Fort Laramie. Added to this, he had a handful of starved oxen that the saints could eat. *It should be enough to last us until we reach the supplies,* he thought. *Just barely.* A scripture came to mind. "By grace ye are saved, after all you can do." The food supplies would reach him in the nick of time.

Cyrus whispered, "The prophet himself wanted to be with us. He tried to come and greet you, but he became terribly ill. We had to have a doctor come from Salt Lake and take him back to the valley."

Captain Willie walked back to the camp. The people were shivering violently despite the fires, and he realized that he needed to get them moving again, so that they could warm themselves, and then find a place to set camp away from the icy wind.

As the camp prepared to break, he saw Emily Wall walking through it. One old fellow was lying by the fire, unable to rise, waiting for someone to carry him back to the sick wagon. Emily handed him her onion. He peered up at her with eyes full of gratitude but was too weak to thank her as he began to feed.

Cyrus Wheelock got up on his wagon again and addressed the saints. "Brothers and sisters. We've got a wagon full of food here, and you folks have a ways to walk before you reach the relief wagons. Now, we can come with you if you wish and take care of you until you reach them. But there's a whole passel of saints somewhere on the prairie ahead of us, the Edward Martin Company. Some of you have kin amid that group, and I know you've got to be worried about them as much as I am. We don't know how those folk are faring right now."

Captain Willie grimaced. Cyrus was right. Captain Willie had been able to buy a few supplies at Fort Laramie, but that meant that there was nothing for the saints who came afterward.

"So," Cyrus said, "I'm asking you to vote on it. I can stay with you folks and help you on your way. Or . . . I can take my wagon and my food and race off to the folks behind."

He fell silent for a moment and let the people think. They were freezing, and many had fainted from fatigue. They were starving and could hardly walk. The sick wagons were painfully full of those who could not go on.

"Who wants us to ride with you until we find the relief wagons?"

Cyrus Wheelock looked out over the crowd to count hands. Not one was raised. Captain Willie peered at women who were holding babes that were at death's door and saw that they did not value their own comfort, their own lives, above those of their brethren.

"All right," Cyrus said, seeming a bit confused. "And who votes that I go on?"

There was a shout of triumph as every hand was thrust high in the air.

Cyrus Wheelock took off his hat and held it in his hand, fighting back tears. He fumbled with it a moment and said, "Well, that's it, then. Thank you, folks. I thank you. The Lord love you. There's not a better group of people in this whole church, I think."

Captain Willie's heart swelled with pride. He agreed with Cyrus. Indeed, he wondered if all of their troubles hadn't come upon them just to create this moment, when these people could prove their faithfulness to the Lord, when they could show the proper spirit of consecration.

It's going to take a lot of moments like this, Captain Willie thought, *to prepare the world for the Second Coming.*

Wheelock and his men rode off with their wagon and horses to find the Martin Handcart Company. The saints raised a cheer to hurry them on their way. Then they turned and resumed their march through the snow.

The promise of food made the journey easier, but not by much. People still fainted from fatigue. People still froze. People died from hunger.

Baline had tried on all of the shoes that were cast off of the wagon, for she had nothing to cover her feet but some cowhide, but most of the shoes were too small. Still, one Dane, Rasmus Hansen, who had gotten a fine new coat, had seen her predicament. Rasmus was from Baline's own small island, and he had been a close friend to her father. He kept a special watch over Baline, and so now he took off his shirt, ripped off its sleeves, and wrapped the sleeves around her hide shoes, reinforcing her crude boots.

They worked well for walking through the snow. The enlarged surface area made them feel like snowshoes, so that Baline was able to march on the crust of the snow. Since the snow cushioned her steps, the makeshift shoes did not fall apart too often. Baline had to tread lightly to keep the knotted rags from coming undone, and every so often a bit of snow would work its way between the bits of cloth, so that her feet grew cold.

The snow had stopped, but the temperature had dropped thirty degrees since dawn, and now a wicked breeze chilled the saints.

Even with the hope of rescue just ahead, the children cried from the cold and from their knotted stomachs, and many people fainted in the course of that hard march. The clouds thinned for a few moments and the ghost of a sun whitened the snow until the saints became nothing more than shadows struggling through a field of blazing white. The temperature had plunged below zero, and a strong wind gusted throughout the day, chilling even Baline's bones. If not for her blanket, which Baline wrapped over her head like a shawl, she would have frozen.

The sick wagons became so full that children cried, for the adults were crushing them.

Captain Savage went back and forced some sick men out of the wagon and had them tie handcarts to the backs of the wagons, so that more sick could be carried. One of the frail brothers died as he was pulled in his handcart.

Later in the afternoon, Rasmus Hansen was pulling his cart ahead of Father Jens when he collapsed in the snow. Jens dragged Rasmus to his own cart to give him a ride. Rasmus was in a stupor, and he clung to the sides of the handcart, peering around. From time to time his eyes would flutter closed, and he opened them only with great difficulty. Baline wanted to give him his coat back, but now it was torn and cold and wet.

Father Jens only pulled Rasmus for an hour before Rasmus drew a cold breath, and then a loud death rattle escaped from his throat, his last breath forming a cloud that streamed away in the wind.

By the time that the company reached the Sweetwater, five more people had died. One was Daniel Osborn, a boy of seven that Baline had sometimes played with. He had been excellent at whistling loudly and catching fireflies.

Snow began to fall again in the afternoon, and perhaps because of this, some of the sick wagons missed the trail and got lost.

That night, the company reached the sixth crossing of the Sweetwater. The river was not deep, but it was very cold, and so Jens carried Baline, Else, and Niels over the water. Afterward, Jens's legs were so frozen that he laid on the ground and wept from the pain. As camp was set, Baline also wept bitter tears, for it seemed to her that all of her friends were dying.

For dinner, there was little to eat. Captain Willie handed out the dry biscuits, the last of the provisions. Only six cattle were left to the company, but he dared not butcher them, for he needed them to pull the relief wagons. He sent men out to find the lost wagons, and they did not all make it to camp until midnight.

30

Final Preparations

Days of Hunger

On the morning of October twentieth Captain Willie rose to find that the land was blanketed with fresh snow. Four or five inches had fallen yesterday, and another five or six had been added during the night.

The first order of business was to cook breakfast and then to rake the ashes away from the ground so that the company could bury its dead. The soil beneath the snow was frozen hard, so the saints had learned to wait until they broke camp before digging where the ground had been thawed. Those who had died the previous day were then interred, along with a sister who had died during the night. Captain Willie was surprised to see Ann Rowley's two-year-old daughter among the dead, for he had not heard that she had passed away.

Sometime in the night, the oxen had strayed from camp, and one of them had also died. That left only five head.

Captain Willie held a brief council meeting with the sub-captains. Since Edward Griffiths had been found to be stealing food, the captains now officially released him from his duties, and John Chislett was called in his place. There was not much food to give out, only about forty pounds of hard bread, twenty-five pounds of rice, three pounds of flour, and a few pounds of dried apples. Captain Willie ordered Chislett to dispense the food only to women who had babies and toddlers to feed and ordered that the two poorest cattle be slaughtered for the camp.

The snow kept falling, and by eight in the morning it was a foot deep. The company could move no farther. So he and Joseph Elder saddled their mules and prepared to go hunt for the relief party.

Captain Willie took no bedrolls. He did not intend to sleep until they found the relief wagons. Nor did he take food, for he could not do so in good conscience. It was the first time that he had ridden a mule in the past four months. He had sworn not to do so, but realized now that there are some promises that should not be kept.

Thus they set out in the storm. The snow kept piling as they rode. As one leaves Sixth Crossing and heads up into the mountains, the elevation rises precipitously, nearly a thousand feet over the course of five miles, to an elevation of about 7700 feet. This is the great Continental Divide. To the east of this rise, all rivers flow toward the Atlantic; to the west, they flow to the Pacific.

As the storms blow over this prominence, the clouds are forced to rise. The air grows frigid and turns to snow, and the snow is released on the eastern slopes. Thus, as they traveled, the snow grew deeper during the climb, so that at times the mules were forced to plod through drifts three feet deep.

All through the day they rode, searching for signs of rescue wagons. The rescuers were supposed to have been only a day behind Cyrus Wheelock's wagon, but the company had marched for a day already. Captain Willie figured that the relief wagons had gotten bogged down in the storm.

So Captain Willie and Joseph Elder rode through the day, and on into the night. As night hit, the storm suddenly blasted with renewed fury, until they could not see fifty paces ahead. Captain Willie had not eaten in more than twenty-four hours, and his head grew light, and his vision blurred.

The two men had no lantern to light the way, and it was only by chance that, well past midnight, Joseph Elder noticed fresh tracks in the snow beside the trail.

A sign had been placed in the snow. Neither man could read it in the dark, but they followed the tracks for three miles, down a long hill and into a ravine at the base of a creek where there were enough willows for the horses to graze upon.

It was two in the morning when they found their rescuers and fourteen wagons filled with food. One man, Harvey Cluff, had said that he couldn't sleep. He'd become worried that snowstorm would force Cyrus Wheelock and Joseph Young to return, and that they would be lost in the snow. He said that the spirit of the Lord would not let him sleep until he hiked through the storm in the middle of the night and placed a sign by the road. He had put the sign up only fifteen minutes before Captain Willie found it.

Captain Willie told the rescuers of his predicament and helped round up their horses and get them harnessed. By five in the morning they were ready for the return trip. The rescuers ran their horses down the mountains through the snow, so that a twenty-seven mile journey that had taken Captain Willie seventeen hours on the way up, took only six on the return trip.

❦

There was no bread in camp on the twentieth, at least not for adults to eat. The people mostly sat through the long day, hunger working its dark magic upon them.

Meat was passed out, but the cattle had almost no muscle left on their bones, and what little meat that Eliza got was stringy. Worse, her body had become accustomed to bread. It was the only staple that the church fathers in their grand wisdom had thought to provide for most of the trip. The English laws upon the ship had been strict—a certain amount of fruits and vegetables had to be supplied to travelers. But once the saints reached America's shore, they got nothing but bread. Bread and rolls on Ellis Island, bread on the trains, all of the bread that you could eat—and nothing else. On the trail, it had been the same.

So Eliza had grown sick of bread. Yet the cruelest joke was that as soon as the company ran out, she grew sick from not having it.

The saints ate only some tough old cattle that night, boiling down hooves and tail bones into soup. The result was that, without bread to go with it, almost the entire camp came down with dysentery. The camp became a disgusting, malodorous place, but the people were too sick and weak to move from it.

So it was that Eliza yearned for the bread that she hated and could get none. Those who had had the foresight to purchase a few supplies along the trail now made up their final meals.

Levi Savage took the old flour bags from the wagons and beat them until he got a cup of wheat, then mixed it with warm water and made some "skilly" to drink. He went to Eliza's tent and fed it to John Linford, who was on the verge of death. John drank his final meal, his eyes filled with tears of gratitude, and passed away an hour later.

Sister Caldwell used some buffalo jerky and mixed it with salt and a tiny bit of flour to make some soup. That night, as the storm blew cold, she took it to the young men who were standing guard. They were in such dire shape that for the rest of their lives they swore that she had saved their lives.

Ann Rowley recalled that she had saved a couple of biscuits on their sea voyage. The biscuits, made from ground bean paste, were so hard that they could break your teeth. She'd only kept them as a memento of her trip. But now she put them in a Dutch oven with some water. She had ten grown people to feed in her camp and only two biscuits. So she gathered her grown children around and said, "Jesus was able to multiply his loaves and fishes. If we have faith, we should be able to do the same."

So the family prayed, then left the biscuits on to cook for two hours. When Ann Rowley lifted the lid, the Dutch oven was filled to overflowing. She fed her family first and then passed out the leftovers to children that had been haunting their camp, staring longingly at the food.

So young Samuel Gadd, after eating a miraculous dinner, went and told his mother the news. Eliza arrived at Ann's fire too late to witness the miracle, or even get a bite for herself.

Baline lay in her tent all day on the twentieth, trying to keep warm. Her right ear had swollen up again, and this time the swelling was so great that her ear canal closed off completely. So Jens made her stay in bed, and the whole family joined her with their blankets beneath them and a buffalo robe on top, as they tried to conserve their energy.

In part, Baline knew that Jens stayed in bed hoping to speed his own recovery. His legs had nearly frozen yesterday, and like many in the camp who were getting frostbite in their feet, he was losing sensation in his legs.

Outside it was as white as Christmas, and so that morning, and throughout the day, Else Nielsen heated rocks in the fire, then brought them in to warm the tent, while Jens told the Christmas story in a way that Baline had never heard before. He quoted the Bible and the Book of Mormon from memory.

"In the beginning was the Word," he began. "And the Word was with God, and the Word was God."

He began the story from the foundations of the world, quoting prophecies of the coming of Christ from Psalms and from Isaiah, from the Book of Abraham and others. Then he went to the New Testament, and gave the account of the births of Jesus and John the Baptist. In an hour he had completed his tale, but there was far more daylight left, and so he told Baline and little Niels about Jesus' ministry and teachings.

Hour after hour he continued, relating miracle after miracle—the healing of lepers, the blind, the deaf, and the palsied. He told of the times when Christ fed the multitudes, calmed the raging storms, walked on water, and raised the dead.

He related the temptations that Christ suffered, and how he taught in the temple as a child, and how he was rebuked and scorned by the learned men of his time. He quoted the Sermon on the Mount from memory, pointing out the subtle and instructive differences between the Bible and the Book of Mormon.

At one point, Baline stopped him and asked, "Have you memorized all of the scriptures?"

Jens laughed. "No child, not all of them—only the words that Jesus has spoken. Why should I not? How can I follow in his footsteps if I refuse to hear the words he has spoken? How can I hear if I do not truly listen? How can I truly listen if I am not willing to take his words into my heart?"

As evening came and night drew on, Jens told how Christ had suffered in the Garden of Gethsemane and how he was taken by the Romans and the Pharisees, put on trial, and nailed to the cross.

The story thrilled Baline and kept her mind from her hunger. She had heard bits and pieces of the tale from time to time in church, or read it in her own scripture studies, but she had never heard it all in one telling, by someone who expertly wove the bits and pieces from various Gospels together to form one bright tapestry that was greater than all of its parts.

Finally, Jens told how Jesus arose from the dead, appearing to hundreds of his followers in Judea and to the people on the American continent, ending with Joseph Smith, who said of him, "And now, after the many testimonies which have been given of him, this is the testimony, last of all, which we give of him: That he lives! For we saw him, even on the right hand of God; and we heard the voice bearing record that he is the Only Begotten of the Father—"

Last of all Jens bore his own solemn testimony that he, too, knew that Christ lives.

By then it was growing dark, and Baline became afraid. Jens had told her months ago that he was worried that someone in his family would die on this trip, and she knew that his legs were still hurting from the freezing water. She was afraid that by him telling her this story of Christ's death and resurrection, he was saying good-bye. He was trying to prepare her for his own death by promising that someday, like Christ, he hoped to rise again.

Everyone in the tent huddled up that night, for the temperature dropped, and the night became bitter, bitter cold—far colder than any night that Baline had ever suffered through. With no food in their bellies, the inmates in the tent could not seem to hold their body heat. Thus everyone in the tent cuddled—Baline sleeping next to Niels to keep him warm, and then sleeping next to one of her tent mates, Sophia Larsen, who slept next to her own mother.

Baline suffered through fever dreams and night sweats all through the darkness, and in her dreams Jesus preached from a little ship out on the flat waters of Galilee, while fish leapt high in the air all around him, and he raised the centurion's daughter from the dead and told Baline that someday he would raise her too.

At dawn the twenty-first, Baline woke to find Sophia Larsen, the girl sleeping next to her, frozen to death.

Baline discovered it by accident. She rolled over and put her arm over Sophia, unconsciously, and found that Sophia was far colder than a living person could be. Baline's eyes flew open, and she witnessed an expression of mild distress on Sophia's face.

Sophia was eleven, only a few months older than Baline, and it seemed astonishing to find her dead, for when Sophia had gone to bed, Sophia had seemed weak and tired, but otherwise healthy.

Thus Sophia joined three others who had died in the night, including the last man in Eliza Gadd's tent, the longtime family friend John Linford.

As Sophia's family mourned, her mother weeping and muttering in grief, Baline whispered to Jens. "It is as if death is creeping nearer every day, taking those closest to me."

The relief wagons reached camp shortly before noon, with Captain Willie riding his mule ahead at a trot. The saints called out to one another, until everyone who was able to crawl from their beds had left the tents and burst into celebration. The women in camp broke into tears and many of the sisters lost all restraint as they deluged their rescuers with kisses upon their necks, tears streaming down the women's sunburned cheeks.

For their part, the rescuers stood looking at the gaunt inhabitants of the camp, many of them so far gone that they could not stand, and held silent for a long moment, overpowered by their emotions, until finally even the hardest men among them broke into tears.

Some rescuers had family in the camp, Captain Willie had learned. He'd been regaled with inquiries as soon as he reached the rescue wagons. Sister Tait, a woman from India, had a husband and family that had traveled to Salt Lake a year earlier. Her husband had been a colonel in the English Army and had come to Utah when his enlistment was up. But his wife stayed behind in India, for she was pregnant and feared losing her child. Her daughter was born safely, but had died as their ship crossed rough seas off the coast of Africa; but Sister Tait had made it this far. Now her husband, who had learned that she was in this company from newspaper accounts, nearly flew into her arms.

Another young man, Robert Bain, nearly dead himself from Rocky Mountain spotted fever, had to be propped into the seat to keep from falling off his wagon as he drove to the aid of his mother and siblings.

The leader of the rescue team was William Kimball, a man that Captain Willie had known for years. They'd served together on their missions in England. William had been among the missionaries to travel west with Franklin D. Richards, and as soon as he had reached Salt Lake, he had helped put together the rescue effort.

Now, by order of the prophet, he was to take over the handcart company.

So he rode into camp, weeping as he looked down upon the sick, and did something that Captain Willie had never imagined. He pointed out a young lady in the camp and shouted, "Brother Cole, there's your dream girl!"

One of the rescuers, a young man mounted on a fine red gelding, rode to the woman in question. Her name was Lucy Ward, and she was a very formal young woman.

Brother Cole leapt from his horse and just stared at her in surprise. He took his hat in his hand, put it over his chest, and fumbled with it, then begged, "Ma'am, would you like to ride on my horse with me?"

Captain Willie saw it coming. Lucy reared back and slapped the young man so hard that spittle flew from his mouth. "Sir," she said stiffly. "We have not even been introduced!"

Everyone burst into laughter. Captain Willie rode up next to William Kimball and asked, "What was that all about?"

Brother Kimball smiled. "That young James Cole boy told me about a dream he had a couple of weeks back. He said he dreamt that he saw a woman who was supposed to be his wife among the handcart folks. Said she was a beautiful woman with black hair and a fancy black fur cap, and that she tied it over her head with a green scarf. I told him, he wasn't likely to find anyone fitting that description among the handcart folk. Then first thing when we rode into camp, I saw her standing there, just like he said!"

Captain Willie smiled at their good fortune. After months of despair, it felt as if the Lord was with them once again. He had no doubt that, proper introductions or no, James Cole and Lucy Ward would soon marry.

The rescuers immediately went to work building up a fire and passing out food. The aroma of bacon filled the air, and the folks sat nibbling on onions, the first fresh produce they'd had in three months, as they waited for their bread to cook.

Children too young to understand what the excitement was all about fairly danced with glee.

Finally, Captain Willie thought, *I get to rest. My mission is complete. Brother Kimball will take over from here.* Yet Brother Kimball dashed that notion almost instantly. He made an announcement to the camp as the dinner was cooking.

"Brothers and sisters," he said. "Captain Willie will be stepping down as captain of this handcart company. But if he will, I would like to ask that he continue serving as the captain over his hundred."

He looked to Captain Willie to see if he would accept this calling, and Willie nodded his consent.

"Good," Kimball continued. "Now, we have fourteen wagons of food here. We're going to send eight of them on tomorrow, to meet up with the Martin Handcart Company, and six we will keep with us.

"Rest tonight. Eat well, get some good sleep for once. None of your men will need to stand guard. My teamsters will do it for you.

"But tomorrow we head to the base of Rocky Ridge, and the day after that comes the hardest part of your journey—the crossing of the Great Divide."

The words made Captain Willie uneasy. He looked at his haggard people, mere skeletons barely clinging to life, and he knew that many of them would not be able to endure that climb. They were too starved, too ill.

When Captain Willie had some time alone later that day, he begged William Kimball, "Are you sure about this? These people need food and rest, a week of it at the very least."

"Winter's coming," Kimball said. There were no trees here beside the Sweetwater, and the wind was a constant menace, blowing day and night. "We can't spend it camped here. Every day that we stay brings a greater chance of another storm."

Captain Willie knew that Brother Kimball was right. He also felt in his bones that a lot of his friends were about to die. He wondered what other help might be coming.

"Is Elder Richards coming?" He wasn't sure why he asked. In part he hoped for more help from the church. But even more than that, he still wanted to have some words with Elder Richards, asking what in the hell he'd been thinking, and hopefully find an explanation that could satisfy him.

But William Kimball shook his balding head. "He won't be coming. He and the prophet aren't exactly seeing eye to eye." Now his voice became a whisper. "The prophet chastised him in public, in the conference. He said that Richards was proud and boastful, and said that 'if he does not repent and humble himself, he will soon find that he has no more of the spirit than a hollow pumpkin.'

"I hear that the prophet said worse things about Richards in private. He chastised Richards for sending the handcart companies out so late in the season. He said that Richards had told John Taylor that he was willing to accept full responsibility for the handcart immigrants, and to that Brother Brigham said, 'Amen. The deaths of these people shall be upon the head of him who sent them.' "

William Kimball added softly, "Joseph Young can tell you this better than I. He was in the room. But Brigham chastised Richards. Joseph got to Brother Brigham before any of us and told the prophet everything that had happened. So now the prophet reminded Richards how he had told your handcart people to 'humble themselves like little children, and to consecrate all that they had to the Lord,' and promised that 'if they did, then the blessings would follow.'

"But Brigham asked Richards, 'Did you ever think, for even one second, that the Lord might have been speaking to you, instead of through you?'

"At that, Elder Richards's face paled, and he began to shake.

" 'How much of a blessing you might have been,' Brother Brigham told him, 'if you had heeded your own advice—if you had humbled yourself as a little child, consecrated your labor and energy, joined that handcart company, and offered them the use of your carriages and wagons. The old gray-headed men and women, bowed down with age, could have ridden in style in your fine carriages, borne with ease. The wagons could have been used to haul the flour and provisions. Your sixteen missionaries could have lent their strong backs to the efforts, pulling those handcarts when the women and children had given all that they could. Those who were riding in the independent wagons would have been shamed by your example and would have followed in your footsteps. Thus, you could have taught them by example instead of just by precept. You could have lifted these handcart folk up, as if on eagles' wings, and sped them to Zion. I believe that the Lord would have taken delight then, and blessed you. But you chose to ride in a fine carriage instead; and that alone shall be your everlasting reward."

Captain Willie stood there, astonished to hear that an apostle of the Lord had been rebuked so harshly.

If Brigham had said such things to me, Captain Willie thought, *I would have fallen to the earth and wished myself dead.*

So it wasn't just me who thinks that Elder Richards is a glory hound. The prophet sees that flaw in him, too.

Yet I was fooled by his promises, Captain Willie thought. *Or was I?*

Captain Willie had felt the spirit of the Lord when Elder Richards spoke, and Richards's prophecy might have been true. If Richards had humbled himself, the handcart company would have been saved.

Yet the Lord has not forgotten me or my people, Captain Willie thought. *Elder Richards may have failed us, but the Lord provided another means for our rescue.*

For the first time in weeks, Captain Willie felt a little peace. *If only I can get my people over Rocky Ridge*, he thought, *I will die a happy man.*

31

THE BITTER TRAIL

ROCKY RIDGE

On the morning of the twenty-second, the dead were dragged from their tents and buried, and camp broke at noon.

The temperature stood at eight below zero, so that even a few moments outside left the people brutally cold. It had grown too cold to snow, but thankfully the wind was still that morning, and as Captain Willie exhaled, his breath hung in the air. The twelve inches on the ground was a thick, dry powder. It covered the rocks and sagebrush, leaving only indistinguishable humps in a field of white.

A prayer was said, and the company took off for the base of Rocky Ridge in good spirits. With six new wagons in the company, and with the people traveling over flat ground beside the river, the company moved well. But the heavy snows hampered travel. Those who absolutely could not walk were allowed to ride, and those who could not pull their handcarts were allowed to put them on a wagon and have their goods carted.

The company traveled only ten miles during the day, yet in that short time, Captain Willie saw too much heartbreak. Several men and women gave out in that trek, simply crumpling to the ground, lying down to die.

He would stand over them, enlisting the aid of their friends, and try to urge them on with promises of food and warm shelter, with pleas from women who loved them. He'd appeal to their desires to reach Zion and be embraced by the prophet. He'd tell them of the love that their children had for them and talk of warm summer days to come in Utah, with the children swinging on their rope swings or taking a dip in a swimming hole.

But nothing he said could reach them. Their dreams had all died, and it seemed that their souls had fled with them. In most cases he left these people, so bereft of hope, wrapped in thin blankets as they lay in the relief wagons, and Captain Willie despaired that they would live.

A man named Jens Nielsen came up with a better solution. When one of their men lay down in the snow to die, his family and friends gathered around and tried to give him the courage to continue. When they had failed, the leader of his tent, Jens Nielsen, said, "Let me speak to him." He then explained to the man, "Everyone here has done their best to encourage you to go on. But I don't care if you die, you piece of filth. Before you die, I have only one desire. I want to knock your teeth out!"

Jens then slugged the man in the face.

The fellow was so outraged that he got up and chased after Jens until they reached camp, at which point Jens laughed and said, "Aha, it worked!"

The Dane stood for a moment, outraged and confused, and then suddenly realized that he had reached the safety of camp after having given up all hope. Suddenly he hugged Jens, began to weep, and thanked Jens for saving his life.

But not all situations turned out so well.

Some of the children had no proper shoes. Mary Humphreys, a girl of fourteen, tried walking with nothing more than some cow's hide wrapped around her feet. By the time that she collapsed just outside of camp, ten miles later, Mary's feet were frozen, her toes black. Captain Willie could not get her to walk farther, and the relief wagons were so far behind that he carried her half a mile to camp.

The sick wagons were so full of people, and the oxen so close to death, that the wagons did not reach camp until nearly midnight.

Here at the foot of Rocky Ridge, the snow had piled deep. Those who could took tin plates and used them to shovel the snow away from the camp sites to the best of their ability. But even then, some of the women were forced to sleep on snow-covered ground, throwing blankets and buffalo hides over the ice. Some of the children got frostbite in their fingers from holding the plates.

The weather was so cold that many of the mothers stayed up late to heat rocks to keep their children warm. At ten that evening, one of the women in Captain Willie's group, Sister Philpot was heating rocks when she collapsed from exhaustion. Though Captain Willie rushed to her side and tried to get her warm, she succumbed within minutes. Her husband had died only five days earlier. She left her two daughters as orphans, Martha, age eleven, and Julia, age thirteen.

On the morning of the twenty-third, as the company prepared to cross Rocky Ridge, the people were exhausted. The terrible cold had prodded them awake all through the night, and months of starvation had left them worn through.

The first task at hand was to bury the dead, each captain attending to that task. Captain Willie could not sleep. A raging wind struck up at four in the morning, making the tent snap like sails. The cold driving underneath the sides nearly froze his backside, so he arose before dawn and dug a shallow grave for Sister Philpot. Though others had died during the night, they were not from his hundred. As he dug, a light snow commenced falling, tiny crystals so small that they swirled around his head, and the slightest inhalation drew them into his lungs, but he managed, with pick and spade, to dig a small trench for Sister Philpot, and then he called out her daughters and family friends for a brief prayer.

By nine his little group was ready to begin the trek up Rocky Ridge.

William Kimball called the camp together for prayer and announced his plan. "The road is easy to follow here," he said. "No one is in danger of getting lost. But it will be hard. We will travel in three groups. In the lead will be children and old folks, those too weak to pull a cart, but strong enough to carry themselves. I want them to go quickly. The wind is growing boisterous, and it's going to be cold. I want the children and old folks to get to Rock Creek Hollow as quickly as they can and then warm themselves by the fires. You will go in groups of no less than three at a time. If at any time someone in your group grows too weary to travel on, I want you to do all that is in your power to urge that person forward. But if you can't urge them forward, wrap them in a blanket, put them in some shelter away from the wind—a rock, or a gully, or against a tree, so that they can await aid.

"After the children will come the handcarts. These will be mothers and fathers, and all of those strong enough to pull. The snow is deep along the hillsides, so this will not be an easy task.

"If you find a child or an elderly person beside the road, it will be your duty to do all that you can to save them. This may mean that you will need to pull someone who is in need. Failing that, you should minister to them to the best of your capacity, and ensure that they are well as they await further assistance.

"If you find that you faint and cannot go on, take shelter, bundle up, and wait for rescue.

"Last of all, come the wagons. It will be the teamster's jobs to pick up the stragglers. No one is to be left behind, even those who appear to be dead. You must get them on a wagon, take them to the fires, and give them a chance to recover. Is that understood?"

When everyone had said "Aye," the journey began.

The road wound up along the hills for four miles, rising about eight hundred feet in elevation during the course. But it was not a steady rise. One might climb several hundred feet, and then descend a few hundred feet, and walk along a level portion for half a mile before climbing again.

The air was so thin that even walking at the most conservative amble left the heart pounding, and a man would have to stop and gasp deep breaths every hundred yards. But in doing so, he would be frustrated, for the air came into his lungs so arctic cold that the lungs rebelled at its touch and would constrict involuntarily, forcing the air out as fast as it came in.

The snow grew deep, more than eighteen inches along the trail, with some places where it drifted three or four feet.

A storm was coming in. It did not unleash a fierce blizzard with vast amounts of snow, for the air was far too cold to hold moisture. The temperature held steady through most of the day at near ten degrees below zero. It was blowing straight out of the Wind River Mountains, and the wind began to scream and moan as it tore over the frozen earth at thirty to fifty miles per hour, blowing snow and ice into the faces of the pioneers.

The children bundled up in blankets and led the way, resolutely marching. In less than an hour, they disappeared into the storm, and Captain Willie found himself overwhelmed by the tasks that faced him.

Captain Willie's little group of handcart pioneers tried to forge a path through the snow, climbing the hills. Among his hundred, he had only three men who were still healthy. Most of the men in their fifties and sixties had already died. The young men in their late teens and early twenties had all been called off on cattle drives, while the older men, the fathers in the group, had already either starved to death as a result of their ceaseless toils or were lying prostrate in the sick wagons, unable to lift their own heads.

That meant that only women were left to pull the handcarts, and none could manage to get them through the snow. Not everyone had the strength to forbear sending their little ones ahead, and so mothers tried to pull their six-year-olds or have them walk at their sides, much to the child's detriment, for they could not endure the cold winter blast as well as an adult.

Captain Willie climbed the hill until he found a handcart or two in trouble, mired in ice up to its hubs, and he would enlist the aid of as many women as were needed, and four or five women would pull one handcart a couple hundred yards, then return and grab another. Thus, for every handcart that he pulled a hundred yards, Captain Willie had to travel three or five hundred yards.

But the bitter winds had their way, and soon began to carry his people off into death's embrace. A quarter of the way up the hill, they found a young boy, only six years old, wrapped in a blanket, so cold that he was in a stupor. Captain Willie wrapped him in an extra quilt and laid him in a handcart and began pulling it through the snow.

The winds blasted Captain Willie's face and were so chill that when he opened his mouth to breathe, his teeth seemed to freeze and a wracking pain stole through his jaws. He tried turning away from the wind, letting his teeth warm, but that meant that he had to stop to do so, and he was reticent, when so many people were suffering.

Groups of children passed his handcarts as the second and third and fourth hundreds set out in waves, and among the children were a few doddering old men, most of them more feeble than any five-year-old.

Many of the adults began to fail as they climbed Rocky Ridge. At places, spikes of rocks thrust up from the ground to a height of six or ten inches. The rocks were almost as sharp as an Indian's stone ax, and they were hell on wheels, and even harder on a man's shoes or a horse's hooves. It was from these peculiar formations that the ridge got its name. Thus the rocks began to slice through people's shoes, both those of the women and the children. Captain Willie saw bloody footprints in the snow and worried about what they portended.

Some men and women had no proper gloves, and wherever a finger was exposed, it soon froze. Sister Kirkwood had a crippled son, a large boy of nineteen, and she was trying to pull the handcart up the mountain, while one of her older boys pushed from behind. She clutched onto the handle of the cart, wrestling it, while her shawl was pulled so low that it left only her right eye subjected to the elements. The wind was so cold that after an hour she sat down weeping, for she could no longer see. Captain Willie went to minister to her and found that her right eye had turned milky white and was frozen in its socket. The skin around it looked black and bruised.

Only then did he begin to realize how severe their predicament might be. For many long hours he toiled to reach Rocky Ridge, struggling to get his people to the top, but they did not make it until the day was fading, and even when they reached the top they still had a dozen miles to go before they could attain the safety of the camp

Captain Willie began to worry for the children ahead. The trail through the wilderness was lonely. Wolves prowled the gullies and ridges. There were broad streams to cross, covered in ice, where old folks or children might fall through. Worst of all, there was the wind to contend with, ceaselessly screaming over the prairie, cold and relentless.

32

Beyond Rocky Ridge

Father Jens had made it only a mile up the mountain before he collapsed. In the brutal cold wind, his legs would not work. He'd tried to let little Niels ride in the back of the handcart, but the deep snow defeated him, and Jens sank into the snow, weeping.

"You go on without me," he cried to Else. "Take the children and walk." Baline had never seen Jens cry. He was a mountain of a man, and she had not thought that he could cry. She thought that he must be in terrible pain.

"Let me see your feet!" Else demanded.

Jens did not answer. Instead, he fell into a swoon.

Else was a tiny woman, weighing less than Baline, and so she called out, "Baline, help me!" She was trying to wrestle Jens onto his back. Baline looked up and down the road for help, but no one was near. So she went to Else and helped roll Jens over. He was gasping for every breath. Once they had him on his back, Else pulled up his pants leg.

What Baline saw horrified her. Jens had only one pair of pants, thin cotton pants that had been appropriate for the summer. The knees were nearly worn through. When he had waded into the Sweetwater yesterday and carried the women across, it had cost him dearly. His legs were blackened by frostbite and severely swollen. His right foot was frozen solid at an angle, so that it pointed inward.

Baline marveled that he had been able to pull the handcart at all for the past two days. He must have done it at a terrible cost.

Else broke into tears and reached up and began raking her hands over her head, as if she would tear her hair out. "Why didn't you tell me?" she demanded. "Why didn't you say something?" But Father Jens was too far gone to speak.

"Niels," Else said, "get out of the handcart. We must make room for your father."

At first, neither of the children moved. Father Jens weighed a good two hundred pounds. There was no way that the three of them could pull him through eighteen inches of snow, in this raging storm.

"Do it!" Else cried. Baline leapt up and pulled Niels from the cart, then grabbed Father Jens by the right arm while Else took the left, and they dragged him up onto the cart and dumped him there, like the carcass of a deer.

Else was in a panic. She went to Niels, who had only just turned six, and tucked his blanket around his head, inspecting him carefully and then kissed him good-bye on the cheek. "Niels, you will follow Baline and do what she says, understand? She is going to take you to the fire, where you can get warm and get some food, yes?"

Little Niels's teeth were chattering, and he had begun crying, but whether it was from cold or hunger or fear, Baline did not know.

Then Else came to Baline and made a show of tucking her blanket around her. Baline's right ear was so swollen that the canal was still closed. So Else leaned close to Baline's left ear so that Baline could hear and whispered, "You must be brave now. I am going to pull Jens in the handcart. He is a big man, and I am not that strong. So I am counting on you. If I do not make it to camp, you must take little Niels to Peder Mortensen, the cripple, you understand? He will know what to do. He will take care of you until your mother and father come to America."

Baline burst into tears. "Yes, I understand."

Despite being a cripple, Peder Mortensen was a wealthy man with many strong sons. More than that, he was as good a man as Baline had ever known.

Else clutched Baline's blanket, pulling it tight, almost as if clutching her throat. "I am entrusting my only child to you. He does not understand the English, and he will rely upon you. It is up to you to lead him. Understand?"

Suddenly Baline understood. In the grove at Winter Quarters, when she had prayed, the spirit had told her that she would lead others to Zion. Now the task had fallen to her.

"Do not be afraid, Else," Baline said. She reached down and retied the rags that served as shoes in preparation for her journey, then took Niels by the hand and led him away.

Slowly they climbed, for the terrible wind raged at them, flinging ice crystals into their faces, and it seemed bent on taking their breath. Baline grabbed one of Niels' hands and had to keep pulling him, for often the child would turn to look back at Else, struggling through the snow, her back bent double, as she pulled Jens in the handcart.

It was futile, Baline knew. Father Jens would be dead long before Else could reach camp, and Else's heart would burst from this labor and give out somewhere along the way.

So she climbed, leading Niels by the hand. The Danes were near the rear of the column, and Father Jens had given out quickly, so that nearly everyone else was ahead.

As Baline climbed Rocky Ridge, she passed handcart after handcart that was mired in the snow. Everywhere, people were struggling valiantly to keep moving. She saw one old woman who had collapsed by the side of the road, and Baline did not dare to peek under her shawl to see if she was still breathing. Something about the way she lay so still told Baline that she was not.

As she walked, Baline found other men and women who called out to her. Sister Jensen begged, "Baline, take Sonja with you too. We cannot keep her in this cold." Sonja was only eight. She was a strong girl who would not slow Baline down. Then Brother Rasmussen called out, "Baline, you have the English. Take Christian with you." Christian was twelve and he was older than Baline, but he was a slow-witted boy, and his parents did not trust him to walk on his own. Soon she had half a dozen children in her wake.

The children were frightened and did not want to leave their parents. "What if there are Cheyenne on the trail?" one of them asked. "Wolves," another said. "I heard wolves howling." Thus they magnified each other's fears.

At last one old woman called, "Baline, take Lars Vandelin with you. You should have an adult!"

Brother Vandelin was an old man with long white hair. He walked with a cane, and his back was so stooped that he looked like a human fishhook. He was just up the road. He turned back and smiled to see the children. So Baline walked in his shadow. The children felt better about having him there, but Baline soon found that Brother Vandelin, who labored manfully through the storm, was among the slowest of her little group. Yet he was in high spirits, and he told the children jokes as he walked, in order to keep their minds off of the cold, in order to keep them from weeping in terror.

The walkers quickly outpaced those with handcarts, and in the next hour, Baline's group passed all of the English carts, and some of them saw the little group trekking through the hills and begged them to take their own children.

Eliza Gadd spotted Baline. Eliza was courageously pulling her own little handcart with William beside her, while Jane pushed from behind. Eliza had little Sarah holding baby Isaac in the cart. Mary Ann and Sam Junior trudged behind, both of them shivering frightfully. Eliza eyed the little group skeptically at first but then saw that Baline was with an adult.

"Baline," Eliza said. "Take Samuel with you. Samuel has been sick. He won't last in this wind."

"Yah, ve do this," Baline said, happy to have all of the company that she could get, for the wolves had been howling for days, and she was afraid to go too far into the wilderness without others around. She had heard how the wolves had attacked the cattle, so that even full-grown men could not drive the wolves back.

Baline's friends Agnes Caldwell and Mary Hurren both stayed with their families, but others joined her troop. James Kirkwood, a boy of eleven, was forced to abandon his mother and bring a little brother, Joseph Smith, who was only four. The Kirkwoods were another family that was hauling a cripple. James's older brother could not walk, and so his mother and another brother were pulling the young man in his handcart.

So Baline found herself in the midst of a large group of children that soon numbered about twenty, with one old man. The cold was monstrous, and the children huddled behind Baline and Brother Vandelin, to get some shelter from the wind. They kept close, so that Baline could feel their body heat even through their clothes.

Baline walked carefully in her useless shoes, but as she crossed Rocky Ridge, the jagged stones tore through her shoes, slicing the old coat sleeve that bound it together, so that time and again Baline had to stop, kneel over, and try to re-tie the mass of rags in some fashion. Her feet were numb from the cold, and her fingers grew numb from trying to re-tie the rags, and once when she bent over, she spotted blood on the ground beside her and realized that her foot was bleeding. She peered back in surprise and saw blood in her tracks. But the cold was so fierce, she felt nothing at all.

Blood will attract the wolves, she thought.

Brother Vandelin must have seen her worry, for now he stopped and had her sit on his coat while he re-tied the rags better than ever.

Then they were on their way again. With each step up Rocky Ridge, the little group was climbing higher and higher, and the mountain winds grew fiercer. Down in the flats below in the morning, it had seemed to be raging. But up here the wind stole Baline's breath away. It was gusting to fifty miles per hour, and sometimes she felt that it was so strong, she was like a kite. She could feel it almost lifting her, as if to make her fly away. The blanket that she clutched around her shoulders fluttered in the wind like a cape, and though Baline tried to keep it close, to protect her swollen ear, the cold still reached it and made it feel as if it was frozen like a chunk of ice.

They reached the flats above Rocky Ridge and then walked down in a small gorge to get some shelter from the wind. There, Brother Vandelin demanded that they rest, for he could not catch his breath no matter how much he gasped. So he stood telling jokes, puns that only Danes would understand, and thus he lightened the children's hearts.

They were alone now. All of the adults with their handcarts and wagons were mired in the snow behind them. A couple of other groups of children had already forged ahead, like tribes in the wild.

After twenty minutes, their blood had cooled enough so that the children were beginning to freeze, and Baline had to get them moving. She suggested that they have a race to a large rock, and though most of the children were not up to it, they made a game of it. This way she kept them going hour after hour.

It was only sixteen miles to camp, but it felt farther. In part it was because they had not had enough to eat for months. In part it was the thin air at this height, which kept everyone struggling for a breath. In part it was the bitter cold combined with deep snow.

Up here on top of Rocky Ridge, the snow had thinned a little. It was no more than fourteen inches deep, except in a few places where it had formed drifts.

The real problem was thirst. After climbing the ridge, all of the children were thirsty, and Baline did not dare let them eat even the smallest amount of snow, for fear that it would make them too cold.

So they slogged through the snow. The littlest ones grew tired. James Kirkwood put his little brother up on his shoulders, and as soon as he did, all of the other little ones wanted a ride, too. Baline let Niels climb on her, so that he could rest, but Brother Vandelin, with his fishhook back and his cane, could not carry anyone.

So they trudged on for eight more miles. The land stayed fairly flat, and sometimes the company had to cross over frozen creeks or leap broad streams.

Hunger kept them company—hunger and cold. Sometimes they had to stop, and all of the children would form a circle with their blankets over their heads, and they would just stand together, in order to warm one another with their body heat.

In the late afternoon they came to a creek or a river, some forty feet across. The water had frozen solid over it, but the weight of those who passed before had made the ice collapse, so that the gray water stood out. Baline didn't dare try to cross through it. Father Jens had frozen his legs that way. Some of the children looked at the gray water and began to weep in fear.

"What do we do?" Niels asked.

Brother Vandelin studied the situation. The river narrowed off to the left, and the ice there was still frozen. A nice layer of snow lay over it.

"Let us cross up there," Brother Vandelin suggested.

A narrower channel meant that the water would be deeper, and perhaps swifter. The ice might be thinner, too. Baline was afraid to try to cross there, for she could not tell by looking at the stream how deep it might be. She didn't want to break through the ice and fall into water that went over her head.

"Someone should test the ice," Baline suggested. "We should cross one at a time."

"Good idea," Brother Vandelin agreed. Baline didn't want to go first. Nor did she want to send one of the children.

James Kirkwood said, "I'll go."

He trudged through the deep snow until he reached a spot where he could descend the riverbank easily. Then he climbed down and put his weight on the ice. It held.

He carefully crossed, then stood smiling on the far side. "Come on," he said. "You can make it."

Baline followed in the trail that he had broken, then sent each of the little ones across one at a time. When they had all made it safely, she crossed herself, and then Brother Vandelin followed in her tracks, as nervous as an old woman, trying to find a place to set his cane with every step. He made it halfway across the stream before the ice broke.

He was standing there one moment, and the next there was a splitting sound, and he plunged into the water. All of the children cried out in shock, and Brother Vandelin disappeared for a moment, then bobbed back to the surface amid floating chunks of ice. He peered around a second, bewildered. There was such a look of shock upon his face from the cold water that Baline feared that his heart would stop. He got his bearings and then began striding for shore. The water only came up to his chest, but he had to break the ice ahead of him by hitting it with his cane, until he reached solid ground.

Baline and James and Samuel each grabbed onto his wet coat

and helped pull him from the water. They dragged him out of the creek as if he were a fish.

He stood shivering terribly, clutching his wet coat around him, and Baline begged, "Are you all right?"

"Yes, yes," he said through chattering teeth. "I am fine. I will be fine."

But she knew that he would not be fine. They were still miles from camp and had no shelter, no way to make a fire.

"Take my blanket," Baline suggested. "You need to be dry."

But Brother Vandelin, through his shock and pain, peered into her eyes in a way that said good-bye. "You keep the blanket. I will be fine. Come, we must hurry. We must keep moving, or I think my feet will freeze."

So they marched along with a renewed sense of urgency. Niels was worn through and through, as was little Joseph Smith, so Baline and Samuel took turns carrying Niels upon their shoulders.

Brother Vandelin walked for fifteen minutes, but soon his faltering steps became slow.

She told the children, "Go with James. Hurry up and go to the fires. Dinner will be waiting for you. It is not much farther!"

Most of them were eager to do so, for hunger knotted their bellies and the cold was overwhelming. But little Niels argued, "Mother told me to stay with you," and he was right. So Baline and Samuel decided to stay with Brother Vandelin, bringing Niels with them, while the others forged ahead.

The other children had only walked out of earshot when Brother Vandelin stopped. With trembling hands he reached into his coat pocket, and through chattering teeth he told Baline, "This is my watch. It is very valuable." He pulled out a beautiful silver pocket watch that was very ornate. "When I die," he continued, "you must give it to Captain Villie. It is worth seventy dollars, maybe more. You tell him to give the money to the Perpetual Emigration Fund, so that someone else can take my place in Zion. Understand?"

"Yes," Baline said, very seriously. He tried to put it into her hands, but he was trembling so badly that he could not unhook the watch chain.

"You keep it for now," Baline said. "Maybe you will make it to camp."

But he was fading so fast. She could see him dying right in front of her eyes, and she knew that he would not make it. Still, he ambled on, and Baline took his left arm and helped him walk while Samuel trudged on as best he could, carrying Niels on his shoulder.

Niels began to cry from the cold wind. The sun was lowering on the horizon, a pale disk behind a veil of cloud, when Lars Vandelin stumbled and lay in the snow. His eyes were closed, and he was trembling so bad that he could not talk.

"Come," Baline said. "Get up. It cannot be far now!"

But Brother Vandelin would not get up. "T-t-take watch," he said. Baline did as he begged. She unclasped his silver watch chain from his vest, but she could not leave him like that.

So she pulled off her blanket and wrapped it over Brother Vandelin, tucking it in as best she could, and left him in his stupor, hoping that someone with a handcart could come along and save him.

Baline still had her dress, her apron, and a thin jacket on, and for now that was enough.

"Come on," Samuel said, "we've got to hurry."

They had been out in the cold all day. Even in the warmest part of this fearsome day, the temperature did not reach zero. Samuel could hardly stay on his feet. He had recovered from his pneumonia and his dysentery, but the diseases had left him weak. Little Niels slumped on Samuel's shoulders, asleep. The cold nights had kept them awake, and Baline felt glad that the child was getting his rest.

So they turned and hurried as fast as they could. Baline felt surprised. After she took her blanket off, she realized that it did not feel so cold anymore. An hour ago, it had been bone-chilling, and she had trembled from it. Now, it felt as if the cold was at an end. The wind still blew viciously, but it was definitely getting warmer. *Just like the apostle promised*, Baline thought. God was tempering the elements for her benefit.

So she trudged beside Samuel for a bit, holding her right ear.

Night was coming swiftly, and Samuel grew so tired that he could not carry Niels. They traded off, every hundred yards, and after a bit Baline realized that Niels should have wakened when they traded. *The cold is making him weak,* she realized. But she knew that he was alive. When she pulled him up onto her shoulders, she could feel some warmth in him.

She could see no sign of camp ahead. The road wound over relatively flat terrain, through a broad valley of sagebrush. Up to her left she could see a line of aspen trees with bark as white as snow. Some of the trees still clung to their golden leaves. Behind her, she could see other children, and some adults now—those pulling handcarts.

She carried Niels on her shoulder, gingerly picking each step as she went, lest her makeshift shoes unravel. She had never felt so terribly weary, so weak.

But she recalled the story that Jens had told her, of how Jesus had been whipped and forced to bear his own cross as he climbed the hill at Calvary, and she felt it only right that she should bear a similar burden.

Samuel began to stagger off the trail, and so Baline talked to him, begged him to recount his dream of Zion, of a city with walls of light, where God was a consuming fire in its midst.

Samuel muttered about how he had seen the Prophet Joseph there, riding his fine horse, and spoke of restful chairs that God had made just for him. This seemed to revive his spirits.

Baline grew weary and traded off with Samuel again. He did not go far before he stumbled and fell in the snow, spilling Niels.

She held her freezing ear and cried, "Get up, Samuel. You have to get up!"

He crawled around a moment, blind with fatigue.

He is not a Dane, she reminded herself. *He is not strong, and so I must be strong for him.*

She shook little Niels, picked him up off the ground, and called his name, shaking him awake. Niels roused himself enough to walk.

They climbed a small rise and suddenly found themselves staring down at camp. A few dozen children huddled amid some willow rushes that were so covered with snow that they looked strange, like statues or animals frozen in the ice. A silver stream wound through the snow, and dozens of children were huddled in a circle, with blankets covering their heads, sharing their warmth.

The cruel wind cut through the valley, and Baline climbed down with Samuel and Niels. An older boy shouted to her, "We have to get a fire going. Help us get a fire!"

Most of the children were sitting in the huddle, in a daze. The little valley looked as if it should have offered shelter, but the wind was blowing out of the northwest, straight down the throat of the canyon. The terrain did not slow the wind at all.

The boys had piled little bits of willow in the snow, and one was trying to light it with flint and steel. Eliza laid Niels down, wrapped in his blanket, and begged Samuel to come lie beside him, to keep him warm.

She took out Brother Vandelin's watch and gave it to the oldest boy, for he seemed to be in charge. "Brother Vandelin asked us to give this to Captain Villie. He vants to sell it and use der money for der emigration fund."

She felt light-headed herself as she stalked along the stream, looking for something to start a fire. Any buffalo chips she might have found were covered with snow, and the willow fronds had been too wet to light. She needed something better, so she walked among the snow-covered humps, searching for some dead sagebrush that might be dry. She found lots of sagebrush, but each time that she grabbed it and pulled, the sage held to the ground by its thick roots.

Baline lost track of time. Darkness was falling, and she could hear some men shouting back at camp. Some of the handcarts were finally rolling in.

She stopped near a willow thicket. The wind was gusting terribly, blowing snow and ice into her face. Her right ear was frozen, but Baline heard the sound of tweeting birds from her left ear. She stood by the willows, listening, trying to see them. The willows only rose to a height of five or six feet, and their stems were deep red, the color of wine. They still had yellowed leaves on them, and Baline heard birds twittering in the shadows near their roots. She stood for long minutes, her stomach cramping fiercely, and imagined catching a sparrow and eating it. For weeks now she had dreamed of getting some fresh meat.

Suddenly she jerked awake. She realized that she had fallen asleep. She looked around and heard the birds tweeting softly, so softly. But she could not see any sparrows in the thicket. Then she saw it—leaves twisting in the fierce wind. As they did, the wind whistled through them, making it sound as if a flock of sparrows hid there.

I'm wasting time, Baline thought groggily. She turned and climbed up toward a canyon wall, searching for fuel for her fire. She wondered how long she had fallen asleep. Night was almost fully upon her.

She stepped into some snow, and her foot went through a crack. There had been a low bit of sagebrush hunched on the ground, and as she pulled her foot back, her "shoe" got caught in the trunk and unraveled. Blinking stupidly, unable to think, she sat down in the snow and wrapped her foot back up. Everything felt numb—her feet, her hands, her ear, her bottom.

I should get back to camp, she decided. She worried for Niels and Samuel. She didn't have much sagebrush, only a couple of pieces, but she knew that the handcarts were coming. The adults would help. So she turned and walked in a seeming fog, heading for camp. She staggered part of the way, feeling very tired.

On the outskirts of camp, she found some handcarts parked in the snow. She was so weary that she lay down. The wind was still blowing fiercely, driving tiny crystals of snow into her face, but the snow no longer felt cold. All in a rush, she realized that the temperature had changed. The snow was as warm as summer!

Baline lay down against the wheel of a handcart to rest, and for a moment she clutched her bit of sagebrush, unsure if she needed to carry it to the fire anymore.

The winter has turned to summer for our benefit! Baline thought. She wept in gratitude and turned for a moment, peering off to the west, toward Zion. The sun had already set, and the clouds were like a shade drawn tight over the heavens, blocking out the stars.

Yet, suddenly, Baline saw a great light. *Zion*, she thought. *I see the lights of Zion.*

33

Attaining Zion

It was after sunset when Captain Willie reached the banks of Strawberry Creek. He found women there before him, sitting on the banks and weeping. They studied the ice, as if calculating some way past it, but others had tried forging new paths through the ice, and in the fading light, Captain Willie could discern the disastrous results.

"Go through the wide part," he warned the women. "Keep to the shallows."

"Captain Willie, can you not help us across?" one of the women asked. She was a frail thing. The trail had nearly done her in, and her teenage daughters, sitting in the snow by her side, were in even worse shape.

If they step in that water, he thought, *they'll die on the far side.*

All through the trip, Captain Willie and his men had carried the women and children across the streams, especially once they reached the Sweetwater, which ran so cold. They'd made a game of it, racing to see who could be first in the water. But today was different. Today the cold had teeth, and it was borne on a killer wind.

If I step into that water, I will die, Captain Willie thought. So he took a deep sigh, affected a smile, and said, "Certainly I will carry you, Sister Barnett."

He stepped into the water and was shocked at how cold it was. It seemed to drive all thought from his mind, and it was all that he could do to hold down the curses that sought to escape his throat.

Sister Barnett stepped forward daintily, and he slogged through the stream.

He could feel rounded stones beneath his feet for a moment, until his feet went so numb that he could feel nothing at all. He waded across. The water only reached his knees. He slogged back and carried Sister Barnett's daughters. A third trip let him bring their handcarts. By then a few more women had arrived, and he carried nine more over the stream.

When he got the last one across, he climbed out of the water, and almost instantly the chilling wind crusted his pants with ice. He couldn't feel his feet, and he knew that if he just stood, he would freeze.

So he excused himself, then set off at a run. It was four long miles, running through snow that sometimes reached his knees, to get to camp.

He had not gone far when he found Brother Vandelin lying in a heap by the road. Captain Willie halted for a moment, gasping for breath in the thin mountain air, and checked to see if he was alive. Brother Vandelin was frozen solid.

Captain Willie pulled the blanket off of him and wrapped it around himself, then took off again, trotting as fast as he could toward the camp at Rock Creek.

He was terribly weary. Two days ago, while his people rested, he had ridden fifty-four miles through a storm. The cold had kept him awake most of last night, and he had walked down and back, down and back, down and back as he helped pull the carts up Rocky Ridge. By the map, camp was sixteen miles away, but he knew that he'd walked at least thirty today.

He'd made his peace with God. *If I die tonight*, he thought, *I'll die with a clean conscience, and I'll leave my people in good hands.*

But he wanted to live. He still had a wife in Logan. He'd been on his mission for more than four years, and he had not seen her in all that time. He longed to be in her arms again. When weariness and cold drove all other human thought from his mind, he clung to this.

He was not fully conscious when he reached Rock Creek. He was stumbling down a hill through the snow and suddenly realized that he saw a bright fire, burning like a lover, there among the willows. In the firelight, the faces of dozens of children and adults peered up at him, too many people to be huddling around one fire.

"Here comes someone else," a woman cried, and Captain Willie staggered toward them.

"Get a blanket around those legs," one of the sisters cried. "They're nearly frozen." Captain Willie peered up at her but could not put a name to her face.

They drew him close to the fire, and Captain Willie sat down on a cold wet blanket, while someone wrapped his legs. He leaned back, thinking to grab a moment's rest, and blacked out.

When his eyes fluttered open, he had to think for a long time before he could remember where he was. He couldn't feel his feet. *Someone has cut them off,* he thought.

He roused himself enough to look down. He was lying on a blanket in the snow. There was a light in the eastern skies, the coming of day, and Captain Willie realized that he'd been out all night. His feet were still attached. He tried to move his toes, but struggle as he might, they wouldn't budge.

Nearby, a dozen people were laid out in the snow, corpses waiting for burial.

There was shouting, the rattle of wagon wheels and the plodding of oxen hooves. Moments later, two men dragged a body over and laid it out beside Captain Willie. It took several seconds for Captain Willie to recognize Levi Savage in the wan light of the campfire. It took longer still to recognize that Savage was still alive.

Savage turned and peered at him, his eyes dazed and unfocused. "Is that you, Captain?"

"Yes," Captain Willie said.

"I got the sick wagons in," Savage reported.

It took a moment before Captain Willie realized that Savage had been left behind to bring in the sick wagons. Given the number of people that had fallen along the trail, it must have been a daunting task.

"You all right?" Savage asked.

"Feet are froze solid," Captain Willie said.

Savage let out a little laugh, something of a guffaw. "You wade through that danged river, too?"

"Yes," Captain Willie said. Savage leaned back, his mouth thrown open in a silent laugh. For an instant, Captain Willie thought that Savage had died.

Then he laughed. "I'm froze up solid, too," he said.

Savage had sacrificed himself to bring folks across the river, and for the moment at least, Captain Willie felt grateful to see him alive.

Captain Willie reached over, slapped Savage on the shoulder in congratulation, and said, "Hell, Levi, ain't we two peas in a pod?"

34

Eliza's Angels

At the top of Rocky Ridge, Eliza released her oldest children, Jane and William. She sent them ahead, determined to drag the handcart the rest of the way herself. The older children had made their trips down and back all day, and she wouldn't have them wasting any more energy. To do so would put their lives at risk. It was simple mathematics.

So she pulled Mary Ann, Sarah, and Isaac over the flats under her own power, grunting and straining. Her back and calves felt like cords of iron, she had been pulling for so long. Her belly felt so empty, it was as if it had caved in.

It was two in the afternoon when the blindness struck. One moment she was toiling ahead, peering through the snow, just a bit of sun shining on it so that it blinded her, and the next moment Eliza found herself blinking madly, trying to see anything at all. White. Everything went white. She chuckled grimly at life's cruel little jest. So, now I know what it's like to go snow-blind. She'd heard of the condition before, of course, but even Doctor Boyle had never treated a case, as far as she knew.

"Mary Ann," Eliza said. "Mary Ann?"

"Yes, Mother," Mary Ann called out.

"Can you see anyone around us? Someone ahead or behind?" The saints were strung out on the road for dozens of miles. Most of them seemed to be back with the sick wagons.

"No one, Mother."

"Get out of the wagon then," Eliza said. "Come over here by your mother."

Mary Ann climbed out. Eliza soon felt her daughter there, just beside her arm.

"Can you see the road ahead?" Eliza asked.

"Yes, Mother."

"Is your little brother all right? Is he bundled well?"

There was a moment of quiet, the only sound the ceaseless wind coursing over the prairie. "He's all right. Sarah is holding him. They're both asleep."

"Good," Eliza said. "I'm going to need your help. I can't see. I need you to hold onto my sleeve and lead the way. Can you do that?"

Mary Ann began to weep. She was only eight years old, and Eliza knew that she would be frightened. She'd already lost her father, her little brother. This trip was making orphans out of far too many children.

"Don't cry," Eliza told Mary Ann. "Don't you ever cry. It doesn't help anything."

Mary Ann took Eliza's hand and began leading her along the path. Eliza pulled the handcart, feeling her way through the snow with her feet. For long miles she marched over uneven ground, while Mary Ann guided her, calling, "This way, Mother" or pulling at her sleeve. At one point Mary Ann stopped and said, "There's a woman in the snow."

"Is she breathing," Eliza asked.

"I don't think so."

"Never mind, then."

Eliza plunged forward, through a world transformed to white. The sun was going down. Eliza could barely detect its warmth on her face, but now it was growing cold.

She felt thin and worn. This trip had taken everything from her—not just her family, but her self-respect, her hope, faith in her own judgment and abilities.

I'm next to die, she thought. *I'm the one pulling the cart. I'm the one who will be up all night with the babies, or heating rocks for my children.*

The thought of death did not frighten her. She felt weary of life, overwhelmed by it. Almost, she longed to go. It was the natural order of things. The old had to die to make way for the young, and Eliza felt very old, ancient and timeless beyond reason. So Eliza surrendered her life.

She kept trudging, taking her babies to safety. But after she reached camp, if she had to lie down and die, she did not care.

"Mother, there's a river in front of us," Mary Ann said at last. Gingerly, Mary Ann led her mother down the embankment, and Eliza stood for a long moment listening to the burble of flowing water, smelling the wetness of it. By listening very closely and reaching out with her imagination, she could almost measure it.

"What do you think," Eliza asked, "forty feet across, sixty? How deep does it look?"

"I can't tell," Mary Ann said. "It's getting dark. But it looks too deep for me."

It sounded deep, too. She could hear the depths in the way that it gurgled. She could almost feel the water tugging the roots of the willow on its shore. For a child to try to wade it in this cold weather would be fruitless. Even if Mary Ann didn't drown, she'd freeze on the far shore.

"Climb into the handcart, sweetheart," Eliza said. "I'll pull you across."

Now I have become Charon.

Mary Ann climbed on. "Okay, Mother. Go straight."

Eliza took a step into water that was only an ankle deep and felt as if her foot had been packed in ice. No words could describe how cold it was.

"Lord," she whispered, "into thy hands I commend my spirit." Then she stepped deeper into the ice, and it drew a shrill cry from her mouth. She gasped for breath as she tried to pull the handcart over the rounded rocks. She tripped and staggered, nearly falling headlong, and after a dozen strides she began climbing the far shore.

She reached it and pulled the cart up into the snow, then lay gasping for a long minute, while Mary Ann climbed down out of the handcart.

"Did you get wet?" Eliza asked.

"No."

"And Sarah and the baby?"

"They're dry, too," Mary Ann said.

Eliza could feel a sheen of ice building on her legs. Her skirt was heavy with water that was turning to icicles. She chilled rapidly in the cold wind and knew that in moments hypothermia would set in.

"We have to hurry and get to camp," Eliza told Mary Ann. The next words came harder. "If I don't make it, you need to stay with Isaac, all right? If I fall down, you just leave me and keep Isaac warm."

"All right, Mother," Mary Ann said. She tried to sound like a big girl, but her throat caught.

So Eliza pulled quickly, running over the snow, trying to keep blood flowing to her extremities. She stopped sometimes and rubbed her icy legs, trying to bring blood to the surface. Full night had come, and still the world was a solid white to Eliza.

"Mother, there are two dead men by the road," Mary Ann said.

"Are you sure they're dead?" Eliza asked.

"Their eyes are open, and there is ice on them."

"Someone will come to pick the bodies up shortly," Eliza said. *Or maybe the wolves will drag them off*, she thought.

She asked hopefully, "Do you seen any fires ahead, any sign of camp?"

"No."

Eliza put her back to it and pulled faster. Too soon Mary Ann begged, "Mother, I can't walk anymore. I'm so tired."

"I know," Eliza said. "I'm sorry. But if I stop, I think I'll freeze to death. Can you go a little farther?"

"Just a minute," Mary Ann said.

So Eliza stood for a long minute and counted to a hundred. Mary Ann took her by the sleeve again and began to pull, but Eliza's blood had gone cold in her veins, and she could barely stand. Her head reeled, and she staggered a few feet. She'd never felt such a deep lassitude; it was overwhelming.

Suddenly the cart hit Eliza's legs. She was standing in front of it, holding the handle, trying to rouse the energy to get moving, and the cart just hit her.

"Mary Ann, don't push," Eliza begged. She couldn't let the little girl try to push this little wagon for the miles that they had left to go.

The handcart nudged forward a second time. Softer, not so urgent. Eliza hadn't imagined it. She had not pushed it forward herself. She cocked her ear, to hear who might have crept up on them.

She whirled. "Is someone there?" All that she could see was a field of white in every direction.

"There's no one there, Mother," Mary Ann said. "We're all alone."

But Eliza could feel the presence of others nearby, the way that one can feel the heat of another body in a darkened room, the way that one can feel air swishing as another walks past.

"Who's there?" she demanded.

She heard a baby cry. She knew that voice. It wasn't Isaac. He lay asleep in the handcart, wheezing softly. This was the full-throated cry of her other twin, Daniel.

"We've come to help," her husband Samuel said. "You rest now. We'll push." The cart nudged her from behind.

Samuel? she asked with a thought, not in a whisper.

And baby Daniel, came a reply.

I'm here too, Sam Junior said. *I've come to help.* That is how Eliza discovered that Samuel Junior had died.

For the next half a mile, the handcart seemed to fly over the ground as if propelled by thought itself. Mary Ann had to rush to keep up, and Eliza had only to lift the handle enough to keep it from falling into the snow.

Baby Daniel kept up a constant babbling, as if happy to be in her presence, and Samuel said, "I love you too much to leave you alone. We had to come back."

Eliza reached out with her senses, with her ears. Samuel was pushing the handcart from behind, and Sam Junior raced along beside the cart while the baby Daniel rode in the cart beside his brother. Yet Eliza felt others around her. She peered over her shoulder, and saw one bright spot in the darkness.

"The problem is," Baline said, "all of you people are so vorried about dying. It isn't dying that you should be vorried about: it's living. You should vorry more about how to live for der eternities." She sounded so childish, so carefree. "Look at me: I'm dead, and I'm all right."

Then the dead fell silent and merely pushed the handcart. Little Mary Ann had fallen silent long minutes ago, and she finally whispered in a small voice, "Father's here, isn't he?"

Eliza wondered how she knew. "What makes you think so?"

"I can smell him," Mary Ann said. "He's pushing us from behind. I heard him say something. He said he loved me."

"Yes," Eliza said, "your father is here."

"And Sam Junior?" Mary Ann asked. She sounded very sad.

"Yes," Eliza admitted.

So Eliza marched, with the dead at her back, until an hour after sunset when she reached the camp of the saints, and Mary Ann led her to the fire.

Eliza was starving, but she wanted nothing to eat. She was freezing, but needed nothing to warm her.

This is no gypsy's trick, she realized. There was no fakir or mystic uttering nonsense, only the clean pure certainty that her family lived, and they were well.

Eliza dropped into the snow at the camp and lay there with her head spinning, dizzy and exhausted and thrilled, her heart pumping madly and the blood coursing through her veins.

It was not until I was dead that I finally came alive, she realized. *It was not until I fell blind that I could finally see.*

She felt the spirits thick around her. Sam Junior whispered, "Mother, I've seen it now. I see everything so clearly—the way to Zion."

35

A Parting of Ways

The Mormon camp was filled with sounds of weeping on the twenty-fourth, mothers sobbing for their dead and dying children, toddlers weeping fiercely over the corpses of their frozen fathers.

The only other sound was the steady bite of shovels into stony soil as the gravediggers did their work.

Mary Hurren lay abed in her tent all morning, while her mother warmed rocks and brought them in, trying to revive Mary's frozen feet. She would lay the rocks under the buffalo robe while they were warm, and sometimes she would wash them with warm water and rub them fiercely—all to no avail. Her toes and heels were black with frostbite.

"Have Auntie Gadd fix them," Mary begged. "She's the best with frostbite." It was true. As the camp nurse, Eliza was developing a reputation as a miracle worker.

"She'll be of no help to anyone," Mary's mother said. "She went blind yesterday, and no one knows if she'll ever see again."

Mary had never known anyone who had gone blind before. "Did anyone else go blind?"

"Sister Kirkwood got her right eye frozen deader than Moses," Mary's mother said. "One of the Danes got her ears frozen so badly, she's gone deaf."

Mary was trying to imagine that. The tale of human misery was hard to imagine. Just about anyone who had walked through

Strawberry Creek the night before had frozen their feet. Even stalwart men like Captain Willie had been brought down.

Lots of people had died in the night. Fourteen were counted dead, but one woman, Sister Stewart, who had thrown away everything that she owned so that she could pull her dead husband into camp in a handcart, while she strapped her baby around her neck with her shawl, had gotten up in the morning to wash her husband's dead body, and in doing so found that the warm water revived him. Even as one revived here and there, others were dying.

About noon, the gravediggers finally stopped, and it seemed that the whole camp went silent.

Mary's father came into the tent moments later, his hands and face covered with dirt. He was one of the few men in camp who was still strong enough to dig a grave.

"Mary," he asked gently, "would you like to come say good-bye to your friends?"

Mary had rarely had death touch anyone close to her. She nodded her head soberly, tried to keep her lower lip from quavering.

Her father bent over and picked her up in his strong arms. His hands were covered with callouses and blisters, and as he held her close, she could smell the mineral tang of open earth on his shirt, the smell of the grave. "You're getting as light as a feather," he said, then kissed her on the forehead.

He took her outside, and the sun shining on the snow made everything harsh and white. Mary had heard stories about the temple, how the women had ground up their finest bone china and mixed it with paint so that the temple was whiter than snow outside. But it could never have been this white.

God has made a temple of the world, Mary thought as she looked around. The white tents huddled in the white snow, and everywhere along the hills the snow lay so thick over the sagebrush and rocks and willows that nothing could be seen but snow.

Her father carried her to the banks of the creek, where a congregation had gathered. He pushed his way through the crowd so that Mary could get a moment's view.

The dead were dressed in white. One of the Danes, Sister

Mortensen, excelled at making fine white linens with fancy trim. She'd been saving dozens of tablecloths to sell when she reached Zion, but now she had taken her precious tablecloths and wrapped the bodies of those who died crossing Rocky Ridge.

The grave was a huge circle, and the dead were laid out in it toe-to-toe, with their heads radiating out from the center. Like spokes on the wheel of a handcart, Mary thought.

It was not hard for Mary to pick out her friends. She saw James Kirkwood first. She'd known that he was dead last night. He was one of the larger boys. He'd carried his four-year-old brother for nearly sixteen miles, then had brought him into camp, laid him down in a blanket, and fallen over dead. Mary had found his body shortly after reaching camp. He was worn-looking and tired.

Next to James lay Sam Gadd Junior. Mary hadn't been told that he was dead, but it did not surprise her. He'd been fighting his dysentery for weeks, growing weaker day by day. In death he smiled, as if he'd just won a great race and his heart stopped beating when he crossed the finish line.

Next to him was five-year-old Niels Nielsen. He'd been alive when Baline and Samuel got him to camp, but had frozen in the night sometime before his mother reached Rock Creek. His face was serene, restful.

Next to him lay Baline. She had her head crooked to the left in an odd way, frozen in that position. Her right hand clung to a bit of her sagebrush, and her left hand hovered near her mouth. She'd chewed almost all of the skin from her hand, so that it looked bright and red beside her pale face. The joint of her forefinger had been gnawed through, and Baline's mouth was frozen open, as if she were trying to take one last bite when she died. Mary had never seen such ravenous hunger on a human face, though she'd seen dozens die from starvation in the past two weeks. *So different,* Mary thought, *she looks so different in death than she did when she was alive.*

For a moment, Mary remembered Baline smiling, urging her along on the trail when she was too tired to walk anymore, saying, "Look, there's a pretty flower ahead!"

For a moment, she was in the hold of the ship, rocking on a stormy sea, teaching Baline her first few halting words of English.

For a moment, Baline sat in a trading circle among the Omahas and sold a snip of hair for a fine necklace.

She was the strongest of us, Mary thought, *and the bravest and kindest. How could she die?*

But the answer was easy. The best had been giving their lives at every step of the journey. The captains had jumped into freezing rivers, acting eager to be the first to help carry the women and children across. Strong men had given away their food, choosing to die rather than watch their children suffer.

She gave her life for me, bit by bit, Mary thought.

"That she did," her father said. Mary hadn't realized that she'd said the words aloud. "Now it's up to you to be strong, and learn from her example, and try to live worthy of her sacrifice."

Across the grave, Agnes Caldwell stood shaking, wracked with sobs, as if the sight of Baline's body would rip the sanity from her.

Mary recalled the times that they'd called Baline, "Baline-tay, Baline-tay, won't you come out to play?" How eagerly Baline would always run out of her tent at that sound.

"I wanted to live next door to her," Mary said. "I was hoping that we could always be friends."

"You'll have that chance," her father said. "When she rises in the resurrection, she'll be glorious, and you if you're worthy, you can live next to her in Zion. You'll be able to touch her, to hug her, to laugh with her. You'll be able to thank her for her friendship and for her service, and for showing you the way."

Mary's heart broke then. She had thought over the past few weeks that she had grown accustomed to death, and that with each passing, it would grow easier. But some deaths are harder to bear than others.

"Say good-bye," her father said, "just for awhile." He held her high then, up on his shoulders, and she felt as if she were riding through the clouds, peering down upon the crowd in this great field of white.

For a few moments Mary forgot her own pain, the freezing in her feet.

"Good-bye, Baline," Mary said. "Until we meet again."

As she turned away, she could hear Baline's laughing voice echo the call. "Good-bye, my friend, until ve meet in Zion."

Afterword

Brief Biographies of People in This Book

Mary Hurren, age 8, lived to reach the Salt Lake Valley and meet the prophet Brigham Young, who wept when he saw the gangrenous condition of her frostbitten feet. He immediately sent for a doctor, who wanted to amputate, but her father warned the doctor, "My daughter did not walk a thousand miles to lose her legs. If she is to die, she will die with them on."

So she was taken to Brigham City, where an old nurse told the family to wrap her feet in steak. They did so, and a few days later the rotten flesh fell from her feet. Mary Hurren was left crippled, but learned to walk again two years later.

Mary grew to womanhood and married a man named Joseph White. She bore him thirteen children and passed away in Brigham City at the age of 88.

Agnes Caldwell, age 9, said that she never suffered much on the journey due to her mother's good care. Indeed, she felt that her mother was inspired to save worthless beads and trinkets in Scotland, trinkets that she used to buy meat from the Indians, and to save money to buy food. Because of her mother's forethought, the family not only made it across the plains alive, but Agnes's mother was able to feed some of the starving men who guarded the camp on a bitter cold night, thus saving their lives.

Agnes reached Utah in good health. She married, had thirteen children, and was called by the church to help homestead towns in Utah, California, and Canada. After her husband's death in 1911, she returned to Brigham City to live near her friend "of my youth," Mary Hurren. She passed away at the age of 77.

Eliza Gadd, 41, recovered from her snow-blindness several days after the climb up Rocky Ridge, and along with her remaining children survived the trek to Utah. A week after arriving in Utah, she was baptized, though she remained silent for years about her reasons for doing so.

Eliza never remarried. She was a quiet woman who made money by gardening, raising flowers, and, like Emily Hill, making straw hats, which she decorated with her dried flowers.

But her greatest accomplishment came through her nursing. Shortly after reaching Utah, she became a midwife. Her level of care was considered phenomenal. It was said of her that upon hearing that a woman was pregnant, she would often walk twelve miles, just to pay a visit. On warm days she would take off her shoes, tie them together by the laces, and throw them over her shoulders, and walk lazily beneath her big straw hat.

For her services she charged almost nothing—two dollars paid for the delivery of a child, along with two weeks of care afterward for both the mother, the newborn infant, and all of the other children in the household. One man, at the end of his two weeks, burst into tears and declared that he did not have the two dollars to pay her. So Eliza, upon seeing a pair of boiled eggs on the table, said, "Well then, I'll have these instead," and she walked home, eating her boiled eggs.

Eliza brought over two thousand children into the world, and was awarded the Guiness World Record for the number of live births delivered by a midwife. After thirty years, when a doctor finally moved into her area, Eliza spoke with him at length about the few mothers and children that she had lost, and she wept in relief to learn that with the current science there was no way to save any of those that had passed away.

Eliza never spoke publicly about her conversion, but it was apparent to all of her family members that she had become a "true believer." She made great sacrifices to help support her sons when they were called to be missionaries later on in life.

The incident where the dead appeared to help Eliza pull the handcarts is drawn from inference. Others on the trek wrote about such incidents. Perhaps the most famous account comes from William Palmer. He was in a Sunday School class in southern Utah, decades after the Willie Handcart Company incident. Nathan T. Porter was the teacher and the subject under discussion was the ill-fated handcart company that suffered so terribly in 1856. (Note that they were discussing the Martin Handcart Company, which was following two weeks behind the Willie Company. The Martin Handcart Company suffered similar death tolls.) The account that follows is taken verbatim:

> Some sharp criticism of the church and Brigham Young was being indulged in for permitting any company of converts to venture across the plains with no more supplies or protection than a handcart caravan afforded. One old man in the corner sat silent and listened as long as he could stand it, then he arose and said things that no one in the room would ever forget.
>
> His face was white with emotion, yet he spoke calmly, deliberately, but with great earnestness and sincerity. He said in substance, "I ask you to stop this criticism. You are discussing a matter you know nothing about. Cold historic facts mean nothing here, for they give no proper interpretation of the questions involved. Mistake to send the Handcart Company out so late in the season? Yes! But I was in that company and my wife was in it, and Sister Nellie Unthank whom you have cited here was there, too. We suffered beyond anything

> you can imagine and many died of exposure and starvation, but did you ever hear a survivor of that company utter a word of criticism? Every one of us came through with the absolute knowledge that God lives for we became acquainted with Him in our extremities!
>
> "I have pulled my handcart when I was so weak and weary from illness and lack of food that I could hardly put one foot ahead of the other. I have looked ahead and seen a patch of sand or a hill slope and I have said, I can go only that far and there I must give up for I cannot pull the load through it. I have gone to that sand and when I reached it, the cart began pushing me! I have looked back many times to see who was pushing my cart, but my eyes saw no one. I knew then that the Angels of God were there.
>
> "Was I sorry that I chose to come by handcart? No! Neither then nor any minute of my life since. The price we paid to become acquainted with God was a privilege to pay and I am thankful that I was privileged to come in the Martin Handcart Company."
>
> The speaker was Francis Webster. And when he sat down there was not a dry eye in the room. We were a subdued and chastened lot. Charles Mabey, who later became Governor of Utah, arose and voiced the sentiment of all when he said, "I would gladly pay the same price to personally know God as Brother Webster has."

The sentiments expressed by Francis Webster were prevalent among those who traveled in the Willie Handcart Company. The spirit of love and unity that was felt in that company was so strong that decades later many wrote longingly of how it was the best time in their lives. People who suffered frostbite and amputations, people who watched friends, husbands, and their own children die wrote later that they had never regretted a single moment.

Others wrote of their own feelings of sensing the presence of spirits helping them pull their handcarts across the plains, and it seems likely that Eliza had a similar experience, for one of her descendants relates the following: When Eliza was growing old, one of her daughters asked her why she had joined the church, and Eliza is reported to have said, "How could I not, having watched all of my children turn into angels?"

Eliza died at the age of 78, in Nephi, Utah.

Ann Howard went on to Utah. Apparently she never married and promptly was lost to history. All of the accounts related about her here are fictitious.

Bodil Maline "Baline" Mortensen froze to death on October 23 while trying to save the lives of other children. She made it safely to camp, but went out for firewood. When she did not return, searchers went to look for her, but it wasn't until morning that she was found lying against the wheel of the Mortensen handcart, still holding some sagebrush in her hand for the fire. So much snow had blown over her that she could not have been seen in the dark.

Baline's parents left Denmark in the early spring of 1857 and raced to Utah just ahead of the US Army, which was marching upon the state, intent to put an end to Mormonism.

Her parents had not heard about Baline's death, and upon learning of it, Baline's mother suffered a mental breakdown and fell into a deep depression from which she never recovered. She passed away four years later after suffering numerous illnesses.

Baline's father moved to southern Utah, to the town of Parowan, near Jens Nielsen, and the two remained close friends for the rest of their lives.

Captain James Gray Willie suffered severe frostbite after crossing the Sweetwater for the last time. With his legs frozen, he had to be carried to Utah in the back of a wagon. He eventually recovered and moved to northern Utah after his journey, where he helped found the small town of Mendon. He served as mayor in the town for many years and ran a general store and post office.

Levi Savage also suffered from frostbite after crossing the

Strawberry. James Hurren and others wrote that Savage kept his covenant to "do more to help the saints reach Utah alive than any other man." He had to be carried the last three hundred and fifty miles.

Two years later, in 1858, Levi married Ann Brummel Cooper, a widow from England who had also crossed with the Willie Company.

Levi moved to Southern Utah in the 1860s, where he lived with his three wives. There, he developed a reputation for industry and helpfulness until he passed away at the ripe old age of ninety.

Jens Nielsen gave away all that he owned to help the Danish saints cross the plains. He was a large man of 225 pounds. His legs also froze on the journey. His 98-pound wife pulled him in the handcart for nearly a week, until a space opened on one of the relief wagons, and this saved his life. He became crippled, walking with a cane, with his right foot twisted inward, for the rest of his life, but he always retained his habit of taking an evening walk while he quietly meditated.

Though Jens never managed to learn to speak English well, his spirituality was greatly admired by those Danes who knew him. They often said that if he only would have learned English, he would have been called to be an apostle.

He moved to Southern Utah and bred fine horses while his wife planted mulberry trees and raised silkworms. In his late fifties, he was asked by the Church to create a new community in Utah, called Bluff, which was deep in the interior of the rugged Grand Escalanate Staircase. For many years he served as the bishop in this small community, and is credited with saving it from an attack by a hundred hostile Navajos who once came riding into town, intent on destruction.

The men of the town were off on a cattle drive, so Bishop Nielsen, who had endured more than any of the Navajos could have imagined, simply limped up the center of the street, forcing them to stop. The Navajos, dressed in war paint and armed with rifles, were astonished by his courage. Jens hailed them and through an interpreter invited the Navajos to dinner. He had a fat steer slaughtered for them and gave them gifts of bacon and coffee. The attack was abandoned, and the Indians that came to kill him became lifelong friends. The Navajos revered him for his courage and dubbed him Chief Kagoochee—Crooked Feet.

Though Jens and his wife Else lost their son crossing the prairie, they later had three daughters. Two were named after Baline's friends—Mary and Agnes.

Jens died peacefully in 1906, at the age of 78.

Susannah Margetts, age 34 at the time of her abduction by the Cheyenne, was sent to a Cheyenne village, where she was kept without guard. Upon hearing that a team of army surveyors was in the area, she made her escape in late September of 1856 and returned to Utah. This caused great consternation for the Cheyenne, since William Hoffman still had their men held hostage and would not return them until Susannah was freed. Word of her escape did not reach the fort until late October or early November.

Susannah died in East Mill Creek, Utah, at the age of 96.

Major William Hoffman, age 49 at the time that he commanded Fort Laramie, apparently never was able to lure a woman to his bed. Though some young women abandoned the Willie Handcart Company and returned to Fort Laramie, I have not been able to find evidence that any of them stayed with Major Hoffman. He continued his career in the military throughout his life, marching to war against Utah during the campaign of 1857. During the Civil War, he presided over Elmira "Hellmira" Prison, where he earned a reputation for being the North's most hardened and vindictive prison warden, creating unsanitary conditions that caused the deaths of more than 25 percent of his prisoners.

Joseph Oakey, age 12, left his family on the shores of the Missouri and returned to Council Bluffs, Iowa, where he took the name O'Kee. His mother, who could not be consoled, received a blessing from the Mormon elders in which she was promised that she would see Joseph again. Twenty years later, when the railroads were running, the family found him in Council Bluffs, Iowa. He had gone to fight for the North during the Civil War and claimed that he had miraculously been spared. In a battalion of nearly one thousand men, he was one of only thirty-three that survived.

His ten-year-old sister, Rhoda, froze to death on the trek on November 9, 1856, while trying to care for her father, who was suffering from frostbite and starvation.

Joseph Wall, age 18, was left for dead on the plains until his sister Emily remembered the promise of an apostle who had said that they would both survive the trek. She returned to stay with her brother, and eventually Captain Willie sent men back to bring them both into camp. Emily pulled Joseph with the help of "a little girl" for more than a month. Joseph was later allowed to ride in a sick wagon until he regained enough strength to pull the handcart once more. Both of them survived to reach Utah in good health, and they credited their apostolic blessing for their good fortune.

Julia Hill, age 20 at the time of the exodus, went on to Utah, where she married one of her rescuers, Israel Ivins. She bore eight children, four of whom died at young ages, and she passed away at the age of 65.

Emily Hill went on to become a noted poet among the Mormons. As a result of her ordeal in helping her sister and Martha Campkin cross the prairie, she wrote a poem that was later put to music by Janice Kapp Perry. The song, "As Sisters in Zion," has become one of the favorite hymns sung in the Mormon church. As an early champion for women's rights, Emily helped make Utah the first state in the union to grant women the right to vote.

Mary Griffith reached Utah and entered a polygamous marriage with a prosperous man named Philo Farnsworth. Her grandson, Philo T. Farnsworth, was the inventor of television and thus gained the title "The father of modern communications."

Martha Campkin, 36, achieved her goal of bringing her children to Utah without any of them dying. In fact, none of them suffered from frostbite or any other harmful effect. A few months after reaching Utah, apparently upon the recommendation of Brigham Young, she married a young man from England named Joseph Young, who was 20 years old. Martha's first husband had asked Joseph to take care of Martha after his death, and he did just that. Martha and Joseph had three children together. She died at the age of 74.

Lucy Ward, the young woman who appeared to James Cole in a dream, married her rescuer only nine days later when they reached Fort Bridger. Lucy's feet were frostbitten and took nearly a year to recover. They went on to Utah and had eleven children. Lucy passed away at the age of 86.

Parley P. Pratt, the Mormon apostle, went on to serve his mission to the eastern states after meeting with the handcart pioneers. He was assassinated in Arkansas by a man named Hector McLean. Though the murder was witnessed by several men, McLean was never brought to justice.

Opponents of the Mormon church will often claim that McLean was justified in the murder because Parley had "seduced" McLean's wife into joining the church and later married her. While it is true that he married her, he didn't meet her until years after her conversion. McLean's criminal treatment of his wife and children—along with the fact that he was a self-confessed alcoholic and that alcohol made him murderous—gave any sane person ample reason to leave him.

The whole story is far too involved to relate here, and certainly deserves its own book. For an interesting look into it, see: jared.pratt-family.org/parley_histories/parley-death-stephen-pratt.html

Franklin D. Richards, 36, was publicly chastised by Brigham Young for his handling of the disastrous immigration of 1856. We do not know exactly what he said in private, but we can well guess, given that in public Brigham told Richards that unless he repented of his pride, he would find himself as "empty of the spirit as a hollow pumpkin."

Franklin D. Richards served as an apostle for nearly fifty years. In that time he became a state legislator, a highly respected attorney, an educator, and a brigadier general. He also served as a church historian for nearly forty years. When he died at the age of 78, he was the senior apostle in the Quorum of the Twelve.

Orrin Porter Rockwell became the most famous gunslinger of the century, with more kills than Wyatt Earp, Doc Holliday, Bat Masterson, and Tom Horn combined. No one knows for sure just how many men he did kill, but estimates range between forty and more than a hundred. (Rockwell didn't brag when he killed a gunslinger. He would simply bury the fellow.)

Porter Rockwell died in his sleep at the age of 65, from a heart attack.

General William S. Harney developed a reputation for brutality with his massacre of the Sioux. He furthered that reputation during the "Bleeding Kansas" episode in 1856, where he attacked the slavers that had been causing so much trouble. As part of his solutions, he emptied out entire counties.

In 1857, the newly elected President James Buchanan was seeking to stave off the Civil War. He decided that the least expensive way to do that would be to send the army to Utah to make an example of the Mormons, and General Harney, who had earned the names "the Butcher" and "Woman Killer" for his outrages against the Sioux was considered the best man for the job.

Harney began a large and costly campaign to eradicate the Mormons in 1857, but the Mormons held back the army by salting waterholes, burning the prairie, and burning or stealing military supply wagons—so that the US Army was brought to a standstill for nearly two years, with nearly zero casualties on either side. (Orrin Porter Rockwell helped lead the forces that stalled the US Army.) The US troops were forced to winter on the prairie in 1857 and became intimately acquainted with the kinds of deprivation and suffering that the handcart pioneers had endured. The entire affair became so costly that it nearly bankrupted the United States. The press eventually began to side with the Mormons, who seemed bent on defeating the army through nonviolent means, and the Utah War suddenly gained the nickname "Buchanan's Blunder."

Harney had to be called off of the campaign in order to put down another rebellion in Kansas in 1858, and Brigham Young took that opportunity to quickly arrange a sort of "mutual surrender" to his replacement, thus avoiding the bloodbath that Harney was expected to unleash.

Of course, the next presidential election was won by Abraham Lincoln, a Republican who had vowed to rid the United States of slavery, and the Civil War began.

The US Government Response to the Handcart Tragedy. As the Willie and Martin Handcart Companies froze to death on the prairie, newspaper accounts of the tragedy circulated in the East. For example, in the *Liberty Weekly Tribune*, 6 Feb. 1857, we get: A Salt Lake correspondent of the *Baltimore Sun*, under date of October 31, says: "We have dreadful accounts of the sufferings among the Mormon immigrants by the hand-cart train, which is now in the mountains. The train contained 350 souls. One-seventh are already dead, and they are dying at the rate of fifteen per day.—There are some 600 more behind, of which we have heard nothing. We hope that they stopped at Laramie. It is impossible for them to get through this fall. The Mormons estimated that there are not less than 1500 of their brethren yet to come in, and the snow is reported to be not less than 3 feet deep in the mountains."

In some accounts, the fates of the poor deluded Mormons was bemoaned in a smug, almost celebratory tone, anticipating that the whole affair would give a black eye to Brigham Young.

Despite the fact that help was available from Fort Laramie and could either have been rendered before the fact or could have been offered once the snows hit (Fort Laramie was only a week away by horseback), no aid was ever sent.

The Cheyenne that the pioneers so greatly feared reestablished peace in the fall of 1856 under a new treaty, but even as the US officials signed the treaty, they were secretly planning another military expedition for the spring to "punish" the Cheyenne for the murders committed that season.

Blame for the Handcart Tragedy. Over the past 150 years, many have tried to figure out who to blame for the Willie and Martin handcart tragedy.

Some have concluded that Brigham Young should hold the blame. It was his plan, after all, and he is the one who urged Franklin D. Richards, as president of the European Mission, to give the plan a try in an effort to save money. The funds that the church was using to help the immigrants had been depleted, and the handcart system seemed a practical way to travel. In fact, Brigham Young himself, a cabinet maker and carpenter by trade, designed the handcarts. But his views on how easy the journey would be were wildly optimistic. In a letter to Elder F. D. Richards, in Liverpool, dated September 3, 1855, Brigham Young said: "We cannot afford to purchase wagons and teams as in times past. I am consequently thrown back upon my old plan—to make handcarts, and let the emigration foot it." To show what a pleasant trip this would make, he added, "Fifteen miles a day will bring them through in 70 days, and, after they get accustomed to it, they will travel 20, 25, or even 30 with all ease, and no danger of giving out, but will continue to get stronger and stronger; the little ones and sick, if there are any, can be carried on the carts, but there will be none sick in a little time after they get started." *Millennial Star*, 7:813.

Of course anyone who has tried pulling a wheelbarrow full of children through the wilderness can tell you that it is not done with ease.

Brigham Young concluded that Franklin D. Richards should shoulder the blame, pointing out that in his letters, Brigham had told him to send the settlers "in due season."

Richards, due to various pressures, mostly coming from the settlers themselves who were eager to travel to Zion, sent the settlers out too late in the year, and then compounded the problem by sending them on once he saw their desperate situation.

But to be fair, Richards was simply trying to implement Brigham's plan to the best of his ability. Brigham had sent encouraging letters telling him that the Lord would bless the handcart pioneers and temper the elements in their behalf, and so Richards's prophecies only echoed those that he'd heard from his superior.

The real problem here is that the immigrants were thrown behind schedule by a whole series of events, creating a domino-effect.

A single event caused most of the delay. The Crimean War kept the settlers from booking passage on ships for two months. At this point, Franklin D. Richards could have asked the settlers to stay in England for another season. But that seemed to place an impossible burden on the saints. The immigrants had already sold their homes and put all of their funds into the hands of the church in order to book passage. As with my wife's great-great-grandfather, many had already given away all that they owned to other members of the church. Thus, they had nothing to pay for housing and food to last them through a whole year. So sending the immigrants out late in the season seemed the lesser of two evils.

Once that choice was made, it led to another delay. The church agents in Illinois were supposed to make the handcarts for the settlers and get their beef and milk cows out of Kansas. But when the decision was made to send the settlers two months late, it was impossible for Richards to send word so that the church agents could prepare for another two thousand handcart pioneers.

The church agents didn't learn of the coming immigrants until they actually showed up at the door. Immediately, the agents went to work trying to round up suitable materials for the handcarts, along with cattle and food, but they were unable to find the cured wood needed to build the handcarts.

To be honest, the church agents in Illinois had a history of failing. Three handcart companies had preceded the Willie and Martin companies, and the church agents hadn't had the time or materials to build the handcarts for any of them, either. So it appears that they had settled into a pattern of letting the handcart pioneers build their own carts—a pattern that had disastrous consequences.

There is no record that I've seen which indicates what the exact problem might have been. The agents arrived in Iowa about six weeks before the first handcart companies reached them, and it appears that in those six weeks the church's agents searched in vain for the necessary wheels, rims, axles, and seasoned wood, and ended up having the immigrants piece together their own handcarts as a last resort.

Just as they finished outfitting the first company, a second showed up, and then a third. After the emigrating season was over—surprise!—the fourth and fifth companies arrived. In any case, this secondary delay was disastrous.

Had the immigrants reached their rescuers up on the Continental Divide three days earlier, the losses due to starvation would have been far less.

Of course, the settlers spent more than three days just looking for their lost cattle. The accounts are about evenly divided as to how the cattle got lost. Did they stampede solely because of the buffalo, or did Indians drive them off? The young man who was on guard duty at the time said that he saw Indians driving the buffalo that stampeded the cattle, and in several other attacks by the Cheyenne that season, cattle were driven off before the attack. So it seems reasonable that the Cheyenne drove the cattle off.

Not only did the Willie immigrants waste three days hunting for their cattle, the loss of the cattle slowed them substantially. By having to carry a hundred pounds of flour on each handcart, the handcarts wore out more quickly, and the settlers spent several extra days just fixing them. Beyond that, the handcarts moved slower, and the men who pulled them wore down quickly as a result. In the week after the saints began trying to pull their carts with the flour, they moved quite slowly, averaging about ten miles per day instead of the normal sixteen to twenty.

So, one can expect that if the Willie Handcart Company had not lost its cattle, they would have reached their rescuers a good week or ten days before they did.

But other mistakes were made. While some apologists suggest

that the independent wagons that stayed behind at Fort Laramie proved to be a boon for the folks in the Martin Handcart Company, one of the captains in the Willie Company, John Chislett, bemoaned the loss. In fact, while Chislett seemed to be a deeply conscientious man, his outrage over Richards's handling of the affair caused him to leave the Church. He notes that he could not decide if Richards was just foolish or completely insane.

Another captain that apostatized, John Ahmanson, a Swede who served as captain over the Danish saints, blamed George Kimball for much of the tragedy. Once the relief wagons reached the immigrants, Kimball decided that it would be too difficult to bring wagons of food and clothing down the steep grade at Rocky Ridge, and then try to take them back up. So he decided to have the immigrants go to the food in a forced march. By sending children and invalids to walk over the ridge in sub-zero weather in harsh winds, without proper shoes or clothing, Kimball showed extremely bad judgment.

Little has been said about the fact that the food seems to have run out prematurely. John Chislett records, "The brother who had been our commissary all the way from Liverpool had not latterly acted in a way to merit the confidence of the company; but it is hard to handle provisions and suffer hunger at the same time, so I will not write a word of condemnation." In short, he believed that Griffiths had stolen some of the food. How much, and where did it go? That's hard to tell.

Early reports suggest that the food stores procured in Nebraska were supposed to last for seventy days. But even with extra provision being added, and with a shortening of rations, the food ran out after 66 days. Since it took roughly 250 pounds of flour per day to feed the company, and since we know that over a thousand pounds of provisions were added near Fort Laramie, and since we know that rations were cut dramatically after October second, it appears that about two or three tons of flour disappeared.

Where did it go? Perhaps some was ruined by wet weather, or maybe it was pilfered. It may be that he handed it out to friends. Oral accounts from some descendants say that he was "choosing who would live and who would die." That accusation seems reasonable.

Given such a position, and such a temptation, few would be able to resist the pleas of starving friends, particularly those that one cared about or admired.

However, ground wheat can easily become compacted, and I suspect that this played more of a role than anyone has imagined.

Also, there is a rather odd statistical anomaly. The death rates of the English saints was about 19 percent, and the Danish saints was 23 percent. But the Scottish immigrants had only about a 10 percent death rate. Could it be that the commissary was favoring some of the Scots?

Possibly, but I don't see it as a realistic possibility. William Woodward was the captain in charge of the Scottish saints, and he says that when Levi Savage warned how hard the journey ahead would be, many of the elderly and infirm in his company "were persuaded" to stay for the winter in Council Bluffs. But he doesn't say who persuaded them. I suspect that Woodward did the persuading himself. Other captains actively dissuaded their weaker members from staying behind. The Danes were proud of the fact that they didn't have any slackers in their company, but it appears that Woodward may have contradicted Captain Willie and secretly warned some to stay behind.

Some prefer to blame no one at all. There was no single human culprit. Certainly, no one ever wanted or expected such a tragic outcome. Rather, there are those who say that winter came early that year, and that alone led to many of the deaths.

Even John Chislett noted that winter didn't just come early, it came with unprecedented ferocity, as if God in his heavens sought to reprove the immigrants for their audacity.

But winter wasn't that early. I went up to Rocky Ridge on September fifteenth of 2006, just to see what the fall colors would have been like during this trek. I was struck by a storm that hit with winds of fifty miles per hour. It dumped a foot of snow on Rocky Ridge in the space of a couple of hours, and though the temperature was more than thirty degrees warmer than the storm that hit the Willie Company, the wind-chill factor was still sub-zero. Such storms are frequent in the high country, and any seasoned traveler in the area knows to expect them.

But in all of my readings on the subject, no one has ever named the real culprit. Here it is: we can easily measure the number of calories required for a two-hundred pound man to pull a handcart sixteen miles, set up tents, and stand guard for four hours. We can also measure the number of calories provided by his bread.

Calories Required: 6000
Calories Supplied: 1100

The settlers died because they were completely ignorant of their own dietary needs. The amount of food they were allotted sounded sufficient to the men who planned the expedition, but no doctor today would recommend such a diet, even to someone who was struggling to lose weight. Once cold weather sent in, the caloric requirements climbed even higher.

This problem didn't just occur on the trek. It had been going on long before. Many of the immigrants were poor, crippled, and stunted from malnutrition. They left at the tail end of winter in 1855–56 and probably hadn't had much in the way of fresh fruit and vegetables for months. The diet provided on the journey was deficient. Aboard ship, English law required that passengers be given some produce—onions and apples—along with their bread and beans. But the church outfitters didn't plan as well. Even when the saints landed in New York, where produce and meat were plentiful, the only food provided was bread. In short, the handcart pioneers were already suffering from malnutrition when they reached the plains, and the condition only worsened as the journey progressed.

Lest we look back and condemn the church outfitters, I might point out that our own dietary sciences are very crude. We can actually measure how many calories it takes to perform labor with accuracy, but most people are ignorant of the fact that the calories listed on a can of soup don't really measure how much energy the soup provides. Calories are measured by burning foods and seeing how much energy is released. This would be a fine way to measure them if the human body had a furnace for a stomach. But the truth is that when we digest foods, we are able to transform only a portion of certain substances—fats, proteins, and carbohydrates—into usable energy. Thus, an oak log or a pint of oil, if measured for their caloric content, would appear to be excellent food—but the body can't use them.

The Apostates. In the early Mormon church, apostasy was considered to be rather scandalous, and many members of the Willie Company believed that the deaths of Thomas Margetts, Almon Babbitt, and other "apostates" from the church were signs that these persons had suffered the wrath of God in the flesh.

They also worried that those who turned back from the voyage to "wait until the next season" were showing an extreme lack of faith. It appears that most of those who decided to wait did in fact emigrate the following season.

One of those who waited was Thomas Evans, who helped build handcarts for others but ultimately decided not to trust the fate of his wife and family to one. Thomas's grandson, David O. McKay, later became the prophet of the church and was one of the most beloved church leaders of all time.

Descendants of the handcart pioneers now number over two hundred thousand. As I was writing this, it seemed that half of the people that heard about this project would say, "That's interesting, I'm related to . . ." And they would tell me stories. So I've met descendants of Eliza Gadd, Captain Willie, Levi Savage, Baline Mortenson's sister Margrethe, and many others.

Early handcart pioneers often developed a reputation for their faithfulness, their kindness, and their willingness to work tirelessly, and those qualities raised them to prominence. Their descendants include scientists, church leaders, and an endless succession of civic leaders, athletes, and entrepreneurs. Fortunately for me, my wife and children are also numbered among those descendants.

What's True and What's Not

Early readers of this manuscript have sometimes become confused. They have wanted to know what's true and what's not. In short, where did I draw the line between fact and fiction? Often, they would read a passage based entirely on fact and think it fictitious, and vice versa. So here are some notes.

The Prologue

The prairie around Rock Creek, Wyoming, is much as I describe it. The "Temple of Wyoming" attracts hundreds of thousands of tourists each year and is reputed to be the burial spot of Baline Mortensen. Many people claim to feel the presence of the early pioneers there. However, some scholars dispute whether this is indeed the right location for the burial.

Chapter 1: The Saints Enter Council Bluffs, Iowa

The town of Council Bluffs, Iowa, was as described. I won't go into its history, but the old hills that once afforded the early settlers shelter from the wind have long been bulldozed over. My description of the city is taken from pictures created in 1853.

I am uncertain when the notion that "Mormons have horns" came into being, but I joined the church at the age of sixteen. A few weeks later I went to my maternal grandmother's house for a visit—while wearing a hat. My grandmother attacked me with a broom and demanded that I show her my horns. In this scene, I tried to capture my grandmother's demeanor.

Eliza Gadd and her family are described as closely as possible. Eliza was a proud woman, an educated nurse who wore a fancy white hat across the prairie. She was from an upper-class family and was the only non-Mormon to cross in the Willie Handcart Company. However, not much has been written about her life before she came to America. Oral tradition holds that her father was a wealthy spiritualist and that he hired mediums and fakirs from all across Europe to come to his house and hold séances. Eliza saw through the fakirs and became hardened in her unbelief.

Eliza's husband, Samuel, seems to have been a genuine saint. One of his tent mates described how Samuel would leave camp when food was cooking so that his own children could eat, even as he starved. While some have suggested that Samuel might have bullied his wife into coming to America, perhaps even threatening to take the children and go without her, no such accusations ever came from Eliza or her children. The relationship between Eliza and Samuel appears to have been a loving one. Rather, it seems that Eliza kept her husband and family in England for more than a dozen years—until a reversal of fortune, pressure from the children, and perhaps her own loss of status in English society (for having such a strongly Mormon family) persuaded her to leave England.

The fight between Elder McGaw and the apostates in Council Bluffs was documented by Levi Savage, John Chislett, and others. As the settlers came through town, folks ridiculed them as noted, and one woman stood at a gate, pleading for women to give up their babies. In the center of town, the apostates, whose names are lost in history, were warning the settlers of impending doom due to that year's "Grasshopper War"—in much the language used here. They also offered to hire any man who would stay. But the final straw came when they began reviling Brigham Young and the practice of polygamy. One must suspect that Elder McGaw had had earlier run-ins with these people. After all, three handcart companies had passed through town that summer already, along with some wagon trains. In any case, McGaw leapt in and began to brawl, and beat up the apostates. There is no evidence that Eliza Gadd ever had anything to do with the fight.

CHAPTER 2: CROSSING THE MISSOURI RIVER

Bodil Maline (Baline) Mortensen was much as described. Her older sister, Margrethe, had traveled to Salt Lake the previous year, and Baline went with Jens Nielsen in 1856. In trying to understand why Baline's parents sent her on such a long journey, I researched what was going on in her neighborhood and learned about the priest Peder Kock and his efforts to persecute Mormons—which included the attempted murder of two missionaries in the fall of 1855, along with mobbing of new converts to the church and the destruction of Mormon-owned homes and businesses. Persecution was particularly strong in Baline's hometown. As the schoolmaster, Peder Kock was free to abuse and intimidate Mormon children as he liked. Hence, Baline's parents sought to protect their children by sending them across the ocean but were unable to afford to travel with them.

The incidents of abuse against the handcart company are all based on historical fact. The laws enacted against Mormons in the 1800s—which included bounties on Mormon scalps—stayed on the books for well over a hundred years. In fact, the bounty on Mormon scalps in Illinois was not repealed until the late 1970s—when I happened to be a missionary serving there.

Most Americans do not realize how dangerously close America came to starting a civil war in 1856. Once again, the battles that were taking place in Kansas have filled books of their own.

Jens Nielsen had given all that he had to help his fellow Danes reach America. The incident with Hansen seeking to steal the pans is based upon actual facts. The lawsuit that Hansen initiated against the handcart company went to trial. The Secretary of State for Utah spoke in behalf of Jens Nielsen and won the case.

CHAPTER 3: ELIZA CAMPS AT THE STAGING GROUND OF THE OLD WINTER'S QUARTERS

There is some argument as to whether women would have taken baths in the nude on this trek. It appears that for the sake of modesty, most baths were taken while dressed. But on at least one other occasion on the journey—more than a month after this—the men called a halt so that the women and children could bathe and wash at some hot springs in an effort to get rid of lice. The main camp full of men appears to have kept a respectful two miles distance. Thus, I suspect that the women bathed with their clothes on most of the time, but did bathe in the nude on some occasions—a circumstance that could not have helped but make Eliza feel vulnerable.

The Willie Handcart Company's official journal entry never mentions how or when papers for the lawsuit against Jens Nielsen were delivered, but one autobiographer mentions that a bunch of men "who were devils that acted like angels and strutted around in boots and suits" came to make trouble in camp either that night or shortly after. Other autobiographers concur. Since we know that there was a beating in town on the day in question, one might assume that the men were out to exact retribution. But it appears that the only person who was really affected by the suit was Jens Nielsen. Ultimately, a lawsuit was brought against him and the Church. Jens ultimately did use the pans for hubcaps—a practice that was fairly common in the company—but we do not know for sure what day he made them. Since the company complained of the dust ruining their wheels while crossing Iowa and since the rest period at Mormon Camp afforded several days for repairs, I suspect that he carried out the repairs here.

I have Captain Willie bear his testimony to things that he may have seen—Joseph Smith raising the dead, flocks of quail falling from the air to feed the hungry saints, fire descending from heaven to envelop the temple. These incidents are based on historical accounts of others from the life of Joseph Smith, and in some cases Willie certainly might have been present, since all of these incidents were witnessed by large crowds, but I have no way to know for certain if Willie was there. The incidents, rather, are meant to be a type of the thing that he might have borne witness to.

I also have Eliza Gadd telling of her father's spiritualism. There is no written account of this that I could find, but it was related from one of Eliza's descendants as Eliza's professed reason for being an agnostic.

CHAPTER 4: CAPTAIN WILLIE ARGUES FOR TRAVELING TO UTAH IMMEDIATELY.

The "mammoth meeting" held on August sixteenth is the single most documented event on the handcart trail. Levi Savage recounted his words in his own journal, and the church's clerk gives an account, as did the official clerk for the Danes. Others in the audience told how they felt as the meeting progressed. Many of Levi Savage's words are confirmed verbatim. So I've taken the various accounts, quoting as much as possible, and merged them into a single narrative. Sister Panting's story of escaping her husband is just one example of the kind of testimony that "several" people were said to have borne as they tried to convince the group to continue.

The one thing that might be controversial in this narrative is Captain Willie's outrage toward Savage—and the vindictiveness that becomes apparent later. I cannot emphasize enough that Captain Willie was a tremendously decent man. He gave all that he had in order to help the saints. However, it appears that he honestly felt that Levi Savage was not only wrong but that he was destroying the faith of others.

CHAPTER 5: BALINE'S PRAYER FOR GUIDANCE.

We do know that Mary Hurren and Agnes Caldwell were Baline's best friends. The rhyme that they used to call Baline from her tent is adapted from one that Agnes's friends in Scotland used to call her out to play.

The visit by the Omaha Indians that day was mentioned in several journals; the Indians drew a large crowd.

More than a hundred settlers turned back on the morning in question. One of them, twelve-year-old Joseph Oakey, fled from his family and never returned. He went to Council Bluffs and hid there with a local family that later adopted him. In a blessing given on this date, Joseph's mother was promised that she would hear from her son again. His parents did not hear from him for twenty years, and when they did, he recounted how he had been miraculously spared as he fought in the Civil War.

In handling Baline's prayer, I find myself in a bit of a quandary.

The saints had been counseled to pray, and one must suspect that Baline—like the others—did pray. As a believing Mormon, I also suspect that she got an answer. But answers to such prayers are not always easy to understand. In my own life, I have felt prompted at times to do things that were almost impossibly hard. In the end, the only reward that I got for my actions sometimes seems to be the personal growth that came by doing what I believed was right. I am convinced that sometimes, more than anything else, God wants us to grow. Whether Baline prayed, and what her answer might have been, I do not know.

CHAPTER 6: ELIZA MEETS WITH ALMON BABBITT IN AN ATTEMPT TO MAKE AN INFORMED DECISION ABOUT WHETHER TO GO WITH THE SAINTS.

In the opening to this chapter, I wanted to try to fill in a bit of the history of what had happened to the handcart company—the cause of the delays that had cost them four months, and so on. I hated putting these details in one huge lump, but I felt as if you needed to see just how emotionally draining this trip had been already.

I mention here that Levi Savage seems to have been secluded from the rest of the camp on this day. In his own journal, Savage says that he stayed in his tent and wrote letters all day. He does not say that he was forced to do so. It may be that he felt embarrassed by his actions and therefore secluded himself voluntarily. However, over the following weeks, Captain Willie worked hard to keep Savage away from the general populace—sending him out of camp on long errands each day or having him scout ahead of the company. I suspect that Captain Willie either asked Levi Savage to stay in his tent—or ordered him to do so.

There is no evidence that Almon Babbitt actually talked to Eliza about the Indian problem, but certainly he would have been intimate with all of the details, and he was in camp at the time. Within two weeks from this date, the Cheyenne would attack on a number of fronts. I mention the major battle in Kansas, but the Cheyenne renegades massacred settlers in several wagons. We do know that some renegade Sioux had stirred them into a fighting frenzy, and that as the cold winter hit, the Sioux carried out a massacre of their own in Iowa. Crazy Horse might have been among those Sioux. Little is known about his history at the time, but we do know that he had escaped the massacre at Blue River and that he had had his vision of himself as a proud warrior, fighting without war paint. It would be another couple of years before his prowess in battle established him as a legend.

In handling Eliza's line of reasoning in determining whether to go forward, I've had to look back at what would seem the sanest course from my vantage point. There is no evidence that Eliza ever asked to take her family to Kansas City, Missouri; however, other immigrants at the time did mention that it was one of several proposed destinations that they discarded.

CHAPTER 7: CAPTAIN WILLIE LEADS HIS PEOPLE INTO THE WILDERNESS.

The events of these first couple of days in the handcart train after setting out into the wilderness are fairly well recorded. We know that Captain Willie's hundred and Levi Savage's hundred moved out ahead of the rest of the camp. Captain Willie met with Almon Babbitt, who refused to sell wagons or carry food but who did go back to Council Bluffs to defend the church from the lawsuit regarding Jens Nielsen's pans. We also know that the company's cattle were "accidentally" left behind, that Levi Savage was made to go fetch them in a terrible storm, and that on the following day he was given similar make-work in bringing a lost cow to camp. This pattern would be followed in the coming weeks.

CHAPTER 8: BALINE JUMPS OVER THE RATTLESNAKES.

The story of "jumping over the rattlesnakes" was related by both Agnes Caldwell and Mary Hurren in later years. Mary Hurren mentions only herself and Agnes being there in her version, but Agnes mentions the others. Though they said that they sang a rhyme as they jumped over the snakes, the rhyme was never recorded.

The tale of Baline praying to catch a horny toad roughly corresponds to an incident that happened with my own daughter when she was six. A friend had found a deer antler, and my daughter asked me whether, if she prayed, she might find one, too. I was about to tell her no, when I suddenly felt strongly inspired to tell her yes. I felt that for reasons that only God knew, it was important for her to get an answer to that prayer. So she went into the backyard and returned three minutes later with her own deer antler—and a firm conviction that God answers prayers.

Though the immigrants were hounded by mobs through much of their journey, in one case a wonderfully kind deed was done—when a man known as "Good" John Goode gave shoes to the children in the Willie handcart company. He did it even as others ridiculed the people and sought to drive them from town. His gift not only saved the feet of some of those children as they marched through the snow, it surely saved lives. I do not know for certain whether Baline ever got any of those shoes.

CHAPTER 9: ELIZA WITNESSES HER FIRST MIRACLE.

Though the tale of Sophia Geary's crushed foot is well documented, I don't know if Eliza helped to treat her or not. At least one other woman in camp had some training as a nurse, but Eliza appears to be the only one in camp who was accredited. There was no doctor traveling among the group. Hence, it is probable that Eliza was called upon to help Sophia.

CHAPTER 10: CAPTAIN WILLIE PARTS A STORM.

The story of Emily Wall staying back to save her dying brother was recorded by several people on the day that it occurred and of course was told in later years both by Emily and her brother Joseph.

The tale of Captain Willie parting the storm was also recorded by several individuals.

Eliza's reaction to the various miracles that seemed to be happening all around her is not recorded.

CHAPTER 11: BALINE MAKES A TRADE WITH THE OMAHA INDIANS

Emily Wall pulled her critically ill brother in a handcart for nearly a month, with the help of a "little girl." The name of that little girl is not recorded. I suspect that it might well have been Baline simply because no grown woman seems to have ever stepped forward and taken credit for the feat, and while a couple of other girls of the appropriate age did die on the trek, none of the parents of those girls ever mentioned that their daughter helped pull the Wall's handcart. So the evidence points pretty strongly toward Baline, unless there is some dusty journal that I don't know about that says differently.

Mary Hurren tells of finding Indian beads at about this time.

The description of the immigrants' meeting with the Omahas is drawn from several accounts. The Danes in particular were terrified, since most of them could either not hear or understand the warning from church leaders that these were friendly Indians.

Several families described how they bartered in the Omaha "trading circles," and many of the purchases listed here are taken from those descriptions. It is doubtful that Baline would have entered a circle, since she probably had little or nothing to trade; however, blonde hair was highly prized by the Indians. Many of the settlers were frightened by the sight of scalps from blondes and redheads that hung from spears and lodge poles in the Omaha camp that day. In fact, blonde hair was so highly prized that friendly Indians sometimes did purchase locks of hair as decorations; and it may be that these Omahas did just that—or that they bought such scalps from other Indians. Given their very strong reputation for friendliness, it is not likely that they had scalped any white settlers recently.

CHAPTER 12: ELIZA STUMBLES UPON THE SITE OF A MASSACRE.

Just about everyone who wrote an autobiographical account tells the tale of finding the massacre site for the Babbitt wagon train. Most of the information here is as accurate as I can get it. Namely, the army had found the bodies of two teamsters and the Wilson baby and had gone to search for the "Wilson woman." When the saints reached the spot, wolves had dug up the graves, and the bodies were reburied.

But there is one interesting point of discrepancy. The army went searching for the "Wilson woman" but never found her. The

Cheyenne braves that had attacked the wagons were eventually caught, and they said that they tried to take her captive but found that she could not ride well enough, so they clubbed her and knocked her off her horse a few miles from the massacre site, leaving her for dead.

Only one person from the handcart company mentions finding Mrs. Wilson's body and then burying it. I strongly suspect that as the Willie company came upon this and other massacre sites, Captain Willie was sending men to clean up the mess before the women and children arrived. In at least one case a few weeks hence, it seems likely that he steered the company away from the Margettes' massacre site, which should have been in plain view.

Hence, we do not know for certain whether any of the women or children ever saw the body of Mrs. Wilson.

CHAPTER 13: CAPTAIN WILLIE DEALS WITH PETTY SQUABBLES IN CAMP.

Thomas Caldwell's injury with the wild cow was documented by a number of people. Thomas himself says that he was trying to milk the cow for "some little girls"—who would most likely have included his younger sister Agnes, Baline, and Mary, who always traveled in a pack at that time.

CHAPTER 14: BALINE HELPS HOLD TENT PEGS INTO THE GROUND DURING A STORM AND A BUFFALO STAMPEDE.

The events surrounding the buffalo stampede are well documented. The handcart pioneers wrote about it in their journals or described it years later. Emily Hill even wrote a poem about it. What doesn't become clear when you study their descriptions separately is just how violent the storm was that preceded the stampede. We know that men and boys had to go out and try to hold the tent pegs into the ground to keep the tents from blowing away. We also know that this area flooded terribly during that storm. No one knows exactly where the camp was, but I have hiked around the area where this was supposed to have happened, in about a three-mile radius, and I think I know where it occurred. There is mention of "flooded streams nearby," and there are some rather deep little streams that meander about in this area. There is also mention of the buffalo running over a small "hill." Now, you have to understand that this area looks almost as flat as a tabletop for a hundred miles in every direction. There aren't any real hills. But the Platte River often left little ridges, places where the sand deepened as the river deposited sediments during floods, and if you are on the floodplain, as these pioneers were, a sand ridge might look to be a small "hill," perhaps as much as ten feet high. Vegetation growing on these ridges—tall grasses and brush—would form a screen that might block the view of people standing on the ground. Whether Baline helped hold those tent pegs, we can't be sure. Boys her age were all asked to come help, and some single women and girls also went out.

CHAPTER 15: ELIZA'S HUSBAND BRAVES THE STORM IN AN ATTEMPT TO FIND THE COMPANY'S LOST CATTLE.

The actions taken during and after the storm are documented in dozens of biographies.

CHAPTER 16: CAPTAIN WILLIE STRUGGLES TO HANDLE THE COMPANY'S FIRST REAL CRISIS SINCE CROSSING THE MISSOURI RIVER.

From accounts given by the pioneers, many in the company began to wonder if their trek was "cursed." In this chapter, I try to reflect some of the various feelings expressed.

It's hard to know whether the Cheyenne actually did stampede the buffalo through camp. Levi Savage said that the cattle "wandered" off in the storm. Others said that that the "cattle began to run with the buffalo," and still others said that Indians were driving the buffalo. The young man who was in charge of guarding the cattle said that he saw Indians chasing the buffalo. Given that certain Cheyenne renegades had sworn to "kill every settler" who tried to cross the prairie that year, it seems likely that it was an attack. In fact, the survivors from the massacre the week before described how they'd gone to retrieve animals that had "wandered" eighteen miles just before the attack. In the subsequent attack on the Margett's wagon train, which took place a few days later, the Cheyenne seem to have followed a similar pattern, attacking while some of the settlers were separated from their wagons, off hunting buffalo. Given that the settlers represented a company that was too large for Cheyenne to attack directly, and given that a study of the renegade's movements at the time could easily put them at that location, it seems not only credible to me—but highly probable—that the Cheyenne really did drive the buffalo through camp in an effort to stampede the herd.

CHAPTER 17: BALINE MEETS THE LAWMAN ORRIN PORTER ROCKWELL.

Orrin Porter Rockwell was a legend on the plains, and his visit would have been a comfort to Captain Willie. He did indeed enter camp at the time mentioned and offered help in the way of hauling supplies, but Captain Willie never took him up on the offer. The reason, of course, is that the saints would have had to ferry their goods across the Platte, which was both treacherous due to quicksand and was still flooded at the time. It was simply too dangerous for women and children to cross.

The incident with the Cheyenne losing a battle in Kansas had happened only a couple of weeks earlier. I can't be sure if Orrin Porter Rockwell knew about it yet, but he was traveling on the south side of the Platte, which was heavily patrolled by the military, and he was also near Fort Kearney—so it is extremely likely that he had heard of the battle.

I was reminded of how strong a Native American's fear of an owl crossing his path might be while driving with a Navajo friend recently. We were going down the freeway when an owl flew across the road. My Navajo friend veered off the road, slammed on the brakes, and just sat for a long moment, trembling. "It is my grandmother," he said, nearly in tears. "The owl is coming to warn me that her time has come." We immediately had to turn around and return home in order to avert his grandmother's death. When I was a child, my Sioux and Blackfoot friends used to react to owls in the same way. Hence, I used it in the book.

Of course, the incident with Baline Mortensen talking to Rockwell is fictitious.

CHAPTER 18: ELIZA MUST CONTEND WITH HER STARVING CHILDREN.

Captain Willie sought to get the pioneers in the "independent wagons" to live the highest law of the Mormon church—the law of consecration, but the saints in those wagons refused as a whole. Those who were traveling by wagon had good reason to refuse in some cases—many were crippled, elderly, or infirm in one way or another. While as a group they voted to reject Captain Willie's plea, it is evident that some of them as individuals accepted the challenge.

Much is made here about Eliza losing her milk. Although we do not know precisely when this might have happened, it most certainly did. Other women in camp wrote about how they went about searching for a wet nurse when their milk failed at about this time. Of course all of the women had gone dry. As a result, the infant mortality rate in camp spiked in late August and remained high through the coming months.

CHAPTER 19: CAPTAIN WILLIE GETS NEWS OF A SECOND MASSACRE.

At least one reader was offended by the description that Boutcher offered of the murder of the Margetts family, feeling that it was too lurid. However, the description that I gave matches the reports made on that day by Levi Savage and others. Boutcher's description was shocking and calculated to put the Mormons on guard. I felt that it was more important to express the horror that the description aroused in camp at the time than to save a reader's feelings.

Levi Savage was shocked at being publicly attacked by an apostle for warning the pioneers against coming so late in the year. He wrote at this time that he had believed that Captain Willie held no grudge and was dismayed to find out that he was wrong.

One of the captains, John Chislett, was deeply offended at what he thought was the callous behavior of Franklin D. Richards. In writing about this, I find that dealing with Richards is perhaps the most difficult chore in this book, trying to make sense of just why

Richards acted as he did. It is obvious that Richards believed that the pioneers really would make it across the prairie without further hardship. I suspect that he took the letters that Brigham Young had sent to him as evidence that all would go well, for Brigham had promised that if the people kept the commandments, God would bless them. Personal experience from his journey across the plains ten years earlier simply reaffirmed all of this. Richards also believed that the pioneers would be safer if they traveled on the south side of the Platte, away from the trails being used by the marauding Cheyenne, and so on. So most of what he did was reasonable. But some things that he did really don't make much sense.

CHAPTER 20: BALINE CROSSES THE PLATTE

When the pioneers crossed the Platte River, it proved to be a Herculean challenge. John Chislett's words condemning Franklin D. Richards are drawn from Chislett's biographical account from years later.

We know that "Father" Haley died almost as soon as he reached the shore. The account here is perhaps a little dramatic, but follows his death as closely as I can tell it.

The meeting with the "Arapahos" is interesting in that Levi Savage and others all say that these Indians "called themselves" Arapahos. Apparently there was strong suspicion that these were hostile Indians trying to lead the settlers into a trap.

In the journals of that night, little is said about what happened during the Indian attack. Indians were spotted, shots were fired, and the Indians ran away while the Indians' camp dogs were heard barking. The reason that so little is written about it, of course, has to do with the fact that the next week was spent on the run. The tale of Baline making an owl noise is fictitious and is drawn from experiences from my own childhood. We had screech owls living in our little neighborhood in Oregon, and I recall that we had a young lady named Suzanne Castleberry whose voice was so high that she had an uncanny knack for imitating a screech owl. It is a sound that no male or grown woman could ever imitate—only a girl. Hence, I gave the skill to Baline, for it certainly would have frightened an Indian.

CHAPTER 21: ELIZA AND THE SAINTS FLEE THE INDIANS.

The threat posed by the Cheyenne was so great that Captain Willie tried to flee with his little group of handcart saints by moonlight, making a grueling march through heavy sands—after already having made a hard march during the day. The struggle left a trail of dead in the settlers' wake, but it might well have saved them from a gun battle.

In having Eliza talk about energy, I try to strike at the heart of the starvation problem. The male pioneers here were consuming about 1100 calories of bread per day, with very little in the way of meat or vegetables—less than a hundred calories per day on the average. But a large man who pulled a handcart 20 miles, pitched tents, cared for the lame, stood watch, and hunted for food would use in excess of 6000 calories. In short, the pioneers weren't dying because of their own lack of faith or because God had abandoned them, but because they were ignorant of their own basic nutritional needs.

We do not know the makeup of the entire camp, but interestingly we do know exactly who was staying in Eliza Gadd's tent. One of John Linford's sons describes how he had seen "men in my own tent" who went without food in order to feed their families. Since there were only two men in that tent—Samuel Gadd and John Linford, we must suspect that both of them starved themselves for the benefit of their children.

CHAPTER 22: CAPTAIN WILLIE HAS TO DEAL WITH DESPAIR AND APOSTASY.

Many of those who journeyed in the Willie Handcart Company said that it was not the starvation that troubled them most, not the freezing cold, but their own struggles with grief and doubt. John Chislett left the church because of it. Johan Ahmanson, leader of the Danish hundred, went even farther and wrote an anti-Mormon book, which he had published in Denmark. Others also left the church. But interestingly, most of those who survived this trek came away from it much stronger—and the better for it.

The journals mostly fall silent on this part of the trek, once the saints began their race to Ash Hollow. The mind-numbing cold combined with the brutal marches that occupied all hours of the night and day (in hopes of foiling any attempted Indian attacks), accompanied by the lack of rations, all take their toll.

CHAPTER 23: BALINE FINDS REFUGE IN ASH HOLLOW

The journey into Ash Hollow was grueling, and I try to tell the tale much as it occurred, incorporating accounts from several autobiographies into one—including those from Eliza Panting, Emily Wall, Jens Nielsen, John Chislett, and Levi Savage.

While we know that Baline Mortensen was ill with an ear infection when she reached Ash Hollow and we know that Eliza Gadd was the most-qualified nurse in the company, there is no evidence that they ever spoke. Their conversation here is meant only to reflect the themes that arise during the course of the novel.

CHAPTER 24: ELIZA LEAVES ASH HOLLOW TO TRAVEL OVER DEAD PRAIRIES.

Several biographers tell of witnessing horrific events that began to occur at this point in the trek—of men who stole food from the mouths of their own children, of women who dared hope that their children would die so that the mothers could have a bit more to eat. The names of the people who perpetrated these deeds were withheld by those who witnessed them, and so the characters that I attribute them to here are all fictitious.

I should point out that I have traveled the trail above Ash Hollow in late September, and it is astonishingly bleak. By this time of year, the grass has all died under the cottonwood trees and then been eaten back by prairie dogs. In short, there is nothing that even a goat could eat. It is hard to imagine how the cattle could survive this portion of the trek, and in fact the cattle were all starving, though they would not die en masse for a few more weeks.

Levi Savage was horrified that a representative of the US Army would steal his horse, as were those who witnessed the deed. I don't know if guns were drawn, but it seems clear from the accounts that the Mormons were afraid for their lives when they were forced to surrender Levi's horse. One young man tried to go back and warn Captain Willie what was happening, but the soldiers forcibly stopped him.

CHAPTER 25: CAPTAIN WILLIE REACHES FORT LARAMIE.

The tale of Tippets demanding bribes from the Indians before paying the monies owed is a matter of public record. The story of Major Hoffman trying to buy a bride is taken from the account of the woman who was propositioned, and so on.

We do not know what Parley P. Pratt might have said when he preached to the saints near Laramie. The words were never recorded. However, the sermon that he delivers—in which he prophesies about airplanes and automobiles—is one of his favorites and might well have come to mind as he tried to ease the journey of these travelers. Parley P. Pratt was murdered a few weeks after this meeting; since he was murdered in a state that had bounties on Mormon scalps, his killer was never prosecuted. Indeed, the sheriff of the town where Pratt was killed knew of the murder plot. He was helpless to stop the killer and had even tried his best to get Pratt out of town safely.

Eliza's son Daniel died on October third as described. We can imagine that Eliza felt bitter and hopeless, perhaps even outraged, but the incident related in which she throws the child's corpse at Captain Willie's feet is completely fictitious, meant only to dramatize the despair that she might have felt.

CHAPTER 26: BALINE STRUGGLES AGAINST STARVATION.

According to journals written at this time, the Danish saints burned their bedrolls as a sign of faith that the Lord would temper the weather. Later, when the Martin Handcart Company came upon the ashes, they did the same.

It is not certain when the children began eating leather in order to quell their hunger pangs, but most stories that deal with it seem to begin showing it in early October. There are tales of families eating their shoes for dinner, of one camp guard who boiled a girl's shoes to make soup but then felt guilty and therefore returned them, and of course of children eating leather from the handcart wheels as well as eating pieces of hide from dead cattle found along the trail.

CHAPTER 27: ELIZA'S HUSBAND SAMUEL DIES.

The events leading up to the death of Samuel Gadd are fairly well described in various journals. We know that he had given up eating in an effort to help his children; we know when he fell due to lack of food; and we know how and when his children discovered his death. But I would like to emphasize here that there is no evidence that he believed his wife had tried to feed him their child's food. Surely he felt guilty and somehow responsible when Daniel died, and that probably hastened his demise, but the accounts of the struggle between him and Eliza are fictitious. Rather, they are told simply to illustrate the fact that when a child dies, the marriage nearly always suffers. What we do know is that Samuel Gadd gave up his meals and let his children eat while he starved.

CHAPTER 28: BALINE WITNESSES SIGNS AND WONDERS IN CAMP.

We do not know if Baline ever had her shoes stolen for food, but at least two other families in camp mention having their shoes stolen and eaten at this time.

The illness of Eliza's son Samuel Junior at this time was a huge burden on Eliza, according to her children. To lose a husband and an infant within the week was hard—to watch a third child suffer seemed to break her. One of Eliza's daughters said that she would look into her mother's eyes and see only a dead thing inhabiting her body.

The death and revivification of Elizabeth Cunningham are referred to in several biographies, as is the incident with the poisoned parsnips.

There are at least three biographers who refer to the miracle of an angel delivering buffalo jerky to Eliza Panting at this time on the trail.

CHAPTER 29: CAPTAIN WILLIE MARCHES INTO THE FACE OF A STORM.

This chapter cobbles together stories from a number of autobiographies, but of all the incidents along the trail, one thing intrigues me the most: in August, Captain Willie was marching with his people when he saw an approaching storm and by the power of his faith and priesthood it is recorded that he parted the storm. Yet now, when the situation was at its worst, he saw a more terrifying storm roaring toward him and he simply told his people to march right into it. Why? I think that the answer can be seen in what he said the night before, when he told one of his men that he believed that they were all going to die anyway. Captain Willie was having his own crisis of faith.

The story of Edward Griffiths stealing flour from the stores and passing it out to his friends is one that was believed at the time. I have not seen any records that indicate whom he might have been feeding, and for various reasons I'm not persuaded that he took much, if any, of the flour. However, in order to try to comply with what witnesses said happened, I present him in this story as being guilty. There's just one bothersome thing here. It is said that he was giving flour to his friends, and I wondered who those people might have been. But in analyzing who lived and who died, it appears that men over the age of 30, along with small children, made up most of the deaths. Yet none of the six captains died. If indeed Griffiths was feeding his "friends," it seems logical to suspect that he might have been boosting the rations of those who had entrusted him with his position. That's not a pretty thing to contemplate. Given the staunch, self-sacrificing natures of both Levi Savage and James Willie, I cannot believe that if they were given extra rations, either one of them knew of it. Both men would have been outraged.

George Cunningham and others all related the details of his prophetic dream of the rescuers who came that morning.

Stories of the rescuers, such as James Cole (who described Lucy Ward to other rescuers from a dream, and married her a week later), are well documented. By combining all of the accounts given about the meeting with the advanced team, we get a fairly detailed picture of what happened.

We also know that the rescuers brought along a copy of a recent newspaper so that the Willie Company would know exactly what Brigham Young had said about the rescue efforts in general conference. William Kimball read from it upon meeting the saints, and then dispensed the clothing that had been donated by church members in general conference, which would have included various coats and scarves donated by Brigham Young himself.

The vote by the Willie company to send the advance teams forward with supplies to help the Martin Company while knowing that some of them would die because of it was a powerful testament to these people's faith. Some historians doubt that the vote took place. However, I suspect that something like a vote took place. In other instances when their rations were cut, the settlers were asked to sustain their leaders' decision by raising their hands. It seems reasonable that they would have been asked to sustain their leaders on this occasion.

CHAPTER 30: CAPTAIN WILLIE RIDES TO SAVE HIS DYING PEOPLE.

Captain Willie's ride, taken without food or water, was a desperate mission to find the relief wagons. The story here follows his account as precisely as possible. However, there is one discrepancy. Some people say that he "rode" off on his mule; other witnesses said that he refused to ride anywhere, in order to keep a vow that he had made earlier, and that he walked. But those who say he rode in this case outweigh the number of those who say he walked, and it seems more reasonable that he would have ridden on such an important mission.

The tale of Ann Rowley multiplying her food is taken from her own biography and from the biographies of her children, who witnessed it.

We do not know the specifics of what Baline went through that morning, but many biographers give accounts of how the starving saints spent the day in prayer and scripture reading. One woman describes how "an old man" sat reciting the scriptures that told of Jesus' life until at last he fell silent—frozen to death.

Though we know that Sophia Larsen was found that morning frozen to death, I have not been able to ascertain who her tent mates might have been. Nor do I have any real reason to believe that Baline found the body. We do know exactly how Eliza's tent-mate, John Linford, died that day.

CHAPTER 31: CAPTAIN WILLIE BEGINS TAKING HIS PEOPLE OVER ROCKY RIDGE.

The winter of 1856, according to those who suffered through it, was perhaps the coldest winter of the entire century. I say in the opening here that on October 22nd the temperature stood at eight degrees below zero. I arrived at this figure by taking the temperature as recorded from a nearby fort and adjusting for altitude. The figure may be either high or low by two or three degrees, but it is reasonable to assume that the temperature fell below zero.

The tales of those who died in this chapter are all taken from biographical accounts.

The account of Jens Nielsen enraging a man who had given up on living and threatening to beat him was given by several biographers at the time, but in many cases Jens was not named. It was said only that "a Dane" had done it.

The plans for crossing Rocky Ridge and the directions given by Captain Willie and others are all taken from historical accounts. Unfortunately, things get a little confusing. It appears for example that some of the rescuers were supposed to remain at camp and welcome the women and children in as they came. However, as the snow proved more difficult for the handcarts than first imagined, it appears that these rescuers were asked to go back up the trail and help bring out those who were sick and injured. This may be why so many of the children who reached camp that day froze to death—the fires that were supposed to have been there to keep them warm weren't burning. However, I also find it plausible that the fires just couldn't stay lit—not in such high winds. I've been up at that camp in a blizzard, and I don't see how any campfire could have been kept burning.

CHAPTER 32: BALINE MORTENSEN TAKES THE CHILDREN TO SAFETY AND REACHES THE END OF HER JOURNEY.

It is not easy to piece together precisely what happened to Baline. We do know that Jens Nielsen's legs were frozen and that he fainted and had to be pulled in his handcart by his wife Else. Baline was apparently then put in charge of leading several children to safety, including barely six-year-old Niels. Pushing the handcarts up Rocky Ridge in the ice and snow was so grueling, especially given the raging winds and snow, that it was felt that the children had a better chance of survival if they could get to camp.

We also know that several people froze their legs while trying to cross a creek at this juncture, which was probably Strawberry Creek, swollen and flooded. I have walked this portion of the trek in late October, and ice runoff leaves small streams and pools in the road in many places, but most of these can easily be skirted, and few are deep. It was the custom for Captain Willie and several other men to carry the women across the larger creeks. Thus Captain Willie and Levi Savage both froze their legs on this day. The old Dane, Mr. Vandelin, is credited with giving up his watch and asking with his dying breath that the money from its sale be used to bring others to Zion.

I went to Rocky Ridge during a blizzard in order to get a feel for what it was like, and at one point while wandering through the willows, I was fascinated to hear a large flock of birds whistling from nearby bushes. On closer examination I found that it was only the waxy leaves of the willow twisting in the high winds, momentarily mimicking bird sounds. I imagine that Baline might well have been fascinated by this, hoping that she might find a bird to eat.

We do not know precisely when Baline died, but witnesses at the time say that her body was found just outside Peder Mortensen's camp, leaning against the wheel of a handcart, while carrying sagebrush for the fire. Some recent biographers have suggested that "no one knows" how she died, and some say that she died on the trail, but in the Daughters of the Utah Pioneers Museum in Cedar City, a handwritten note by one of the Mortensen girls gives the details of Baline's death.

CHAPTER 33: CAPTAIN WILLIE RECONCILES WITH LEVI SAVAGE.

While I can piece together some of what happened with Levi Savage and Captain Willie from other accounts, neither man tells about his experiences during or after their climb up Rocky Ridge. I suspect that it was humility that kept them both quiet in later years, but at least at that time both men were very near death. Levi Savage normally kept a daily journal, but after this near-death experience he fell silent. Even when he did take up the pen months later, his handwriting was transformed from a fine strong script to a nearly illegible scrawl. Both men froze their legs that day while helping others and spent the next two months hovering near death.

CHAPTER 34: ELIZA GADD'S VISION.

We know from the accounts of Eliza Gadd's daughters that Eliza went snow-blind while crossing Rocky Ridge, and she had to be led by her young daughter.

The incident where Eliza felt the spirits of the dead is not based upon her account, but on the accounts of others on the trek—several of whom said that they "felt the spirits of the dead" helping to pull the handcarts on this stretch of the trail. However, according to an oral account given by one of Eliza's descendents years after the journey, one of Eliza's grandchildren asked her why she joined the Mormon Church. Eliza reputedly said, "How could I not, after having watched all of my children turn into angels?" Because of this, and because of the way that Eliza changed and grew from her experiences, I suspect that she is referring to a spiritual experience similar to the one that is related here.

CHAPTER 35: MARY SAYS GOOD-BYE TO BALINE.

Mary Hurren's final good-bye to Baline Mortensen is taken from Mary's own account and from that of her father.

For Further Information

The tales of the handcart pioneers here are drawn in part from autobiographies, in part from the biographies written by the pioneers' descendants, and from articles by military personnel and newspapers from the time. Many of these can be found in the archives of the Daughters of the Utah Pioneers, in special collections at Brigham Young University, and on the web.

Some of the people mentioned in the biographies became famous enough in their own right so that information about them is readily available through libraries or online resources. These include General Harney, Major Hoffman, Crazy Horse, Wild Bill Hickman, Orrin Porter Rockwell, Levi Savage, John Brown, and others.

A Final Note

If you enjoyed this book, do the author a favor and tell a friend.

If you'd like, you can find information on this and other books at www.InTheCompanyOfAngels.net, which you can then forward to friends on the Internet. If you would like to contact the author, you can email him at davidfarland@xmission.com.